Dedication

Decisions on branding, connecting everything from organizational competences to latent consumer needs, are made in a company every day. Their leadership patterning can add value by being organizationally motivating and strategically purposeful. Or, in companies that are too lazy to lead through learning, what happens is that branding decisions are made by default, tactically, and to suit the political agendas of individuals – especially high-fliers. Divide and conquer rules, OK?

Excitingly, two great change forces, shaping a new epoch of marketing 'glocalization' and 'new intelligent information media' mean that consumers are peering through to see which companies are which. Climb on to the intelligent 'brandwagon' now. Slow learning organizations, ignorant of branding's interconnections, will be looked back on as the late 20th century's corporate dodos. What right have these organizations to exist in the year 2010? 2005? 2000? . . .

'One of the global good fortunes for our third millennium is that the Japanese and the Chinese are the most fussy consumers in the world. Many western organizations urgently need to learn a painful lesson unless they wish to become prisoners of the value-added chains of other companies. It is vital that all employees realize that one can sell the world's most fussy consumers anything once, but unless it lives up to its promises (current and future implicit in brand) then that consumer will never think of purchasing from your company again, nor will his or her peers, nor will his or her peers' peers . . . Belief in this 'world class' dynamic suggests that company learning concepts such as purpose of brand organization, Chartering of 'living scripts' and marketing of lifetime consumer relationships are among the most valuable just-in-time thought pursuits that turn-of-the-millennium business leaders can employ.'

© 1995 WCBN co-workers at MELNET
http://www.brad.ac.uk/branding/

We dedicate this book to curious turn-of-the-century readers: be they fussy consumers or hard-working business people.

Contents

ThinkPieces

Acknowledgement

The pronoun 'we' is used throughout this book as many co-workers have helped in the iterative development and practice of Brand Chartering. In particular, the author wishes to thank the following:

- Helena Rubinstein and Simon Broadbent at Leo Burnett Brand Consultancy, London
- Josh McQueen at Leo Burnett, Chicago
- Professors Mark Uncles and David Weir at the Management Centre, University of Bradford
- Professor Peter Farquhar, The Strategy Institute, Claremont Graduate School
- Professor Stephen Parkinson and Janette Sheerman at the University of Ulster
- Professor Malcolm McDonald at Cranfield Management Centre
- Melanie Cocks at Bournemouth University
- Jeff Devlin at Arthur D. Little, London
- Jacques Blanchard at Novaction, Paris
- Charles Penn, Chris Mole and Stephen Greenhalgh at Coopers & Lybrand, London
- John Moran at Coopers & Lybrand, Kuala Lumpur
- Ken Munro and Lucy Cannington at Coopers & Lybrand, Sydney
- Professor Chris Halliburton at EAP, European School of Management
- Simon Flemington and Lucy Oulton at BBC for BUSINESS
- Bill Ramsay at Templeton College, Oxford
- Roger Brookin at Petal KK, Tokyo

- The Economist Intelligence Unit
- Companies that interacted with us as Brand Chartering has evolved

As mass marketing's era of concentrating brand equity on individual products passes into history, any attempt to explain how to Charter newly evolving service and system forms of brand organization is likely to be prejudiced by omission or exaggeration of emphasis. The author apologizes for these to both co-workers and readers.

We have connected up an eclectic mix of perspectives on brand process which give the architecture of Brand Chartering a practical breadth and depth befitting a process approach to brand organization. Please choose components of Chartering the 'living script' of your branding process suited to its contextual purpose of adding value for consumers, inspiring employees, partnering winners and killing off competitors whose organizations change too slowly to add value as business chains rapidly go 'glocal' global and local at a furious velocity.

We also foresee other changes like new media transforming brands from dealing in an era of semi-intelligent mass communications media (for example TV broadcasting) to being leading business processes embodying far more intelligent systems of communicating. We advise a 'do now' sense of urgency in editing the future of brand organizations as Unique Organizing Purposes; in contrast, the twentieth-century notion of a brand as merely a Unique Selling Proposition is past its sell-by date.

Publisher's acknowledgements

The publishers wish to thank the following for permission to reproduce copyright material on the cited pages.

Pages 6, 23, 85, 201, 218-9, 247: extracts from Competing for the Future by Hamel and Prahalad © Harvard Business School Publishing. Pages 8 and 73: extracts from brand strategy newsletter reproduced by kind permission. Pages 13, 125, 137, 224, 256, 257 © The Financial Times, London. For figures on pages 33 and 269 thanks to Leo Burnett Brand Consultancy. Figures on pages 54, 220, 229, extracts on pages 264, 277-9, 281, 355, 361-4, and extract from Maucher on page 320, sourced from EIU publications. Pages 51. 250-3, 275-6, 358-60: extracts © The Economist, reproduced with permission from issues of 10 November 1990, 9 April 1994, 3 February 1990 and 21 October 1989 respectively. Pages 55-6, 93, 96, 158-9, 172, 192-3, 242, 247, 370-1, 383-4: extracts from Branding – the Marketing Advantage © Copyright 1995 BBC for BUSINESS. Figure on page 60 supplied by JWT Advertising Agency, London, and Unilever Malaysia. Table on page 98 and extract on page 142 © NTC Publications Ltd, Henley-on-Thames. Page 110–11: extract from a speech by Jeremy Bullmore © The Institute of Practitioners in Advertising, London. Thanks also to Jeremy Bullmore for permission to print this partially edited extract from the speech. Pages 124 and 352-4: extracts from The Journal of Brand Management © Henry Stewart Publications, London, reproduced with permission from issues 2(1), 1994 and 2(2), 1994, respectively. Thanks also to Henry Stewart Publications for permission to reproduce extracts from articles by the author which originally appeared in The Journal of Brand Management. Page 133–4: extract © The Independent, reproduced by permission. Page 208: extract from Stevenson reprinted by permission of Canadian Business Magazine © 1995. Page 210: extract from Marketing Week reproduced by permission © Marketing Week, London. Page 224: extract from Blackston, M, Beyond Brand Personality in Brand Equity and Advertising (Aaker, D and Biel, A eds) © LEA Publishers Inc. Page 247: extracts from September 1992 edition of Marketing Research © The American Marketing Association. Page 274: extract from Belasco © Crown Publishers Inc. USA, reproduced with permission. Pages 145 and 365–7: extracts from an article by Alan Mitchell © Marketing Week, London, reproduced by kind permission. Page 367–9, extracts from speech given by Raoul Pinnel, Director of Marketing, NatWest Bank: thanks to Raoul Pinnel, NatWest Bank. Page 373: extract from article by James Lynch in the Journal of Marketing Management, issue 10, 1994 © The Dryden Press, an imprint of Harcourt Brace and Company Ltd. For World Series articles appearing on pages 375–384, thanks is due to the BBC for permission to reproduce this material.

While the publisher has attempted to trace all copyright owners and to obtain permission to reproduce material, in a few cases this has proved impossible. Copyright holders of material which has not been acknowledged should contact the publisher at the above address.

Forethoughts on revolutionary times for brand owners

An open letter

To CEOs who invest in brand organization – and all who serve the brand

Behind ubiquitous nonsense headlines on 'the death of the brand' which have surfaced in the 1990s, there is a serious need for a worldwide forum for those who see brand equity in the following terms:

- cultural empowerers allowing an organization to take advantage of change;
- often the company's only commercial licence to invest beyond the short term;
- the strategic architect's means for building smart relationships harmoniously with all corporate stakeholders, not just end-consumers or retail customers;
- wealth-expanding leaders which serve to accelerate future innovation and added value that the company musters as a corporate citizen;the CEO's editorial assistant in cross-checking the essential direction of the company's core competences;
- mixers of partnership strategy as well as competitive strategy in pursuit of delivering world class quality and value, globally and locally.

In contrast, much that is now written about brands tends to elevate a specific professional discipline or business function above the rest. The high cost and power of branding within a company are used to claim the CEO's support of one managerial perspective and then another. Branding is also introduced as a consultancy spin to sell a mega-proposition such as downsizing the organization or investing heavily in IT systems.

If your company is interested in considering our alternative proposal – proactively to exchange thinking on how to earn the rights of leadership through brand organization – please read on.

Two introductory ideas follow this letter:

- Competing and partnering in a brand new world;
- Brand Chartering: what and why it is.

Yours sincerely

P.S Relearning brand organization. All great brand organizations embody two beliefs.

(1) Employees like all human beings want to be leaders, in the sense of being respected in their own spheres of business, and to be part of a winning team. It is much more motivating to be part of an organization which keeps on winning, and it can make hard work worthwhile or even a joy.

(2) The brand organization leads by:

- discovering new ways of delighting consumers;
- being faithful to trust that has been accumulated;
- making the consumer feel smart in repeatedly electing to renew a relationship with the brand;
- focusing consistently on essential values that the brand's consumers uniquely have the right to expect;
- cultivating character and presence of mind through style rules that feel rewardingly familiar;
- serving consumers' perceptions of what is socially significant.

In short, the brand organization strives to stay ahead as its consumers' 'editor-of-choice' (Mazur and Lannon, 1993).

There are other customers and potential partners which the brand organization must involve too, but brand mortality starts to creep in when employees stop focusing on the end-consumer.

A principal aim of this book is to put the classic form of Western brand management on trial, to cross-examine where and when it got in the way of brand organization, or interfered with the organization-wide learning ability that companies need to leverage change if they are not to become hostages to the added-value foresight of others. In this process we may all need to go back and cross-examine our own instincts on the way world class brands work.

Competing and partnering in a brand new world

1994 was the year, when *The Economist* opined on the death of the brand manager (Reid, 1994), *The Financial Times* (1994) declared that manufacturers who do not realize that global marketing is uniquely challenging will go to the wall, and McKinsey's advocated that companies would henceforth need to earn the right to brand (Freeling, 1994). However, 1994/5 saw two seminal sources of information published which – once they have diffused their way into the thinking of senior management – will change the way that western companies manage brands. For some companies this may come just-in-time and others just-too-late.

One of the two seminal sources is the book *Competing for the Future* from Harvard Business School, the other a video from BBC for Business. Before looking at these let me start with my personal bias as author which led to my research of a subject that has come to be known as World Class Branding.

A personal view

Ten years ago I first travelled to Japan. Like other Westerners before and since, the trip was a shock to my system. It turned thinking and practice in my chosen profession upside down. In Japan – and indeed in much of Asia – companies invested in brand equity at the corporate level first and the product level a distant second. In Tokyo, in one of those garbled conversations which is the best I can manage as a *Gaijin* among Japanese, I first heard about the sub-brand. I was asked: 'Why is it that so many foreign advertising campaigns in Japan carry only sub-branding messages? Don't you know that, without the accompanying guarantee of the corporate brand, many Japanese consumers will not attend to a commercial, however much you target the message of the sub-branded product? Why do you hide the company behind the brand instead of leading with the company?'

While my Western-style CV had proudly stated that I was highly qualified in brand positioning (which I thought I had been consulting on for a decade), the reality was that I knew a lot about positioning sub-brands, a little about umbrella branding and nothing about corporately branded architectures. In 1989 I wrote a book on the subject called *World Class Brands* which made two vaguely right predictions. It also leaned heavily on quotes from experienced interpreters of Japanese business practice, particularly those with an optimistic passion for informed management of change.

The predictions were as follows:

- Western companies are in danger of overbranding. The risk of owning too many brands (configured around local and temporary product lines) is far greater than that of investing in too few.
- Corporate brand processes work by establishing smart business relationships with all audiences. They must serve the 3 Cs – consumers, channels (for example, retail customers) and company (for example, employees) – not just one of them.

In 1989 I was lucky enough to make the acquaintance of Bob Heller, one of the expert Western interpreters of Japanese business practice. Box F.1 contains some of his thoughts.

Box F.1   Some of Bob Heller's thoughts

The concept of the continuously evolving business unit is neither customer-led nor market- driven; it leads the customer and drives the market. Effective change management insists on getting the right answers to six basic questions:

(1) Are you selling the right things?
(2) Are you supplying these in the most effective way?
(3) And at the lowest cost?
(4) Are you as good as or better than your best competitor?
(5) Are you tapping the widest possible market?
(6) Do you have an edge, that is, a unique system of business skills?

None of these questions can be permanently answered 'Yes' unless the company is continuously changing and genuinely committed to innovation. That in turn will not be effective unless the following six barriers are removed:

(1) Red tape
(2) Lack of funds for innovation
(3) Preoccupation with today instead of tomorrow
(4) No innovative thinking
(5) No top management support for innovation
(6) An organization structure that discourages innovation

The task and test of change management is how nearly it removes such barriers and closes the gap between the ideal and the real, which starts from having a clear idea of the ideal, then correctly assessing the reality and then acting to close the gap. The process is also the model for successful planning and successful product development.

The most effective change masters are the Japanese who founded adaptive management on 10 tenets:

(1) Take a long-term view
(2) Grow internally

continues

continued

   (3) Go for the largest attainable and profitable market share
   (4) Get all the information you can about the business and the markets
   (5) Follow the leader, and pass him
   (6) Develop new products and services
   (7) Compete on everything except price
   (8) Concentrate on your strengths
   (9) Build a customer franchise
(10) Minimize risk

Change leadership rests, like democracy, on the consent of the governed, but it earns that consent by doing what is right, regardless of the impact of established traditions and conventional wisdom. The examples of Japan and of great commanders in war confirm the formula: the leader changes the 'corporate culture' by personal example, symbolic change, moving rapidly into successful action and observing the 10 pillars of leadership:

   (1) Trust
   (2) Teamwork
   (3) Atmosphere
   (4) Objectives
   (5) Clarity
   (6) Confidence
   (7) Back-up
   (8) Performance
   (9) Humanity
(10) Competitive aggression

(*Source*: Extract from a management seminar held at Templeton College, Oxford, in 1989)

The book *World Class Brands* drew some polite compliments, such as 'it reads well', but ultimately the feedback from most practitioners was: so what can we do about that? With the benefit of hindsight, it is clear that all of us have underestimated the complexity of organizational inertias built into the classical brand management system. Many marketing departments have come within a whisker of killing off both themselves and their companies. The following paragraph provides an illustration.

Until recently the world's leading consumer goods businesses could look forward to profit by competing with fragmented brands which carved up or segmented markets within both nations and product categories. This was organizationally convenient, since brand managers could report to managers with national or product territories. It also made the accountants' job easy, since all they had to do was count up the contributions of separate business units and within these stock-keeping units. So these interested parties, and many others including suppliers of the classical brand concept, like market researchers and creative agencies, were happy with the convention that targeting was the objective of brand communications. Large Western multinationals such as Unilever or Procter & Gamble could manage 5,000 separate targeting devices if they wanted to, and it seemed so much simpler to divide up the brand's need for support into piecewise specialist functions, as opposed to organizing a more integrated teamworking process.

Seminal source: *Competing for the Future*

The book of this title is the first seminal source for companies intent on relearning branding. It is written by Professors Gary Hamel and C. K. Prahalad, and published by Harvard Business School Press (1994). These authors develop a 'strategic architecture' which should be studied by all those who want their companies to profit from the changes that lie ahead. In the context of branding these include:

- delivering glocal (global and local) standards of quality and value to end-consumers;
- knowing what learning processes make the company uniquely competent in advancing added value;
- developing partnerships as well as competitive strategies because continuously delivering the world's best products and services is a process which few companies will master on their own;
- foreseeing how to take advantage of change.

Specifically, Hamel and Prahalad introduce a top-level branding dynamic which they call the 'banner brand'.

'Marketing experts have opined that it takes in the order of $1 billion of advertising to build a significant share of mind with consumers across North America, Asia and Europe. Yet what is the marginal cost for Sony, in terms of brand building, when it launches a new product bearing those four famous letters? Sony's new product introductions benefit from instant street credibility. Now one can legitimately ask which came first: great products or the great brand? Of course it was the product. But what Sony and other global brand leaders have done is consciously to build "banner brands" that span multiple products and businesses and which help customers transfer great experiences with today's products into great interest and enthusiasm for tomorrow's products . . . We believe that any company that fails to take advantage of the logic of banner branding will find itself, long-term, at a competitive disadvantage.'

One of Hamel and Prahalad's architectural metaphors makes a particularly striking plea for the underestimated powers of intangible assets. A company's two most powerful sources of advantage are depicted as a house with banner (for example, corporate) branding as its roof and core competences as its floor. Within these boundaries the service capabilities of business units and core products are conditioned. Some of the connections that can be drawn around these terms, interpreted in our own words in the list below, can be quite revolutionary. Many Western companies appear to have got their organization, of at least one of these power sources, upside down.

- **Core product** opportunities are revealed through their pre-marketing platforms and their foresightful direction towards future leadership goals, not just in their sales performance.
- **Business units** should be the focus for customer delight, and networking centres coalescing with external partners to connect up the core competences of different companies.
- **Core competences** are the company's focused learning processes. These systems determine how value is added and whether the company is capable of leading a sphere of business. Tellingly, core competences act in combination. Benchmarkers, quality gurus, and so on, need to understand that a good definition of global market competition is one where no two companies can continuously expect to profit from owning precisely the same combination of competences. A corollary is that in optimizing leverage of 'glocal' (global and local) added-value chains, partnership strategy can be even more important to leaders than competitive strategy.
- The **banner brand** is directed as a top-level brand in which corporate reputation, awareness and leadership foresight are invested. It works as a unique organizing purpose. It embodies a uniquely relevant service purpose which transforms into a feedback loop between employee pride in winning and consumer satisfaction with the best. It acts as the consumer's editor of choice by transferring high-level values, such as trust and delight, across temporary product manifestations of the branded organization. Banner brand impact is 'glocally' multipliable by linkages to other brands including sub-brands (for example, Gillette as banner, Sensor as sub-brand, Series as sub-brand, and so on).

We wanted to explore some real multidimensional examples of branded businesses which worked at being unique organizing purposes. How could a brand's living script be revealed so that everyone who served the brand could realize its added-value totality?

Seminal source: BBC for BUSINESS: 'Branding – the Marketing Advantage'

We were lucky enough to have a meeting of minds with BBC for BUSINESS. Its video 'Branding – the Marketing Advantage' (© BBC FOR BUSINESS), made in 1995, is the second seminal source of information on branding; not in our judgement because of the part we played, but because five strongly branded companies – American Express, 3M, Singapore Airlines, Hägen Dazs and Club Med – were prepared to be cross-examined on everything their brands stood for. The results are available for academics and practitioners to view, wherever they work in marketing's global village, courtesy of the BBC's worldwide distribution.

Box F.2   Review of video

Both product quality and creative communications are important, but they are only temporary manifestations of branding. The really vital brand is one whose organizing culture loves its end-consumers so much that all employees run and win marketing's equivalent of an Olympics marathon, only to pick themselves up as they cross the winning line in eager preparation for the next marathon. All this because of sheer pride in serving not only goods but what's really best for consumers – the leader who delights all customers by consistently setting new world records on quality and value.

(*Source: brand strategy Newsletter*, 31 March 1995)

The heroes of this video are brand processes, their people and the organizational networks supporting them. Employees of the companies illustrate the extraordinary panorama of value-added elements which a passion for brand leadership can leverage. The plot unfolds that the brand is limited only by restricting an organization's collective imagination, which is easy to do over time via hierarchical systems like classic brand management, or through the loss of consumer and customer focus, which happens in companies where excessive financial caution takes over from the passionate conviction of adding value. Many of the marketing practitioners interviewed in the video candidly admit that organizational barriers like these have only recently been overcome by them reinventing their own jobs, and that a vital service culture involves top-level commitment to the teamworking joy of constantly needing to learn.

We have conducted extensive research on what benefits people derive from the BBC's video. Branders will need to consign many twentieth-century brand management practices to the history books if they are to take advantage of the marketing challenges that lie ahead.

Box F.3   There has never been a more exciting time for marketing and branding

- World class marketing is going global and local.
- Media are going worldwide-broad and personally- narrow; casting is becoming interactive.
- The post-industrial electronic information-service era promises both intimate customization and mass cooperation on a heroic scale, for example, ECR and BPR. (These are two of the giant management consultancy propositions of the 1990s: ECR stands for efficient consumer response, which aims to build information technology and logistics partnerships between major manufacturers and retailers; BPR stands for business process re-engineering.)
- Distribution, manufacturing and media competences are becoming inseparable. With the emergence of computerized multimedia, you do not have a total business strategy unless your organization knows how to network across all these competences.
- Partnership strategy is becoming as important as competitive strategy.
- Unless brand organization is top of the CEO's agenda now, the company will not be fully capable of taking advantage of change. Would-be global companies which place the brand marketing process below other disciplines (for example, those governed by short-term financial performance) may implode.
- The end-game of brand organization may be 10 years away, but moves being made today will determine the allocation of wealth between business winners and losers, and correspondingly between nations and regions which happen to be the closest investors in these businesses.

The experiences of the BBC's interviewees concerning relearning brand organization add a sense of urgency to finding a way through today's extraordinary marketing challenges. The following is one taken from a compilation listed in ThinkPiece 7.

'The idea of the classical brand management system was that you would have in a relatively junior role someone who would champion a product as brand within the company. But as soon as you get umbrella branding, this becomes a terrible political system because the real purpose of brands these days is to extend across territories, whether they are product territories or national territories. Instead you end up with a system where fairly junior managers are trying to save their job or save their brand; you end up with just a sea of politics, and a lot of internal brands fighting with each other, and a lot of internal departments fighting with each other.'

The BBC video provides a unique debating opportunity for people on the Internet, swapping notes on challenges to brand processes. Its global availability makes it a reference point from which many new ideas on brand organization are emerging. Without this global forum this book would have had a far narrower range of viewpoints to reflect. More generally, this experience has led to the development of MELNET discussed in ThinkPiece 11.

Our opening invitation to you, the reader, is to join the debate on what your brand organization will need to focus on by picking out what interests you. Brand Chartering is an early learning tool for exploring what value-added leadership means to whom in your organization, and how best to harness these insights and motivations in an integrated way.

Brand Chartering: what and why it is

Our original contribution to the BBC for BUSINESS video was a list of questions the BBC's journalists could use to find out how companies brand value-added and leverage corporate advantage. For several years we have been collecting questions which probe the depth and breadth of the organizational and strategic strengths that can be interwoven in a vital corporate branding culture. Some are listed below.

Questions on the vitality of organization-wide branding

(1) What leadership values would people – for example, the 3Cs: consumers, channel, company – really miss if this brand did not exist? Is there a common interpretation of the brand's essential meaning throughout the organization?

(2) Was this brand process ever in danger of being anchored too narrowly to a product or local platform? How did your company stop this happening?

(3) Is the brand's communications mix integrated and able to leverage changing media economies? Is it flexible for global and local marketing?

(4) Does this brand offer a world class 'balance' of quality and value? What future discontinuities in the added-value chain – globally or locally – could undermine this balance?

(5) Do all added-value departments of the organization contribute to auditing this brand's opportunities and risks? Has the marketing department had to be reorganized to serve this brand globally and locally?

(6) Is everyone agreed on this brand's claim to resources relative to other brands? Who is ultimately responsible for this brand's goals? Are measures of business team performance well aligned with the specific goals of the brand?

(7) What core competences does this brand represent? How does this fit with your overall foci for corporate competences?

(8) Is the brand's platform linked to any other brands in the organization? Does your company use banner brands and product sub-brands?

(9) What aspects of the brand process does the CEO sponsor?

(10) Does your organization's culture promote a sensitive joy of change and a focused teamworking spirit? Would your people be proud to be called manifestations of your brand?

This approach mimics what we try to do in Brand Chartering. Inputs to Brand Chartering are suitable debating questions, or management workshop frameworks which help to forge a consensus on what unique keys relate to a specific brand leadership process. The output of Brand Chartering, a 'living script', provides everyone in a business team with a shared understanding of the unique purpose of the brand they serve.

Usually Brand Chartering is done privately within a company, and the Charter aims to summarize the brand's top- line living script on one updatable piece of paper or a few communal computer screens. By making this short, teamworkers can be encouraged to bid passionately for what 'do nows' need to appear on the Charter to promote the brand's leadership strengths. By ensuring that the output of the brand's living script is shared, consensus on how best to serve the brand organization is renewed. 'Video Brand Chartering' of the sort executed by the BBC may one day prove to be the acid test of a brand leader which is so strong that it is prepared to make itself publicly transparent.

Three driving forces

In this book we will try to show that brands reflect corporate and organizational brainpower. We will see that a lot of intricate connections can be made across different branding junctions. These are crossroads in the process of branding where informed direction shapes the right to lead.

- Inside the company people's productive and creative efforts can harmoniously come together at branding junctions if employees share the same script on the brand's purpose.
- Outside the company perceptions of the brand – for example, among end-consumers and retail customers – can be worth much more than the sum of the parts whose composite meaning is clarified by decisions made at branding junctions.

The brand interconnects three driving forces which we will label create, manage and direct.

- **Create** involves thinking about why a communications platform will have enduring value for everyone.
- **Manage** involves balanced decision-making, often under urgent pressure for action, but with a consistency of purpose which makes marketing a different discipline from selling. We hope new accounting methods will be developed which recognize that the health of world class companies increasingly needs to be counted over longer time spans than the financial accident of the calendar year. But managers of the 1990s must be pragmatic enough to live with both the historical burdens of corporate governance and the world of the new brand organization.
- **Direct** involves the style of corporate leadership which motivates a passionate organization-wide (service) commitment to fitting the brand to other competences invested in by the company, as well as having the capability to learn how to take advantage of change.

We will refine these terms in the main part of the book. It is important at this stage to recognize the principle that enduring brands must continuously and harmoniously connect these three driving forces. All managers need to share this understanding of the process of branding from the outset. Otherwise, tensions will occur wherever groups of people try to win at three different things at the same time.

The biggest threat to many companies today, as they strive to build a core competence in global and local branding, is that departmental politics will take over and different internal visions of brand leadership will proliferate. This risk is particularly strong wherever:

- no practical consensus exists on organizing priorities as people strive to balance everyday decision-making on the branding of competitive quality and value, globally and locally;
- the economies of traditional ways of competing are in a state of revolution, thanks to changes as broad as what world class marketing will be, and as personal as how one will use multimedia (like computerized communications) in ten years' time;
- the corporate/global banner brand uses new marketing rules to defeat (or complement) the targeting rules of one-product brands (which

were until recently the profitable basis of most brand management systems).

Box F.4

'1994 will probably go down as the year the gloves came off in international business . . .

. . . global marketing is uniquely challenging . . .

. . . it demands that companies attain a flexibility and focus that few have yet achieved . . .

. . . technology can be a marketing curse as well as a blessing . . .

. . . there is the question of communications . . . companies can no longer hide behind the carefully manipulated images of their brands . . .

. . . consumers are more demanding than ever before – and competitors more ruthless. The manufacturer that fails to appreciate these facts will go to the wall.'

(*Source*: 'Soap and chips', editorial in the *Financial Times*, 21 December 1994)

Chartering the breadth and depth of brand processes as leadership systems

Our present vision of top level brands as leadership processes is summarized in Box F.5.

Box F.5 Foreseeing brands as leadership processes

The enduring brand process will be a leadership system which shares an organization's competences with consumers, employees who serve the brand and other stakeholders of a company, such as intermediary customers between company and end-consumer. The basic needs of any brand are to be profitable as a communications investment, and to be competitively closest to its end-consumers in delivering quality and value (real or perceived). To thrive among world class competitors, leadership systems will need to:

- adapt proactively to change;
- connect up and renew unique organizational competences;

continues

continued

- commit those who serve a brand to a consensus sense of focus;
- be consistently motivating both as consumer lifestyle and as employee workstyle;
- exhibit a fine balance between competitive and partnership spirits (reflecting corporate responsibility for global purpose and local presence).

A Brand Charter provides a living script which is short, so that the brand's directional vision is easy for everyone to remember, and updatable as the brand evolves. The communications techniques suggested in this book on how to make Brand Chartering work for you have arisen from asking marketers, creative practitioners, CEOs and business teams around the world the following question: If you were to choose the form of a top-line living script for your brand, what would you like to see in it?

Unlike other planning systems, the Brand Charter is kept short by concentrating on top structural know-how, just as an architect does. All workers connected with the brand should be organizing round this if they are consistently to serve the smart business relationships, which are essential to trust in the brand and attracting consumers to it. The Chartering process can, of course, be indexed to much longer supporting documentation and quantitative aspects of business planning, but this is not pivotal to everyone's understanding and communal sharing of the unique sense of direction of a brand's added value. Brand Chartering should also index outstanding strategic or policy issues which need top-level contemplation and response. For example, the CEO may not be a day-to-day member of most brand teams, but he or she does need to be a branding party to issues which connect up to all of the company's goodwill and he or she should have the best vantage point for advance detection of any common patterns of branded 'illness' across the company.

Best practice organizational development of Brand Chartering often starts with a company's 'banner' brands (semi-corporate or other brands connected to a significant proportion of the organization's goodwill). Try to pilot a Chartering format for these top brands. Other brands and sub-brands can then follow a similar format.

Once a company has established an organizational format for what will be a Charter, it becomes practical, should the CEO or other senior managers wish, to scan through the company's whole brand architecture. The strategic direction of investment in branding can then be based on up-to-date and organizationally aligned knowledge. Whenever it is necessary for people to hand over top responsibilities for brands, this can be done with a strong sense of continuity.

As a procedural system, Brand Chartering should be organized so that it continually brings the brand alive for the whole business team. This can be done by generating communal feelings for the brand's living script which are so directed that everyone in the business team feels a 'do now' sense of urgency.

Branding junctions: where Charterers take the opportunity to organize integrated branding

In taking up the challenge of Chartering a living script for something as intricate as a global brand process, we soon found that we were embarking on a worldwide search for the most practical ideas for locating and orchestrating branding junctions. These are:

- **organizational**, where many people's inputs come together to form part of the added value of the brand process; and
- **perceptual**, where consumers experience a brand's relationship holistically. We stress that this is the way the public interprets brands. There is a danger that a brand will become a misfit if it is served piecemeal by experts in different functional silos of a company.

Because the character of a brand's relationship with consumers lives on in their minds, time is the third dimension which intersects every branding junction. Consumers value a brand which not only knows where it is going but also shows it is proud of its history. It should never be economical with the trust it has already won, nor with the expectations it creates by being in the news.

Internally, company managers have to balance such potential conflicts as returns and investments, short-term requirements and long-term goals, creative brilliance and institutionalized discipline. Do not underestimate the complex interpersonal expertise which needs to be brought together in producing and directing a vital brand. Branding junctions are vantage points for synthesizing views and goals of the brand as a business process, among staff whose collective contributions determine what brand equity evolves.

To gauge the differences which organizational alignment can make at a branding junction, consider classifying three levels of know-how:

(1) Ignorance is where every member of the business team has a different perspective on what the brand is about and where it is going.

(2) Mediocrity is where every member of the business team has a communal perspective, but this is not continuously and actively focused on leading consumer wants.

(3) Excellence is where every member of the business team has a communal perspective, and this is interactively focused on leading consumer wants.

World class competition means that branded companies will need to practise excellence at branding junctions to survive, or at any rate to seize the greatest advantage to be won from branding. If you work in a company which aspires to excellence at branding junctions, and then to perpetuate this standard, Brand Chartering, or something similar, will become a necessary organizational tool.

We would bet on the 20th century turning out to be the first and last in which companies believed that brand marketing could be organized as a departmental function. Henceforth, brand marketing needs to be a service skill which is networked across an organization. This does not necessarily signal the end of the professional marketer, but the marketing curriculum vitae will need to be revised to encompass the role of added-value coach across the organization's business teams, instead of being functionally revered as the high priest of consumerism. Internally, marketers should act like drama teachers, seeking to get everyone in the business to fulfil themselves in the parts they play and knowing the added- value script by heart. At the same time they need to be constantly on the lookout for signs that the script needs to be changed. Ten years ago we heard a brand marketer in a consumer goods company (Nestlé) say: 'Every meaningful brand is really a service which the whole of the company can add to.' Today we applaud such foresight from a company which many would then have regarded as needing only a manufacturer's orientation.

Introducing any new organizational system requires political tact. But radical reviews of branding practice are now in order. The mid-1990s have witnessed CEO contributions to articles (such as the aforementioned ones by McKinsey and *The Economist*), surveys (Coopers & Lybrand, 1993) and speeches (such as those made by Ed Arnst while CEO of Procter & Gamble) signalling the need for urgent changes in the organization and practice of brand marketing. Readers of this book will see why we believe that Brand Chartering is a user-friendly and pertinent organizational tool for enabling branded companies to evolve as both fit to serve their customer constituencies and capable of winning the strategic contests that competing for the future involves.

References

Coopers & Lybrand, (1993). 'Marketing at the Crossroads', report on a survey. London.

Freeling, A. (McKinsey). 'Winning the right to brand', speech at the Marketing Forum on the Canberra, 1994.

Hamel, G. and Prahalad, C. K. (1994). *Competing for the Future*. Harvard: Harvard Business School Press.

Macrae, C. (1991). *World Class Brands*. Harlow: Addison-Wesley.

Mazur, L. and Lannon, J.(1993). 'Crossborder marketing', The Economist Intelligence Unit.

Reid, M. (1994) 'The death of the brand manager', *The Economist*, 9 April

The Financial Times (1994). 'Soap and chips', editorial, 21 December.

References

Overview

In the main section of the book we consider 15 of the most important branding junctions currently encountered in organizing brand processes. We aim to reveal the kinds of Chartering insights that accrue from these focal components of the brand as a business process. We review experience-based questions which have been tailored to these junctions and which are a growing part of the Brand Charterer's tool bag.

In practice, however, organizations usually develop their own Chartering formats from a handful of branding interchanges. This is because most of the branding junctions are closely interconnected. They have been delineated in this book to make it easier to choose lessons which directly relate to everyday brand decision-making in any organization. Many readers may not yet be in a position to suggest that their organization needs to look into the benefits of Brand Chartering. We hope they will find that branding junctions, one by one, provide a stimulating framework for a personal investigation of why, when and how they could make branding work. Eventually companies that win the right to brand will need to ensure that branding serves to interconnect everything they do.

Companies have often piloted Brand Chartering principles by beginning at a focal point of interest then building across to other brand junctions as they become relevant to their own branding processes. The ways in which a company chooses to view its primary branding interchanges usually depend on how it organizes its branding system and the most urgent challenges to its current brand processes. CEOs' decisions to adopt Brand Chartering have often stemmed from their corporate recognition that a revolutionary market challenge is appearing on the horizon. Although the impact on profits of this revolutionary scenario may be five years away, leaders who have adopted Brand Chartering know that they are well placed to orchestrate how and when to take advantage of change.

Brand Chartering is constructed so that everyone can play a part in integrated branding. Find an organizational junction where you contribute to branding's added value and ask: What if everyone teamworked around here? As far as possible, the three main sections of this handbook are written so that the reader can choose where to start. Junctions are also arranged modularly for those who wish to browse through topics of current interest. We go first to the centre of each branding junction and then clarify the most typical ways it interconnects with other junctions.

An overview of the 15 branding junctions is shown in Figure O.1.

Figure O.1 illustrates the breadth of Brand Chartering. Depth comes from the fact that every branding junction can repay a lot of detailed thinking, as you can see when you refer to the relevant chapter. If Figure O.1 seems too detailed an introduction try the exercise below first. Some of the questions will always be worth asking wherever Chartering is being used to take a fresh view of a brand process.

Practical exercise for brand organization

Select some of the following questions. Ask a few people who are key to controlling or adding value to your brand process to answer them independently. Compare answers. If everyone shares the same vision of the brand process then you probably do not need Brand Chartering, or, more likely, you are already doing something similar. (The chapter relevant to each question is indicated in brackets.)

Create

(C1)   What leadership values would people – such as the 3C's: consumers, channel customers, company – really miss if this brand did not exist? (Chapter 1)

(C2)   Is this brand being anchored too narrowly to a product platform? How can you stop this happening? (Chapter 1)

(C3)   What perceptual codes uniquely remind people of this brand? How is each of these identifying property rights actually being leveraged? (Chapter 2)

(C4)   How do we help consumers to interpret where this brand is going to in a manner consistent with its past relationships and personal basis of trust? (Chapters 3 and 4)

C R E A T E	Chapter 1 Essence **What is the brand's leadership domain, and what is the core connecting message? What would people miss if this brand did not exist?**	Chapter 2 Identity **What inventory of consumer codes are invested in the brand? How is each code actually being leveraged in branding smart relationships**	Chapter 3 Heritage/Friendship **What else carries over from yesterday's relationships with consumer/clients which explains why we are who we are? What effect does past culture have on the future?**	Chapter 4 Future News **What else should we 'do now' to keep brands newsworthy and fit for competing in future business environments? What sorts of products/services will we have in five years' time**	Chapter 5 Other Create **What else can (re)create leadership and ensure that we cannot be outpositioned by competitors?**
M A N A G E	Chapter 6 Masterbriefing **As the economies of new types of media proliferate, how do we ensure consistently efficient integration of contributions from all of our creative agencies? 'Glocally'!? What jobs are the different media channels doing?**	Chapter 7 Quality and Value **How do we get perceived competitive quality and value consistently right for every product and service directed in the brand's name? How do we set goals and measure performance?**	Chapter 8 Flow/ Team Networking **As brand formation flows across the organization, is every department contributing optimally to the success of the brand? Are experts sharing their top-line know-how on process opportunities and risks?**	Chapter 9 Umbrella Connections **Are we making full use of new marketing rules associated with umbrella and banner brands? Do managers understand how marketing's 'rules of targeting' must be balanced by 'rules of connecting'?**	Chapter 10 Other Management **What else would enhance teamwork and support balanced manaagement of the brand's objectives? For example, how do we appraise managers for what they contribute in the medium term as well as the short term?**
D I R E C T	Chapter 11 Architect **What is the brand's role within our brand architecture? (for example, corporate brand, product sub-brand?). Is the architecture focused at the right levels and suitably interconnected to lead our sphere of business whatever types of world class competitor emerge? Which employees may feel threatened if we change our brand architecture?**	Chapter 12 Strategy Architect **Are there any other disconnections between our strategic visions and the totality of our brand architecture? For example, do we have the right core competences? Who will be our competitors and our partners?**	Chapter 13 Organization Architect **Are there disconnections between our organizational missions, roles, culture, etc, and our brand architecture? For example, do we set the right performance goals for branding to keep control of the added value chain?**	Chapter 14 Drama of Leadership **Is the brand's purpose motivating enough and so well understood that everyone in the business team urgently senses what to 'do now'? Who is really responsible for the brand's goals?**	Chapter 15 Other Direct **What else connects each brand and the brand architecture with prioritized organizational capabilities and strategic competences?**

Figure O.1   Brand Chartering: vantage points from the top 15 junctions.

Manage

(M1) Does this brand offer a world class 'balance' of quality and value? What future discontinuities in the added-value chain, globally or locally, could undermine this balance? (Chapter 7)

(M2) Is the brand's communications mix integrated and able to leverage changing media economies? Is it flexible enough for global and local marketing? (Chapter 6)

(M3) Do all added-value departments of the organization contribute to auditing this brand's opportunities and risks? Is everyone agreed on this brand's claim to resources relative to our other brands? (Chapter 8)

(M4) Do we make full use of new marketing game rules associated with umbrella and banner brands? Is this brand separate from all others or linked to a corporate brand architecture? (Chapters 9 and 11)

Direct

(D1) What core competences does this brand represent? How does this fit with our overall foci for corporate competences? Is the most being made of Hamel & Prahalad's concept of the 'banner' brand? (Chapter 12)

(D2) Have we fully explored partnership strategies for this brand as well as competitive strategy? As well as successful in-market products, does brand vitality depend on pre-marketing/post-marketing strategy? (Chapter 12)

(D3) Who is ultimately responsible for this brand's goals? Are measures of business team performance well aligned with the specific goals of the brand? Which leadership skill do competitive world class brands prioritize: cost-cutting or value-adding? (Chapter 13)

(D4) What aspects of this brand process need CEO involvement? (For example, corporate reputation; organization-wide communications of stretch targets and teamworking culture; leadership alliances leveraging change in the added-value chain.) (Chapter 14)

What other integrated perspectives of branding appear in this book?

Chapter 16 presents a case study of Brand Chartering in action. It is followed by 'ThinkPieces' related to Brand Chartering and/or the future of branding. We have sought to include the views of as diverse a collection of strategic and practical thinkers as possible.

We have also been able to select case studies and leadership practices originating from research conducted by the Economist Intelligence Unit. There is much for us to choose from because many top-level strategic and organizational insights are available in this extensive library of management materials. We must thank many other journals and publications which have allowed us to quote from them, especially the *Journal of Brand Management* and the *brand strategy Newsletter* where many questions on branding processes were first exposed in print.

In a book where our 'architectural' concepts of company branding are heavily influenced by our understanding of how Japanese companies communicate communally, it is appropriate to redress the balance with quotations from three American sources (see Box O.1). These demonstrate that new ideas about how world brands work to connect up communications are becoming a preoccupation of executives in world class companies everywhere.

Box O.1   American views of priorities for future brand processes

'The 3M logo is the primary symbolic representation of 3M's people, products and values. This is why it is the most valuable property we own.'

(3M corporate brochure)

'In the old days, it was up to the worldwide business manager to make the case that a new product was right for local markets. Now it is up to the local manager to demonstrate that it is not going to fly locally. Our expectation is that every new product will find a global market'.

(Anonymous US executive quoted in Hamel, G., and Prahalad, C. K. (1994). *Competing for the Future*. Harvard: Harvard Business School Press)

continues

continued

> 'Global brands are emerging because companies that make and market them are becoming global organizations. . . . The brand is a by-product of organizational experience and business systems (which is what we truly leverage rather than some catchy name). . . . So why do organizations, including my own, continue to strive for worldwide brands? I believe that they are rallying points or symbols for the organization itself, for the experience and knowledge it brings to the marketing of soft drinks, cigarettes or beer.'
>
> (Michael Jordon, CEO Westinghouse, former president of PepsiCo International)

A training and facilitating tool

Another way to introduce Brand Chartering is as a training and facilitating tool which enables consumer-facing companies to think and act, globally and locally. It is arrogant to believe that a brand offers consumers an enduring lifestyle unless the company also understands how to live the brand.

Many talented people in a company can contribute value to an integrated branding process. Chartering offers them the opportunity to explore how many of this book's 15 'branding junctions' are relevant and to form a consensus on the brand as a leadership process creatively, managerially and directionally.

What risks does the integrated approach of Chartering set out to overcome? Try this exercise. Consider your biggest current branding problem. Navigate over the 'branding junctions' using black spots to mark where the multiple sources of your problems are embedded. Ask somebody else to navigate the same problem. From the debate which ensues, you may conclude that the bad news and the good news are that the problem is mainly organizational. Bad because sustainable brand teamworking may involve time and effort, commensurate with a cultural change in which employees across the globe have to come out and stay out of their departmental silos or hierarchical closets. Good because organizations today still have the power to solve most branding problems.

We will take as a 'black spot example' our subjective view – for debating purposes only – of Unilever's problems in the 1994 'European detergent wars' involving Persil Power and Omo Power in a fabric-rotting controversy. 'The greatest marketing setback we have seen' was the retrospective judgement of Unilever's co-chairman, Sir Michael Perry, in

CREATE	ESSENCE	IDENTITY	HERITAGE/ FRIENDSHIP	FUTURE NEWS	OTHER CREATE
				•	
MANAGE	MASTER- BRIEFING	QUALITY AND VALUE	FLOW/ NETWORKING	UMBRELLA CONNECTIONS	OTHER MANAGE
			•		
DIRECT	BRAND ARCHITECT	STRATEGY ARCHITECT	ORGANIZATION ARCHITECT	DRAMA OF LEADERSHIP	OTHER DIRECT
		•	•		

Figure O.2   Navigate branding junctions: integrated teamworking across these junctions reduces the risks of organizational black spots.

February 1995. An explanation of the black spot pattern shown in Figure O.2 is:

- **Future news**. In 1987 you did not need to work in the detergents industry to spot the product form that would be the next great technology breakthrough. Anyone working in Japan would have noticed the launch of a detergent brand called Attack by the Kao Corporation. It was a micro powder which took up four times.less space than competing products. It took under a year to overthrow Japan's previous market leader (in a market worth close to $1 billion annually at current prices). You could brainstorm several reasons why this product form would have future world class potential including those immediately observable in Japan: retailers saw an advantage in needing less shelf space, and consumers found smaller packs easier to carry home and thought them more environmentally friendly. The world's detergents markets are dominated by branded manufacturers because the category is driven by product innovation. Understanding the destiny of Attack's product form was therefore at the top of the agenda for the future of any world class manufacturer of soap powder.

- **Flow/networking**. Unilever's explanation for having to reformulate Power products, within weeks of launching them in Europe, was that a mistake occurred somewhere between research and marketing. In the critical period prior to the launch the flow of information between departments on the branding process was below par.
- **Strategy and organization**. These are often over-hyped words. But basic components of organizational strategy revolve round taking a view on the future, above all constantly searching for any foreseeable market discontinuity; and making sure that everybody in the organization is determining how to turn prioritized challenges into corporate advantage.

So what should Unilever's employees and its customers understand from the firm's own PR of its 'Power' branding?

Initially, in April 1994, Power brands with a manganese 'accelerator' catalyst were claimed to be the product of a core strategic investment. An article in the *Sunday Times* on 3 April 1994 stated:

> 'Across Europe, executives at Unilever, the Anglo-Dutch consumer-goods giant, are gearing up for one of the most important product launches of their working lives. Project Clover is the culmination of 10 years' research and development costing £100 million to produce Europe's first super-concentrated washing powder. In the words of Unilever's Andrew Seth: "This is the biggest step I can remember in the last 30 years. Persil is the heart and soul of the Lever business, and this is the powder of tomorrow." '

By 13 August 1994 the word passed on to the Lex column of the *Financial Times* was 'since concentrated fabric powders represent less than two per cent of Unilever's turnover, the European soap wars are not material anyway'.

The alignment of organization and strategy in regard to this branding process was somewhat less than you would expect for a core business of a world class company. If this can happen in a company that is widely referred to as a text-book model for brand marketing, it is probably time for everybody who works with brands, or strategy, or organization, to think about how to integrate these corporate investments if world class marketing processes are to serve us all.

1

brand Essence

Introduction

Please forget what you may have read in marketing textbooks for a few minutes. Before you think of targeting, concentrate on 'connecting up'. This is the defining – and literally essential – communications purpose of powerful brands.

Peter Drucker says that 'the business enterprise has two basic functions: marketing and innovation. Marketing and innovation produce results; all the rest are costs' (Drucker, 1982). The power of branding is greatest when it draws on both these functions and communicates the business mission to all the company's audiences from employees to consumers.

The essence of a brand is the communications connections:

- which it has the founder's right to propagate and own;
- which give it an evolutionary right to a unique leadership domain, that is the brand's service or adding value objective.

By directing brand essence all kinds of reasons why the world values the declaration of independence implicit in a leading brand (or indeed any other leadership identity such as a great nation) can be interconnected. Three immediate consequences of essence are as follows:

- In the ideal brand world, everything that is done in the brand's name should be a confirmation of its essence.
- Choice of essence permeates everything an organization will be able to do strategically with the brand. We will see that, when other things

27

are remotely equal, the history of marketing communications shows that the most meaningful and communicable essence wins out time after time.

- It is vital that companies project the essence of brands properly and to maximum organizational advantage. It has been estimated that it now takes about $1 billion of advertising to build up significant recognition among consumers throughout North America, Asia and Europe (Hamel and Prahalad, 1994). Consequently, a tragic loss of resources can befall any brand owner who projects a brand's essence such that its meaning is unable to evolve beyond the first product to carry the brand's name.

As an intellectual concept, brand essence sets a trap for anyone who tries to define it more precisely than we have. Essence can involve everything at the core of a brand which works to the brand's unique advantage as a communicator. From this perspective, a brand is vacuous as a consumer promise unless it is also a core business purpose. Fortunately, recognizing key aspects of the essences of particular brands is a job, although perhaps not an easy one, that any business team concentrating passionately and inquisitively on living a brand's objective is qualified to do.

Looking back at twentieth century market categories, many of the world's biggest essences are remarkably transparent:

- The leadership essence of cigarettes is embodied in Marlboro. This brand was founded with the brief of being 'the cigarette for men which women like' (Watkins, 1959). The cowboy icon and later stereotyping, such as American Independence and Marlboro's Wild West Country, were identifiers which translated the meaning of this essence into an image for generations of consumers.
- The biggest communications essence for soft drinks is 'the refreshing and most friendly drink in the world'. These were the connecting visionary slogans of the brand from the early 1900s. Subsequent identifiers translating this lifestyle into reality include Coca-Cola's designer bottle, red for visible packaging and logos, familiarization as the real thing and the friendship of the 'American Dream', which Coke's advertising brings, like an ambassador, to the world's youth and young at heart.
- The world's most powerful essence for fast foods is McDonald's 'fast foods served consistently with home-from home values'. This was the connecting vision repeated in most of the published scripts emerging from McDonald's proprietor, Ray Kroc. This resonates through the training manual which every new employee receives.

When you line up essences founded on communication of such 'great ideas', it becomes apparent why these brands could be destined to lead the social values that matter most in their marketplaces. This does not happen unless organizations also set about living these essences internally (that is with all the product and service contributions inspired staff can make) as well as promoting them externally (that is cost-effectively to consumers and retail customers). So, for example, Coca-Cola's formative distribution goal was set to be 'within arm's reach of desire'. An early inspirational act for ensuring continuous improvement of staff training at McDonald's was the founding of Hamburger University.

Many of history's most famous brands grew when they were nurtured by a business person with a consistent vision, the power to command long-term corporate commitment to taking the vision to market and the creative passion which leverages the company's capabilities to distinguish product and market values.

If a brand does not have a vital consumer meaning it is not worth investing in its leadership organizationally; the enormous financial resources needed to publicize it continuously; or the time and political resources required to make it a rallying point for the skills of the company's people. Nor is it worth living the value relationships which feed through the brand process to trading customers, their endconsumers and back again. Conversely, if a brand does have a vital (and self-perpetuating) consumer meaning, companies discover that there are more significant similarities than differences among consumers in their sphere of business as they market a brand's essence around the world.

The fact that a product-oriented and impulse-grabbing essence like 'have a break, have a Kit Kat' could also establish a global and local 'time-out' meaning in consumers' diaries was never appreciated by Rowntree. It was appreciated by Nestlé, which acquired Rowntree because it thought its leading brands had enough of these kinds of meanings to be worth buying. They would then be served up globally as brands which could stand out as unforgettable in their own right, as well as playing a strong supporting role as entries on Nestlé's menu as the world's leading foods company. Although some accountants' renderings of commercial history may say otherwise, it was not the past performance of Rowntree's brands that Nestlé valued at $4.5 billion – record-breaking five times book value – when it acquired the company in 1988. It was the future advantages which Nestlé, as the world class packaged foods company, could create out of the latent essences of these brands.

The story of Kit Kat as part of Nestlé's global vision is amplified in Chapter 13. So too is the story of Guinness as a brand whose essence – beers whose visible characters are so distinguished that brewers around the world prefer to partner them rather than compete against them – is reflected at such different levels as:

- Guinness products – beers instantly recognisable by their unmistakeable physical appearances (stout's black and white poetry, the red beers from Kilkenny, Kaliber's zero alcohol);

- Guinness corporate style – the frothy confidence of a company that knows where it is going with almost as much focus as the record-breakers chronicled in its annual publication, *The Guinness Book of Records*;
- Guinness country – the brand that represents Ireland more than any other. (The idea that a brand which is a country's major export can take over the essence of the world's stereotyped images of the country of origin is a subtle one discussed in more detail in Chapter 3.)

Test the following essential hypothesis. A strong leader is humanly attractive if:

- leadership is transparent;
- values added are fairly shared.

Before testing this on brands, test it on other great organizing identities such as nations. These are clues to why powerful brands work. Another clue is that brands are the most democratic of independent competitive beings. The day that a brand process loses its essence by ruining its reputation or loading itself with too many organizational costs is the day that consumer votes will ebb away in all free competitive markets.

Living and breathing an appropriate cultural philosophy of why branding really matters is particularly important as more companies realize that competing for the future will involve something more important than product branding. This is the banner branding of global business domains with organizational support systems that are specific to the brand and its unique service objective.

Some banner brand essences may seem to be as simple as focusing on being the world class branded company which leads a designated sphere of business. In fact, electing to be both world class (capable of offering the world's best quality and value) and branded is not a simple matter. Branding is not one of those core competences that a business can choose to add on to other competences. Rather other core competences need to be chosen in a way that will enable branding to be worthwhile. Specifically, brand-oriented organizations need to go beyond the purposes of other organizations by aiming to have:

- sufficiently unique control over the added-value chain glocally so that other companies prefer to partner them rather than compete against them;
- economical ways of staying in the news that excite both staff and consumers, and share the brand's leadership essence as closely as possible between them.

For example, the essence of British Airways aims to do both these things through the medium of its slogan 'the world's favourite airline'. This declaration of intent is a mission for staff to live up to as well as a meaningful consumer promise. It also connects up competences, which were underexploited in the old British Airways, such as the routes and hub for a global network and world class engineering staff. (See ThinkPiece 1, brand benchmarking of British Airways.)

In another example, the founder of Honda was once asked: How did you originally decide that Formula 1 motor racing would be a worthwhile consumer promotion? He replied that he had not thought like that. His actual reasoning was: engine technology is a core competence of Honda; therefore we want the best engineers working for Honda; the challenge of winning Formula 1 will be a timely way to ensure this.

As long ago as the 1920s Marks & Spencer developed a philosophy which the Japanese were to (re)invent decades later. The aim was to develop continuous relationships with suppliers who would then be asked to improve their offers at regular intervals. The distinguishing feature of this policy was that Marks & Spencer would choose, at each of these steps along the learning curve, whether the next improvement should be in terms of better quality or better value. Through control of this partnership strategy, Marks & Spencer determined that it would always stay quality steps ahead of the competition.

The essence of a brand-oriented culture should be that a restless spirit of improvement pervades the organization. The Japanese have a notion of cultural duality which is hard to translate into English but whose spirit can be interpreted as 'organized self-improvement means mobilizing selforganizational improvement'. From day one, Sony's cultural essence (for the company's staff) began with the founder's mission statement:

> 'If it were possible to establish conditions where people could become united with a firm spirit of teamwork, and exercise to their heart's desire their technological capacity, then such an organization could bring untold pleasure and untold benefits.'

Over the years this has been translated into the consumer essence of 'Sony being state-of-the-art electronics'. Sony's cultural and consumer essences are thus reflections of one and the same branded being.

Research by Hamel and Prahalad concludes that the four top-level communications investments in branded businesses are:

(1) domain
(2) recognition
(3) reputation
(4) affinity.

If essence guides everything you think and do, these four communicators are the top-level and continuing ends that branded businesses seek in order to know themselves continuously.

Consider how close to perfection Sony's branding investments score:

(1) Being state-of-the-art electronics is a great business domain unless you are a competitor, in which case, as one company told us: 'It's Sony's unfair advantage. We innovate new features in our product category, but whenever Sony replicates them, within a few months the word-of-mouth among the public ends up being that Sony innovated everything.'

(2) Sony's identity system deserves its near universal recognition (see ThinkPiece 1, brand benchmarking of Sony).

(3) Sony (subsequently joined by other Japanese companies) deserves its place in history for taking the quality of corporate guarantees to new consumer heights.

(4) Sony consumers are a loyal club by any standards. For new generations '–man' strikes a pretty hip chord as an integrated part of Sony's brand architecture.

We will see that implementation directives associated with 'connecting up' brand essence can permeate every level of Brand Chartering – creative development, management, organization and strategy – and all 15 branding junctions. Indeed, defining the essence of a brand-oriented organization, and aligning this with employees who serve the brand, makes the vital difference between essential branding processes and fairly useless ones.

Brand essence workshops: dancing with your core values

To focus on competing for the future, Brand Charterers frequently use brand essence workshops as a navigational tool for aligning business team understanding of the adding-value objective of the business and the strategy for propagating it. There are various reasons why the branding process needs essential communications clarity to thrive. As we discuss these reasons bear in mind that:

- the essence of 'branding' is 'uniquely purposeful creativity';
- the essence of 'process' is 'teamworking and connecting up'.

Team consensus and virtuous spiralling

Leadership qualities can be clarified by questions spiralling round a brand's outstanding virtues (and weaknesses) in order to confirm a business team's belief in why the essence of its business is of unique and enduring value. For example, in the case of brands which aim to be world class leaders of product categories, the framework shown in Figure 1.1 has proved to be an invaluable way of connecting up a virtuous spiral of themes to a brand's core. By concentrating on this methodology, business teams can converge on both a consensus statement of the mission of the branded business and why this is the essential communications perspective for directing values that are developed in the brand's name.

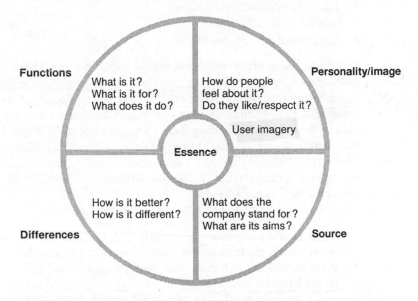

Figure 1.1 Brand essence. (*Source:* Leo Burnett Brand Consultancy)

In consumer terms, strong brand essences are apparent when there is a link between each inner quadrant and where the whole has a degree of clarity. Essences begin to weaken wherever:

- confusion exists in the consumer's mind about what the brand does or is for;
- real performance differences over competitive offers are no longer apparent;
- personality or image lose their unique relevance;
- the source of authority declines in credibility or in its base for admiration.

Inner and outer core questions can be tailored as a function of a brand's purpose and domain of influence. By questioning the core of the brand, the aim of virtuous spiralling is to refine team consensus down to the simplest statement of the main, distinctive characteristics that make the brand unique and represent its future source of power.

(Re)focusing the brand architecture

Directors of branding organizations cannot afford to rest on a blind belief in the company's brand architecture. Brand owners must be flexible, particularly in the competitive environment of the late 1990s which is characterized by an extraordinary congruence of change trends including:

- business internationalization
- retailer concentration
- integration of new media.

As business organizations confront these changes, corporate leaders must deal urgently with the problem of owning too many brands, representing fragmented product or geographic territories. Survival of the fittest will require firm decisions on which brands to demote, by either culling them or sub-branding them to appear not in isolation but as part of a corporate or 'banner' brand's family. Conversely, companies must find ways of identifying with higher-level branding platforms, which act as banner brands (that is quasi-corporate umbrellas) in the ways discussed in Chapters 11–14.

One way forward is to ask some essential questions:

- What would consumers really miss if this brand did not exist?
- What would trade channels really miss if this brand did not exist?
- What would the company really miss if this brand did not exist?
- If this brand was our company, and if we pumped all our resources into it as our only brand, would its essence be transformable into a leading domain for one of our core spheres of business?

This simple visioning exercise provides an acid test of whether there are any hidden jewels in the existing brand portfolio worthy of investing in and directing at higher levels of corporate advantage.

Stretch-domains

Box 1.1 Japanese tuition

Recently, in a letter from a Japanese pen-pal of mine, I was reminded that our first conversation on umbrella branding got off to a sticky start. It was 10 years ago and my first visit to Japan. Typically, I had adopted expatriate defensive posture in being slow to immerse myself in the power of corporate branding. I had argued along the lines that:

continues

continued

'Perhaps it is only in Japan that a company brand can represent salmon, steel mills and electronics at one and the same time.' The reminder in my friend's letter began: 'Perhaps we see now that it is only in the UK that a brand (Richard Branson's Virgin) can stretch its virginity from pop music to airlines to colas to personal pension plans.' The letter concluded 'By the way I hear that your nation's biggest grocery brand (Sainsbury's) now advertises itself as able to supply everyone's favourite ingredient.' Fair cop guv.

Memories came flooding back. My friend had taught me with exquisite patience that there is a right and a wrong way of asking how brands work at making connections. The wrong sort of question relies on literal consumer research. Sadly, a lot of academic research of brand equity perpetuates this by asking: 'As a consumer who knows this brand's existing products, what else could be manufactured in this brand's name?' A question framed in this way will elicit the response that the manufacturer should at most stretch its knitting to neighbouring product categories.

A vaguely right kind of questioning needs to be asked of the company. If we started with one brand as the company's topmost brand which brand would this be? And, more importantly, what stretch-domains of leadership can the brand represent in consumers' minds?

(*Source:* Diary entry by Chris Macrae, 1995)

It is particularly valuable for those who might be tempted to classify themselves as product manufacturers to ask: What if we were to project ourselves not only in this way but also as a fashion styler (for example, L'Oréal, Dunhill); or a service club for our consumers (for example, American Express); or a media owner (for example, Disney, Cosmopolitan); or a world class guarantor of competences (for example, Sony, Nestlé); or in any other way that prevents the brand being too closely anchored to individual products instead of an evolving business?

Sir Adrian Cadbury once said that chocolate needs to be marketed as both function and fashion. A similar realization turned Gillette-Sensor into a winning combination of a 'Best a man can get' lifestyle and a visibly innovative product. Previous branding efforts communicating the functions of local best-selling lines had come within a whisker of turning the shaving market into a commodity market, with a generation of young men perceiving Gillette's leadership image as little more than cheap, blue and plastic.

We should not assume that manufacturing is an essential competence of operating a brand franchise. Manufacturing for Nike's flexible range of merchandise is largely contracted out. Similarly products are sourced

[handwritten margin notes: CNET: young "hip" "in the know" — ZD: old conservative in the know mainstream]

for Body Shop or the Virgin range of drinks without these companies needing to own manufacturing plant.

The right origin for (re)developing a high-level brand is not necessarily a product. The brand should consider drawing on any or all channels of access which the company has already won, such as communications, distribution and world class competence.

The way that your company projects the essence of a brand has a simple but vital consequence. If you think of a brand's essence as being a single product then potential consumers will too; if you ever want to move the brand on to endorsing something else it may be almost impossible to do. This has been a costly lesson for many late twentieth-century manufacturing companies. So much of the brand power they invested in was dedicated to individual products that it is now hard to transfer these investments to higher-level branding domains on whose future playing fields world class branded companies are assembling.

One constructive approach is to consider what the essence is of particular world class domains from the consumer viewpoint.

- The essence of manufacturing: best quality? best value? really innovative products we did not know were possible? safe and caring?
- The essence of retailing: best prices? exclusive offers? widest range? at our doorstep? a socially rewarding atmosphere?
- The essence of the service company: all the information/help we need in one place? worth knowing for a lifetime? helps us learn about costs and benefits? warm human feelings?
- The essence of the fashion company: new ways of making impressions? escapism?

Swatch evolved from the great idea of reinterpreting the watch to have more than a manufacturer's hallmark of excellence by being fashionable too. Swatch marketers now reckon that their brand's equity extends to any category that can potentially be reinterpreted in a surprisingly fashionable way, but not to neighbouring product categories such as clocks.

Given time and consistency of presentation, apparently intricate details can help consumers widen a brand's horizons. For example, it is noticeable that Ariel's UK advertising in 1994 began to move away from the standpoint of the detergent product. With the help of a mere preposition – 'At Ariel we believe in . . .' – the brand appears to be taking on the form of a company with competences such as stain removal instead of being confined to the product domain of the detergent.

In other cases, brands which hone their characters to epitomize a product category's strongest emotional values, such as soothing and trusted in the case of cough mixtures, may proceed to unlock a character whose extendability across other categories is the envy of competitors' brands whose characters have not been envisioned beyond those of aggressive product salesmen. Choosing the right founding product for a new brand involves a lot more than first appearances suggest.

There is a never-ending list of human needs for brands to portray and serve. Consequently, it is sad to see companies investing a lot of money in product-obsessed brand essences whose stretch capabilities are less than vital. We believe that *the* essential opportunity for every brand-leading business is to make a valuable difference emotionally as well as functionally; a double act which makes it hard for any other organization to follow.

Connecting up other core strategic properties

For higher-level brands, including corporate and banner brands, it is crucial that everyone in the company understands the strategic direction (vision, culture, mission, values, and so on) which a brand's essence represents by being:

- a corporate source of advantage (over competitors and for partners);
- a continuous pathway for added-value leadership; a uniquely relevant consumer meaning;
- a reference point in the sphere of business.

The brand-oriented business also seeks to broaden strategic perspectives on every operating matter. A particular advantage of a strategy being expressed in terms of brands is that it is perceived as alive and thus more stimulating to work with than, for example, an abstract level of return (Urde, 1994). (Organized purposes of leadership are discussed in Chapter 14.)

Some approaches for clarifying essential connections are as follows:

- Big meaning for company and consumer. Providing everything coheres and is relevant in a self-perpetuating way, a bigger brand beats a collection of smaller brands.
- Connections to sub-meanings (usage meanings, performance differentiation, source/platform of values owned, personality/image that is consumer-smart).
- Uniqueness that company can protect and which cannot be outpositioned by a higher-level appeal.
- A capacity for continuous growth, for example by coining its own legends/heritage and creating buzz and selfperpetuating momentum.
- Consistently adds value, should ideally encompass highest quality points in core markets (as well as other value points) if it is not to be outpositioned.
- Strategic fit with company's core competences, that is brand pathway matches corporate advantages to deliver (although not necessarily to produce; for example, Nike sources products as do top retailers).

- Has sufficient flexibility to be proactive to change (whether this is in environment, consumers or competitors). Robust as a competitive survivor even when not optimally supported.
- Clarity of its own territories versus rest of corporate brand portfolio. Focused so that company organizes around: for example, NPD (New Product Development) for this brand.
- Competitive impact: easily lends itself to great identities, news-worthiness, and so on. Here again company must be clear on which brand services it can profit from and which are vital for brand's essence as image-maker, and so on.
- Consistency/integration, alignment in everything done in the brand's name, for example, masterbriefing or 'intuitive feel' of serving this brand. Ideally, a very simple core so that it is never misinterpreted by corporate personnel, and so on.
- Global prestige (from staff pride and motivation to communications channel newsworthiness, that is free PR to distribution channel partnership), for example, to be perceived as world's number 1.
- Values/vision as if it were a company brand intent on two-way smart relationships with every audience.

Global and local ownership

We have observed two common organizational models where brand essence is king and the brand process is directed in an action-oriented way.

(1) The benign dictatorship, where the quality of being benign comes from a brand owner or founder recognized by the team as having a dedicated and true belief in the gospel that if consumers' needs are not properly met then the brand's franchise will surely die.

(2) The soft-wired culture, where the brand's essence is networked as the operating culture for everyone who serves the brand. For many organizations this is the ideal model provided there exists a will and a way. The will must come from seeing branding as the ultimate service that organizations can seek to deliver; one systematic way is continuously uniting organizational action and vision by Chartering the brand's essence and living script.

When a business has previously fragmented branding responsibilities to operating territories – countries, product streams or business units – whose divisional managers were free to rule as long as they met their revenue targets, the challenge of becoming an integrated, brand-oriented organization should not be underrated. Visioning the brand's essence will ultimately be a way of achieving strategic bonding. Sometimes it is necessary first to agree on the most important strategic elements or the business. Focus on elements that must be developed consistently by all involved because they are the value-differentiation heart of the business. By formalizing a consensus among managers that they are organization-ally interdependent, you acknowledge that a communications strategy is needed to harness value-creating commonalities and that someone has to have leadership responsibility for directing it. If you cannot reach an agreement then you may conclude that either you do not have a brand-oriented business or you do not have the right people skills to serve one.

The craft of preparing any workshop is to be forewarned and forearmed. If the participants have not previously had much in common, start with some team-building procedures. These may range from rehearsing strategic essence for someone else's business, such as a competitor's, to dramatizing extreme organizational cases where other companies have, in a crisis, resorted to a not-so-benign dictatorship and profited from mandatory pulling together.

Most of the time, however, brand essence workshops serve to develop constructive tensions out of natural and healthy diversity. Brand decision-making is frequently a balancing act between imperfect alternatives. Judgements should be transparent to all teamworkers and not hidden away in expert silos. Thus essence forums are a constructive way to initiate or revitalize multifunctional teamworking. When we have done this with brand teams around the world focusing on a global brand process, it has almost invariably been a privilege to participate in such progress towards global and local thought and action. Unlike many other teambuilding events, globally organized workshops of this kind are guided by an essential purpose.

Audit of lead opportunities and risks in systemizing and (re)vitalizing essence

A brand-oriented business focuses on organizing unique added values. Throughout this book we will see examples of why organization systems of branding need to feed back and forward through brand essence. In a sense brand essence is like taking out a contract on what particular business relationships you wish to form. Some examples of leading questions which drive organizational form through perpetuating the value and realizing the investment of brand essence are as follows.

(1) What focal points evolve from brand essence in terms of value creating functions? Specifically, what needs to be developed inside the organization and what needs to be contracted out?

Example: being Benetton (1994) includes organizing the following value functions

(handwritten margin note: "% of "BRAND ESSENCE" GENERATED")

	% of value function developed within Benetton
Design themes	100
Design options	5
Catalogue	100
Store range	0
Material procurement	100
Knitting	1

(2)   For every function, what opportunities or risks particularly interact with brand essence?

Example: essential risk audits

Wherever brand essences of global businesses represent the key to billions of dollars of goodwill, you might think that companies would audit the functions most at risk of destroying their perceived value. At the time of writing this book a surprising number of companies did not do this.

- The 1980s essence of Perrier was about purity at a single source, but then trouble at the source of production caused Perrier's essence to temporarily self-destruct (and many feel that it has not fully recovered to be the brand it once was).
- In the summer of 1994 one of Body Shop's founding family was alleged to question whether being positioned as an ethical company was worth the candle. This was prompted by press reports that part of Body Shop's US operations had been charged with some local misdemeanours relating to waste disposal. It was specifically because of Body Shop's ethical brand image that this issue raised serious questions about whether the company was being faithful to the essence of its contract with the public.
- 1994 also saw the European launch of Unilever's 'Power' detergents. Seldom has a company invested so much time, money and reputation in a marketing war that was lost before it started. In spite of the imposing battle cry of a PR campaign revealing 'Unilever's largest launch in a decade' and a continental launch process costing close to £250 million, an unintended part of the launch mix was retrospectively confirmed by the company's co-chairman, Mr Tabaksblat, as 'a product which had a defect which we had not detected'. As another Unilever executive subsequently opined, 'We were very enthusiastic about an exciting new product and did not look closely enough at the negatives. Somewhere between research and marketing something went wrong.' (See also Chapter 14 for reasons why world class companies cannot afford to imagine that the reputation of the corporate brand is separable from the essences of their product brands.)

In conducting risk audits of a brand's essence it is very important to explore acute sensitivities which can arise from the following:

- Interaction with the uniqueness of a brand's essence; for example, Perrier's problems were greater because its positioning was purer than pure.
- Extremities of a product's use, particularly if the consequences can be dramatised by a competitor; for example, the critical weakness of Unilever's Power products was evident for only a few special fabrics/dyes, but was dramatic enough for Procter & Gamble to obtain European news coverage of the crisis. Earlier, in a 1980s UK relaunch of the Persil brand, Unilever's initial failure to clarify that the new product was biological caused a highly publicized row with a UK pressure group, The Eczema Society, which had previously endorsed the Persil brand.

(3) To vitalize brand essence across internal departments or external business partners, are there lessons to be learnt from brand franchising?

Many of the world's most consistent branding operations employ franchising mechanisms ranging from the fully franchised McDonald's to the part-franchised Coca-Cola. In the latter case, Coca-Cola headquarters effectively franchises the latest marketing concept for worldwide use to sales organizations around the world, many of which are independently owned bottling companies. Franchising kits offer advantages, including consistency, speed of global implementation and shared know-how. As management structures in organizations flatten, marketing skills will increasingly need to be networked instead of departmentalized. Franchising modules as communications-sharing toolkits will play an increasingly active role in experience-based marketing.

Clarifying essential keywords and picturing the big ideas that embody them

There comes a time in any branding when a creative agency needs to be briefed, and the brand will have to be turned into messages which translate as simply as possible into consumer values.

Brand essence is not usually a slogan that can be directly campaigned on (British Airways being an exception). Moreover, the essence of the branded business mission, for example from a team's virtuous spiralling (see above), may be stated in terms that include the industry sector you wish to lead. Thus the essence of a business vision will often need to be translated into consumer vocabulary. For example, in the clothing industry product lines range from 'haute couture' to 'basics'. If your brand is to be the leader of an everyday clothing sector, 'basics' is not a keyword for external consumption even if this is part of the essential vocabulary of the internal mission statement of the business team directing the brand.

To ensure an optimal strategic fit between brand and business purpose, the business team should envision the brand essence as a summary of relevant leadership qualities that a good agency will be able to work into big ideas. However large your communications budget, simplicity is a core operating principle of branding because of the practical working hypothesis that your public is never there, in mind and spirit, simply to listen to you. The intriguing and defining characteristic of all commercial media is that you are trying to propagate a message to people whose primary reason for being there is very different from your own. This is the common denominator: from reading a newspaper, to watching television, to playing a computer game, to sifting through correspondence, whether it be postal or electronic.

There are various tools for the business team that wants to transform brand essence into a transparent creative brief. One of the best and simplest is keywords. Get every member of the team to write down one word they hope consumers would most associate with the brand; then another if it has a valuably different meaning. Repeat this until no more unique value triggers are forthcoming. When a brand has a weak essence the team will have produced a very long list of conflicting words, which is a finding in itself. When a brand has a strong essence, a handful of keywords capture it. Reaching consensus on a handful of essential keywords is an excellent achievement for a brand team. A creative agency may, for example, transform these words in a single picture, such as Marlboro's cowboy, which will prove as useful as any verbal translation of brand essence. Note that most consumers picture a brand in their mind's eye much more clearly than they can verbalize it. We will come back to this topic when discussing the identifying property rights of branding investments in Chapter 2.

Brands exhibit a knack of their own when creating personal relationships. They take on unique characters, express themselves – and their businesses – through particular tones of voice, and may even be capable of offering a change of mood to the consumer, as well as a lifestyle image. In these and other essential style rules of branding, any way of prompting and retaining a commonly held feeling for a brand's essence across the brand team is to be valued. While we are not advocating that every CEO should dress up as the legendary Kentucky colonel who founded the world's leading chicken fast-food takeaway (KFC), this organizational means of globally identifying with the brand's service disciplines is not as corny as it might appear.

Summary

Many brands these days are supported by business teams comprising hundreds of people. Alignment makes a vital difference to the power of the brand. Imagine the contrast between the brand where every member of the business team shares a common belief in a leadership purpose, and one where every team member has a tangentially different perspective on the brand.

Higher-level brand leadership bundles up the communications of everything that a company has accomplished, such as product competences, know-how, trading partnerships, reputation and consumer values, and projects it forward to tomorrow's marketplaces. We do not believe that it is now cost-efficient to think of the origin of a higher-level brand process as merely a product: there should be a lot more for a leading company to serve.

Within the branding of a business process, essence is a vital branding junction. It works to keep branding faithful to its leadership purpose. The transparency of brand essence as an organizing contract helps to guide a business team in thought and action, through the short and long term, and keep it aligned in an integrated and value-added direction. You may make your own list of reasons why brand essence matters wherever business strategies are highly dependent on organizational goodwill. A shortlist of leading connections made by orchestrating brand essence thought processes might be as follows:

- The valued meaning of a brand both for the company and the consumer.
- The clarification of what is in the brand for other stakeholders, for example, trading channels, company shareholders.
- A tool for aligning a brand's resource allocation and focus within a company relative to other brands and in relation to a company's core competences.
- A way of maintaining integrity for a brand at all points of delivery.
- An engine for new product delivery.
- A procedure for driving communications and advertising briefs.
- A means for inspiring (new) personnel both inside and outside the company with the meaning of the brand.
- A system for defining the organization required to deliver the brand and to take proactive advantage of change.
- An approach for ensuring that a business culture has foresight and is value-oriented.

(See ThinkPiece 2 for an agenda of a typical brand essence workshop.)

References

Drucker, P. (1982). *The Practice of Management*. Harper & Row

Hamel, G. and Prahalad, C. K. (1994). *Competing for the future*. Harvard: Harvard Business School Press

Watkins, J. L. (1959). *The 100 greatest advertisements*. Dover Publications.

Urde, M. (1994). Brand orientation – a strategy for survival. *Journal of Consumer Marketing*, **11**(3)

2

brand Identity System

In Chapter 1 we advocated focusing brand communications on the integrated connections a branding process needs to make before contemplating any targeted messages. Readers who felt inhibited by this apparent relegation of market targeting to a secondary status may enjoy the multidimensional freedom of expression inherent in the concept of a brand's identity system.

Nowadays powerful branding employs a visual design language of symbols, colours, sub-brands, flagship products, service promises and other identifying reminders, which shapes the way we recognize a brand's sphere of business. Brands navigate human associations and perceptions with a variety of reminders, each of which acts as a consumer code. A powerful corporate or umbrella brand is capable of conveying multiple messages with particular relevance to different audiences, as well as other mind-expanding interpretations of its essence. In the case of global brands, identities need to be crafted as component forms of an international design language. In this chapter we will see how analysis of the brand identity system enables us to explore the breadth and depth of the universe of associations which a brand has invested in consumers' minds.

Some well-designed identity systems

It is difficult to over-estimate the power of a well-designed identity system. We begin with some examples.

McDonald's

If you are aware of McDonald's, you are likely to make many of the following associations with the brand's identity system: Big M logo, Ronald, Big Mac, Mc named menu items, Red and Yellow, and so on. The identity system is a communications tapestry. The brander must keep asking two questions:

- What identifying 'threads' are known to everyone who knows the brand?
- How are they working for the branding process, both its consumer heritage and its future business?

These questions should be guided by an informed belief in design impact and aesthetics. Remember:

- There is no point in cluttering the tapestry with another thread unless it is serving some vital purpose.
- The identifying threads must all fit together. As part of a pattern, they should provide overall confirmation of a brand's essence. Identities should not directly clash, but subtle tensions can be good. For example, the most fascinating human characters are those who intrigue because they are at once familiar and continuously capable of surprise.

Box 2.1 contains some interpretations of how the identity system of McDonald's works for the brand. Use this and add your own insights by asking the sorts of questions listed.

Box 2.1 Exploring the identity system of McDonald's while confirming the essence of fast food served with home-from-home values

WHAT?	HOW?
What brand identifiers (for example, colours, symbols, stereotypes, slogans, platforms, famous moments in brand's history, product features, design icons, other appeals to senses, etc) are in the minds of your consumers?	An identity system: • casts leading identifiers with different roles; • connects everything up to achieve multiple effects such as "multi-positioning", "multi recognition" . . . What leading interpretations can you find when exploring McDonald's identity system? Which identifiers would you show off where if you were directing the McDonald's brand?

McDonald's integrates	
M	Signpost for distant media; nicknamed destination (golden arches)
Ronald	Children's aspect of multipositioning; local community visibility; anchor of family personality
Big Mac (also Big Breakfast, Mega Mac)	Adult appetite aspect of multipositioning; Big codes (eg value); Familiarisation slogans, eg Mac Attack
Mc	Linking identity for broadening product menu
Moscow	Global and local PR platform
Red & Yellow	Heartwarming impact

To appreciate fully the significance of these identifers to the goodwill invested in – and stewarded by – those who direct the business of McDonald's, read benchmarking McDonald's in ThinkPiece 1 and then take a second look at the box.

Marlboro

Some would say the cowboy has proved to be the most valuable branded identifier ever created considering the internationally popular image he conferred on the brand and its smokers. But do not underestimate the powers of other Marlboro identifiers such as red, the device of the red chevron with white backdrop and Marlboro (Big) Country scenery.

The red chevron has always done a great job in ensuring that Marlboro's pack stands out from the crowd. Think of how many ways this works: from making the Marlboro pack visible on a retailer's crowded shelves to being Marlboro's signature wherever one smoker shares a cigarette with another. Twenty years ago one of us, as a rookie market researcher, was talking to a Marlboro brand manager in the UK. We were expressing bewilderment over instructions from Philip Morris New York headquarters that while much of the marketing mix, such as advertising, allowed for a high degree of local flexibility, if the brand manager wanted to change one iota of the brand's packaging design, this had to be signed off in triplicate from HQ.

These days we would be bewildered by any owner of a global brand who did not regard packaging design as a strategic property that requires global control. The consistency of Marlboro's red flag is the connecting thread which keeps the whole history of the brand's equity alive. In some countries cigarette marketing is so highly censored that only two image-building acts remain to support your product:

- sponsoring an abstract global flag, for example Marlboro's red chevron around the world's grand prix motor racing circuits;
- showing your package off on retailers' shelves and in consumers' hands.

By owning red in a product category, the brander enjoys the most popular bold colour which has the greatest impact. Most Marlboro smokers are also reminded of Marlboro's wild west legends by their pack's identity – as Marlboro's continuous flag of independence – even if these associations are only reinforced by memories.

In China you can see a remarkable modern rendering of a brand's identity system with the Marlboro brand using its red and big country identifiers to extraordinary effect. Imagine a commercial which mixes footage of a popular sports event sponsored by Marlboro and attended by Chinese youths waving red Marlboro flags as part of their supporters' ritual, with Big Country scenery.

The rapport of Chinese people with the Big Country dwarfs even that of Americans. In this oriental context Marlboro's red flag connotes the dreams and aspirations of China's youth as well as being a visual reminder of their symbol of patriotic familiarity. At a stroke the brand becomes the passport to imagining China's evolution from being a great power to an era already beckoning where the Far East is the most dynamic place on earth and where China will have a great international role to play.

Budweiser

The American Budweiser brand is an example of how identifiers can be threaded together as consumer codes to portray a national institution. This analysis of Budweiser's identity draws on a book by Sal Randazzo in which Budweiser is described as the archetypal male mythology brand:

> 'The unique power of advertising goes beyond its ability to build and maintain successful, enduring brands by creating perceptual entities that reflect the consumer's values, dreams and fantasies. Advertising turns products into brands by mythologising them – by humanising them and giving them distinct identities, personalities and sensibilities that reflect our own. In some sense, advertising brands have, in our consumption-driven society, come to serve a similar function as the ancient Greeks' pantheon of gods. They function as projection holders wherein we project our dreams, fears and fantasies. . . .
>
> 'The connection between advertising and mythology seems fairly obvious to me. Myths are more than entertaining little stories about gods, goddesses and heroic characters. The universality of myths, the fact that the same myths recur across time and many different cultures, suggests that they originate from somewhere inside us. Psychoanalyst Carl Jung said that myths, like dreams, are really projections that emanate from the soul or unconscious psyche. Myths represent humanity's collective dreams, instinctive yearnings, feelings, and patterns of thinking that seem to be hard-wired in humans and that function somewhat like instincts to shape our behaviour.'
> (Randazzo, 1993)

Box 2.2 helps to explain 'Budweiserness' by suggesting seven of the brand's most significant consumer codes (together with our attempt to translate meanings for non-American readers).

Box 2.2 Inventory of American consumer codes identified with Budweiser

Brand identity	Context as American consumer code
Clydesdales	Shire horses used by Budweiser at promotional events; they were previously used for delivering beer. They fascinate Americans and connote macho images of power, strength and working pride
Cvolski	Most famous execution of a long-running series of slice-of-life ads featuring blue collar workers as the USA's real heroes
This Bud's for you	Budweiser's long-running brand slogan
Red, White & Blue	Brand's packaging colours (corresponding to the USA's national colours)
American eagle	The company's oldest trademark modelled on the bald eagle (the USA's national symbol)
Beechwood aging	As Budweiser's product legend declares on every pack, this proprietary process 'produces unique taste, smoothness and drinkability' – we know of no other brand of beer that costs so much to brew or age
Genuine article	The heritage of being the USA's number 1 brand of beer

Some points to digest from Budweiser's inventory of identities are:

- Each identifying code is a valuable property right as a contributor to Budweiser's image bank. Each code required a large and continuous marketing investment to imprint its association with Budweiser on American consumers' minds.
- Each identifying code is intimately related to Budweiser's essence as a leader, namely being the product hero of the American working male by portraying the American male as (unsung) hero. Budweiser's identities are engineered to work with each other in developing an integrated picture. They link product connoisseurship with images of working males and with the integrity of traditional American values and overall pride in belonging.

Once you have examined how intimately a brand's vital reserves depend on its inventory of identities in consumers' minds, it is difficult to attach credibility to any analysis of brand positioning, brand valuation, and so on, unless it includes an integrated analysis of brand identity.

Kodak

It is prudent to think of the brand name as an audio-visual symbol. It can serve to link customers around the world only if they all find it readily pronounceable. Early world class branders like George Eastman knew this. He christened his camera Kodak because this name was 'short, vigorous, incapable of being misspelt . . . and meant nothing'.

Kodak's identity system, nicknamed 'Big Yellow', remains a source of competitive advantage for the brand today. The ways in which the brand's colours grabbed Japanese attention in the late 1980s would surely have made George Eastman proud (Box 2.3).

Box 2.3   Sky wars

At a time when Fuji and Konica were committed to heavy spending abroad, Kodak spent three times more than both of them combined on advertising in Japan. It erected mammoth $1 million neon signs as landmarks in many of Japan's big cities. Its sign in Sapporo Hokkaido is the highest in the country. It sponsored sumo wrestling, judo, tennis tournaments and even the Japanese team at the 1988 Seoul Olympics; a neat reversal of Fuji's 1984 coup when it won the race to become the official supplier to the Los Angeles Olympics.

Kodak's cheekiest ploy was to spend $1 million on an airship emblazoned with its logo. It cruised over Japanese cities for three years, mischievously circling over Fuji's Tokyo headquarters from time to time. To Fuji's chagrin, Japanese newspapers gleefully picked up the story. The Japanese firm was forced to spend twice as much bringing its own airship back from Europe for just two months of face saving promotion in Tokyo.

Half of all Japanese consumers can now recognize Kodak's goods instantly. Kodak's recent growth puts it within sight of second-place Konica in Japan's market for camera film.

(*Source: The Economist*, 10 November 1990)

A creative break

Before examining further how identities work to create and renew brands, it is worth noting some of the organizational implications of investing in brand identity. Like most of the components of Brand Chartering, the identity system seems to be naturally anchored in one area of branding, in this case creativity. But interconnections with all other areas of the brand as business process must be constantly reviewed.

Identifiers represent valuable property rights of the branded communications process. They have often required significant investment costs to become symbols whose power is proportional to the global recognition that they have accumulated. In spite of this, archaic national laws do not always provide protection against visual counterfeiting, so branded manufacturers must be wary about the extent of their possible exposure.

Cola wars

An example is Coca-Cola, which at the start of 1994 was the largest manufacturer's brand in the UK monitored by audits of packaged goods products carried out by Nielsen market research. One year later a proportion of its business was lost to partnership combinations involving Cott colas, major British retail chains and in some cases host fashion brands, such as Virgin. Coca-Cola's vulnerability is not due to replica products, since well formulated own-label colas have been around for years. The new cola warriors have been 'lookalikes', deploying two key identifiers that had previously been Coke's own: red livery and classic associations with Americana.

How did this gap in the brand's defences emerge so suddenly, in spite of Coca-Cola's wealth of experience? A technical answer is that a manufacturer's 'me-too' reaction to another's famous branded identity never proves profitable when both are competing on level playing fields. This is because some of the me-too's communications will be mistaken by consumers as messages for the real thing. Even more will be interpreted by consumers as an impostor's challenge to their loyalty to an old friend. But the mechanics of competition from a major retailer (such as Sainsbury's, whose distribution power represents over 10% of grocery purchases made by UK consumers) are different. With only marginal overheads (instead of advertising and other marketing budgets) the retailer can offer the product at a lower price, although this did not make previous own-label colas particularly big business. The sting to the manufacturer's brand comes from the retailer's control over shelf space. In some British stores consumers have seen red American lookalike colas being given up to four times the display of Coca-Cola's facings where the points of sale are made.

For Coca-Cola this UK lookalike phenomenon is insidious. Its image is becoming diluted and its value undifferentiated, because confirmation of the brand's essence was invested in Coca-Cola's whole visual language, not the mere name.

The drastic impact of lookalikes is so far confined to the UK and a few countries whose attitudes to designer's rights might be labelled as 'third world' (like any country that refuses to recognize artistic copyrights protecting audio, visual or computer software). The UK's isolation in Europe on the lookalike issue was evident in a recent test case in which the UK's leading brand of wine, Le Piat D'Or (positioned as a French blend for the British palate), was able to negotiate a halt to a lookalike offer from the same British supermarket chain that started the cola wars. Appeals were won not in British courts but under French law which was applicable because the wine was bottled in France. Until the UK's laws are changed, no manufacturer's branding strategy is secure from the possibility of a lookalike invasion without:

- development of a design that is protectable but more complex than consumers really need;
- ownership or long-term partnership of retail channels;
- ownership of a scale or other product advantage which cannot be replicated.

Another major organizational issue connected with identity systems involves the networking of design skills. These are increasingly relevant at the interface between tactical and strategic decision-making on the branding process. In Chapter 11 we discuss how many brands a company needs and how high-level banner brands can be designed to connect up much of the company's goodwill with lower-level sub-brands targeting local consumer needs. Nestlé assigns a lot of its detailed thinking on these matters to visual communications experts who are specifically charged with two major jobs:

(1) To arbitrate in a balanced way between strategic brand requirements from Nestlé's headquarters in Vevey, Switzerland, and ideas on brand identities related to marketing initiatives of national subsidiaries.
(2) To control the design formats used to ensure that Nestlé's banner brands are communicated with global consistency compatible with the consumer image of a world class company and yet sufficiently flexible to connect up with every sub-branding presentation. Figure 2.1 is an example taken from the design catalogue of approved ways of representing Nestlé's corporate brand (Mazur and Hogg, 1993). (See also ThinkPiece 1, brand benchmarking of Nestlé.)

Box 2.4 contains extracts from recent speeches by an executive from American Express. It highlights some intriguing points about the importance of taking corporate identity systems seriously.

The Corporate Identity

1. The Nestlé Horizontal Corporate Logotype. Where the first priority is the legibility and the recognition of the Nestlé name, this version, which puts emphasis on the Company name, should be used for stationery, fleet vehicles, annual reports, etc.

2. The Nestlé Vertical Corporate Logotype. Where the Company philosophy or its corporate role needs to be expressed, this version, which puts emphasis on the nest as a Company symbol, should be used on sign-posting, buildings, etc. Preference should be given to this version wherever possible.

NB. *These versions are not to be used on packages (see below).*

The colour for the NESTLE corporate identity is always grey as defined in the NESTLE Corporate Identity Guidelines.

The Brand Logotype

When NESTLE appears as a corporate range or product brand, the solid version should be used. Positive or negative, any colour can be used.

Where NESTLE appears as a corporate brand, it shall, in all applications, be given increased prominence in size, position and colour.

The Nestlé Seal of Guarantee

This version is exclusively for use on packaging, on the side or back panels only of the unit pack, display or shipping carton.
It should never appear on any other material.

For exact application, refer to Nestlé Corporate Identity Guidelines.

Any use of the Nestlé logotype and/or the 'nest' device not in line with the above has to be approved by the Trademark owners.

Figure 2.1 General guidelines for the use of the Nestlé logotypes. (*Source:* Nestlé.)

Box 2.4   Keeping a brand image up-to-date (at American Express)

I'd love to be able to claim that everything about our brand is the result of thorough research and careful deliberation, but I guess we all know that in real life things don't always work out that way.

Take our Centurion, for example. You see him on our cards and our travellers' cheques, embodying such brand characteristics as security, integrity, strength, protection, service. We couldn't have created a better symbol if we'd employed droves of researchers and designers and branding consultants. Which we didn't. The truth is altogether more serendipitous.

We owe our Centurion to an explosion of forgery after the Second World War. In the post-war years our travellers cheques became hugely popular, not only with travellers but also with counterfeiters. We desperately needed a harder-to-forge design, but at the time new engravings could have taken a year or more. So we asked our printers, the American Bank Note Company, to help – and from a dusty shelf they produced this guy; he'd been engraved for another job which had never been printed. From the obscurity of a printer's store-cupboard he's gone on to become one of the best-known brand marks in the world – proving that great symbols aren't always made to measure. You can sometimes get them – literally – off the shelf.

In 'Project Jigsaw', we recently undertook a complete revamp of our visual identity. We laid out all our direct mail packs and product literature and they looked as if they had come from a whole bunch of different companies. So we needed to reassert a consistent visual style that every part of the company could use. But Project Jigsaw went far deeper than a routine rethink of graphics and typography: it examined the style and tone of voice we use when we talk to our customers and potential customers.

Let me quote you a few sentences from the internal manual that resulted from Project Jigsaw:

> 'The transition from the 80's to the 90's was traumatic. People who were happy participants in our "prestige dream" have changed. They now speak about getting value. Words like "exclusive", "privilege" and "select" seemed to permeate every level of our communication. The tone and manner generally suggested someone who felt he was better than most . . . but attempts to apply this florid (and, to today's ear, pompous) language across a wide array of marketing communications ended up working against us . . . looking old-fashioned and out-of-date. People talk about the world moving forward and American Express lagging behind.'

continues

continued

In short, our brand attributes and values might have been as good as ever, but the way we were presenting them had lost its relevance. So what are we doing about it now? Again, I quote from the manual:

'Our tone and manner should reflect those of a service company . . . a group which consistently reinvents itself to meet and exceed it customers' changing needs and expectations. Our voice should no longer be from the "Chairman of the Club's Membership Committee" or from a disembodied global corporation that's full of itself. Rather, it should be the voice of a consultant . . . a skilled, flexible and entrepreneurial advisor and supplier. Someone who earns his customer's trust through performance not promises. A competent, confident professional.'

And that, I think is the essence of everything we're doing to bring our brand up-to-date. The values don't change but the audience's perceptions do. The attributes don't change but the presentation must. In conclusion, I think the most important step we've taken in renewing our brand image is to be honest with ourselves; to listen to what customers were saying and admit that our corporate style had become outmoded. Once we'd taken that on board, we could see that a new style of advertising would help, but that advertising alone would not be enough. A brand is a very public thing.

(*Source:* Extracts from speeches by Russ Shaw, head of advertising and brand management, American Express Europe)

The brand identity system offers immense power to the brand oriented company, but the use of this capability by many twentieth-century brand owners has been underwhelming. Why?

One reason, frankly admitted by American Express, is 'honesty' about an organization's current weaknesses. The biggest impediment to valuable evolution of service values in every great company is often arrogance. It takes a subtle blend of modesty both to be proud of being number one and continuously to ask whether your presentation values are up-to-date.

Marketers have sometimes tended to enjoy advertising as a sexy activity where dream-making is contracted out to an external agency. In contrast, designing a corporately branded identity immediately involves the laborious business of serving the lifestyles you present. The point to reiterate from Amex's confession is that true service unites performance and promise. In fact, one good test of a design consultant is the extent to which he or she converts you to the service theme. Avoid those who fail to make this point, because they may hit you with artistic brilliance but run away from the deeper organizational issues involved. Conversely, one of the best design consultants we know was adamant that the first slogan of marketing should be that 'all brands are services'. We last met him preaching this gospel at every operating level of a world class packaged goods company, and promising to excommunicate anyone who referred to the company as a manufacturer.

Having developed a feeling for identity systems, we now take a deeper look at some of the initial questions we suggested all branders should keep asking about the identity systems they are operating.

What consumer codes are identified with the brand?

The brander will often end up with quite a long list for each brand. If appropriate, cluster them where they have similar meanings and try to locate the one which most clearly represents each cluster. Then start classifying.

- Which of these associations come free with the product's visibility? For example, the colour of your pack if one has been consistently chosen, or if you are really lucky your personifying icon, such as the Centurion of American Express.
- Which involve a heavy investment to keep in consumers' minds? For example, an advertising slogan is usually a heavy investment. It needs a lot of repetition if it is to stay in consumers' minds. It may take 5% of all your advertising time spent and probably more than that in terms of your share of consumers' attention. It will usually be at the expense of establishing some other consumer code.
- Which of these consumer codes are strategic? For example, a vital confirmation of the brand's essence or a permanent part of the brand's visual recognition.
- Which of the codes are tactical or transitional? For example, helping the brand to compete as a fad in the local market but something that you do not expect to be permanently associated with the brand.

These details are worth clarifying before the brand team addresses the purpose of each consumer code:

- How are we using this identifier in the brand process? For example, what does it do for the brand in consumers' minds in relation to recognising, purchasing and enjoying the brand?

There are a number of answers, some of which are listed in Box 2.5. You may want to add more.

> ## Box 2.5   How is the brand's identity system working?
>
> Strong brands use identifiers to work in many ways. How do they do this? Make a list of all the ways in which your brand's identity system must compete for consumer attention, such as:
>
> - General recall of brand as top of mind.
> - Specific recall of brand as top of mind (for example, occasion of use, calendar of mind).
> - Heighten visibility/recognition of brand (for example, impact in a specific media or on a new platform).
> - Badge brand with personality or other image to wear.
> - Extend a brand.
> - Endow a brand with a stereotype bringing instant cosmopolitan appeal.
> - Local buy-in to a globally branded phenomenon. Develop architectural strengths of high-level brands (for example, corporate/banner brands, see Chapter 11).
> - Build linkages between brands (for example, corporate brand and product sub-brand).
> - General reminder of brand essence.
> - Pre-emptive (for example, symbolic) ownership of brand essence.
> - Souvenir of brand essence (or other empathy translator). Connect up values of flagship brands to benefit other brands.
> - Seed a brand's cachet.
> - Brand a word-of-mouth legend.
> - Identify a brand's own PR platform.
> - Transition a brand through evolution of its identity system.
> - Translate essence into lifestyle or service guarantee.
> - Express a corporate tone of voice; a cultural style.

Identity for brand recall

Packaging and product design have often been sidelined from their role as a brand's first (and almost free) medium. We are now witnessing the end of an era of mass communications where advertising agencies, as their name suggests, had certain biases as creative suppliers. Their main bias was towards the provision of TV advertising, and away from helping to integrate design and other forms of communications that holistic brand identity systems need to exploit.

Notably, brand recall is a richer source of brand power than many branders realized when results of communications campaigns were routinely judged by superficial measurements of advertising and brand name awareness. These measurements were made by market researchers who were paid for 'precision', defined by the amount of data they collected and the standardization of formulae used in number-crunching.

Now that brands are increasingly aiming to be umbrellas for various products, there are new subtleties in the ways that brand awareness works in consumers' minds. They cannot be calculated merely from such basic market research questions as: Which brand names (or advertising) do you think of spontaneously when I mention a particular product? Or which brands do you know when I prompt you with a list of names?

One way to identify valuable brand recall involves uniquely associating a brand with an occasion of use that is a vital part of every consumer's diary. For example, from Malaysia we see how simply 'Showertime is Lux Time' associates the Lux brand with taking a shower (Figure 2.2). What a suitable diary entry in a humid country for the Lux brand's core range of beauty cleansing products. It is easy to see why a Lux brand manager would rather have Lux spontaneously return to mind every time a consumer thinks of taking a shower than when questioned generally and out of the blue by a market researcher.

Identity for taking advantage of new and global media

Today's global media calls often provide only a fleeting glimpse of the brand, whether this is as the sponsor of an advertising hoarding behind the goal on a football pitch or of the player's shirt or of the backdrop to the interview after the game. Clearly, concise brand identifiers like the capital M of McDonald's or the Coke of Coca-Cola work to ensure that their brands can play with the best in front of global audiences. So do such gems for brand names as the fourlettered Mars and Sony or the three-lettered Lux. One consequence of the natural visibility of short brand names is that you are now unlikely to find any name which is globally pronounceable and clean (that is, free of unfortunate connotation in someone's mother tongue), with four letters or fewer, which has not already been registered as somebody's trademark.

Figure 2.2   'Showertime is Lux time'.

Box 2.6 provides an Italian souvenir of how the suitably identified global brand stands out from the crowd.

Box 2.6   Worldwide footage

Unlike local brands, the world class identity also enjoys making cost-effective use of such global media spots as trackside hoardings at the Olympic Games. Being seen in the neighbourhood of other world class brands is to inherit a state of international approval which local brands cannot muster. Subliminally, historical replays of such global media events create a cumulative sense of discrimination between brands with world class status and those with something rather less.

Alongside the footballing superstars of Italia's 1990 World Cup, the serious competitive pitch was reserved for brand hoardings. As events turned out, many of these identities looked under-rehearsed to play their part behind the scenes, being handicapped by over-long names or graphic logos designed to exploit media opportunities offering more time or space in front of the audience. In contra-distinction, one four-lettered word made use of every camera angle. The Mars house colours – dramatic red with gold bordering and black background – proved to be a stylish flag for the confectioner's global panache. By easily scoring the most global rating points, the Mars branding was the visible winner of the championship.

(*Source:* Macrae, 1991)

It is not just global media sponsors that are prone to materialize in fleeting glimpses from the crowded brandscape of our mass communications society. Think how many identifiers flash by city workers on an average commuter journey, or the shopper travelling with a trolley through the aisles of a hypermarket.

Identity for brand image and brand personality

Marlboro without the cowboy would never have got started as a global brand; Lacoste without the alligator would have no fashionable meaning. The competitive make-up of brands whose products are primarily consumed in social settings requires an identifier which badges the brand with an image for consumers to wear.

Throughout this book you may detect many subtle ways in which we suggest personality icons – in human and animal forms – give their brands extra metamorphic powers. The following is a short list of illustrative examples:

- Introduce a dramatic new value to the brand; for example, Amex's centurion.
- Make the brand more personally recallable to occasional purchasers; for example, Johnnie Walker in the seasonal market of Scotch whisky.
- Give the brand child, and therefore family, appeal; for example, McDonald's Ronald or Disney's cast of animal characters.
- Authenticate a slogan through the brand's announcer; for example, the way Tony the Tiger establishes that Kellogg's Frosties are Grr..rreat.
- Stereotype a brand's essence without saying a word; for example, the power of any advertising copy which features Esso's Tiger.
- Merge fantasy and fashion; for example, Lacoste's Alligator.

Identity for brand extendibility

A particularly interesting challenge facing many companies which find that one-product brands are no longer economic involves extending (some would say stretching) the brand. The example in Box 2.7 is only a slight exaggeration of how a poor frame for brand extension decision-making is something which brand decision-makers can ill afford.

Box 2.7   Which of these alternative approaches to brand extending is more sensible?

Option 1: Stretch the brand instantly by announcing that new product X is now offered by the brand.
Option 2: Review whether the brand has any identifying codes which are relatable to product X.

- If yes, brief your advertising agency to help consumers interpret the brand's extension to the new product by portraying the brand in a

continues

continued

> way that emphasizes the relevant codes as signposts to and from the brand consumers know to the new product you wish to announce.
> - If no, and in the absence of other brand alternatives, integrate into your brand's identity system a relevant new identifier and once this has been cultivated proceed to announce the new product using the new identifier as signpost.
>
> Through the process of extending a brand, the ultimate difference between these options can be 'all or nothing'. By enabling consumers to interpret where you are going, option 2 allows a brand to become all that its leadership essence is capable of. By confusing consumers, option 1 can end up diluting consumers' feel for brand essence until the brand's relationship has lost all its meaning. Yet in the 1990s, as brand extendibility has increasingly become the most valuable creative talent associated with branding, many companies have adopted option 1 either in an ill-considered rush to obtain new product revenues or through failure to develop an organized understanding of brand identity systems.
>
> Unfortunately, faddish frameworks, often compounded by measurements of so-called proven – that is historical – brand power like brand valuation and early American research into brand equity (Barwise, 1993), seem to have been accessories to the folly of disorganized stretching of brands. The acid test for any framework on the future power of the brand revolves round prioritizing the following line of questioning: Does this framework recognize that a brand's future power is largely leveraged, positively or negatively, by what you creatively make of it? In particular, is it agreed that the most relevant communications creativity involved in extending a brand is that which helps consumers to translate their imaginative connections between where your new products and service values are going to, and where they think your brand is coming from?

Identity for enabling global and local communications

You may find some clues to construction of strong brand identifiers by brainstorming how human languages work.

- Brands contribute characters to an experiential language designed for human exploration of quality and value; a language which is the first truly global and local one. Presence in the mind depends on the consistency, creativity and visibility with which a brand makes particular values its own. Key identifiers assist in this process both by adding particular nuances to a brand and by being devices which heighten recall. Ultimately, just as familiarity governs which words you choose most regularly to express yourself, familiarizing devices breed a comforting inclination towards certain brands. Just as some words appear to have a particularly distinguishing tone, some brands strike irreplaceable personal chords.

- One particular power of the brand is to mix image with reality. For example, brands can work like package tours that transport the human imagination without the physical strain of leaving home. Most consumers now enjoy perceiving a mixture of local and international offerings to be at their doorsteps. Appeals to our local senses remind us of our roots; offers of cosmopolitan experiences broaden our horizons. Indeed, John Naisbitt advises that one of the megatrends for our third millennium involves 'the blending of global lifestyles and cultural nationalism'.

- Unsurprisingly, identity themes which dominate branding's universal design either resonate with appeals to human fantasies or are stereotypical of human needs. Much of this canvass of branding concentrates on the themes shown in Box 2.8. To be effective communicators, most identifiers refer to some extent to the interpretive conventions which other brands or widely known entities have already established. It is unwise to identify yourself in a competitive vacuum since it is necessary to relate to codes which consumers already know how to read.

Box 2.8 Predominant themes referenced by branding's universal design codes

- Countries
- Clubs and other affiliative institutions confirming belonging or belief systems
- Male/female roles (more specifically: male for impressing females, male for males, female for males, female for females)
- Friendships, smiles, humour
- Fun, appeal to children's imagination, family rewards
- Mothering, growing, environmental concerns, home-from-home comforts
- Rebels, youth, adolescence, artistic freedom, power to the people
- Sun, seasons, nature

continues

continued
- Purity, good health
- State-of-the-art, science, modernity
- Self-indulgence, treat, pleasure, fantasy
- Status, self-achievement
- Biggest, world's number 1, leader's guarantee
- Celebration occasions: anniversaries, rewards
- Symbol of good fortune, tradition Safety, simplicity, stability
- Power, strength, confidence

The inclusion of local identifiers gives a global brand identity system much needed flexibility. It can also give local consumers the pleasure of feeling that they are improving a global institution.

Identity for brand architecture and high-level brands

As we have seen, the McDonald's brand language demonstrates one way of establishing a multidimensional communications format facilitating all the linkages that high-level corporate and banner brands need to exploit. Its multiple communication territories include:

- the geographical – global and local;
- consumer segments – from children to adults;
- usage occasions – from breakfast to driveaway snack;
- menu of products – from burgers to nuggets to pizzas.

When constructing the constellation of identifying effects that a coherent brand architecture needs, remember that:

- each brand or sub-brand has its own essence, but there should also be transfusion synergies between these essences;
- each identifier should make at least one specific 'how to use' contribution, either to a particular brand or as the linkage between two or more brands;
- the constellation of effects of all the identity systems in the brand architecture should be more than the sum of the parts.

It is because of McDonald's constellation of consumer codes that it is difficult (indeed almost impossible) for any business to attack

McDonald's directly. Is McDonald's fast food? A family entertainment centre? A cosmopolitan meeting place and break from city pressures? It is all of these at the same time.

Identity as an essential advantage

Hershey's is the USA's favourite chocolate company. It has never seemed to share the passion for global marketing of its major indigenous rival, the Mars company. Hershey's has therefore had to try that much harder to stay close to American hearts and minds in a business environment where, in Sir Adrian Cadbury's words (Macrae, 1991), 'you cannot afford to be in the second division' because recognition as an industry leader, economies of scale and world class production competences are critical success factors. Hershey's achieves its special rapport with American families to a large extent through its 'Hugs' and 'Kisses' brands which are notable identities for the following reasons:

- In English these are cosy brand names for playing confectionery's role in family bonding.
- 'Hugs' and 'Kisses' are bite-size chocolate morsels that are probably the smartest individually packaged brand units that a few cents can buy.
- The brands' shape, wrappings and product patterns (Kisses are a mosaic of dark and white chocolate) involve a production complexity that required a large upfront investment. Hershey's therefore feels confident that neither manufacturer nor retailer could affordably imitate Hugs and Kisses. Regarded as a marketing platform – over the long lifetime of the Hugs and Kisses brands – the high cost of investment in production technology is really a low-cost branding delivery system.
- As flagship brands in Hershey's brand architecture, Hershey's Hugs and Kisses are affordable entry tickets for each new American generation to the chocolate world of Hershey's. Arguably, the success of every Hershey brand depends on its familial connections to Hugs and Kisses. While these identities may be largely American, they are the foundations of a world class branding process judged on the criteria of the unique values they deliver to their consumers and to their corporate owner.

Seeding or identifying a brand's cachet before mass marketing

From Lacoste to Häagen-Dazs, a remarkable number of famous brands seeded their reputations, in some cases up to haute couture levels, by winning stylistic acclaim or becoming word-of-mouth cult fashions among opinion leaders before they spent money on mass-marketing media. Box 2.9 shows that Lacoste was one of the first brands to cultivate its image from an individual sportsman's prowess.

Box 2.9   Looking into the legend of Lacoste

The brander should never forget that the typical consumer test of a symbol is: how pleasing is it the hundredth time your eyes meet up with it? This helps to explain why the most productive symbols have a certain cleanness of style, a hidden simplicity rather than a showy complexity.

Consider Lacoste's alligator. This is one of the world's most successful brand trademarks. It is pitched on the advertising hoarding with the greatest impact: people's breasts. It works both subliminally and supraliminally to confirm the brand's stylistic essence of 'being abreast of an adult sense of humour'.

How was this brand conceived? René Lacoste was a French tennis player and a hero in Davis Cup competitions of the 1920s. He acquired the nickname of the alligator and a girlfriend embroidered an alligator on a blazer he wore on the courts. That is where the brand's star was born.

(*Source:* Macrae, 1991)

In the benchmarking of Häagen-Dazs (see ThinkPiece 1), it is noted that the brand's exotic, Scandinavian-sounding origin suggested by its diphthong was the invention of a New York ice cream manufacturer. The brand's global expansion through seeding methods of communications has pioneered new standards of creative efficiency. Do not be critical of this inventive process. All global brands have a duty to exploit almost free mythological transfer to the utmost as this provides a brand's stakeholders with a better deal than the multibillion dollar scoops of advertising that may otherwise be required for a brand to gain global recognition.

Identity as a brand's own PR platform

Beaujolais' global birthday party as a branded PR event is world class. The 'new Beaujolais' arrives. Can you think of any brand which has established its own PR day on the world's calendar with greater economy of resources?

Identities for transitioning a brand

By investing in a system of interconnecting identities, brands can be moved through major evolutionary stages by phasing identifiers in and out while maintaining sufficient identities at any moment to ensure perceptual continuity. This process needs to be thought about very carefully, particularly where a brand derives a great deal of impact from action replays from the past. These replays take place sometimes metaphorically, in consumers' memory traces, and sometimes literally, for example, because a brand was a prominent sponsor of an event at which a world record was established. Three examples of transitioning a brand's identities illustrate the diversity of this process.

McDonald's

Ronald was preceded by a completely different human icon, Mr Speedy. He was caricatured as a hamburger-headed man and helped to popularize the notion of fast food while this consumer category was in its infancy. Mr Speedy retired from the McDonald's identity system in 1962 once 200 McDonald's franchises were up and running.

From Marathon to Snickers

During the 1980s the Mars company tidied up several local brand names. For example, in the UK the Marathon chocolate bar was rechristened with the product's international name Snickers, so that British consumers could in future relate to the global sporting stages where this brand was increasingly billed to appear. It is claimed that Marathon's consumers had little difficulty in adapting to this name change. The bar's traditional brown, blue and white packaging was so clearly differentiated on shopping shelves that visual identification with the brand took over while the brand's name was changing.

'Pandemonium in a toothpaste' was the headline in the New York *Herald Tribune* during the controversy over Darkie in the late 1980s. The brand was a sufficiently strong market leader in various Asian countries that Colgate decided to acquire an interest in the Hong Kong company which owned the brand. Unfortunately, the Darkie trademark, which gave the brand's packaging a prominent identity, was a black man with shining white teeth. While not distasteful to Asians, sections of American society, including some of Colgate's shareholders, found this racist.

Identity as a corporate tone of voice, service lifestyle and cultural state of being

As illustrated earlier in this chapter by American Express and McDonald's, and as investigations into most meaningful banner brands will show, top-level opportunities in branding come from unifying investments in a company's communication processes as much as possible. Can branding, corporate identity, PR, cultural mission, service training, and so on, be directed as an integrated communications process instead of being managed as separate activities? All communications should be organized to confirm a business's leadership purpose and to serve the various stakeholders of the company equitably. Increasingly, corporate goodwill is cultivated most consistently by recognising that many stakeholders interact with each other and people of the most importance to a company will often play a variety of stakeholding roles through the lifetime relationships that really valuable branding offers.

Summary

Branding (or whatever word you use for an organization's added-value communications process) invests identities in the minds of consumers (and all stakeholders of the company). Identifiers go beyond a brand's name creating a design language which includes symbols, colours, subbrands, flagship products, service promises, slogans and other perceptual prompters. This investment needs continuous and integrated cultivation if it is to be properly harvested tactically and strategically.

An organized branding process depends on:

- business teams sharing up-to-date knowledge on what consumer codes are owned by the company;
- being committed to serve the values and differentiated meanings that stakeholders may globally and locally interpret to reside in the codes which identifiers represent;
- coherently foreseeing connections between investments in branding's identity systems and other process parameters which contribute to organizational form and successful evolution of core businesses.

Every widely recognized identifier owned by a company is a communications property right which should be making a purposeful contribution to added value or competitive advantage. This chapter illustrates the range of capabilities that identity systems can be used to develop and the values they (re)create.

Throughout a company's brand architecture, identifiers contribute to a constellation of essentially differentiated sources of power (that is brands) and the ways in which goodwill connections can be interweaved to be more than the sum of their parts (that is linkages between different levels of branding from corporate/banner brand to product sub-brand).

(See Thinkpiece 2 for an agenda of a typical brand identity system workshop.)

References

Barwise, P. (1993). Brand Equity: Snark or Boojum?, *International Journal of Research in Marketing*, **10**(1).

Macrae, C. (1991). *World Class Brands*. Harlow: Addison-Wesley.

Mazur, L. and Hogg, A. (1993). *The Marketing Challenge*. Harlow: EIU/ Addison-Wesley.

Randazzo, S. (1993). *Mythmaking on Madison Avenue – how advertisers apply the power of myth and symbolism to create leadership brands*. Probus Publishing.

3

brand
Heritage/Friendship

The communications power of the brand is amplified by:

- its history – the defining moments which made it famous, exciting and relevant as a cultural leader;
- its consumption meanings at an intimately personal level, for example its values as a friend and character;
- its accessibility – there is no point in being famous or a friend unless you are there when needed 'in mind (for example, breadth and depth of recall) and in body (for example, strength of distribution)'.

The brand's power to make relationships can become an in-depth exploration of connections made with any audience. For example, in Chapter 1 we emphasized the importance of the brand's essence to each of the 3Cs: consumers, channels (for example, retail customers) and company (for example, employees).

Consumers admire a brand which seems as if it knows where it is going and is proud of the leadership standards it has displayed in the past. Every meaningful brand has a lot of company know-how built into it and is an essential platform for consumer reference.

Neglect of a great brand's history of meanings can be very costly to a company. There are eight reasons why organization-wide appreciation of this statement matters. We begin with memories from the consumer heartland, and build up to the thesis that branding values are most strongly perpetuated when consumer and company lifestyles are bound up in one enduring relationship.

Heritage beliefs

In many product categories brand heritage is the most important property of all. For example, the average age of the world's top 30 spirits brands is over 100 years old. German lagers market themselves as brewed to the purity regulations of 1516, which probably sets a record as far as the history of quality control goes. Make your own list of why heritage values have vital meanings to consumers in your markets. Examples may include:

- a family or seasonal habit passed through generations;
- a heart-warming souvenir of good times;
- a well-known quantity, for example, something which you can give to someone else and know it will be appreciated;
- trust in something which has never disappointed you;
- something which turns you into a connoisseur.

We will discuss some of these examples later, but for the moment note that you could dig deeper into each of them and develop detailed relationship scripts. For example, is connoisseurship in your brand's script mainly about pride in a personal possession (for example, reminding the consumer of his or her own expertise) or being a social talking point (for example, a subject which you can use as a conversation opener)?

Organizational forms and communications media may be changing fast, but basic human motivations do not. Most of branding's most compelling interpersonal keys are in the history of branding for everyone to see, dig deep into and bring up to date in appropriately analogous settings.

Powerful as heritages are at a personal level, their superpowers are derived from being recognized by society as part of the fabric of life. Some of the biggest institutionalized meanings may not even seem to be brands. Why are diamonds (instead of some other substance) so widely recognized as an essential symbol of marriage? Because De Beers has consistently marketed them as such. Why is champagne the drink for the biggest celebrations? Because the champagne houses in Reims cooperated to brand this essential meaning as their collective objective.

The symbiotic way in which mass communications work means that branded beings can go further than their organizational parents. For example, they may come to be leading ambassadors of the countries that founded them. Ask the world's consumers what Americana is and you will see how branded heritages like Disney, Coca-Cola, Marlboro, Levi's, and so on, dwell in the minds of people around the globe. Or look into the mirror of Ferrari in Box 3.1.

Box 3.1   What sums up Italian culture?

'Ferrari – it is all that is beautiful' is the consensus reply in Italy. Author Andrew White in *The Centenary of the Motor Car* is only a shade less passionate: 'Motoring would not be the same without Ferrari; in the case of motor racing it can be said with certainty that "Ferrari is a cult; Ferrari is Italy".'

Ferrari is the ultimate dream car. It has speed, grace, beauty and a roll of honour that runs from here to Le Mans. Ferrari has won nine drivers world championships, eight Formula One constructors world championships and 14 sports car championships.

Certainly Ferrari is symbolic of Italy. Stylish, cool, sophisticated – it could not have been built anywhere else. To Italians it is more than that. Throughout post-war Italy's troubled times Ferrari was contributing to the rehabilitation of national pride, gaining respect throughout the world both industrially and in sporting terms.

Ferrari's universally known insignia – a prancing horse, the *cavallino rampante* – is further steeped in Italian history. Legend has it that it was the personal emblem affixed to the fuselage of a fighter plane by a gold medal winning pilot in the first world war. He died, but his parents presented a portrait of the horse to Enzo Ferrari when he won the 1923 Circuito di Ravenna. Ferrari adopted it as his firm's logo, representing it against a yellow background, the symbolic colour of his native city, Modena, where Ferrari's production facilities remain to this day.

(*Source: brand strategy*, 28 October 1994)

Making friends

It has been said that most of the world's city dwellers now see more brandscapes than landscapes. (The term brandscape was coined by an anthropologist, John Sherry, and popularized by Alexander Biel (1993).) Brand messages are projected all around us. We probably see 1,000 or more commercial propositions every day but we screen most of them out. We all make personal dichotomies of 'in' and 'out' brands. Some of our 'in' brands we just about tolerate, or may be on the verge of dismissing to 'out-that-was-in' (a third state which marketers would technically be right to classify as different from a brand that has never been 'in'). But others among our 'in' brands are good friends in various senses of the word, sometimes as a virtue of necessity, sometimes as characters we are really attracted to.

You can add to this personal list of examples of sources of brand friendship:

- Familiarity. It's become a routine part of my day; for example, does the same brand meet you at every breakfast time?
- Simplicity. It makes choosing easy; for example, among dozens of purchases for the household I make every week, most are routine or frankly boring. In all honesty, I shop on auto-pilot in many categories. If I'm buying replacement batteries I just want them to last a long time, fit the appliance and be safe. The brand which I recognize as communicating simply is a good sort to know. It saves my time and is hassle free.
- Habit. I have been a customer there for 20 years and I am too lazy to change; for example, my bank.
- Best friend. If you don't think `that some brands make deep friendships, you have probably never let your children near Ronald McDonald!
- Image. Like the clothes I wear, being seen with this brand is part of my image and the impression I make on my peers, and myself.
- Mood changer. When I want a break from writing/reading this book I have been known to reach out for my favourite chocolate bar.
- Fan club. I have bought that brand so often that to tell you the truth when I see it in the news I applaud it and myself, rather like you might applaud your football club when it's had a winning day.

We can use a list like this to make some observations on ways of forming brand relationships based on consumers' viewpoints. It is strange how quickly executives in smart offices can forget some of these basic points. This applies especially to committees of executives, which is one reason why this chapter emphasizes the importance of brand history to every teamworker involved in Brand Chartering. Please expand this partial listing of communications mechanics which brands work with in forming relationships with consumers.

Befriending devices

Many of a brand's befriending devices can appear corny if you are not 'into' the particular brand. For example, this can apply to caricature ways of presenting a brand whether in personified form like Ronald or logo form like Nike's swoosh mark. Some of the designed-in histories which people who are 'into' the brand may be seeing are as follows:

- With all-the-family brands, it is highly appropriate to be able to appeal to the youngest member of your audience even if the device is twee to adults. Similarly, with brands intent on being multicultural, naive symbols often work best. For example, if a logo like Lacoste's alligator raises a smile in any culture we would rather own that than something that is more sophisticated.

- Loyal consumers meet their brand thousands of times. What really matters to them is the impression the brand confirms, not the first impression it makes on a stranger. For 'in' consumers a brand will also be a bundle of connecting memories. Many of the more significant ones cannot be experienced unless you have actively participated in purchasing-consuming-witnessing the brand.
- Brand recall is often designed to be associated with situations so that brand memories come flooding back at significant times such as when a purchasing choice is being made or a consuming experience is taking place. There are many brands whose real power is reserved for these occasions. Consequently, if you ask a consumer about a brand out of context, as much market research does, you are likely to miss many of the most subtle points of the brand's relationship.

Purchasers' roles	Purchasers	↔ Consumers	↔ Witnesses
Image to wear	self	self	peers
Self-consolation	self	self	nobody
Gatekeeping	housewife	housewife/family	family/neighbours
Gifting	self	friend	friend's peers
. . .			

Figure 3.1   Role playing of brand by purchaser as a function of P-C-W meaning. (*Source: Branded stage management, in Macrae, 1991*)

Consistency

Consistency is vital to branding relationships of the sorts we have described. Changes to the brand's core communicating devices need to be made in emotionally caring ways. Subtle branded values are most at risk of being murdered by any brand management system where frequent rotations of marketing personnel and brands are made. If a brand has a deeply meaningful relationship with consumers, it would seem to be common sense that a new manager has a lot to learn to get a real feeling for the brand. This is particularly the case if there is no system such as Brand Chartering for effecting the handover of care for a brand.

Pitfalls

Brand relationships can have costly side-effects. Because many of branding's lesser relationships are trading on consumer sufferance owing to lack of urgent need to change a habit, organizations allow themselves to be lulled into a false sense of security. Typically branded goodwill can protect an organization even as it becomes less competitive, until suddenly the poor value of the offer makes even the most loyal consumer think again. If your business team is not fully aware of empirical brand diffusion patterns of this sort, the way consumers are prone to flock together can be quite a shock. This may happen because of a price rise that has gone over some common psychological precipice or, in the case of a brand leader, the loss of its goodwill halo effect – which can account for up to 25% of its business – once the brand has visibly lost its number one status to a rival contender. An aim of Brand Charterers is to fuse together branding analogies so that unnecessary organizational shocks like these never take place.

Reflections of human nature

If you want to gain a deeper understanding of the quality of your brand's emotional relationships with consumers, most of the analogies with human relationships are worth exploring. For example, consumers can give revealingly consistent answers to what kind of person a brand would be or what kind of mood they associate with a brand. Similarly, most of the ways that people express themselves are applicable to brands. Valuable brands have their own tones of voice, style rules, idiosyncrasies and creative ways of coping with conflicting tensions which have over time made their characters pleasingly multidimensional. In other words they are mature.

Brand friendships are reflections of human nature. People's relationships with brands have many similarities to interpersonal ones. For example, you probably have an inner circle of friends with whom you feel familiar. While not always being able to explain what might appear to be logically borderline classifications between good friends and mere acquaintances, there are usually deeply emotional reasons even if some of these are sourced in the historical serendipity of being in the right place at the right time.

Extraordinary recognition

The making of 'in-out' relationships is a primary purpose of branding because of the advantage of being closer to end-consumers and their purchasing decisions, but it is certainly not a solitary purpose. Consider this extract from Sal Randazzo's excellent book *Mythmaking on Madison Avenue*:

'The Green Giant is counted among the so-called Leo Burnett critters that include Tony the Tiger, Charlie the Tuna and Morris the Cat. The Green Giant's humble beginnings were the Minnesota Valley Canning Company, founded in 1903. The company chugged along until the early 1920s when it developed a seed that produced peas that were unusually large and tender. The code name for the new peas was "Green Giant", and in 1926 the image of a Green Giant became the trademark for the company's superior peas.

'Then in the early 1930s, a young copyrighter named Leo Burnett entered the picture. Burnett changed the image of the Green Giant and made it more friendly and appealing. He also introduced a new descriptor "jolly".

'Through the years both the brand and the company prospered. The Green Giant became one of the most widely recognized trademarks, and in 1950, on the advice of The Leo Burnett Advertising Agency, the Minnesota Valley Canning Company changed its name to the "Green Giant Company". This proved to be a wise decision for many reasons, not the least of which is the fact that, when the company went public in the 1960s, the name carried with it instant recognition and respect.

'The Green Giant character works on a number of levels:

- It works to engage and entertain the consumer by lending a sense of drama and intrigue to an otherwise unexciting category.
- Once the consumer is engaged, the Green Giant character communicates important product attributes: quality, freshness, and consistency.
- The character also works as a mnemonic, an immediately recognizable brand trademark and symbol.'

As a friend puts it: 'I have never bought any canned vegetables in my life. But I still recognize jolly good characters like the Green Giant as standing out above and beyond the duty of branding consumer loyalty. They embed themselves in the human imagination even when you are not a target of the company's current products.' That is a great asset, because brand recognition and reputation also count with every kind of non-consumer stakeholder including those featured in the above extract (company staff, shareholders and trade).

Action replays

Powerful brands make the most of action replays in many ways. A simple way into this realm is having the equivalent of a brand's photo album at the business team's fingertips for every PR occasion. International brands are getting more and more photo calls as journalists write up their stories. They often appear as the props if not the stars of news features made for cosmopolitan audiences. Which comes first in terms of celebrity status: basketball as a famous sport? The world's best basketball player? Or Nike? Any brand which successfully travels across international markets and decades needs newsworthy aspects of its heritage to propagate its own source of (hi)stories as a leader. Once you appreciate that lifestyle journalism for cosmopolitan consumption can instantly refer only to the relatively rare icons that already have internationally recognized meanings, you may plot the particular advantages of having an internationalized press kit assembled for your brand.

Market histories are dominated by leaders who leave traces of brand memorabilia behind both physically and in the popular imagination. This is evident in museums of technology, from cars to electronic products, and in public retrospectives of fashions, as well as more privately treasured possessions. Brand memorabilia also plays a part in themed settings such as those that create the atmosphere of many bars and restaurants.

Increasingly brands, by investing in sports and other forms of dynamic media, circulate through timepaths which work in far more diffuse ways than the specifically scheduled 30-second spot of television's commercial break.

Defining moments in history are now global stages on which branders aim to play their part. The opening of McDonald's in Moscow captured a symbolic moment of a new era in history; so did Coca-Cola's sampling at Checkpoint Charlie as the Berlin Wall fell. One moment with the historic impact of McDonald's Moscow opening gains goodwill for the branded organization among a wide variety of stakeholders. There are valid grounds for believing that this single corporate act has improved the power of McDonald's in the eyes of all of the following:

- Consumers in Moscow and globally
- Society in Russia and globally
- Staff in Moscow and globally
- Franchise owners, current and prospective
- Journalists in Russia and globally
- Shareholders and city analysts

(*See* ThinkPiece 1, brand benchmarking of McDonald's.)

For all these kinds of stages to be valuable, there must be sufficient visual continuity of the brand for action replays to be recognizable when consumers of today and tomorrow revisit history and review all the parts the brand has played. It also helps if every product ever associated with a brand looks like a leading representative of its historic time zone. Every long-term brand should consider using design as its first media, and moreover one that it owns.

Brands can also become the heros of global legends. Some of these plays have consciously been scripted to turn the brand into a commercial myth – a classical icon – for their corporate owners (Lannon, 1993). For example, in the brand benchmarking of Coca-Cola (Thinkpiece 1) we relate the legend that Father Christmas is today turned out in a smart red and white uniform as a consequence of Coca-Cola's sponsorship, which gave Santa's image a facelift during the second quarter of this century. (Before this relaunch in Coca-Cola's red and white livery, Father Christmas's appearance had become that of a bedraggled wizard.)

There is still a lot to learn about how some brands capture the global imagination and others do not. Every time you come across a globally famous reputation it is worth asking yourself whether you know how it came to be like this. For example, how did Manchester United become so famous around the world while some other English football clubs with comparable records have only local pockets of affinity or recognition? Was it because many of Manchester United's successes coincided with the Swinging Sixties to the extent of becoming a symbolic association of the era? Was it to do with the legends associated with Busbee's Babes, including those of tragic heroism when most of Manchester United's team died in an air crash? Was it because the club has always had an ebullient mix of a strong team plus some especially colourful stars, such as the Charltons, Best, Giggs and Cantona? How much of this did the club promote? Not all these clues could ever be transferred to another branding situation, but many of them can.

Do you know whether your brand owns any magic moments in local consumer histories? For example, has it inherited any peculiar founder's rights as a market pioneer? Lux is an example of a brand which not only introduced the world to glamour in a soap bar but was also, in many developing countries, consumers' first affordable access to branded glamour of any kind. So in Lux's world of beauty what kind of brand essence works best for Unilever? A first kind which scripts the brand as being soap and neighbouring categories? Or a second kind which sees the brand's relationships as able to evolve through a broader range of cosmetics provided they are about introducing consumers to life's simple luxuries at affordable prices? As we have previously pointed out (Macrae, 1991), Unilever's historically soap-confining view of Lux may mean that the brand has largely had its day in the USA and Western Europe, but the business opportunity of building the Lux Company out of relationships of the second kind is potentially one of the branding world's most exciting platforms in emerging high-growth economies such as Japan, South East Asia, Eastern Europe and China.

Some companies do not seem to have realized the magic that can be associated with a brand which happens to have been at the right place at the right time. Take Bass, for example. It is probably the only brand to have sat for an impressionist painter, and what a painting Renoir's barlady at the Folies Bergère turned out to be. This would seem to be a great brand 'seeding' opportunity. Admittedly Bass has only truly envisioned its business as international in the last decade since its acquisition of the Holiday Inns hotel chain, so there is no point in debating whether there might have been an opportunity to internationalize the Bass brand in the way that Guinness has with its globally visible ales. An item for Bass's current agenda is: why not create within Holiday Inns a Renoir (or Folie) Brasserie format, including the kind of French food that is washed down best by ales, using Folies Bergère-style memorabilia with the Renoir print as centre-piece, and offering commemoratively branded lines of Bass? Would a format with unique elements of this sort provide a powerful seeding platform for establishing Bass as a worldwide brewer?

Two questions contribute to a debate of the above proposition:

- Are there historic precedents of brands which have succeeded in trading off a double image made for home-based and international consumption?
- Is the 'seeding' of brand fashions a successful investment strategy?

Going for 'glocal' organization

Many brands have used the power that is granted to a globalizing business to exchange values between different cultures. For example, in the evolution of Sony, the company took great pride in introducing to Japan interesting Western customs. Whether it was for newsworthy impact associated with Sony's image or sheer exotic delight, Akio Morita's biography (Morita, 1986) demonstrates that he wanted Sony's first building in Tokyo to be different from any other. He thus decided that the building's plaza would feature a French restaurant, a cuisine that had not previously been available in Japan but that he rightly foresaw as having a lot of fashionable potential.

Inside Japan Sony consciously developed quite a reputation for being one of the first gateway companies to the rest of the world, just as outside Japan Sony set out to develop as a pioneering standard bearer for the quality of Japanese products. As other Japanese corporate brands have become masters of this craft, they have created a visionary terminology – for example, being a global citizen or a 'glocal' insider – to highlight what cultural values an organization should nurture in striving to achieve the best of both worlds: global leadership know-how and locally sensitive customization.

Brand seeding

The strategy of brand seeding focuses on refraining from mass market expense until the essence of a great brand has been planted. Our research suggests that 'brand seeding' is one of the strategic marketer's best kept secrets, although it may be less of a secret these days. In the experience of the author and co-worker Chris Mole, it has proved to be a popular topic for conference talks. In a BBC2 television documentary "The ice cream wars", Chris Mole explains why brand seeding strategies break with conventional rules for launching new brands. Brand benchmarking Häagen-Dazs (ThinkPiece 1) provides ideas for those who want to develop a global brand without risking the high advertising costs that are classically associated with launching a brand.

Typically, a valuable seeding opportunity may stem from:

- the reputation of a thriving and fashionable business in some foreign country;
- high-quality products which become talking points when sampled among opinion leaders;
- legends of magic moments associated with the brand;
- mechanisms for strong PR and visibility.

Box 3.2 contains some lessons from brand seeding across national markets. These illustrate how seeding sets about transferring market histories to the cumulative benefit of the brand.

Box 3.2   Some lessons from implementing brand seeding across countries

Key elements of seeding mix include:

- premium product and pricing
- strong design
- PR
- word of mouth
- visibility in fashionable places.

Roll-out criteria include:

- Go from one success to another, that is do not necessarily go to the biggest market or channel first.

continues

---

continued

- Do not use mass-marketing techniques until your exclusive image is thoroughly planted; for example, mass advertising can kill off a seeding strategy if it is executed before the brand's cachet is firmly in its opinion leaders' minds.
- All opinion-leading audiences – for example, journalists, business partners, prestige retailers, consumer opinion leaders – can be seeded in parallel.
- Diffusion (or transfer) tactics can be aimed within a group, from one group to another, across cities/countries (for example, jetsetters-word-of-mouth), across distribution channels.

Tricky addendum

Some seeded brands form a mixed range of product lines including flagships that are never intended to be profitable because they are made as limited editions or specifically placed in a high- visibility arena where the distributor charges the brander for the privilege. In this case, the brand team (including marketing and financial personnel in particular) must be absolutely clear as to which product lines are image-making flagships and which are to be best sellers. Corresponding performance criteria and measurements require subtly different monitoring instruments.

While we are advocating orchestration of brand seeding as a conscious option for strategic marketers, it is interesting to note that the origins of many famous brands were seeded in the past by accident as well as design. These include:

- Coca-Cola (the drink of the smart set in turn-of-the-century drug stores, the American equivalent of Parisian cafe society);
- Dunhill (the leather goods attire of early car drivers);
- Del Monte (produce originally associated with a famous hotel);
- many of today's 'haute-couture' brands.

The marketing analogy with Aladdin is irresistible. Marketing geniuses now search for old brands, symbols or commercially magic properties which can play the lead role in fashioning brand new presentations.

In an emerging area of smart multimedia channels, we believe that seeding know-how will become increasingly important in developing new brands and revitalising old brand essences.

The first global language

Global brands aim to pre-empt association with 'big idea' identifiers as their own universal property rights. For example, if an international competitor to Marlboro tried to advertise cowboy imagery for its cigarettes, the chance of profiting from this would be remote because (even without any legal redress from Marlboro's owner) the two most likely consumer outcomes would be that many would misread such advertising as being for Marlboro; and many others would see no point in choosing an imitator instead of the real thing.

A cultural stereotype such as Americana can also work to the benefit of a group of brand leaders – Marlboro, Levi's, Disney, Coca-Cola, and so on – each with distinctive competitive domains but American theming in common. A symbiosis results. The more famous these brands become, the more they become leading reminders of why the American way of life is appealing to a global public.

We believe that brand teams need an increasingly high literacy rate in reading branding's glocal (global and local) language. It is not just a case of being able to read what stereotype codes are embedded in the market histories of your brand and those of your traditional competitors. These days it is necessary to have coding antennae attuned to attack scenarios that might come from any kind of territory:

- from ostensibly different products as Virgin's invasion of cola and other drinks markets illustrates;
- from different geographic territories, for example, the globalizing brand;
- from a different zone of history, the seeded brand. For example, Häagen-Dazs's long established heritage in the USA has been a pivotal component of its recent global scripting.

Whether national governments like it or not, two trojan horses of our emerging era of global networking are joining to form humankind's first global language: brands (whose unique essences reserve their own memory traces); and computerized icons (which are making human communications more symbolic and less verbal). Both these systems of thinking work to draw on (and deposit in) a global reservoir of accessible cultural stereotypes and symbolic forms. In multimedia's global high-ways, these communications phenomena will be an integral part of the way that global society learns, as well as keys to the commercial influence that branded organizations will exert.

The time to perfect and the time to market

The brand organization needs to make these time zones coalesce, but pay each the distinctive organizational respect that is its due. Leading brands are unique business systems. They often represent a long learning curve. Quality product formulas, vibrant staff cultures, efficient supply and delivery systems, know-how networks and partnerships, overall reputation and track record take years to build. A leading brand often emanates from a core format or a winning element which took years to refine. Ask yourself how often the actual development process of a strong brand follows this three-stage pattern of evolution:

(1) The winning element is cultivated as core component of an improved consumer benefit.
(2) The integrated system is refined for commercial viability.
(3) The competitively efficient format is replicated in a mass way, and at this stage amplified by mass-market branding.

Strong brands sometimes appear to have come from nowhere, but this is often because stage 3 is both the visible and the fast-moving one. In contrast, the foundation stages are often painstakingly slow.

How old do you think McDonald's is? The business was actually born in 1937 when two hard-working brothers opened a hamburger restaurant in California. Another site was opened in 1939, but after that 17 years were spent on stage 1 by the McDonalds as they perfected the way an outlet could serve food fast and economically to a maximum number of customers.

Stage 2 of McDonald's began when Ray Kroc entered the scene in 1954. At the time he was a 52-year-old milkshake-mixer salesman who had visited the McDonalds in California to find out why they needed eight of his machines at a single site. Ray was amazed at what he saw: fast food being served through a process of world class efficiency and being operated only at the two McDonald's sites. He watched this spectacle for two days before approaching the brothers with an offer to franchise their concept.

Stage 3 involved a local and a global branding exercise. It had taken Ray seven years to licence the USA's first 200 McDonald's franchises. But along this learning path Ray's special genius created the family values of McDonald's that made the restaurant so consistently welcoming across the country. Families with children needing personal refuelling on a highway miles from home knew that McDonald's would be a safe haven. Would-be American franchisees were lining up to join McDonald's. Mass-market advertising budgets rapidly increased both to pre-empt the family image and to transform it into the brand's leadership essence. A core purpose was to ensure that franchisees were proud of both their service role and their contribution to the history of the marketplace.

Brand expansion then progressed to a worldwide race to lead the fast-food business with the McDonald's branding franchise across the world. By 1990 the prize for being the fastest on the accelerator to this global market could be recorded in terms of McDonald's daily customer base of 23 million people.

The lesson appears to be that once evolution of a winning business system is fully proven, the painstaking stages of development can turn into a hectic race to global markets. Once you have innovated the world's best business system, the last thing you want is for a competitor to do the replicating. This is how Hamel and Prahalad (1994) describe the evolution of winning businesses from learning curve to lift off:

> 'Developing new competences and reconnoitring new competitive space can be the work of a decade or more. Yet despite the studied space of competence acquisition and market exploration, the final dash to the finishing line can be an all-out, pell-mell sprint. This is particularly likely when several competitors have been working in parallel to develop needed competences and marketing insights, and simultaneously come to believe, after a round or two of expeditionary marketing, that the market is finally ripe. This last, mad scramble to the finish line is a race to pre-empt competitors in key markets, to capture market leadership in the biggest and fastest growing national marketplaces, and bank the rewards in pioneering. . . .
>
> 'Managers have given much attention to the very important task of reducing product development times. Speedy product development is an important component of the capacity to pre-empt competitors. Yet the time interval to be minimized is not just "concept to market" but "concept to global market". A product development cycle that is 50% shorter than a competitor's is of little benefit unless it is coupled with a strong worldwide distribution capability. Although being first to market is important, the real returns go to companies that are first to global markets.'

Global races need to be scripted carefully. Branded ones are so visible that the CEO must keep on checking that local scripts are not being misinterpreted. On one occasion, even McDonald's had to take strong corrective action to keep its image together (see Box 3.3).

Box 3.3   A French affair

At the beginning of the 1980s the motherly McDonald's had a fleeting French affair. France's tradition of gourmet food did not make it seem likely to be one of the most important lead-countries in the company's European advance, so the business in Paris was licensed to a single franchisee. The McDonald's fast food concept soon proved itself to be just as welcome to busy Parisian families as other Europeans. Unfortunately, McDonald's franchisee, flushed with the success of the business, was tempted to choose such prime takeaway sites as a shopping arcade dominated by St Lazare's pornographic movie house as he was to select respected boulevards for all the family. McDonald's had to buy back the franchise as a matter of urgency.

Strategic imperatives associated with globalization imply revolutionary changes to the architecture of brand, strategy and organization (Chapters 11, 12 and 13) that companies will need to compete in the future. An organization will be unable to compete in a global business world with the kinds of brands that were effective in the local business world.

Gillette provides an early example of a company which has successfully re-engineered its branding architecture. The changes which Gillette made to its communications mix are chronicled in Thinkpiece 1, so here we will concentrate on Gillette's strategic commitment. What Gillette did was to amalgamate all its historical goodwill which had been fragmented at local (and low-value) product levels into a credible corporate architecture where everything connects through to the essence of Gillette as 'the best a man can get'. Gillette now has a serial global platform for launching all new world class products (stage 2 proven performers) at a stroke. This ensures that no competitor can be faster than Gillette at Stage 3. This is Hamel and Prahalad's summary appraisal of the Gillette-Sensor launch:

'After spending more than $100 million over 10 years developing its revolutionary Sensor razor, and conducting an initial round of customer research, Gillette launched the product in 19 countries simultaneously. Followers, like Warner-Lambert's Schick division, were quickly buried under Gillette's worldwide promotional avalanche.'

If you do not have your own access to an appropriately global banner reputation, a franchise model of global branding may be attractive. In the race to global markets, you will need partners locally to replicate your brand's indomitable spirit in the eyes of consumers everywhere. You need to write up the system developments of stages 1 and 2 together with a branding kit that your local partners/customers around the world find a joy to use. The fact that a franchisee is an external partner makes for good discipline. You are likely to specify the strategic controls that must operate glocally more carefully than you would if dealing with a local office of your own company. Examination of the franchiser's craft can provide excellent insights for the disciplines which need to be practised by any business team which finds itself involved in their organization's stage 3 race to global market.

Lifestyles for lifetimes

Hamel and Prahalad also shed more light on how purposeful corporate branding seeks to leverage the most important consumer connections between the history and the future of the business.

> 'The goal of the corporate umbrella brand is simple: to help customers transfer the goodwill that has been built up through positive experience with one of the company's products to other products it offers or intends to offer. Besides having a Canon copier at home, one of us also possess two Canon 35mm cameras, a Canon 8mm camcorder, a small Canon electronic typewriter and a Canon fax machine. There was never a decision to be a Canon home, it just worked out that way. Whenever confronted with Canon as a choice in a purchasing decision, one instinctively reflected back on the reliability, performance and value of other Canon products. Imputed with those virtues, each additional Canon purchase looked not only like a "safe" buy, but a "smart" buy. As the pace of life has continued to accelerate, and as the complexity of what people buy has accelerated exponentially, banner brands like Canon and Sony have become mnemonics, standing for quality and value, in the minds of harried, confused consumers.'

Ritual values for revitalizing consistent obsessions

Change is constant. Competitive businesses will always look for new ways to gain advantage, whereas the most basic human meanings of product categories seldom change. Take chocolate, for example. Should children ever be denied access to the joy of chocolate? Should adults ever be denied access to the mood- changing influence that life's least costly indulgence can offer? Of course not, if you are to be a leading chocolate manufacturer who stands up for the democratic meanings of chocolate. Consequently, value for money will always be the leading success factor in the industry and it is not surprising that many of the world's leading chocolate companies – Mars, Hershey and Cadbury – have cultures that are puritanical about value for money. Note that even as distributing supermarkets were insisting on multipacks, the chocolate manufacturers were inventing bite- size and pick-and-mix formats so that in the most hyper of supermarkets, chocolates may be picked up as branded morsels (at the lowest ticket price of any unit sold in the store).

We asked a marketing director who had two careers in marketing – the first in chocolate, the second in spirits (for example, whisky) – about the biggest similarities and differences in branding winners in these marketplaces.

- Biggest similarity: the data trends you need to look at to judge how strong your brand equity is.
- Biggest difference: while you always need to be obsessed with a product category's critical success factors, you need to be prepared for how the focus of consistent obsessions will vary as you go from one product category to another.

For example, to succeed in chocolate bars you must offer unbeatable value and quality. To square the value circle you need to have scale to be the low- cost producer in any bar you market and to offer the consumer the best value for money. In the case of the Mars bar it was important to offer more appetite satisfaction per penny than any other bar. Similarly, the quality obsession with the Mars bar was to look perfect and have a consistent texture, so much so that there was even a Mars bar brand manager's tooth test: bite into it and your teeth should meet exactly at the centre of the bar. Contrast that with marketing whisky brands where you are often concerned with appealing to connoisseur and fashion values. There are places where you would not want your whisky to be available and you are certainly not saddled with the Mars bar obsession of finding every different campaign theme possible to renew the emphasis on value for money such as 'the biggest Mars bar ever offered'.

Rituals turn abstract customer service virtues into reasons for the staff to be proud of the brand they serve. McDonald's organizes crew competitions across its franchises. The prizes for those attaining the highest customer satisfaction ratings are management training courses at Hamburger University. In another example of virtuous spiralling between customer path and staff delivery, the British Airways advertising campaigns (of the late 1980s and early 1990s) featuring the 'World's Favourite Airline' and 'Smiles as BA's corporate body language' justified their high advertising spends largely because of their motivating effects on staff culture. We would suggest this indirect effect on consumer sales was their most important purpose. It is notable that consumers appreciate the amount of organizational effort that goes into making a smile campaign work among every member of staff almost as much as they see through the company that advertises such a message without training staff to live up to it.

It is not only service companies that benefit from ritual celebrations. The leader's knack revolves round an insatiable appetite for searching for strong methods of bringing the whole organization closer to customers and then taking pride in continuing to improve. In particular, celebrating a valid claim to be the world's number one in something is powerful for employees as well as consumers. The world's best is worth going an extra mile for, whether the mile is the extra effort that employees put in as part of the winning company or the distance a consumer is prepared to travel to find the best. The world's best instils pride whether you serve it as an employee or wear it as a consumer.

In a technological world it is tempting to think of core competences in abstract terms. But in fact the continuous cultivation of almost all core competences depends on teams of people building skills through intense dedication and concentrating for long periods of time on routine or systematic elements of work. Any way that branding can be deployed to transform routine into ritual is well worth considering.

Corporate values also act as signals of strategic focus and become associated with a company's right to lead. Opinion-leading audiences are impressed by an organization like Procter & Gamble, whose purpose is guided by the mission statement of only entering markets where the firm can develop and sustain a quality difference against all competitors. See how many additions you can make to this list of the kinds of impressions that are made by such a consistent declaration in a quality improvement culture:

- P&G's selection of markets on quality criteria becomes textbook wisdom among commentators ranging from business journalists to academic scribes.
- P&G's quality reputation among business students gives the firm a lead in recruiting the best.

- P&G's new products tend to be given more serious attention by the trade (including the biggest supermarket multiples) than many of P&G's competitors.
- P&G's employees are empowered to stand up for quality on an everyday decision basis within the firm.

We would emphasize three reasons why a brand's values have a vital influence on the consistency of leadership within an organization:

(1) Provided the brand values are aligned to critical success factors, they anchor the focus of the brand on the fundamental determinants of quality and value that are most relevant to consumers.
(2) They reinforce the employees' sense of mission and pride in fulfilment; and when allied to rituals they go beyond the routine to the nobler kind of craft associated with dedicated customer service.
(3) They empower, that is they provide an employee with the best defence against transient decisions being made somewhere up the hierarchy. In P&G there is a communally felt right of appeal: 'Is this a Procter kind of way of behaving?'

Summary

We have explored eight intriguing nuances of brand heritage and friendship.

From the consumer viewpoint:

(1) Heritage beliefs
(2) Making friends

From the multi-audience viewpoint:

(3) Extraordinary recognition
(4) Action replays
(5) The first global language

From the company (employee) viewpoint:

(6) The time to perfect and the time to market

In relation to the service/leadership guarantees between consumer and company:

(7) Lifestyles for Lifetimes
(8) Ritual values for consistent obsessions

In the process we have noted that various models of global branding rely on editing the future of a brand's history in strategically astute ways. The following models and processes of organising round global brands have been introduced:

- 'Glocal' brand process
- Brand seeding
- Brand franchising
- Brand re-engineering
- Banner/corporate branding

References

Aaker, D. and Biel, A. (1993). *Brand equity and advertising*. LEA.
Hamel, G. and Prahalad, C.K. (1994). *Competing for the future*. Harvard: Harvard Business School Press.
Lannon, J. *Branding essentials and the new environment*, ADMAP, June, 1993.
Macrae, C. (1991). *World Class Brands*. Harlow: Addison-Wesley.
Morita, A. (1986). *Made in Japan*. E P Dutton.
Randazzo, S. (1993). *Mythmaking on Madison Avenue – how advertisers apply the power of myth and symbolism to create leadership brands*. Probus Publishing.

brand Future News

Robert Woodruff was Coca-Cola's great brand leader for much of the 20th century. He had a special way with slogans. He focused the company's investment philosophy by declaring that managers must always ensure that Coca-Cola was 'within arm's reach of desire'. He saw this as a vital core competence in serving the impulsive, that is personally urgent, consumer need of refreshment that soft drinks cater for.

For Woodruff, advertising tag lines and slogans were more than mere consumer messages. They were deployed to turn his business visions for Coca-Cola into perceptions which became realities. Long before Coca-Cola was a truly international brand, Woodruff organized pride in the slogan that Coca-Cola was 'the most friendly drink in the world'. His efforts enabled even greater leadership acts to become embodied in an apparently more humble slogan 'the pause that refreshes'.

This advertising slogan was first used in the 1920s to put the brand into the diary of every American worker. Whereas Europeans might have tea or coffee breaks, Woodruff institutionalized the idea that American workers should have Coca-Cola breaks. The national interpretation of Coca-Cola's meaning became so common that, just as Americans were preparing to enter the second world war, Woodruff lobbied the US War Office until the generals were persuaded that the essential meaning of Coca-Cola's slogan was a vital answer to 'the extreme fatigues of battle'. Coca-Cola thus became the GIs' mascot with the War Office subsidizing investments in Coca-Cola's manufacturing and distribution facilities to ensure that wherever American GIs went, Coca-Cola would be there for them.

People to empower

There is no strategic substitute for empowerment of people at the centre of brand control who:

- are passionate about product, and the service dimensions it can represent now or for the future.
- understand the concept of market exploration of global and local consumer needs; for example, by exploring the subtlety of notions such as consumers do not buy products, they buy solutions to a problem however fleetingly conceived. By moving into this realm of the imagination it quickly becomes evident that buying decisions are triggered by global and local cultural interpretations which a brand must respect, and yet it must take the symbolic lead not the cultural lag.
- know how to interconnect the essence of the brand's past history of friendship with the future focus of products and services which the branded company foresees. This is the way to ensure that core products perpetuate a brand's marketing pathway. Thus the company earns the right to keep focusing its core competences so as to keep turning the perception of brand leadership into objective reality. Leadership is concerned with always being the reference point against which every would-be competitor gets judged.

Today, more than ever, the soul of most world class brands resides in an organization's service motivations and its core competences. It is worth repeating a paragraph from an early review of the BBC for BUSINESS video 'Branding – the Marketing Advantage'. It encapsulates 90 minutes of footage of how marketing practitioners in the 1990s justify their right to brand:

'Both product quality and creative communications are important, but they are only temporary manifestations of branding. The really vital brand is one whose organizing culture loves its end-consumers so much that all employees run and win marketing's equivalent of an Olympic marathon, only to pick themselves up as they cross the winning line in eager preparation for the next marathon. All this because of sheer pride not only in serving goods but also in what's really best for consumers – the leader who delights all customers by consistently setting new world records on quality and value.'

Brand Charterers – and all great instinctive teamworkers on branding processes – have a duty to make the future happen in their brands' presence by asking such questions as:

- What sorts of products/services will our brand have or need to represent to be valued as a leader in a few year's time?
- What do we need to 'do now' to accelerate the future?
- Who will we really be competing against and who do we want as partners to make the most of our added-value chain?
- What fundamental discontinuities and changes will we need to leverage?
- How does this translate into the messages we need to communicate now?

In best practice form, the process of branding is an organizational instrument for 'editing the future' from a true perspective of leadership. It creates and communicates an organization-wide will to sustain a focused combination of core competences in order to deliver unique value. Try out a simple brainstorming exercise. What are the essential qualities of brand leadership which can unite all a brand's audiences (beginning with the 3Cs: consumers, company employees, customers (between employees and end-consumers)? Simple things like:

- focused direction of a leader, a brand organization proud of where it has come from and where it is going to, but not arrogant in exaggerating its worth;
- a company with an indomitable spirit in pursuit of achieving world records (quality/value);
- an identity which is unforgettable and easy to relate to;
- a totality which feels worthy of trust.

Then try a second exercise. Imagine that you are a journalist interviewing a company's people in an attempt to evaluate its claims to be a world class brand. What organizational body language tells you whether brand leadership is real? Some examples are:

- a real 'buzz' and pride among employees;
- consistently aligned motivation/vision expressed by everyone you talk to;
- evidence that customer service trend measurements are as much apart of the operating culture as financial performance measures.

Future now

Built into the framework of brand chartering is a 'living script' philosophy. By this we mean that persistent cross-checking of leadership purpose is a key organizational process for adding value. Two of the most important dimensions of brand leadership editing involve organization-wide viewpoints and envisioning a spectrum of future time horizons: the 'then' and the 'now'.

Later chapters (such as Chapter 8) make a point of cross-checking views of a brand held by people in a company's different departments and regional offices. We place particular emphasis on this because in our interviews with Japanese business people the most common advantage cited for companies of Japanese origin revolves round that of 'internal marketing communications'. We use this phrase instead of the simpler one of 'consensus' because we now have a lot of evidence that scripting a brand organization's internal marketing communications can be an even more complex challenge than that of its external marketing communications. This is especially the case in companies that wish to take advantage of change. As we will see in Chapters 11–14, once companies rid themselves of the inertias of classic brand management systems, the growth opportunities of brand leadership are exciting. This helps to explain why strong organizational leaders are those who instil a joy of change culture.

In order to ensure that Brand Charters clearly understand future time horizons, we take every opportunity to ask questions like:

- Where does this brand as leader need to be in five years' time? And to achieve this what must you do now?
- Where does this brand as leader need to be in three years' time? And to achieve this what must you do now?

We deliberately repeat these questions for different time horizons to understand the extent of brand vision, consensus on brand vision, the urgency and depth of practical details that must be prioritized for the 'then' and 'now' of brand leadership to intersect.

At the same time, other 'do now' questions can be asked, for example: to lead with this brand's essence in five years' time, what sorts of potential partners should be sought now? It is important to clarify action plans not just within the company but also in terms of networking. An increasing number of corporate processes, such as research and development, cannot be performed to world class standards by one company alone. In other words, it is vital that an organization recognizes what its core competences are not, as well as what they are. Meanwhile, proper leadership of the brand's added-value chain may require 'networking in' skills that the company does not have, as well as leveraging those in which it excels.

While cross-checking the charter as a living script, we will see that 'do nows' may be prompted for specific depth at every branding junction, that is, through the particular focus which each chapter of this book provides. For practice – and because this is the first time that we have introduced the future dynamic fully – we will look at the themes of earlier chapters from a future-oriented perspective.

Brand essence

Since essence should be the core connecting message, it is vital to remove any uncertainties people may have about future changes to a brand's essence. For example, if the view of brand essence for leadership in five years' time is thought to be very different from today's brand essence:

- verbalize the essence of today and the future;
- check to see whether a different verbalization could connect the two.

If real differences persist, this is a branding discontinuity which must be addressed as a strategic priority. An organizational consensus should be reached on its causes and plans made to break the discontinuity to consumers in the most coherent way. In principle, you must find a communications mechanism which enables consumers both to interpret what they used to value in the old essence through the new essence and to feel that the leadership move you have made is in a direction they support.

Discussing how competitive and environmental change drivers will create leadership challenges for you to overcome is also an essential part of editing a brand's living script (see Box 4.1).

Box 4.1   Iterative interpreting of a brand's essential future

Looking forward and you actually do need to go out to the future and have a look at a few alternative futures and work backwards and see your current brand, what it stands for, what it means, how that stacks up against alternative futures – if you can do that then you actually have a chance of managing the brand successfully to get the future you want.

(*Source:* Chris Mole in BBC for BUSINESS video 'Branding – the Marketing Advantage')

Brand identity

The multifaceted nature of identity makes it one of the most dynamic mechanisms of the brand. Consequently, identifiers are usually the ally of brand news. From time to time you may invest in new identifiers to tell consumers about a changing aspect of the brand. However, it is important to time the phasing in and out of identifiers to help consumers interpret brand news in the most consistent way.

Brand heritage/friendship

The example in Box 4.2 indicates why this branding junction should constantly be cross-edited to create future values (in spite of what may seem to be a conflict of temporal terminology).

Box 4.2   Creating the multifaceted personality of Levi's

Until quite recently a view prevailed that brand campaigns achieved the most impact by being one dimensional. At the extreme the brand was still conceptualized as a product that was best supported by a unique selling proposition (USP). This had the virtue of management simplicity, but truly powerful brand organizations now direct personalities with more intriguing breadth and depth.

While Levi's has always thought of its friendship with consumers in more broadly empathic terms than purists of the USP school, it is only as the great Levi's 501 campaigns have blossomed since the late 1980s that the brand has fully visualized the multifaceted personality it wants to be. From the consumer viewpoint, Levi's is now offering a menu of feelings which you may select to wear or to keep in your wardrobe.

As Figure 4.1 shows, Levi's now has seven dominant character traits. No advertisement can meaningfully portray all of these. To keep its personality fresh and appealing as a youth brand, Levi's marketers and advertising agency Bartle, Bogle, Hegarty choose a 'do now' selection of traits to be embedded in the next commercial in the epic Levi's 501 serial.

	Launderette	Fridge	Parting	Beach	Pawnbroker	Pool Hall	Swimmer	Procession	Creek
Romance			•	•	•				
Sexual attraction	•	•	•				•	•	•
Physical prowess	•								•
Resource-fulness	•				•	•		•	
Rebellion						•	•		•
Independence			•	•					•
Being admired	•	•	•		•	•			

Figure 4.1 Levi's personality traits (rows) triggered by commercials in the campaign series (columns). (*Source:* Fuller, K. 'The Levi 501 Campaign', ADMAP, March 1995)

Summary

Be passionate about creating news in the image and product/service reality of the brand. Use this to focus marketing of your added-value pathway.

Know that true brand leaders are never afraid to accelerate change. This is the spirit needed to outrun every competitor.

Ask everyone who serves the brand to envision the 'then and now' of where you want to be. Create an organization that foresees competitive and partnership scenarios and takes advantage of changing conventional rules. At the same time keep faith with the brand's essential meaning:

- as a communicator both internally and externally;
- as a creative fountain of know-how.

Turn the process of branding into an organizational instrument for editing the future. Encourage communal curiosity with 'do now' questions, for example:

- Do we agree where we want the brand to be in 3 years' time?
- How do you interpret what you need to 'do now' for us all to achieve this?

Develop a living script which can be acted on as a user-friendly road map highlighting top-line news. Go for a one-page script not a bureaucratic tome.

Enjoy living the script as a teamworking community which knows why and how it is dedicated to leading its sphere of business to win for the consumer.

brand Other Create

Chapters 5, 10 and 15 are different in style from the rest. They are intended to be breathing spaces for you to take stock before considering another dimension of the Brand Chartering process.

For example, what 'creative communications' questions have we brushed over which could be critical to particular brand scripts? One of these is that as well as essential aspects of a brand's leadership objective there are destructive things it is vital that a leader never does. You may make your own list but there are many general aspects of trust which are core to a long-term relationship with consumers. We are very wary indeed about a brand management lack-of-system which is careless in its process with regard to such fundamentals as being consistent in pricing policy, or, if something goes wrong with it in real or perceptual terms, withdrawing a brand's product speedily and with statesmanlike apologies (even if the setback has been blown out of all proportion by a competitor).

Within the one-page living script of a particular brand there is no room for clutter. You cannot write in every 'must not do'. There are other more efficient ways of communicating internally. For example, a generic 'must not do' listing can be compiled as a one-page cross-checking system for application on all of a company's brands. Nonetheless, there are times when a particular 'do not' should be temporarily highlighted in a brand's script.

We have done this when we have sensed that the brand's team is going through an intensive period of change or development of the brand in which the danger is that their eye may be taken off some of the fundamentals. Two examples of highlighting pricing consistency in a brand's script are as follows.

- In the first case it was clear that a brand's geographic markets were converging rapidly but nobody was in charge of converging local pricing policies which had taken a historical liberty of being all over the place. As an independent adviser, the Charterer had to take the unpopular decision, from the perspective of many managers, of writing into the Charter that the CEO must organize convergence of the brand's pricing policy if the brand was to have a strategic future.
- In the second case, explained more fully in Chapter 16, loyal users regarded value for money as part of the brand's essence. But, after a chartering time-out was taken to research the meaning of this, we discovered a highly brand-specific interpretation of value was being made. Crucially, local consumers' driving value motivations did not cohere with future global marketing plans to introduce several new, upmarket lines for the brand. The way this future news was initially conceptualized by headquarters might have had quite an impact but the new lines would have outpositioned the brand's original lines in such a way as to destroy its essence. You can imagine the damage that could be done to loyal users' trust in a brand if you suddenly position their favourite products carelessly as lower-class cousins of some arrogant new brand lines. The 'do not' question which local marketers helped to raise on this brand ultimately meant that the brand's global script needed some sensitive re-editing.

Although you may now want to consolidate earlier points concerned with the creative level of brand process, once you have tried out Brand Chartering you are most likely to hop from one branding junction to another. In other words, branding junctions laid out within the creative process need not be juxtaposed when thinking through a brand process. They all have important roles to play in amplifying the meaningful relationships which a brand leader must promote.

Some marketing pitches like pricing and customer service seem to be embedded at every level of the brand process. We meet them in various chapters of this book, but like the suggested generic 'do not' list they could each be made into one-page ideas for continuously cross-checking every brand script. Figure 5.1 contains suggestions for questions adapted from a list which a client reportedly gave Dennis Cahill recently. It was designed to prioritize learning about overall patterns of response as opposed to 'correct' answers to each individual question.

Customer service	Pricing
How does the customer define great service overall and from us in particular?	What is the price elasticity of our product?
How does the customer perceive our level of service? How does it compare with their expectations? Who provides the best customer service and why?	How does our selling price impact on our reputation/ position in the mind of the customer?
What is the best way of measuring our level of service and making sure we are doing it?	At what point are we priced too low and lose our mystique?
Does better service translate into higher sales or greater customer loyalty? How does customer service fit into the purchase decision?	How does pricing affect our position as the superpremium offer in the marketplace?
Is there a price increase/decrease allowed or expected because of our service level?	Can we get credit from consumers for lowering the price?
What are our customer service attributes that we can own and defend?	How can we most effectively position a price change with the customer?

Figure 5.1 Examples of questions for cross-checking brand scripts. (*Source:* Editorial by Dennis Cahill, (1995). *Journal of product and brand management,* **4**(1))

Figure 5.1 helps make the point that there are those, including ourselves, who question whether a marketing department is a good idea in competing for the future. This is not because marketing curiosity and informed analysis has become unimportant. On the contrary, it is now too important to be departmentalized. Marketing intelligence needs to be continuously learnt and shared by everyone who adds value to the company as an organization-wide network. We suggest ways of implementing this in Chapter 8.

When interrogating a brand's script one question should lead to another in any way which seems relevant to you. There is no reason why a vital line of enquiry should be confined to one of the create, manage, direct strands of the branding. Whereas a book has to follow a single track, consumers' perceptions do not, employees' contributions should not, and organizations' priorities in strengthening their brand processes never do.

We find that marketers' first exposure to Brand Chartering tends to invoke clustered interest in junctions which form particular patterns. For example, many people whose key interest is the essence of the brand find it natural to move on to questions of flow/teamworking. Those who start with a particular curiosity about brand identity systems often move on to questions about brand architecture and then back to brand flow and essence. We are not suggesting that these will necessarily turn out to be permanent patterns of interrogation. They are influenced in part by how many companies currently find a particular branding junction attractive or novel as an introduction to integrated brand organization.

There is also the issue of how open a dialogue practitioners feel able to have when seeking advice.

Open vote:	Closed in-depth discussion:
Brand essence	Brand flow/teamworking
Brand masterbriefing	Brand: all architecture junctions at direct level

Figure 5.2 Chartering junctions where weaknesses most commonly occur in brand processes. (*Source:* A Brand Chartering surgery for marketing directors, London, 1995)

Brand architecture is now, in our view, one of the most critical brand organization junctions of all. But it is seldom the most user-friendly way of introducing Brand Chartering. This may be because it focuses in on such big issues as whether the whole corporate reputation is on the line in consumers' minds even when the company believes it is marketing a brand without a corporate endorsement.

6

brand Masterbriefing

Nowadays any brand process must govern holistically a selection of media options which are fragmenting and multiplying alarmingly fast. Two reasons why masterbriefing of a brand process should be important to you involve the obvious and the not-so-obvious:

- The availability of a lot of different media means the brands' total impact must be integrated.
- All media are not created equal – they are capable of making different sorts of contributions to the brand.

A never-ending choice of media

- Advertising spots (television, video, poster, press, radio) appearing in regional, national or international forms.
- Sponsorship of programme material, ranging from 'this program is brought to you by . . .' to advertorials, that is media forms in which the distinction between programme content and commercial message is blurred.
- Sponsorship of events, from global sports to local community festivals.
- Celebrity endorsements.

- Taking a public stand on an issue. For example, the Body Shop gained continental fame by being one of the first brands to petition against an EU directive relating to cosmetics and animal testing.
- Public relations.
- Word-of-mouth.
- Cosmopolitan visibility, for example, through franchised outlets in all the world's most fashionable shopping arcades to being displayed at airports' duty free shops, a channel which in itself stimulates jetsetters' word-of-mouth.
- Own news stages, from owning the media like Disney to creating a media event like Beaujolais' global birthday party.
- Being an integral part of world news, for example, McDonald's Moscow opening.
- Co-branding, that is where two brands share a promotional platform.
- Corporate identity and brand signage.
- Your people as media who serve the brand's lifestyle or represent its competence leadership.
- Packaging design.
- Sampling, for example, through the letter box, in somebody else's store, in your own boutique (such as Häagen-Dazs ice cream parlours), in high traffic locations (such as your capital city's largest railway station), in high visibility places (from first-class air cabins to spectators at Prince Charles's last polo match).
- Point-of-sale material.
- Points of service contact. For example, in most banks the common point of contact has moved away from the service counter inside to the automated 24-hour cash dispenser outside, and in a future cashless society we will be ordering from 'smart-coded voice-activated in-home banking menus'.
- Fashionable product placement, for example, in films and film stars' wardrobes.
- Promotional competitions.
- A leaflet inside the product packaging.
- Consumer feedback mechanisms such as free telephone hotlines for dialogue about the brand.
- Collectors' schemes, loyalty clubs.
- One-to-one direct/database marketing (postal media, computer media and one day computerized multimedia).
- etc.

It is not easy to choose among such abundant media forms as the practitioner comments in Box 6.1 illustrate.

Box 6.1   Media and practice

'I am constantly bombarded with offers to advertise here, support this, sponsor that. The key focus has to be to know your consumer and how to get at them, but then to say: what are the opportunities? Sometimes the new opportunities can be useful because they allow you to get at a discreet segment of that market, more efficiently or more cost-effectively, particularly if it's new and it's keen to get new advertisers on board.'

(Chris Hobbs, 3M)

'I guess traditionally it has been very easy for marketers to communicate with their consumers because they've had a series of tools – broadcast television, PR, press, etc. – and those have had extraordinary reach among a broad mass of consumers. The problem is that nowadays consumer groups – and the media they use – are segmenting. It's necessary to talk to them in different ways.'

(Claire Watson, Häagen-Dazs)

'A key problem is developing a totally integrated communications mix because different creative suppliers provide these services and historically people have been given briefs at different times and these have not really connected together. It's as if the brand has evolved without a masterbriefing and you end up with components of the brand in conflict with each other which consumers can see even if their brand marketers can't.

(Chris Macrae)

'As a customer you receive quite a bit of direct mail from us and if you lay out all the pieces of communication across the table (we actually did this exercise) and if you looked at each one, you would say, "All these communications look like they come from 20 different companies." And they did. And we were losing impact with the customer. . . . So we said right, we must address this. We've come up with some guidelines and rules for developing a consistent tone of voice and a consistent-looking feel for our brand, so now any type of communication we send you looks as if it is coming from American Express.'

(Russ Shaw, American Express)

continues

continued

'Most brands including product brands are now more or less service brands and they really have to be delivered, irritatingly, by things that walk around on two legs. It's a human thing, and you know humans have to be motivated in order to keep on performing at a high level.'
(Chris Mole, Coopers & Lybrand)

(*Source*: Extracts from ©BBC for BUSINESS video 'Branding – the Marketing Advantage')

As well as the issue of proliferating media there are other questions, such as:

- How are the costs of playing the game changing?
- What performance measurements are used to judge the success or failure of particular media investments?

Many people know that the most powerful branding media work on medium-term consumer loyalty. Many organizations prioritize short-term performance measures which can lead to brand spends that actually demote the brand's command of loyalty. David Ogilvy said this in 1986; he was referring to a blight in American brand management, but much of it is even more relevant today.

'Advertising is going through a bad period. Commercial clutter is worse than ever. The cost of media has ballooned. The cost of commercial production is scandalous. The problem of client conflicts is driving agencies round the bend. Worst of all, the trend to cut advertising budgets in favour of below-the-line deals is out of control. Do you realize what is going on? Manufacturers of packaged goods are now spending twice as much on below-the-line deals as on advertising. To put it another way, they are spending twice as much on price-cutting as on building brands. Manufacturers are buying volume by price discounting, instead of earning it the old-fashioned way using advertising to build strong brand franchises. Manufacturers are in fact training consumers to buy on price instead of brand.'

So as well as day-to-day selection criteria marketers need to have their own guiding principles on efficient use of media. You increasingly need to get your principles 'signed off' by the corporate hierarchy just to steer a consistent course through the high-pressure environment of daily management. For example:

- The media we choose must add to each other both as an integrated representation of the brand to the consumer and as a leadership mission for employees.
- Media effectiveness is not static. The practitioner who takes a pioneer's advantage of a strong new media often gains disproportionately. Then crowds of followers make the novelty of the media or its increasing cost less effective. The pioneer can often continue to win from this situation provided privileged terms of access (or even ownership) of the media were negotiated at the start. Medium-term entrepreneurialism in building media needs to be rewarded.
- Strong use of some media involves a greater learning curve than others. 'Glocal' marketing organizations pride themselves in transferring media learning experiences. Think of a simple medium such as the free-phone consumer feedback loop for a brand's users. It offers the consumer a forum for making suggestions/complaints and receiving advice. The company that has a system for transferring learning experiences across its brands and across different countries can use this medium very powerfully. The company that leaves each brand manager to reinvent the use of such a medium is likely to conclude that it is ineffective, whereas in reality the organization is ineffective. Take this a stage further by thinking about the potential connections between free-phone media and interfacing media such as computer-administered database clubs. This illustrates why many Charterers believe that integration will be a hallmark of brand organizations of the future, with particular regard to investment in overlapping media and the ways in which people who serve the brand will need to teamwork.
- Media need to be played in different ways for enveloping consumers at different stages of brand experience, for example, trial (first ever purchase) versus loyal user rapport.
- Good marketing never overlooks the potential of almost-free media before being dazzled by more sexy (and costly) platforms. (This admonition is issued by a CEO of one of the world's foremost branded companies, which is a good enough reason for us to illustrate it with a detailed example in Box 6.2 before we turn to challenges involving more sizeable media investments.)

Box 6.2   Master execution of the humble product leaflet

Inside every pack of King Oscar 'Brisling' sardines, you, as consumer, are likely to find a leaflet appealing for your loyalty with text like this:

Dear Customer,

The word 'Brisling' is emphasized on the label of the product you have purchased. There are strong reasons for setting Brisling apart from other sardines.

Facts you should know

- No specific fish is called sardine. The word 'sardine' originates from the Mediterranean island of Sardinia. There, small fish were caught and canned for more than a century. It is only after the small fish are put in a can, packed in oil and hermetically sealed that the fish can take the name sardine. This means that there are a large number of species of fish from many countries offered as sardines.
- However, there are no small fish for packing sardines like Norwegian Brisling.
- Brisling are members of the herring family and are caught primarily in the cold, unpolluted ocean waters of the Norwegian fjords.
- Brisling are caught for packing when they are two years old. This is when the species has reached its mature size and the fat content is exactly right. The Norwegian government has appointed federal inspectors who determine when the fish quality reaches its peak.
- Most species used for packing sardines from countries other than Norway are caught before they reach mature sizes (usually 6–12 months old).
- Because Brisling are caught when they are older than other sardines, they have time to accumulate fat which is low in 'bad' cholesterol and very high in Omega-3 fatty acids. Omega-3 is considered of value in the prevention of heart attacks.
- Once the Brisling are caught, they are kept alive in a purse net for three days. During this period the Brisling digest and naturally rid themselves of stomach contents. This self-cleansing process (thronging) ensures that there are no 'sediments' present in Norwegian sardine products. No other sardine packers use this process.
- Brisling, upon arrival at the cannery, are smoked in large ovens using oak wood. The natural flavour of the smoked Brisling creates

continues

continued

a unique taste unlike that of any other sardine product. Sardines from countries other than Norway are either chemically 'smoked' or not smoked at all.

• Brisling sardines, packed in olive oil, mature in the can just like good wine does in the bottle. This has to do with oil penetrating the flesh of the fish and blending with the fish oil. The Brisling in oil, that has been stored in your cabinet for more than two years, may be called vintage.

Our many thanks to you for purchasing King Oscar Brisling Sardines. We, at King Oscar, will continue to keep up our high standards and hope for your continuous support; also, please tell a friend.

Sincerely,

KING OSCAR, INC.

All media are not created equal

This is a very important paragraph (so please consider reading it twice). Media are not created equal; they do different kinds of jobs well. Consequently, if a medium becomes less economic – for example, as has happened with exorbitant increases in the cost of television advertising over the past 20 years – you cannot just transfer out of it to any other medium. A potential substitute needs detailed examination to ascertain whether it is capable of doing the same job. More precisely, to be a proper substitute a new medium must be capable of making the same distinctive contribution to the integrated collection of media the brand uses as the medium it is to replace.

Box 6.3   Advertising and the power of fame

All major advertising media are still – in the original sense – broadcast media. Like the sowers of seeds, they cast their messages very broadly indeed, and the advertiser is left hoping that enough of them fall in the right place to make the whole thing pay for itself.

But that is about to change. Within a startlingly short period of

continues

continued

time, consumers – real people – will be able to demand and receive any medium, any part of any medium, any brochure, any advertisement that they choose, and it could be an advertisement designed for an audience of one.

I believe it to be true that Sheba is one of the successful pioneers of relationship marketing: one-to-one marketing; direct marketing. I believe it to be true that, if my cat is on Sheba's database, on his birthday he will get a birthday card. And should I, as the owner, tell Sheba that my cat has unfortunately expired, I will get a small book from Sheba helping me to live with cat grief. I find it very easy to believe that this form of marketing may be extremely cost-efficient and successful, and many of the new technologies that are speeding our way will help speed the development of relationship marketing.

But what about brands? Just about the only thing brands have in common is a kind of fame. If the phrase global brand means anything, it's not that everyone in the world consumes it, or even that everyone in the world could consume it. It's just that everyone in the world has heard about it. Fame lends a curious value to things and to people. Famous things can be shared, referred to, laughed about. Famous things are, literally, a talking point. We talk about the weather because we know about it, it affects us all, it is a shared experience. Remember the way that Sheba does it; and then think about the way Richard Branson has done it. Not a lot of sophisticated targeting there, it seems to me, but a tremendous amount of sophistication nonetheless, because he's realized (in both senses of the word) the value to Virgin of simple fame. Some from advertising, some from sponsorship, some from stunts and public relations: but a fame so precise and yet so general that it can now add value to music and air travel and vodka and even cola.

There's private marketing communication, already important and likely to get more so. And there's public marketing communication, already important and certain to remain so.

Public communication through the advertising of a big idea maintains the relevance of brands over very long periods of time. It's big and bold and confident and public: look at BMW, look at British Airways. It creates and maintains the brand warmth we (marketers) consciously borrow every time we launch a brand extension. It delivers now . . . and next year . . . and in 10 years' time. It reaches people who will never fly British Airways and people who will never buy a BMW, but whose knowledge and views and opinions are still of immeasurable value, not least to that minority that does fly and does buy.

(*Source*: Extracted, and partially edited, from a speech by Jeremy Bullmore at the IPA President's Breakfast, Savoy Hotel, London, November 1994)

Direct marketing

What are direct marketing's typical capabilities in the middle of the 1990s? Unlike the broadcasting capabilities of advertising, the strength of direct marketing is narrow-casted targeting. It is often an excellent secondary medium on occasions such as:

- administering some of the benefits of loyalty clubs aimed at rewarding/understanding the needs of the brand's heavy users;
- cultivating opinion leaders during the seeding phase of building a new brand's cachet;
- developing niche positions for sub-brands.

Direct marketing by mail is unlikely to be capable of being a lead medium for most major brands for two reasons, which can be fraught with practical misunderstandings.

(1) If a brand, as leading business process, is to have one essential hallmark then we would suggest that this is connecting things up rather than targeting. Imagine the consumer viewpoint of a brand which is led by direct marketing:

- I, the consumer, have no idea what brand image my peers will confer on me for using this brand because the 'privacy' of direct marketing media means that I do not know what, if any, messages have influenced other people's awareness of the brand.
- If the brand is a service, I, the consumer, cannot gently nudge the brand's staff towards living up to the culture which, for example, the brand's advertising has publicly promoted as being it's own essential values.
- Moreover, I, the consumer, am not receiving, for example, advertising's public vote of confidence for my smart choice of brand. (We late twentieth-century consumers subconsciously underestimate how deeply gratifying it can be to see on network television an advertisement for a brand we have used in the past few days.)

(2) There is a world of difference between a brand which goes public with a smart relationship 'democratically guaranteed' to everyone – for example, all audiences of the brand: consumers, channels, staff, critics, nations – and one whose relationships are based on billions of individual transactions communicated in private.

- Generally, a direct-marketed brand's private 'guarantee' is always going to be worth less to me as a consumer than a company which publicly puts its reputation on the line.
- Personally, I, as a 1990s consumer, already feel transactioned to death by direct-marketing offers through my letter box. I get up to 20 of them to every item of real mail. Am I alone in

finding these to be so much more laborious for the individual to compare, let alone dispose of, than mass-marketed offers? Knowing what short-term selling pressures can do to managers of mass communicated brands, I wonder how many more selling pressures will in the future be fed down to me, the consumer, by direct-market branders as computing power makes their offers technically clever with the targeting of special offers.

Today brand marketing seems to be driving across one organizational crossroad after another with yellow lights flashing where no tried-and-trusted route map exists. In the old days of local (not 'glocal') competition and sequential (not parallel) change factors, there were safe branding directions to follow and profit from. Even if this was how most twentieth-century brands worked, those who do not recognize that we are now reaching a fundamental discontinuity in best practices of marketing are at risk of deluding themselves and the organizations they serve.

The risk that companies must now urgently guard against is the disintegration of the brand marketing process. Electing to make direct marketing your brand's main medium could be a bridge too far from broadcasting your brand's essential messages to its consumers, or a leap too fast in the evolutionary form of mid-1990s brand organization. But as every year changes, marketers must rehearse their own positions on what branding jobs direct marketing can and cannot do. The advice of top-level management consultants is that the variety of these media is only just beginning to blossom technologically (just think what multimedia highways may do) and the economies of using them are set to improve dramatically.

Unfortunately, the point that different media do different things well, is often obscured by an industry obsession for converting the reach of one medium to another through such simplified measures as gross rating points, which attempt to convey how large your audience may have been. It sometimes seems that while the majority who add value in a marketing company know that media buying can never be a precise science, financial or other nerves at the centre of control demand a numerical bottom-line anyway. There is an increasing danger of establishing measures which get out of touch with meaningful human thought processes. Numerical blindness can create ignorance even at such simple levels of media comparability as:

- How attentive were your audience?
- How long did they have to think about your message before another medium or programme zapped their minds?

If you as a marketer award yourself the same rating points for putting a piece of junk mail through the door, which an adult opens and immediately bins, as beaming a commercial, which excites all family members in one communal showing, then your brand's economics is likely to lose its way. What starts as a careless symptom of this sort can very quickly become a terminal form of illness, however famous the brand.

Executional differences also provide a lot to play for. Even within an ostensibly simple medium such as sampling through the door, the effectiveness of presenting the brand as you normally package it rather than in some messy image-lacking sachet can be of the order of 300% or more. We have seen repeated evidence of this in simulated test marketing experiments. (For further findings from this international brand experience databank, see Just-in-time market research, in Macrae, 1991.)

Because aggregate and blunt measures of media performance are a widespread distraction to thoughtfully integrated communications, Brand Charterers often find it worthwhile to convene a workshop which goes back to first principles by debating the 'controversy' of:

- How are media equal or different?
- 'For what' are media equal or different?
- Whose job is it to integrate the different media used by a brand organization?

How are media equal or different?

To debate this issue, Brand Chartering workshops often begin with two questions:

- What kind of broadcasting jobs need to be done to keep a brand vital, or in Ogilvy's famous words 'part of the fabric of life'?
- Which media (marketing mix components) take lead and supporting roles in getting these jobs done?

Assuming we are considering brands that are intended to have at least a medium-term future, you might like to edit this shortlist of essential jobs involved in broadcasting a brand franchise:

- Keep the brand in the news.
- Consistently add real value (by increasing perceived competitive quality).
- Sell more.
- Bond smart 'two-way' relationships (for example, market researcher Max Blackston (1993) suggests an appropriate way to probe the depth of a brand relationship with consumers is by asking not only how they perceive the brand but also what they think the brand thinks of them).

Let us consider 'brand in the news', part of the job description for a brand's promotional media first coined by an advertising executive, James Webb Young, four decades ago when agency and client had more confidence in continuity and integration of creative thinking. Some of the interpersonal newslines that he valued in assessing the strength of an execution and a medium employed by a brand are listed in Box 6.4. (Recollecting times when a brand seems to have had a 'buzz' of its own, please add to this list other manifestations of 'brand in the news' which come to mind.)

Box 6.4   Some debatable answers on how 'being in the news' works for a mass market brand

- Convey a popular image of the brand (that is one that a consumer expects everyone to see in the brand).
- Make a declaration in public, for example, a guarantee which the brand will live up to.
- Applaud loyal consumers (most consumers like to see their brand in the news and, apparently, winning against competitive brands).
- Make news items that are reported by journalists.
- Make a brand into a celebrity whose consumption transfers some of its celebrity status.
- Capture and symbolize a mood of the times.
- Establish the brand as a reference point, against which other brands are compared by critics and public.
- Make brand a topic of social conversation.
- Make brand famous and endorsed by opinion leaders.
- Motivating employees.

Continue the debate by asking which components of the marketing mix can play a lead role in endeavours aimed at newsworthy branding (Box 6.5).

Box 6.5   Some debatable answers on which media can play a lead role in making the essence of a brand 'newsworthy'

- Advertising can.
  (Gillette, British Airways for transnational broadcasting; Benetton or Häagen-Dazs for transnational 'word-of-mouth')
- Packaging and design can.
  (Nestlé)

continues

---

continued

- Developing your own retail or display channel can.
  (Body Shop)
- PR and world-staging can.
  (McDonald's, WeightWatchers)
- 'Brand seeding' can.
  (Häagen-Dazs)
- Price-cutting cannot.
- Promotional competitions cannot (unless they are intimately linked to the brand's essence).
- Direct marketing through mail shots cannot?

(References in brackets are to benchmarking of named brands in ThinkPiece 1.)

If you wish to explore the 'how' dynamics of brand communications further construct a matrix analysis by:

- putting other short-listed branding jobs to be done across the page;
- putting types of media mix down the page;
- ticking off which types of media play leading roles for which jobs.

For example, before Häagen-Dazs mass markets in any new country, it dedicates its branding communications to establishing a super-premium fashion platform. The columns in Figure 6.1 show the kinds of jobs to be done if a *haute couture* 'seeding' platform is to be secured. Many of these have been incorporated into the introduction of Häagen-Dazs to new countries with considerable flair. By working back from a choice of key jobs to be done, a masterbriefing plan for seeding a brand among a minimum critical mass of opinion leaders takes shape.

In Chapter 3 we saw that the combination of media used in the seeding of a new brand is very different from that for a classic brand launch relying on a heavy burst of television advertising. Interestingly, most successful 'seeders' confirm that if mass advertising is employed too early – before the cachet has been cultivated among a minimum critical mass of opinion leaders – the brand's opportunity to win a *haute couture* image is likely to be lost for ever.

'For what' are media equal or different?

All good marketing decisions are context specific. Check out typical 'for what' questions which you can then fine-tune and extend to your own business environments.

How to become newsworthy:	How to be seen as desirable:	How to get other people to create the identity for you:	How to get people to try it:	How to move from country of strength:	How to spread the gospel of the world's number one:
• High visibility • Free publicity • International • Journalist's favourite	• Opinion leaders • Success to success • Showcase distribution • Premium prices • Hard to get? • Sexy?	• Legends • Endorsements • Visible consumption • Unique point of sales • Jetsetters' word of mouth • Great photographic images • Great logo	• Sampling • New distributor • Line targeting urgent/impulsive need • Gifting vehicles	• Borrow national identity • 'Seed' local desire for world's favourite • Offer exclusive premieres to partners • Create jetsetting media/stages	• Be the ambassador of the product category • Offer sneak previews to VIP audiences • Lead on quality/service commitments, globally and locally • Make heros of product's unique positive qualities

Figure 6.1 How to create a fashion out of a product.

For what product categories?

The simplest point is sometimes the easiest to overlook. It is very unlikely that the most successful media combination for a brilliant clothing catalogue will also be the best integrated media model for a fast-moving consumer good (fmcg) with a low unit price such as a Mars bar. (For an example of what can happen when an fmcg company is instantly converted from an advertising-led to a direct-marketing led model, see the case study on Heinz UK in Chapter 11.)

For what countries?

If your brand is to compete in international markets, then another obvious point is that there are very different media economies and impacts across countries. A masterbriefing should have a primary model of how integrated media work for the brand, but this must also be thoughtfully edited by country. For example, what different point-of-sales support will your brand organization need:

- in a country like the UK where grocery channels are dominated by a handful of supermarket retail chains which have their own selective agendas about which outsider brands to stock in addition to their own labels;
- in much of South East Asia where retailers are often happy to stock precisely one facing of every available branded line?

If necessary, various primary models of working an international brand will need to be kept up and running with the aim of converging them as countries' marketing environments converge. The most powerful brands tend to be those which dare to seize the initiative with a primary model that creates a new broadcasting form. As of 1995, Gillette's integrated communications still provides an outstanding example of satellite television-led promotion. The format of these advertisements is unlikely to win prizes for creative brilliance and it is conceivable that cosmopolitan consumer boredom will set in if too many other companies clone Gillette's idea. But Gillette is currently exploiting the benefits of having created a cost-effective communications package and, moreover, much of satellite television's staple programming (for example, sports, pop cultures) and corresponding audiences suit the products represented by the domain of the Gillette brand. (See brand benchmarking Gillette in ThinkPiece 1.)

For what goals, and how do they vary by levels and leagues of branding?

Management goals and communications practices must vary by levels and leagues of branding which are classified in detail in Chapter 11. The communications mix for a short-term faddish product is likely to be very different from a banner or corporate brand which strategically connects up a substantial number of products and a significant proportion of corporate goodwill.

For what operating dimensions of an integrated branding model?

When a business team adopts an integrated view of the brand process as being all those vital relationships which develop through organization of a complete business system and service mission, it is appropriate to try to clarify the operating dimensions of the communications process. We believe that business teams should brainstorm their own customized terms of reference. As an example, one classification suggested by McKinsey includes four principal elements:

(1) The breadth of communications from approaches that are mainly mass media to those that are propagated by one-to-one means such as direct mail.
(2) The loyalty of the required relationship which could range from monogamous to polygamous.
(3) The basis for trust, varying from simple faith in a tried or true product to clear logic as to why the selling proposition works.
(4) The complexity of the value chain in which a product or service could be fully integrated, or, alternatively, completely unbundled. (Freeling, 1994)

For what competence-building skills?

It is also valid to argue that some of your brands must be used as testbeds so your company's people can be sure of being suitably far advanced down specific learning curves associated with major new media. As with any competence-building investment, we advise that business teams exercise caution when determining whether a competence which may faddishly be labelled as a direct lane on a future highway is what it claims to be, or merely a diversion. For example, it is not evident to us that the skills of excellence involved in postal direct mailing will have much in common with skills of excellence in those not-so-far-off days when most households no longer own a television but have a computerized interface to a multimedia highway, none of whose facets resembles the passive (that is non-audience interactive) programming of old. Moreover, the technology and information for multimedia leadership is far more likely to be resourced by partnerships of companies than by each company inventing its own database of consumer addresses.

Whose job is it to integrate the different media used by a brand organization?

The organizational challenges of (re)creating environments in which integrated brand marketing flourishes should not be underestimated. Political inertias will surround brands as sources of power within the organization unless corporate leaders insist on a different kind of managerial dynamic (see Box 6.6).

Box 6.6   In the place of eight branding fiefdoms, First Choice is born

In the summer of 1994 there was notable applause in the British business press for Francis Baron of travel business First Choice (previously Owners Abroad). His stewardship was regarded as remarkable because of dramatic gains made in the direction of integrated branding. His company had come to the brink of a marketing crisis. Eight brands were too many for an industry leader. His company's advertising pot was split into £500,000 dollops whereas the leading competitors were Thomson's £7.5 million and Airtours' £4.1 million.

In a frenetic 12-week integration programme Francis appointed different agencies – for example, advertising, corporate identity and consumer PR – and got them working together. Says one of the agency heads: 'Francis exhibited unusual skill giving each agency clear responsibilities and strict deadlines; there wasn't time for the political manoeuvring that you sometimes get in these circumstances.' Says Francis: 'I had made it clear at all agency pitches that their managing director had to be account director. . . . Part of their job was to go back to their agencies and rally the ranks if some of their ideas weren't chosen.'

Key organizational questions to ask when evaluating whether a brand's communications are fully integrated include:

- Is there a masterbrief from which all creative agencies are currently working?
- Does the brand team have a share in Brand Chartering, or something similar, so that medium-term goals of the brand as business process are agreed and verifiable by all?
- What safeguards are built in so that tensions between a brand's short-term performance and medium-term development are properly balanced?
- Who is accountable for the whole brand process? Does he or she have the continuous power to deal at least as an equal with the politics governing the company's processes and manifest in its functional

hierarchy? If the company is international, does the company's global/local marketing theory work in practice?

- How do media and service commitments interact in a brand organization?

For some special insights regarding the latter question, we have collated some of the experiences which Sim Kay Wee of Singapore Airlines illuminated during interviews for the BBC for BUSINESS video (Box 6.7).

Box 6.7   Some components of brand service organization of Singapore Airlines

The Singapore Girl has been the theme of the company's advertising for more than 20 years. She's 'our icon'. She portrays the kind of image we want, and the quality of service that we give. And we are very proud of her.

The most important thing about training is that you don't just focus on technical training, but on the softer aspects too. For example, you can train a stewardess to pour a cup of coffee for a passenger. The technical aspects of that are to make sure it doesn't spill, the cup is in the right position and all that. But we add to that soft training which is about attitude: a warmth, a friendliness, the anticipation behind pouring that cup of coffee. In addition, you've got to recognize your staff. Every year our managing director gives out awards for staff who go out of their way to serve passengers and make sure that passengers are delighted.

It's no good just being good at training your staff or just giving good in-flight service, all these things must happen simultaneously. It is doing things in a coordinated whole, so the value to a customer is compounded and he or she gets an entire package.

We participate in a lot of frequent-flyer programmes with British Airways, Swiss Air, and so on, but that is really buying loyalty. You buy the loyalty by giving travel mileages for passengers. We also think it's important to have the loyalty of the passengers so that they appreciate what you do for them. That's why we have our PPS (Priority Passenger Service) scheme. We collect data on these passengers so, for example, we know not that he is a whisky drinker, but which is his brand and we make sure he gets it in his hand before he even asks for it. The ideal point is reached when the passenger's hobbies or needs are satisfied. For example, if you have a passenger that likes gardening he will get his favourite gardening magazine that he normally reads so that he will not miss out on an issue while he travels. And I think the ultimate will be reached when on his next visit to Singapore you get the director of the Singapore Botanic Gardens which is world famous to bring him around

continues

> *continued*
>
> personally to the Orchid enclosure for example, so I think this is what we are talking about when we say exclusive service.
>
> (*Source:* © BBC for BUSINESS video 'Branding – the Marketing Advantage')

Summary

The next few years will present fundamental discontinuities in the opportunities and risks of media economies, the like of which brands have not experienced since the beginning of the television age. For example, in multimedia channels media will soon begin to overlap in ways that we can only begin to imagine.

Winning brand organizations will:

- flexibly develop suitable patterns of media for specific brand processes;
- ensure that they have developed a masterbriefing capability which is up-to-date and tailored to the essence and level of a specific brand's role within the organization.

Masterbriefing frameworks should also be used to facilitate brand learning across an organization's market-facing business teams, both globally and locally. The communications and service integrity of brand leadership should be one and the same process.

Integrated marketing of customer relationships is the future name of the branding game, but do not promote a media's creative supplier to your brand's lead role just because this slogan is bandied around. Require suppliers to justify how the quality of their communications/ creativity will support integrated brand organization in both its internal and external manifestations.

As a first approach we have suggested a framework for exploring 'how' and 'for what' jobs specific media may be deemed equal or different.

(See ThinkPiece 2 for an agenda of a masterbriefing workshop.)

References

Blackston, M. (1993). Beyond brand personality: building brand relationships. In: Aaker, D. and Biel, A. (eds). *Brand equity and advertising*. LEA

Freeling, A. (1994). Winning the right to brand, speech at the Marketing Forum on the Canberra, McKinsey

Macrae, C. (1991). *World Class Brands*. Harlow: Addison-Wesley

brand Quality and Value

The balancing process of branding

In 1993, around the branded world, pricing earthquakes struck in such far-flung marketing territories as Marlboro (USA), top department store brands (Japan) and brands newly exposed to competition from generic products (especially grocery products in the UK and parts of Europe). Greedy brands were seen to be suffering setbacks and marketing organizations were shaken up.

The quality/value balance represented by a brand and its pricing policy needs to be carefully Chartered. Considerable subtleties are involved. What may seem to be a tactical pricing decision will often turn out to have cumulative repercussions. Two of the long-term reasons for branding – adding value and strategic advantage – are often talked of as organizational goals without any thought for the occasions when they become directly incompatible.

Branding's determining forms of marketing investment, like advertising, often pay their way by adding value rather than gaining new users. It can be far more effective to campaign on increasing the loyalty of existing consumers and their willingness to pay a price premium than to increase sales volume by getting the brand to acquire new consumers.

Box 7.1

The real benefit of branding is often less in creating volume than in supporting the price that the purchaser is ready to pay. It may wrongly be taken for granted that the reason for marketing activities – advertising, for example – is to increase sales volume, which is a relic of the early and expansionist years of this century. In fact marketing is largely a process of adding values, both rational and emotional. The author is indebted to a referee who added a comment at this point: 'I have lost count of the number of erroneous marketing decisions I have encountered due to the failure of many modellers of advertising effectiveness/awareness to fully appreciate this issue.'

(*Source*: Broadbent, 1994)

However, if you keep on banking an extra premium from your loyal consumers your cumulative exploits make you vulnerable to competitive attack. At some stage, either the increasing value of your market or the pricing amounts by which you can be undercut make you irresistible prey for new competition. Consumer price insensitivity often does not obey the response curves which standard econometrics models assume.

What lessons can Brand Charterers learn from 1993? Are there any lasting consequences? We are not privy to the following companies' detailed financial records, but the year's events seem to indicate revealing patterns which relate pricing decisions to branding discontent.

Marlboro's price peak, 1993

For over 40 years Marlboro's branded communications have campaigned on an essence which has been the making of the world's and the USA's favourite cigarette. It is difficult to imagine how any other communications imagery can directly challenge Marlboro Country.

For several years before 1993 Marlboro had led price rises in the USA among premium brands significantly above the industry's extra costs. In the process, an increasing price gap opened up for generic (that is virtually unadvertised) brands to exploit at the price-sensitive end of market consumption. By 1993 generics had risen from being a marginal force a few years earlier to be the leading dynamic of the marketplace, with their volume share jumping from 28% to 36% in just nine months. This meant that the generics sector was selling one and a half times more cigarettes than Marlboro and coming close to it in terms of total consumer spend (Marlboro being bolstered by its price premium of 50% or more over generics).

Technically, Marlboro's market share was just about holding its own. On a short-term view its most recent price rise may have profited the brand's performance in that year. But Marlboro was by now on the edge of a price premium precipice. The stage was set for what newspapers around the world would soon be reporting in excited tones, like this extract from the UK's *Sunday Times*:

> 'On April 2, 1993, Philip Morris, the world's largest consumer-products group, took the biggest gamble of its life. It slashed the price in America of its top-selling cigarette, Marlboro, by 20% – 40 cents a pack.'

Unlike other brand pricing earthquakes of 1993, Marlboro's was started on its own strategic terms and judged as correct by many in the pure world of competitive strategy. It was designed to cut generics down to size. The profit squeeze would hurt Philip Morris much less than its main rival Reynolds. Because Reynolds had inherited a relatively frail financial structure from the days of junk bond management buyouts, it has been conjectured that Philip Morris's frequent price rises may have deliberately lulled Reynolds into a false sense of security. The strategic sting was then dramatically to introduce a deep price cut when it would hurt most.

Most things have turned out the way Philip Morris planned. The generics boom has been halted. Marlboro's leadership (in 1995) looks like being fully restored. But what Marlboro's owners could not have anticipated was the global news coverage associated with the spectre of the world's most valuable brand (as calculated by accountants) having to take a price cut. Accountancy-driven algorithms of brand valuation were popularized in the late 1980s. Their frame of reference, as mathematical algorithms, is influenced by financial regulations and not by marketing foresight (see Chapter 12). The *Financial Times* (13 April 1993) observed:

> 'At a time when corporate performance in many industries depends increasingly on attributes such as reputation and service, there is a genuine need for more precise methods to measure the value of intangibles. But the issues have so far been as much obscured as clarified by efforts to put a price on brands. These methods involve, at best, highly subjective judgements and amount, at worst, to a mechanistic checklist exercise. They offer very few verifiable insights into how and why that performance was achieved, and hence, whether it can be maintained. But in the real world, that is what really counts.'

In the year following the price cut Philip Morris's stock lost about 20% of its value compared with a 5% gain by the Dow Jones market index. What has now become known as 'Marlboro Friday' was taken as a signal for writing down many of the world's major branded companies. 'Life and death stories on brands' proliferated among various influential financial columnists. As a final legacy, even as Marlboro was regaining strength in late 1994, Philip Morris's CEO (in charge of 1993) appears to have taken early retirement.

The lessons from Marlboro are symbolic, but not as generalizable as those from other pricing earthquakes of 1993. They show how widely big brands have become targets for global news coverage. Philip Morris's local strategic manoeuvre might have been flawless in the days before accountants talked so publicly of valuing brands and Marlboro's fame as the world's most valuable property right. Instead the symbolism of 'Marlboro Friday' has opened commentators' minds to the issue of where brand leadership is going right or wrong.

UK packaged goods price peak, 1993

In the UK mainstream grocery chains led by Sainsbury's and Tesco (which each retail over 10% of the nation's grocery products) have been building up their own brands for almost a decade. In the old days, when neighbouring supermarkets fought battles out on high streets, competing on the price of own labels was the primary concern. As consumer shopping moved to superstores at out-of-town sites, own label brands started playing a much more prominent role in confirming the quality of the lifestyle you buy into by making your regular shopping trip to your favourite (brand of) supermarket. Many manufacturer brands were lulled into a false sense of pricing security at this time. They had continuously maintained their category leading brands at price differentials which appeared reasonable, typically 20%, when compared with supermarkets' own increasingly upmarket labels.

Partly in response to this sustained shift upmarket by retailers and manufacturers, foreign discount grocery formats began to target the UK (such as Germany's price-fighter Aldi and American-styled 'Warehouse' clubs for consumers). Consequently, in 1993 the major supermarket chains suddenly changed course, showing that they were prepared to merchandise products down to generic price-saving levels, in addition to their (by now) premium own labels. The *Sunday Times* reported on 3 April 1994:

> 'Britain's equivalent to Marlboro Friday arrived on November 3 1993. On "Sainsbury Wednesday", the supermarket group cut the prices of 300 lines, and David Sainsbury, chairman, predicted that branded product prices would "have to come down very significantly to compete".'

The shock for some UK branded manufacturers was that they were pricing their products at over double the price of the generic product. Some still do not seem to be able to reconcile how so much extra overhead has ended up in their branded cost chain. Was anyone in these companies keeping an eye on how much the cost of marketing and supplying their brands had become relative to the lowest cost supplier?

Our first pricing axiom for Charterers is that it is never safe to take your eye off the pricing ball. The second is that this becomes doubly vital once individual customer channels control a significant proportion of your market, say 10% or more.

At time of writing (two years after Marlboro Friday), it looks as if Marlboro in the USA escaped with a blip on the Richter scale, compared with what may be happening to Coca-Cola in the UK in some supermarket channels for its product. Yet if Coca-Cola had a pricing fault it seems to have been one of perceived arrogance rather than failure to add value. Recent advertising, such as 'Always Coca-Cola', and globally directed visibility have been as good as ever. Up to 1993 the added value of the whole soft drinks category in the UK had been consistently raised by Coca-Cola. How did the company fail to explain the logic of its policy to leading UK supermarkets? They profited from high added value in all soft drinks from the strong leadership which the Coca-Cola brand delivered. Now the UK is being swamped by a multitude of lower priced Cotts. These include own label lookalikes (such as Sainsbury's Classic which has taken the lion's share of colas through this channel); and 'guest brand formats' (such as the three-way production of Cott, signed as Virgin Cola, premiering as the cola of Tesco supermarkets). For more details on strategic interpretations of these manoeuvres, see Chapter 12 on Cott's intention to export retail programmes from Canada and the USA to the added-value chains of packaged goods globally and locally.

Our third pricing axiom is that Brand Charterers should never forget that added-value strategy is not only about competition but also about whom to partner, and how partners may share your expectations from the added-value chain.

In the second part of this chapter we will take a closer look at three basic drives which need to be balanced harmoniously for brand processes to keep on winning. These are:

- Top value
- Top quality
- World class focus

We will also discuss why transactions labelled as 'brand milking' need to be organized with care, unless it is intended that the brand process should keep on losing value.

Top value

During the 1980s one of the authors was involved in managing and reporting on over 200 experiments involving brand launches, relaunches and extensions. Each experiment involved collecting a customized dataset for forecasting the brand's business potential. Our part of the bargain to clients was the competence to forecast their brand's business potential with a modal accuracy of plus or minus 12%, provided they specified market access parameters, defined in terms of:

- awareness (percentage of consumers who would know their brand);
- distribution (percentage of consumers who would find the brand where they wanted to shop);
- market crowdedness, for example, how many brands made up 80% of the market and how many brands were actively rotated in a typical consumer repertoire. (Macrae, 1991, Chapter 7)

These 200 experiments were personally managed in over 15 countries and around 50 product or service categories. This was part of a larger corporate experience databank which through the 1980s comprised about 2,000 in-market experiments, spanning 40 countries and several hundred market categories.

Our modelling approach involved simulating communications, purchasing and usage experiences of consumers. Simulation modules were structured to be comparable across experiments but were not based on normative measurements. This enabled us to take full account of the fact that brand leaders aim to break norms, especially in extending or relaunching their franchises. However, as our experience bank of in-market experiments grew, it was naturally interesting to search them for benchmarks of consumer response. We detected a 25 – 50% rule on pricing which is shown in Box 7.2.

Box 7.2   Pricing: consumer response benchmarks

- Brand leaders can 'perceptually justify' price premiums of up to 25% against other directly competing brands.
- Brand leaders with a discernible product plus are able to 'perceptually justify' price premiums of up to 50% against what are otherwise directly competing brands.
- Higher premiums are 'perceptually justifiable' only where the consumer's need served is actually a 'different competitive marketplace'.

There are some subtly interesting qualifications to note before applying these guidelines in practice. Before coming to these, two clarifications of terms are worth making:

(1) We view these as ballpark figures (that is within a few per cent). If your own personal operating heuristic is 30% or 20%, instead of 25%, that is fine. We are talking the same language.

(2) These guidelines seemed to be general consumer response patterns:

  • over time (or at least the 1980s)
  • across countries/markets, from developing ones to over-developed ones (reporting areas included India, Thailand, Indonesia, Japan, USA, Europe);
  • over different periods of economic health and social mood, from feel-good boom times to depressing recessionary times.

Subtle qualifications on pricing perspectives

(1) There may be many different 'value' markets for the same branded product. Typically, these are defined by consumer need and its specific situation. For example, there are at least three different markets for soft drinks:

  • multipacks to take home from the shopping trolley market (a competitive one in which our rule would apply);
  • on-street consumption out of pack (where we would expect a higher pricing base to apply than with multipacks, and also to suspend the rule at locations where there is little competition or the immediacy of thirst is great);
  • restaurant/bar consumption, where we would not advance any rule because the added value of the service environment dwarfs any value judgement of product value.

France, one of the world's thriving markets for mineral waters, provides an interesting example of how price bases between the three soft drinks markets vary immensely. For decades the price multiplier between the take-home market and the 'restaurant' market has been observable as almost any number from five in a cafe to 10 or more in a restaurant. But it was only in the 1980s that French mineral water companies realized they could also open up the on-street market with a multiplier of about three to five through merchandising small (0.3–0.5 litre) bottles competing directly against canned sodas. Indeed, to this day, in France's local parades of small food stores which provide both for residents' take-home shopping and tourists' impulse purchasing, you can see two strangely different consumer behaviours going on in the same outlet. Some consumers are paying more for a smaller bottle of mineral water – though admittedly often out of a chilled cabinet – than others are paying for a bottle three times the size.

(2) Brands may position products in very different quality/value submarkets by social occasion of use. For example, there are different segments of the take-home ice cream market whose prices bear no relation to each other. A super-premium ice cream brand like Häagen-Dazs is not competing for the same end usage as an everyday block of ice cream for all the family. If in doubt ask consumers. Substitutable selections for Häagen-Dazs may be patisserie cakes, or other desserts fit for an adult dinner party. The ice cream block may be competing against jelly or tinned fruit for the children.

(3) If the top-priced market is a *haute-couture* fashion one, then all generalized pricing guidelines are cancelled. In the highest of fashion markets, snobby behaviour takes over with a vengeance. People are prepared to pay any price, indeed may want to pay any price, if this means they feel visibly superior to all but a self-elected élite. You may debate whether this is ordinary branding territory or whether it is more appropriate to have a different word for it. Kapferer explains that the French do, in their notion of marketing the *griffe* (Box 7.3).

Box 7.3 Beyond mass marketing: the world of the *griffe*

In luxury markets the French distinguish a special term of relationship, the so-called '*griffes*' or literally 'claws'. In reality, brands and *griffes* should be distinguished for the different grounds they cover.

The very word says much more. Its meaning as a 'claw' suggests instinct and violence; something unpredictable, that leaps out and leaves its mark. In this sense, the *griffe* is the mark of an inspired and instinctive creator. The *griffe* also has the same root as 'graphic', and it refers back to the hand. Its reference model is handmade work and craftsmanship.

(*Source*: Kapferer, 1992)

---

(4) The balance of what may be 'perceptually justifiable' makes pricing a fine art. On the one hand, it can be very risky for a brand to stretch its price premium to the upper limit of what is perceptually justifiable. Our evidence is that brand–price elasticity seldom takes on the linear form of economic modelling. Many brands have a critical pricing point up to which consumer response remains robust, but after which it falls over a precipice.

On the other hand, the brand leader which claims no price premium at all will often be underachieving in sales volume, let alone sales value and profit. This happens because new or intermittent purchasers use price as a selection cue to the quality image of the brand. It also happens because loyal users like the reassurance that their brand is superior which a pricing premium, used in moderation, can give.

Towards a robust strategy for competing on value

A price that is 'perceptually justifiable' in current competitive markets is only one aspect of branding a robust value strategy. Two critical points to add to the picture of price decision-making are that:

- taking too high a price premium may encourage a new branded entrant to enter the market;
- taking too low a price premium may not enable you to invest in the future.

World class competition means that being locally the lowest-cost competitor may not now be enough. You need to be low cost vis-à-vis scenarios of global competition, including new ones involving companies outside your traditional competitive set that may become intent on introducing discontinuities to the added-value chain across a sphere of business. This is what Cott Corp is trying to do in colas. Generic priced products can also suddenly emerge because of the branded supermarket's own need for competitive response to foreign retail entrants offering discount formats.

The Brand Charterer must be well informed on all scenarios involving attempts to revolutionize the added-value chain. Some of the most important clues will emerge first from the other side of the world. Organizations will need to hone their networking antennae to collect this intelligence. Among serious attempts to destabilize branded added-value chains, there are two different types of outcomes which condition what branding action must be taken. You must distinguish between revolutionaries who will make a long-term mark on the sphere of business and those who will not.

Foreseeing fundamental discontinuities to added-value chains

If you assess that the revolutionary will win, you must review your own core competences. Business survival may require you to re-engineer value across the whole of the branded business. A partial response, such as cost-cutting measures, however painful, is unlikely to be enough. Like repeatedly fleeing an enemy in war, this can be the start of a vicious circle of self-destruction of your value-contributing capabilities. For example, view the new competence configurations of brands like President's

Choice and companies like Cott Corp in Chapter 12, and then debate what the revolutionary consequences will be for which traditionally branded manufacturers.

Managing the fallout from revolutionary failures

Some generic priced products will have a fairly short life. The UK's leading branded supermarket chains would not be able to survive in the formats which their brands represent if the public unanimously chose to shop generic. But this does not mean that brand-leading manufacturers can afford complacency because some brand processes have managed to get 250% out of line with sustainable low cost, and many more are above our 50% benchmark for a sustainable value-based offer. Even where brand manufacturers are operating processes of unbeatable quality and value, the visibility of generic price differentials of 250% can tar all brands with the same brush. In different ways, this makes end-consumers, retail customers and opinion leaders like journalists take another look at who may be over-exploiting what in the added-value chain.

One likely scenario is that many retailers will continue over the long term to make a show of generics in some categories, just as they make a show of premium own-labelling value in other categories. To some extent, all brand manufacturers are now battling with each other to convince retailers that their categories are genuinely ones where brands add the most value for all: retailers, consumers and themselves. Branding grounds for this justification include continuous scope for innovation in a product category, or valuable closeness to the end-consumer in ways that only a unique brand essence can offer.

Top quality

Quality and value are correlated perceptions. Unless your aim is to turn a market permanently into a commodity market, there will be a pricing point below which your brand's perceived value starts to fall. Too low a price cue conflicts with the credibility of the brand's claim to be a better or differentiated standard from other offers in the marketplace. A brand leader which cuts its reference price is liable to be perceived by consumers as reducing the quality of its ingredients or service even if it is not. We have helped several number 2 ranked brands – which have had advance notice that a leader is going to war on price – to counterposition with a stand on quality and take over market leadership.

Consumers aspire continuously to improve their lives. Some of the implications of this are as follows:

- If a core brand (that is, one which you are not milking or otherwise disposing of) needs to cut its costs, it is usually advisable to do this in ways that are least visible to its most loyal fans. Working out how to do it is much easier if the Brand Charter is in place before you address the cost-cutting challenge.

- Global marketing may bring pressures to smarten up the added value of your brands (and cull those which do not meet this requirement). Yet in local economies which are not growing as fast as your company globally wants to raise value, you are unlikely to win friends by introducing high added-value lines too quickly alongside the brand's traditional offers. A strong global brand lets local consumers feel that they are making local improvements to a global institution. Conversely, a brand presenting itself as having better global things to offer which are beyond local consumers' means is exhibiting its own local weakness.

- A coherent global brand cannot afford to vary its price across countries while presenting itself as precisely the same in all other respects. It helps if the identity system of the brand architecture has established an international coding system which can credibly communicate a variety of quality and value offers. Alternatively, a brand can be presented in an array of different product categories, including some where all products are relatively low ticket items. Thus a premium branded fashion can still make itself available in every locality (see Box 7.4).

Box 7.4   Quality perceptions and the global whisky brand

'When IDV was first taken over by Grand Metropolitan, I got permission to try to promote J & B within the group. I spent half an afternoon telling hundreds of executives from Watney, Trumans, Mecca and Peter Dominic what a magnificent whisky it was.

'My persuasion worked and J & B promptly appeared in optics all over Britain. But then foreigners, used to the idea of J & B as a luxury premium brand, discovered it was just a commodity Scotch in its native Britain and the discovery was beginning to hurt sales in the rest of the world. So, a few years later I had the embarrassing job of telling my in-house customers that they would have to discourage buyers by

continues

---

continued

upping the price and transforming it into the same premium brand as it was everywhere else in the world.

'People outside the drinks business may not appreciate what a serious mistake it was because I'd jeopardized J & B's image, and that's the only asset any drinks brand has – apart from its intrinsic quality – and even a whisky as good as J & B can be hurt if it becomes associated with cheapness.

'The story has a happy ending. J & B is still not a big seller here (in Britain), though an awful lot of people are prepared to pay a premium price for it, but it's the second biggest selling Scotch in the world, and its sales outside the United States have gone up eight times in the last 15 years to more than 4 million cases. And that's not bad for a Scotch which was virtually unknown until the 1950s, and which depended on the US for 90% of its sales until the 1960s.'

(*Source*: Extract from Bull, G. (1990). My Biggest Mistake, *Independent on Sunday*, 25 February)

Moving on from perceived quality to realization of quality, there are some trends in world class competition which need to be actively tracked by managers and foreseen by directors.

- Increasingly, companies claim to be focusing their competences and orienting new product development on products and services which are strong enough to capture world markets. Some of this is hype, but it suggests that world standards in some product categories will be higher than the local standards to which companies have been accustomed. Companies must recognize the opportunities for leaders and the risks for laggards that this trend represents. Brands as processes need to be increasingly tied in to a realistic assessment of a company's combination of core competences.

- A director waving a magic wand cannot produce world class quality. It requires more teamworking, more carefully integrated R&D and the dedication of all involved over long incubation periods. Branded markets will expose companies that cannot organize the pre-marketing brand processes now implied by the development of world class products and services.

World class focus

Six years ago we wrote the following:

> 'The world's best products often depend on highly personalized commitment. Local products of excellence will always be prized, but in an era where the meanings of local and national boundaries will soon need to be questioned more honestly, world class brands should have the confidence and the integrity to symbolize the best produce, services and experiences that transnational cooperatives have to offer.
>
> 'Good marketing involves facilitating offers that are as customized as technology and human endeavour can manage, while maintaining an economic balance which satisfies the customer and the company. Branding provides the power to identify a cause which unites people over time – with an appeal that acts as a centre of gravity – so that customers can benefit from economies of scale while enjoying a feeling of individual attention.' (Macrae, 1991)

This world class philosophy advances the brand's social role as ambassador of free world trade and competition, and motivates staff in a service company to 'reach out for the stars'. But we now have a new interpretation for those involved in projecting the essence of individual brands.

We believe that the anchor points of top-level brands will increasingly move away from products to a consumer bond of trust that – whatever the brand offers as products – it will deliver particular balances of quality and value which the brand's reputation has come to signify. This means that top-level branding will be more corporate. Particular combinations of competences served by specific companies will reassure consumers as meriting differential grades of quality/value. If the architecture of retailer, service and fashion brands already manifests this, why cannot manufacturers' brands? Ultimately, as we argue in Chapters 11–14, the economic models for branding world class quality and value must involve more communications resources weighted towards organization-wide banner-brand processes and less towards product sub-brands, than was practised by the classic fast-moving consumer goods manufacturers of the 20th century. It is a shame if the quality of the structure of a company's communications channels does not live up to the quality of its products.

An understanding of the nuances of quality and value must pervade all aspects of brand and business processes if a company is to compete effectively and be consistently successful in cooperating with partners in the added-value chain of the sphere of business.

Milking brands

We conclude this chapter with a brainstorming exercise on 'milking' a brand. This means consciously or inadvertently taking profit out of a brand in a way which either damages its equity (medium-term competitive standing in its markets) irreparably, or results in the restoration of the brand costing more than was gained from the milking episode. Here are some of the ways in which brands are milked.

Allowing short-term sales tactics to run the marketing mix

Many companies have fostered brand management cultures where people have been rewarded for actions like price cuts whose only purpose was to increase sales for a particular time period, that is 'meeting the targets planned'. This can easily become a vicious circle, with more and more pricing manoeuvres required to push sales along. For example, in the early 1980s most American manufacturer brands spent the majority of their marketing mix on quality-enhancing activities. By the late 1980s most of these mixes were spent on price promotions. From the consumer viewpoint, branded products of this sort increasingly become commodities; they end up with no differentiating qualities other than the price they sell at.

It is not surprising that brands fall sick when organizations are directed like this. One of the most damning indictments of short-termism in late twentieth-century branding is the humble coupon which promises the targeted consumer money off for trying a brand. It is known that in many American product categories the physical cost of sending out coupons exceeds the amount of money consumers redeem. In other words, consumers are ultimately paying for the brand's couponing as well as its increasing lack of quality differentiation.

You get interesting answers when you ask brand managers why they are couponing. A typical one is: to penetrate new users for the brand. In the circumstances cited above, this suggests a brand with a strange mechanism for rewarding consumer loyalty. Probably the most honest answer is because retailers like it. Catch 22 is that retail chains like it because they can see that coupons, in the long run, weaken manufacturer brands and strengthen own labels.

We are not claiming that coupons should never be used. But the dangers and temptations to deploy tactical weapons like these have become so great that it may be time to take a symbolic initiative. For example, requiring that the CEO signed off every couponing campaign would cut down this form of customer disloyalty marketing. Box 7.5 shows that in the summer of 1993 Procter & Gamble may have paved the way with a process which takes the seriousness of this kind of issue to heart.

Box 7.5

Procter & Gamble has revamped its US marketing strategy, introducing a policy of 'everyday value pricing'. This involves cutting down on short-term deep-discount promotional deals, which periodically slash the cost of products to the retailer, and replacing them with a system of more consistent lower prices.

However, the change has stirred up opposition among less efficient retailers, who have relied on deep-discount promotions for a substantial part of their profits.

Typically, P&G is cutting the price of Tide and Cheer liquid detergents by as much as 15% with lesser reductions on some other brands.

(*Source*: *Financial Times*, 15 July 1993)

Allowing a strongly marketed brand to become too greedy

Ironically, 1993 has shown that a form of milking may also be manifest by the reverse phenomenon of a strongly marketed brand mix (for example Marlboro) which over time gets too greedy with the price premiums it accumulates. We have seen that a brand can get too greedy for its own good from the perspective of any or all of the people in its customer chain. In particular it may:

- go a price rise too far for its end-consumers;
- be judged by retail customers as not sharing out enough of the added value it is winning;
- invite a new form of competitive brand process.

Insufficient investment in the brand's essence

Whether a brand leader's price is in balance or not, it is being milked whenever its organization does not invest sufficiently in the brand's essence and inter-related competence building. This may include various kinds of evolutionary qualities such as innovation, customer service and renewing the vitality of the brand image.

Failing to manage the brand's essence carefully

Milking occurs, by default, if the brand team fails to manage the brand's essence caringly. This can happen when previously loyal consumers are left behind by a sudden relaunch of essence which is insensitive to helping them interpret the relevance of the brand's new values (or, indeed, has become a totally different brand in all but name). When new people join a brand team, especially at top levels of management, there can be a temptation to do something different such as attacking a competitor's position. Whether this is done through superficial understanding of the brand (for example, because the whole business team has changed and no Brand Charter handed over) or because of some sort of personal arrogance, consumer research has consistently demonstrated that this is a tragic waste of time and money.

Similarly, brand essence can be milked if it is stretched to represent new products in an uncaring way (see Chapter 1).

Failing to foresee future change

A brand is also being milked if nobody is responsible for foreseeing how to take advantage of future change. There are many ways in which the implications of world class competitive quality and value now need to be tracked. These include:

- the relatively simple, for example, tangible assessments such as are we keeping in touch with world class cost and quality of production?
- the fairly complex, for example, will the scope of the brand's essence be broad enough to have critical mass in a world where competitors may be directing higher level banner/corporate brands, and media economies/effectiveness of the brand mix are changing fast?
- the strategic scenario, for example, what fundamental discontinuities to the added-value chain are foreseeable? How do we take advantage of this, with which partners, and against which competitors?

When should a brand be milked?

Provided no harm will be done to a company's reputation, there are times when brand milking is appropriate. These include:

- before killing off a brand or selling it (if the purchaser does not understand milking);
- brands with tactical (as opposed to leadership) objectives. (See, for example, leagues of branding in Chapter 11.)

Summary

A lot of pricing and quality decisions on brands have been made from the tactical perspectives of junior brand managers when they really needed corporate recognition as fundamental strategic components of the brand process. Training on the dangers of brand milking should be a prerequisite for all who make or influence marketing decisions.

Strong brand leaders act as consumer reference points. They define quality and value standards. To be faithful to these, subtle decisions on balancing price and quality need to be taken from a consistently informed viewpoint. The price of the branded offer can be too low or too high. Competitive value and quality are:

- correlated;
- perceptual as well as real in product terms;
- inclusive of service elements as well as product elements;
- subject, within the same product category, to different consumer frames of reference such as the urgency of the need and the local competitiveness of channels meeting a specific need.

World class quality and value are introducing new dynamics into marketing and business processes. These may affect entire strategic configurations – between competitors and partners – of the added-value chain across a sphere of business. Somebody with high-level responsibility in the company will increasingly need to foresee and take a view on communications scenarios which must be turned to corporate advantage. These include:

- evolution of the quality and value capabilities invested in the company's brand architecture (Chapter 11);
- competitive, partner and organizational strategies (Chapters 12 and 13).

Feedback from managers closest to local customers and consumers will be an important part of the process of developing an informed top-level view of core brand processes. A new world class realism is needed. Organizational survival now depends on recognizing that the essence of modern brand marketing is continuous improvement of quality and value. This belief needs to be sovereign in the way that leaders think, act and direct the company's service culture (Chapter 14).

References

Broadbent, S. (1994). Diversity in categories, brands and strategies, *Journal of Brand Management*, **2**(1)

Kapferer, J. (1992). *Strategic Brand Management*. London: Kogan Page

Macrae, C. (1991). *World Class Brands*. Harlow: Addison-Wesley

8

brand Flow/Team Networking

If a company wants to learn the most from the branding process, employees need to embrace teamworking. The organizational culture needs to be integrated.

Box 8.1   A revolution in brand organization

Integration is the opposite of functionalism that has all too often stood in the way of serving consumers superbly. It was effective when high growth, unsophisticated consumer demands, and weak distribution channels meant that each function could make real progress by itself toward improved customer satisfaction and greater profitability. On its own, manufacturing could cut costs and boost quality; marketing could develop better ads; and sales could improve call patterns and enhance customer presentations. In most industries, however, the opportunities to make progress against such narrowly defined criteria have about run their course.

(*Source*: George, 1994)

Beyond teamworking, it is also appropriate to foresee ways in which Team Networking can be facilitated so that employees from different offices or companies can work as partners in developing added-value

140

chains of business at global and local levels (McHugh, Merli and Wheeler, 1995). How, for example, will partners of General Magic – including Apple, AT&T, Motorola, Philips and several Japanese companies – need to organize their network of employee relationships if inter-corporate vision and team leadership are to work to accelerate the delivery of customer delights? (For General Magic, added-value focusing is about the future sphere of business involving new programming and hardware for personalized multimedia.)

In order to be capable of learning and relearning everything about brand organization, companies must realize from the outset that there is nothing wrong with accessing different learning frameworks. This applies to both an overall process perspective of the business and different conceptualizations of a specific process such as brand organization. You gain consensus from all team members and grow depth and breadth of expertise by synthesizing different expert perspectives, provided the synthesis actually takes place and leaves all involved with harmonious feelings and clarified actions. This is how communications processes become more than the sum of their parts. This is how expert functions are organized to contribute to competent added-value processes, those where leadership worth is represented as continuously being more than the sum of individual components. (Many of which will only be sustainable – in spite of any technological appearances to the contrary – if the architectural dynamics of employees' human motivations are purposeful and harmonious.)

In this chapter on brand flow and team networking we discuss the following:

- Issues to respect and foresee
- Initial guidelines on how to evolve a company's master framework for learning brand organization
- Structural keys embedded in Brand Chartering and similar tools for company learning
- Masterclass learning of brand organization for winning at 'glocal' marketing

Issues to respect and foresee

It is impossible to underestimate the depth and breadth of change management that can be needed to change from a classic departmentalized structure of brand management to the new teamworking process form of brand organization. (This statement is corroborated by companies in the midst of directing this change in Chapters 11–15.)

Once people foresee the nature of the challenges which confront today's company, change is facilitated by envisaging the specific advantages which brand new organizations need to create and leverage. A critical factor in the success of the mission is finding out what learning tools for brand organization are most important for your company. We aim to clarify the extent to which purposeful and focused teamworking dynamics of internal brand marketing can be translated into the heart and the soul of the brand organization.

In 1995 it was quite normal to read of the marketing state of affairs described in Box 8.2.

Box 8.2

At the last industry conference, of the senior marketers attending and responsible for the brands, only one in ten believed that their dedicated distributors could feed back their desired set of brand values. And less than two in ten claimed that an internal staff audience (comprising, for example, product planners, designers and engineers involved in formulating new products) would be able to feed back their desired set of brand values spontaneously.

(*Source*: Extract from an article on the future of the brand by Tim Greenhill, ADMAP, March 1995)

The industry referred to is automotives, but it could have been almost anything. Try this acid test. Pick up the first book you can find on new product development (NPD) process. How clearly does it convey to you that every NPD process should be tailored to reflect the essence of the brand it is due to fit? What sorts of future shocks are in store for 1990s manufacturing companies which on the one hand claim that brands as their channels to consumers are their biggest investments, and on the other hand have no internally acknowledged brand-specific NPD process? (A brand-specific NPD process can be much more than the product-category-specific NPD process that most companies organize.)

In our experience, a similar lack of focus in 'internal brand marketing know-how' often abounds through a wide variety of departments, ranging from raw materials sourcing to specific adaptations of market research, which might be expected to add special values to particular brands.

The situation has not been much better in service industries, as illustrated in the following quotation from an American Express marketer in the BBC for BUSINESS video 'Branding – the Marketing Advantage'.

'The main theme of our recent reorganization was focus. We've set up key dimensions in our marketing team, for example one is customer loyalty, another is new customer marketing. We want our marketing process to operate along the line of key customer processes rather than specific functions. The customer used to start at point A and move through several departments. In other words, the customer moved through horizontally whereas we were organized vertically. We have had to relearn marketing. We are not yet there 100%, but it's been a real revolution for us thinking about how you walk through with the customer in every process.'

We remind you that 1994 was the year when Unilever had, to quote its co-chairman, 'the greatest marketing setback we have ever seen' (see Overview, page 24). This process weakness – dubbed 'A Soap Opera from Unilever' by *The Economist* – was explained as being caused by interdepartmental misunderstandings such as that 'of a slip somewhere between R&D and marketing'.

As the added-value chains of many businesses go global, we should foresee that competitors in some of the largest industries will embark on a third world war. This time the infantry – and casualties – will be brands instead of nations. But it will also be people whose jobs depend on organizations earning the right to brand. In this mother of all branded wars, competitors will exploit any suggestion of a rival's product defect even where these are perceptual in terms of:

- the all-but trifling fault of Persil/Omo Power mark 2 (which the UK's Consumer's Association felt was still abnormal in its fabric rotting potential though significantly less of a rotter than launch mark 1);
- the product whose imperfection will be experienced only once in several billion times like the Intel chip which had to be withdrawn after an expert lobby on the Internet revealed this issue;
- the perfect new product but one which does not match the brand's loyal users' emotional expectations in the light of their brand's history.

You could make a list of other things that you want to foresee in brand new organization. For example, world-winning new products will often involve longer R&D processes than companies have previously had experience of managing. Who is going to ensure the branded continuity? In a classical brand management company a 10-year R&D process could be in marketing contact with five different brand managers as they rotate two-year tours of duty in the management of the company's hundreds of different brands and separately targeted market segments.

In our view, the idea that 'integrated brand marketing begins internally' has to be made a priority in effecting the changeover to new forms of brand organization. Strongly led companies will describe old marketing's follies, pointing out analogies from other companies' disasters. They will make it clear to their employees that this is not a person's fault, but that of an old organization form 'which no longer suits the company we need to be'. The quotation is a phrase Procter & Gamble's CEO of the mid-1980s used when the company first started to embrace the business team belief system. Surprisingly few competitors took notice of this at the time. (Petty, 1985)

You might consider the following suggestions when first embarking on brand new organization.

- Prepare ahead. Scout externally for various practical perspectives on matters such as opening tactics, for example, whom to use as opinion leaders in evolving the new brand organization; and what cultural or other corporate beliefs will need to be turned upside down in recognition of the revolutionary process involved. Was the full extent of these needs-for-change foreseen or does this just have to be learnt by doing? ('Scouting' may involve benchmarking some companies which are ahead in brand organization transformation. We suggest doing this with non-competitors and ideally those with whom you can reciprocate through some other valuable process/know-how coaching.)
- How will performance measures and incentives need to be changed to have a proactive influence on learning to be world class as a brand organization?
- Think through 'ultimate responsibility' scenarios. For example, in a corporate marketing setback scenario – when action must be fast and totally aligned to preserve goodwill's 'kingpiece' corporate reputation (see Chapter 14 for the need to cultivate a culture in which corporate reputation is regarded as the responsibility of every employee) – who do you want to lead what? How will process training be used to ensure that no gap exists between theory and practice of responsibilities at team and individual levels?
- Consider transitionary roles in the forms of managers of specific marketing/customer processes. These can help marketing people to relearn first; this is vital if they are subsequently to act as expert coaches in networking internal marketing learning across the brand organization.
- Architects at the top of the company must separate changeover practices which may be threatening to people's jobs from those which are growth opportunities. If cutting jobs is inevitable, this not only needs to be handled with all the care and attention that the company has used in similar circumstances, but it should also be separated in time and process from fostering teamworking beliefs and introducing a learning tool for brand organization. The successful introduction of these two processes requires building the maximum motivation and openness among employees beyond anything your company has seen before.

Marketing people should be given the first chance to join the brand process revolution. The ironical after-effect of a generation of short-termism in corporate management, which probably peaked with 'Barbarians at the Gate' of companies like RJ Reynolds, is that many marketers may need to be given the empowerment opportunity of relearning what marketing foresight is about. Before marketing processes can be taught across an organization-wide network, we need to teach the coaches. Writing in the mid-1990s we would suggest that you do not consider anyone as a brand process guru who is not prepared to admit that he or she is relearning too.

Box 8.3

'There is a systemic failure in marketing culture and companies' organizations,' says market research consultant David Cowan. Too often, he claims, marketers' pseudo-explanations which satisfy our curiosity but actually explain very little, if anything at all, crowd out real analysis.

Marketers tend to see problems in terms of strengths and weaknesses of individuals. They tend not to give enough weight to the corporate structures and processes that create and mould peoples' behaviours and attitudes. Sentiments like 'if only our agency was more creative', 'if only our researchers had better insight', 'if only the client thought more strategically' are mere platitudes masquerading as explanations: by definition, they are always true.

The real challenge is to understand the underlying conditions that stifle or encourage the human qualities we want. Why, for instance, do companies consistently fail to see the threats and opportunities that are thrown up by emerging technologies and new products?

(*Source*: Alan Mitchell, *Marketing Week*, 21 April 1995)

Initial guidelines on how to evolve a company's master framework for learning brand organization

If company learning is to begin to take place in process mode, different departments and expert functions should be encouraged to bring their various frames of reference to the teamworking table. Departments need to explain these opening frames before they can be edited to differentiate what is truly functional expertise from what needs to be interconnected process-style competence.

Whether or not other departments need to be transformed from separate existence into networking form, we believe that marketing should be encouraged to lead by example. (Lack of continuing credibility in marketing as a departmentalized function was the primary finding of a survey of managing and marketing directors in 1993, 'Marketing at the crossroads', by Coopers & Lybrand.) It should transform itself out of being a department and across the organizational network in the confidence that it will need to act as a vital school of added-value thinking.

The higher-level motivation for marketing disciples should be that the company needs an intangibly led communications process to leverage its most valuable dynamic assets, in the form of brands interconnected to core competences interconnected to any other learning resources of the organization associated with leadership (for example, customer service culture, deadlines prioritized by foresight schools of the future, and so on). The strong marketers of today and tomorrow, that is those who recognize the chance to recreate an internal marketing culture aligned to medium-term leadership foresight, will jump at this promotional opportunity.

If consensus between the company's CEO, senior marketers and interdepartmental opinion leaders suggests that you already have a strong 'master-learning' tool for brand organization, we suggest you give it a light edit by comparing it with this book and incorporating any newly valuable ideas that occur in the process.

If your consensus is that the company needs to develop a master-learning tool for brand organization, we suggest that one or more teams should be set up to compare the Brand Chartering framework in this book with another learning framework chosen from brand marketing, customer service, strategy, learning organization or other perspective on focused accumulation of intangible advantages. If, for example, a strategy-oriented comparison was to be made, we would recommend *Competing for the Future* by Hamel and Prahalad. If a comparison was to be made with up-to-date 'brand change' agendas requested by practitioners and researched by academics then we would recommend the latest available know-how forum originating from the BBC for BUSINESS video 'Branding – the Marketing Advantage'. (The video is being continually supplemented by follow-up notes from Internet group discussions and other knowledge exchange materials – see ThinkPieces 9 and 11.)

The agendas in Figure 8.1 are made in 'junction style' to help clarify both the focus and the interconnections between these critical brand change agendas. In this way academic researchers can synergetically co-partner each other through electronic media such as the Internet.

Brand architecture	**Brand partnership strategy: architecture new rules for externalizing and internalizing; exploiting reputation, top-level values, etc., of banner brands; culling or refocusing brand equity in an 'overbranded' company**	
Brand organizing	**Use of Chartering or equivalent scripts for teamworking; integration of strategy frames for leveraging brand and other intangibles (for example, competences); CEO lead-responsibility for brand organization**	
Brand equity	**How to prioritize marketing advantages invested in brand system; how to align measurement and performance time frames; how to rehearse scenarios of discontinuity threats to brand equity**	
Global branding	**Balancing HQ and local roles and information leads; how to beat locally targeted brands; how model of external and internal priorities differs from local era branding**	
World class culture	**World number 1 culture: how to sustain and how not to lose; stakeholder priorities as global citizen; specific clarification of right to lead (for example, visionary capabilities); manoeuvring corporate environment (for example, abolishing over-accounting)**	

Figure 8.1 Typical practitioner-directed scoping of top eight 'Brand Change' Agendas.
(*Source*: Adapted from © BBC for BUSINESS Video Professorial Exchange, MEG 95, Management Centre, University of Bradford.)

'Glocal' added-value warfare	**Market-partnership networks configured glocally to overthrow classic added-value chains; principles of 'holonic' organizations (beyond process re-engineering)**	
Seeded marketing channels	**New brand targeting of opinion leaders before mass marketing consumers; global and local transfer tactics of haute couture goodwill; co-developing new channels**	
Service smart integration	**Smart consumer relationship integration processes: for example, lifetime focus, two-way feedback loops; employees' delight (through super-motivation mechanisms)**	

Figure 8.1   *continued*

Practitioners can gain from a dynamic curriculum which intentionally stresses:

- breadth, that is interconnections across brand change agendas; and
- depth, that is full exploration of the agenda within its terms of reference.

We reiterate advice given in the Forethoughts that the generic form of Brand Chartering presented in this book also requires a degree of general editing to maximize its relevance as a master-learning tool for the in-situ use of your brand organization. By in-situ use we have in mind factors such as:

- how departmentalized your current organizational structure is;
- who leverages added value the most, and from what expert perspective or leadership competence;
- brand architecture specific issues (see Chapter 11).

Additionally, it is worth asking a simple but sometimes revealing question: what 'user-friendly' factors make learning frameworks look different in either form or substance? Examples are:

- Devised for an educational purpose with a particular user format. (For example, books, word-of-mouth, computerized 'windows' involve users in different kinds of educational flows.)
- Devised for practitioners and the common reference set of know-how which they already use to communicate.
- Starts from a particular lead perspective driven by, for example, a strategist or a service-focused expert.
- Degree of designed-in flexibility – ranging from a learning system which needs to be highly flexible to allow brand organization itself to evolve through a period of rapid change, to a more rigid system where certain conventional-structured rules are built-in because these are assumed to be constant (best practice) beliefs.
- Vocabulary – is this slanted? For example, targeting, segmenting, unique selling propositions as self-proclaimed 'strengths' tend to restrict debate and are anchored to a particular era of marketing assumptions. Mass marketing has already passed through two great periods of brand organization: first, pre-TV and local; second, TV and multinational. The third period is the multimedia, glocal world which is now materializing. If a tool is to encourage learning and teamworking, vocabulary and internal 'learning' media must be recognized as more than an incidental part of people's thinking processes.

In the process of comparing a pair of learning tools for their brand organizational capabilities, you might also want to consider the following issues:

- Does structure enable sufficient breadth and depth to edit everything into the team's living script of the brand?
- How do component terms of the structure appear to influence people's thinking? For example, the way terms are clustered often causes people to envisage particular interconnections of the brand process more easily than others which may be even more critically inter-related.
- What terms are ultimately common to both learning systems? Which of the unique ones do you need to add? How do you tidy up conceptual vocabulary to be accessible to all teamworkers? What examples/ training are needed to induce what level of comprehension of how to use the system? How do you balance ease of use needs of teamworkers with prioritized in-depth qualities which the brand's living script needs? What output qualities of the process matter to you: focus, consensus, comprehensiveness, creativeness, urgency of motivation to action?

Structural keys embedded in Brand Chartering and similar tools for company learning

Key 1

We believe that the form of a learning tool can benefit from incorporating a 'window and junction' structure.

Teamworking learning systems will increasingly be computerized. This suggests that a window–menu structure is vital to allow correspondents to explore the breadth and depth of the brand. Computerized media should allow them to zoom in and out of the windows. By emphasizing that the windows should also be thought of as the primary process junctions of brand organization, people can quickly assimilate the idea that any one junction of thinking could and should lead to the interactive implications of another.

Key 2

We believe that each window, apart from those in Key 3, should stand out for one big topic of enquiry as well as a detailed procedure for holding the specific enquiry. In this way it is possible to use the learning tool for both the breadth and depth of debates.

- For breadth, overview learning can be gained by debating where branding mistakes originated (for example, the black spot technique discussed in the Overview, page 25). Conversely, brand process success stories can be analysed and debated at an overview level. Learning can be facilitated by asking individuals to do these sorts of exercises separately before swapping notes. Organizational learning across brands and over time can be gained by spotting patterns of mistakes that recur (and then finding out why) or looking to transfer one brand's junction success to other analogous brands.
- For depth, workshops for convening a debate on the topic can be scripted. In Chartering's case, illustrations of these are provided in ThinkPiece 2. The author, co-workers and others also find the junction format convenient for indexing purposes; for example, which business schools are pioneering which research agendas related to Chartering's junctions.

Key 3

One or more 'Others' windows are necessary. This enables people to interconnect the master-learning tool with frames of reference in other peoples' minds, whether these are specific to brand organization or in their view inter-related from some other expert perspective. Additionally, with any particular brand process, there are always likely to be a small number of special issues that no general purpose scripting tool can cover. In any learning tool it is important to leave the 'what else?' mechanism of inquiry open.

Key 4

By requiring that people converge on a one-page output for a brand's script at any point of time, you know the common reference point from which all teamworkers start in interpreting the brand. This can also be used as a mechanism for getting the involvement of all departments, because they know that they must participate in both bidding up and buying into the signed-off priorities that are communally expressed as the brand organization's current living script.

Key 5

By following a semi-structured layout in all its Charters, a company can make it easy for employees to learn about as many brands as they need as well as the actions expected from them in support of the brand. For example an impactful layout for conveying the dynamic qualities of strong brand leadership is as follows:

* The top of the page itemizes the brand's essential components in a relatively constant way. These also include the brand's linkages and priorities within the company's total brand architecture.
* The bottom of the page lists the brand's 'do now' deadlines for accelerating future added value.
* The middle of the page can be used to list outstanding questions, such as feedback projects currently under way to illuminate deeper understanding of the brand or to review the impact of a current competitor's initiative. It can also be used to record change trends and so on that are fundamental to the brand, but where deliberation as opposed to immediate action is required.

Key 6

We believe a similar set of keys is appropriate for Chartering any of the company's other core investments in intangible sources of advantage, such as core competences (discussed in Chapter 12 and ThinkPiece 6). Moreover, we believe that every 'core intangible' is also an 'information highroad' for company learning. CEOs and other people at the top of a company need to take the lead in showing business teams how to work these new information highroads in the context of company learning, over and above the traditional ways in which particular intangibles have been viewed functionally by departments of the company. We will discuss the meaning of this sixth key in the next section.

Masterclass learning of brand organization for winning at 'glocal' marketing

There is an easy part and a difficult part to relearning brand organization, which has to start with the CEO and top people in the company before it can cascade down to business teams.

In our work with major multinationals, all the senior executives we have met have subscribed to a strong marketing belief system. Extracts from such a system of thinking, developed by Cranfield School of Management's Centre for Advanced Research in Marketing, are reproduced in Box 8.4.

Box 8.4   Developing a strong market orientation

(1) **Start at the top**. Strong leadership and commitment to customer focus at the top of an organization is indispensable.

(2) **Involve everyone in the organization in the marketing philosophy**. The message has to cascade down so that everyone knows that serving the customer is the ultimate objective.

(3) **Be prepared for structural change.** Lasting step changes in customer service levels cannot be achieved wherever an organization is structured along lines that benefit the company not the customer. Proactivity is needed to foresee how changes in the external environment are leveraged by leading the way with internal processes.

(4) **Use new structure to feed upwards into customer-facing strategy.** The information on which strategic planning is based should come from customer-facing units.

(5) **Review marketing tactics, particularly the alignment of the 4Ps with customer strategy.** Keep looking at the 4Ps (products, price, promotion, place) from the customers' point of view, remembering to look ahead so that customers see you as the leader even as their perceptions are influenced by global and local trends in media and added- value frames of reference.

continues

---

continued

(6) **Accept that change is a way of life.** Involve all employees in 'editing the future' and learning activities, for example competitive information detection, which produce an informed consensus and purposeful focus.

(7) **Understand the difference between quality systems and quality products or services.** Make sure that people understand that systems exist to serve the needs of the customer. Recognize that every product has a perceptual context because all acts of consumption involve human emotions.

(8) **Focus on the customer, not the competition.** Both matter, but leadership essence comes from focus on the first.

(9) **Look at end-to-end processes, not piecemeal processes.** The customer should experience seamless service.

(10) **Keep the end-user in sight.** Immediate customers matter but losing sight of the end-user is a symptom which can quickly lead to terminal illness.

(11) **Develop and empower people down the organization, particularly those who have customer contact.** Ultimately customers experience brands as services whose power to consistently delight depends on the organization's people.

(12) **Understand the relationship between customer focus and profit.** Monitor a suitable combination of measurements for a well-chosen selection of time horizons, tailored to appraise the specific purpose of the marketing approach and gauge levels of successful achievement.

The above agenda is quite intricate, especially for students of marketing or teamworkers for whom marketing is an 'away' discipline to be interconnected with their own 'home' functional expertise. However, for people at the top of marketing companies, a lifetime's experience makes this kind of frame of reference very intuitive indeed. So what is their most difficult barrier to relearning brand organization?

Like the rest of us, senior management's barriers to relearning brand organization vary, but the following over-simplified illustration nonetheless typifies the biggest change barrier for people at the top of multinational consumer goods companies.

Until quite recently the CEO of a company with traditional brand management systems was led to view key control responsibilities along these lines:

(say) 20 core operating countries: control by liaising with 20 strong country managers
(say) 1,000 products: control by clustering into (say) 10 product streams with their managers

(say) 100 brands: leave to junior brand managers to report in to various levels of management, depending on market size, but not to the CEO

But an inconvenient realization grew throughout the 1980s. Leading brands were no longer just consumer propositions but the company's primary communications channels. Moreover, it was posited that these brands had become the company's most valuable assets because they were the first reference points in consumers' minds in crowded markets being joined by a glut of equally able competitors (including many whose business was becoming more international than conventional marketing segmentations had recognized). Imagine being a CEO in this situation. If you take all of the above seriously, you are likely to start a major reorganization so that the customer management of your main brand equities is reassigned to more senior people. This requires a lot of effort and dotted line coordination between managers of country, product and brand becomes quite complex. While people get to grips with this some mistakes are likely to happen, but in your view a stronger organization makes all of this worth doing.

You have just asked everyone in the company's headquarters and local offices worldwide to learn this new complex matrix of responsibilities, and then somebody has the nerve to come along and say 'hum, that's only a small part of the job that needs to be done to relearn brand organization'. Imagine the pain of it all.

As neither the author nor co-workers are CEOs of such a company, we cannot do that. As carriers of the 'hum' message we can, however, tell you what happens next. Quite often we are shot at (but that is normal for a messenger) and we do try to empathize with the shock we have brought. On other occasions we are asked for a view of what to do next.

Suggestions for a brand organization learning system

Everything henceforth stems from recognizing that the brand process is not just about consumer proposition or your communications channels to external customers. Some of the brands you select must be much more. These high-level brands must be what everybody in the company organizes around to input:

- all their added-value talents;
- daily service perspiration; and
- other kinds of communal learning.

As a result top-level banner brands can be leveraged as reflections of corporate core competences, your leadership visions and everything else that your corporate reputation stands for. This can include planning who you will partner as well as who you will compete against. It also involves what societies your company as a global neighbour has most impact upon both environmentally and economically.

Seen from this viewpoint, top-level brand scripts must be, at least lightly, edited by the CEO. Even if you have never projected the company as a consumer brand, your reputation is out there globally and locally, in a way that one severe organizational crisis could destroy more tangibly than a meteorite falling on your corporate HQ. This is a fundamental corporate fact of life in our era of global village media and corresponding competitive communications.

Real brand organization learning will need the dedication and curiosity of everyone in the company. But the following preparations need to be made by the CEO or those who share with him or her an organization-wide remit.

Pilot an internal communications system until the CEO has at least top-level editorial control over the whole brand architecture. Do this by first finding a format which works for both your corporate reputation and a few of your most important brands. Put special teams on this to script the details but in a way that the CEO can quickly read and 'edit the future' for:

* opportunity and risk to corporate goodwill;
* alignment of direction with that of inter-related investments such as the company's core competences.

We believe the system you will need will be similar to Brand Chartering at least to the extent that it integrates the six keys mentioned above and embodies the process philosophy of editing the future into a top-line script.

If developing such a system sounds like involving the CEO in a lot of extra work merely to avoid excess risk, then think of it another way. Now you have your brand organizational learning tool in place, the CEO can prioritize 'do now' goals for teamworkers who everywhere impact the brand. For the first time the CEO and the company share an internal medium in which strategic intent and implementation coalesce. Organizational evolution to leverage change and the proactive detection of external information that leaders need is integrated in one and the same process, and you will discover many other integrated strengths that come from a communal direct line of communication from top to bottom of the company focused on its most dynamically valuable asset: the brand.

Ultimately, 'Brand Chartering' as an organization-wide learning tool works to ensure leadership, control and communal feedback all in one up-to-date exchange of employee know-how. Furthermore, while this chapter has been concerned to show how business teams can learn to brand all intangible (learning) assets as more than their parts, opportunities to integrate tangible assets into the corporate foresight are also worth seizing. For example, the advice in Box 8.5 is included as part of a case study in the video course materials for 'Globalization with Kenichi Ohmae' by BBC for BUSINESS.

Box 8.5   World Class Operations

In this context, the approach to facility location is a response to the projection of future conditions, not current competitive issues and resource prices. It is made by a CEO focusing on marketing, product and operational issues, not by a manufacturing executive concentrating on direct labour rates. The decision is based on the capabilities that conditions in the new location could help the company to build, not on the conditions themselves.

The goal of this strategic approach to facility location is to build a network of capabilities, rather than just a network of facilities. This network is specifically designed to support the company's business and market strategies on a continuing basis. It is structured as much for what it can 'teach' the firm as to take advantage of external location resources. It is dynamic and maintained as an ongoing element in a company's strategic plan.

(*Source*: Bartmess, A. and Cerny, K. (1993). World Class Operations – Building competitive advantage through a global network of capabilities, *California Management Review*, **35**(2).)

Summary

Brand Flow/Team Networking is currently one of the most exciting aspects of the practice of Brand Chartering. There are, however, two big 'buts':

(1) Team Networking does not happen in a sustainable way unless organization is newly structured to facilitate it. The same goes for winning at brand organization. It makes sense to harness both of these initiatives at the same time together with anything else the CEO wants to put on the architectural agenda of becoming a learning company. We have discussed the importance of preparing learning tools on both brand organization and other know-how (intangible) 'dynamic' assets which need to be accumulated and leveraged over time. These then need to be integrated into the working practice of everybody in the organization top-down, bottom-up and side to side. Key principles for implementing this have been summarized. The CEO must take the lead in developing

an 'edit the future culture' and we have suggested an approach. Something like this is urgent because the main window of opportunity for brand organizations to define 'glocal' added-value chains will not extend far into the new millennium. We advise CEO's to adopt Nike's slogan now: 'Just do it'.

(2) We still have a lot of work to do in this book on Brand Chartering. We need to dig deeper into ideas on how to bring internal communications architecture to the company (for example Chapters 11–15) as well as external marketing communications prowess (for example Chapters 1–7 and 9). We need to refresh creativity as well as pride in leadership, and this needs to be instilled into every employee who serves a brand. We also need to train people to catalogue potential changes to conventional wisdoms of old brand management. Where is there most danger of well-intended operating guidelines becoming destructive inertias in the context of the brand learning company? A good starting point is to champion every way in which top-level brands do much more 'connecting up' than targeting. It should be anticipated that this will turn some executional rules of the brand's marketing brief upside down, as we will see in the next chapter.

References

George, M. *et al.* (1994). Reinventing the marketing organization, *McKinsey Quarterly*, December

Hamel, G. and Prahalad, C.K. (1994). *Competing for the future*. Harvard: Harvard Business School Press

McHugh, P., Merli, G. and Wheeler, W. (1995). *Beyond business process re-engineering – towards the holonic enterprise*. Chichester: Wiley

Petty, P. (1985). Behind the brands at P & G. Interview with John Smale, *Harvard Business Review*, November/December

9

brand Umbrella
Connections

Every manager wants to meet performance goals set by the company he or she works for. Moreover, every manager wants to be seen by his or her peers, bosses and subordinates to be doing the right thing. But do those who organize the roles and responsibilities of brand managers take account of these basic human motivations? Who helps whom when it is time to implement new practices across the whole organizational process of branding? We will keep asking these questions in the remainder of this book.

Box 9.1   The threat of overbranding

By overbranding I mean that until a few years ago, particularly if you were an fmcg (fast-moving consumer goods) company – foods, toiletries, things like that – the way to develop markets was within country and within product category. So you had a different brand in each country and product category and that was the level at which brands were operated. But now business competition is going truly international; most brands have become so fragmented that they really do not have any share of voice in the global public's minds; so the result is that having hundreds and hundreds of separate brand channels actually puts the company at a disadvantage.

The real key is the legacy and history of how brands have been

continues

---

continued

managed in the 1970s and 1980s. Many companies are now saddled in the 1990s with huge portfolios of small minority brands which do not justify themselves and are not supportable economically in the current communications environment, nor on any future competitive scenarios.

(Source: Extracts from © BBC for BUSINESS video 'Branding – the Marketing Advantage')

In Chapter 8 we suggested that winning brand organizations will pioneer internal teamworking cultures so that brand processes flow reassuringly as smart service relationships with consumers and customers. The revolutionary topic of this chapter is both more simple and more complex. Most of the literature and inherited conventional wisdom from the era of classic brand management used a vocabulary of marketing that was all about targeting and propositioning consumers. A proper frame for thinking about powerful umbrella branding turns many conventional rules of thumb outside in. Out goes the selling proposition; in comes sustainable marketing of a leader's purpose. Instead of being conditioned to respond like targets, a different world of consumer interpretations evolves with perceptions of all the valuable 'connections' which a smart brand relationship cultivates.

Strong umbrella brands need to embody top-level values like delightful service process, world-leading competence and trust guaranteed by the corporate reputation. This poses extraordinary challenges for companies which need to change from investing in product-based brand equity to investing in higher-level equity platforms for brand organization.

This chapter begins with a short history of what mental baggage marketing people need no longer carry. Then we start to catalogue how umbrella brand campaigns help consumers to make connections with smart relationships of a longer, deeper and broader sort than a locally presented product brand.

Box 9.2   Beyond positioning

Unfortunately, we now have to recognize an episode in marketing history where many marketing and advertising people have set to sea – like *the owl and the pussy cat* of Edward Lear – in a beautiful pea-green boat. It is now sailing into history and must therefore be quickly jettisoned by those who want to enjoy the future of brand organization.

continues

continued

Most of the terms of reference for brand positioning go back to the 1970s when two Americans, Trout and Ries (T&R), popularized a theory of positioning consumers' minds that was anchored almost exclusively in the brand's first power base of 'value'. Their schooling emphasized that effective product positionings required a different brand for every product. Moreover, T&R castigated the mere thought of umbrella branding across product or national territories (of consumers' minds) as a corporate sickness. In effect, T&R positioned positioning to delight managers of the short-term. (Advertising vocabulary since the 1950s has used the word position to reflect the way a brand works on consumers' perceptions. It seeks to position its own points of contrast versus competitive offers. Through the 1970s Trout and Ries popularized the word positioning with a specific interpretation of their own. A result was their best-selling book, *Positioning – the battle for your minds.*)

I first started researching umbrella brands seriously 10 years ago. The Japanese office of a leading fmcg (fast-moving consumer goods) multinational had not been making any headway with product brands and was prepared to tear up T&R's approach to positioning. In Japanese markets, product sub- brands were the lowest form of brand with Japanese consumers wanting to know what quality of corporate guarantee was on the line whenever they chose a product. In positioning umbrella brands in consumers' minds, we started to discover that in addition to the product positionings of T&R, it was necessary to invest in an inventory of identities (enabling consumers to recall, wear and recognize the umbrella brand in as many ways as possible, see Chapter 2) and an integrating brand essence (which works as an emotional platform, service vision or corporate guarantee connecting up a wide range of products, see Chapter 1).

In the 1990s one of the biggest problems facing international consumer goods companies is the ownership of too many fragmented product brands whose marketing budgets just do not have minimum critical mass. You might have thought that the positioning school of T&R would already be defunct. Yet recently, while working for the same multinational but in a different national office, their advertising agency's local account executive made a cautionary presentation on the dangers of line extending drawing totally on the T&R syllabus. Moreover, I have become accustomed to the sad fact that the T&R gospel of the more brands the better has often suited marketing clients (for example, the more brand managers the better) and their agencies (because umbrella branding can expose how poorly many agencies cater for the vital branding need of integrated communications; for example, identities created by packaging design and advertising should always be a unifying source of a brand's impact).

(*Source*: Chris Macrae, personal diary entry, 1994)

From an umbrella frame of reference, which all brand organizations now need to keep thinking about, we suggest retaining what you wish from the classic T&R school of positioning as a framework for 'sub-branding'. Product sub-brands will always have an impact in those contexts where the name of the game is to position consumer minds within product categories or segments thereof. But each of these is by definition a highly fragmented channel of communication whose scale as a marketing platform is no longer a brand strategy in itself, except possibly in very big product categories, and consumers who become used to umbrella brands are smart enough to see that their values play at higher levels. Consequently, many consumers have leaped ahead of marketers in looking down on brand values conceived in only product positioning terms.

Brand Architecture works by linking up high and low levels of branding. High-level brands play by new rules as banners reflecting corporate leadership. If you need a slogan to popularize this, try out that of Haim Oren of Israeli ad agency Admon Communications: 'There is positioning if you want product sub-brands, and there is now compositioning for company brands – integrated messages for organizations whose intent is to lead added value across a sphere of business.'

Brand Architectural know-how requires new explorations of marketing thinking. There are two things we need to learn as rapidly as possible:

- What new rules of the game do umbrella brands play by to communicate connecting messages? (A topic addressed in this chapter.)
- Where does Brand Architecture lead to organizationally and strategically? (A topic addressed from Chapter 11 onwards.)

Cataloguing the new rules of umbrella branding

We suggest compiling a catalogue of game rules beginning with what can be seen to be newly working in umbrella form. We then add some practitioner guidelines which have been issued to contrast good umbrella branding practice with one-product brand rules of thumb. We conclude with some questions, including offbeat ones, which illustrate why we recommend brainstorming the increasing variety of advantages which umbrella branders are inventing.

Figure 9.1 provides an example of a brand organization which has recently discovered its own way of working umbrella branding. We, as consumers, know that we have recently seen Nivea extend itself

Brand	Strategic transition	Execution keys
Nivea international	Transition from long-established image of of Nivea Cream's trusted value for money and understated but uniquely identifiable royal blue pack to cosmetic and treatment ranges including many high added-value applications of female moisturizers/skin care products.	**Starting position** Nivea, circa 1990, has an extraordinarily loyal consumer franchise founded on cream's properties as: • soothing/caring • reference point for skin care (mother of all creams before high fashion/science products targeted this area) • trusted (simple value choice) • impactful ownership of royal blue livery. But the use of Nivea is underexploited owing to the founding product's modestly presented simplicity and singular form. **Typical actions** Each high added-value fashion line appears in own advertising commercial; usually several of these run concurrently; rotations of campaigns also aim to match seasonal needs (eg, sun care). Very successful in translating the following message: if Nivea has for so long been depended on for its expertise in producing the ference point product in orinary creams, then it should now be only natural to look to Nivea as the first source

Figure 9.1 Nivea's brand organization.

Brand	Strategic transition	Execution keys
		for high added-value variants of skin care products.
		• Sub-branded ranges have evolved, such as Nivea 'Visage'.
		• Adverts are usually executed as an essay in blue.
		• Sub-branded technologies are conveyed by word-of-mouth in women's magazines.

Key moves
Leveraging extension potential of extraordinarily powerful brand equity owing to the following combination:

- unique identity system (eg, royal blue and white livery); high impact differentiating brand as simple, pure
- unique essence owing to heritage values of reference product as trustworthy, simple, valued, consistent, caring through generations, the global standard
- developing awareness trigger in consumers' minds as the consisitent leader of skin care's 'mental bridge' between products chosen for cosmetic values and those chosen for treatment values.

Integrated global branding as number 1 consumer authority. Transitioned through being consumers' standard reference point in basic skin care to being the first in mind when consumers wish to try specific (and high added-value) skin care treatments. Buying out global partner (Smith & Nephew) before full appreciation of brand equity's leadership position was widely recognized by city analysts.

Figure 9.1 *continued.*

successfully from primarily the reference point of a good ordinary skin cream to almost anything it wants to be in skin care and neighbouring categories. We know that the essence of trust in Nivea still feels the same as it always has. Umbrella branding cataloguers can debate all the key moves that Nivea has made, some of which you might wish to edit by taking Figure 9.1 as a starting point. Figure 9.2 (see p. 166) provides a similar analysis, but for a highly contrasting situation: the re-engineering of Gillette's brand architecture. (It should be noted that – as throughout our illustrative strategic analyses in this book – the figure has been compiled by people who have not worked on the nominated brand. As reasonably informed interpreters of umbrella brand language, these brand critiques feel right as far as they go but we are not in the business of giving away a company's state secrets.)

Copy department guidelines

From a small straw poll of copy departments at manufacturers and advertising agents, conducted in 1994, fully analysed guidelines for umbrella branding appeared to be lacking. There were some general impressions:

- It is thought that it is often difficult for a TV spot to feature more than one core product (or category) at a time. One solution is to integrate, for example, press advertising, which is thought better for carrying range messages. Another solution is to execute two or more product TV advertising campaigns in the brand's name concurrently (sometimes as spots sharing the same commercial break).
- There is also considerable debate about best practice when extending a brand which has hitherto primarily been associated with one product. This may relate partly to the large number of attempts that have been made without properly re-examining what the brand's future essence should mean. In terms of copy instructions, some companies insist that if a well known brand is to be extended, the new product must appear early in the TV ad on the grounds that consumers will not be attending/expecting a new product at the end of an ad for a brand whose existing product is well known. However, not all mood campaign formats can begin with the new product in the opening seconds. An alternative solution is to feature press ads or PR designed to introduce the product news and inviting consumers to watch out for more on television.

Guidelines such as these illustrate that to be effective umbrella brand advertising must be orchestrated in context-specific ways. Detailed learning is needed to make the most of integrated presentation of such variables as form of media, number of concurrent campaigns and products featured. But the curious umbrella brand organization widens the debate even further.

Brainstorming offbeat questions on umbrella brand organization

In the past couple of years we have met a lot of marketing directors who commented: 'Oh, I did not know other people were also asking themselves that kind of question.' Communicating with umbrella brands is still a new art for most of us, and we do recommend brainstorming some of the 'management of execution' issues with other practitioners from non-competitive product fields. Examples of brainstorming questions are listed below. Questions do need to be raised and debated before an organization can make the most intelligent use of umbrella brands.

- Are the products you sell the most of (or profit the most from) the same as those which are your best image-making flagships? If not, what implications does this have for which products you budget for in allocating resources to advertising of sub-brands? Moreover, how should you rotate advertising campaigns of sub-brands to represent leadership across your total sphere of business? Should calendar or other theming of consumer diaries take precedence over product-specific messages?
- Will parts of the company's umbrella brand architecture be reinforced by flagship products which the organization cannot make itself but should licence out? Are there other partnership strategies you should form to encourage companies to work within the added-value chain of your umbrella branding instead of competing against it?
- Are you making the most of 'double-branding' linkages (for example, Gillette-Sensor) where two or more levels of brand hierarchy both gain from being connected up to each other? At a global level, is it possible to imagine a consumer-facing organization competing for the future without at least one quasi-corporate brand directed from the top of the organization's brand architecture?
- If you are getting less and less bang for your promotional bucks, where is the source of the problem:

Brand	Strategic transition	Execution keys
Gillette USA and Europe	Transition from fragmented, local and low added-value 'best-selling' product brands to international company lifestyle brand 'Gillette'. Gillette company brand to be used as the master brand in a double-branding leadership strategy planned in the following way: • Gillette to have meaning relevant to being number 1 across all target markets (categories and countries); • flagship product sub-brands to be aspirational leaders of categories crafted to give two newsworthy means of added-value linkage: – continuing 'news' campaigns of company brand and product sub-brand could enhance each other – additional 'news' coming from campaign rotation of sub-brands while retaining Gillette as core.	**Starting position** Gillette, mid-1980s, has history of largest volume shares in global markets but fragmented and low added-value positions. There were no linkages across markets other than 'subtracting value' through communications as cheap, blue and plastic. **Typical actions** • Cancelled system of local advertising budgets allocated to campaigns on best selling local product brands. (This had developed over time into fragmented and value-but-not quality positions.) • Execution of New Umbrella Format: interweaved company umbrella lifestyle meassage 'best a man can get' with features on leadership benefits of one or more flagship product sub-brands. Note: Campaigns positioned as international leadership platforms; Gillette (world's number 1); flagship product sub-brands (Sensor, Gel, Series) featured unique high added-value sub-positionings transferring values to Gillette's best selling (but now non-advertised) lines as well as reinforcing Gillette's image as an innovator.

Figure 9.2 Gillette's brand architecture re-engineering.

Key moves

'Double-branding'; company umbrella branding (lifestyle) and aspirational product sub-brands add value to each other

- umbrella branding's essence envisions a world leader of its sphere of consumption – 'best a man can get' has simple but various meanings to purchasers and consumers
- product sub-brands presented as newsworthy with leading features in their category. 'Linkages': between the levels of brands connecting up the Gillette portfolio
- company brand and product sub-brands positioned to lead each other
- company brand is kept as the connecting centrepiece while campaigns for product sub-brands are rotated
- actual best-selling Gillette products feed off the news/fashion created by Gillette and its flagship sub-brands in spite of being absent from advertising. 'Identity system': exploits an internationalized design language
- the umbrella brand and flagship sub-brands are pivotal awareness triggers but not the best-selling products
- other elements of Gillette's identity system recycle Gillette's history of communications/design properties; for example, blue is now the spotlight colour under which Gillette's close-of-ad logo is highlighted.

In core business categories (such as disposable razors), Gillette effectively presents consumers with a full range of value positions while encouraging them to think of trading up to the flagship sub-brand as the only one featured in advertising.

Figure 9.2   *continued*

- creativity of execution
- format of execution
- media used
- brand architecture (for example, too many brands)
- some combination of these?

- Can you still afford the philosophy that it is okay if some of your brands are competing against each other?
- If you were to start again with one brand as a company banner what would that be? What other high-level brands would you maintain? How do the brands' values work to represent your core competences and core businesses?
- Your competitors are playing by some new umbrella branding rules, but what are the implications of this for you? Do you know any longer where your next competitor may come from; for example, some new brand partnership, or a traditional competitor but with a newly evolving brand architecture?

Summary

Brand organizations have a lot to be curious about regarding 'connecting up' umbrella branding. In terms of external media investments, connecting up involves:

- knowing what higher-level values work best for umbrella brands;
- integrating forms and timing of media used;
- maintaining a brand architecture so that linkages can be formed between brands where tactical impacts may still be conveyed by positioning sub-brands, but increasingly the primary focus of your brand equity needs to be changed to higher-level banner brands which represent brand organizations to consumer and customer.

These are important questions to bring out in the open. Answers should be iteratively rather than definitively sought. Ultimately, they need to be diagnosed as part of the wider framework issues of branding process, introduced in terms of teamworking in Chapter 8 and developed more fully in architectural terms in Chapters 11–14.

You may also find that some of Brand Chartering's earlier chapters, for example on essence and identity, take on renewed importance now that we have started to explore the leadership meanings of umbrella brand organization.

Reference

Trout, J. and Ries, A. (1981). *Positioning – the battle for your minds*. New York: McGraw-Hill

10

brand Other Management

You may find that the metaphor in Box 10.1 does not quite fit on first reading but it could grow on you.

Box 10.1 Seven strands of the umbrella brand organization

(1) Creates integrated and urgent feelings (for example, Chapters 1–4)
(2) Knows its quality, value and the economics of an integrated mix (for example, Chapters 6 and 7)
(3) Feeds on proactive team management/learning (for example, Chapter 8)
(4) Plays by competitive rules of umbrella branding (for example, Chapters 9 and 11)
(5) Lives on competences which make all of its relationships smart (for example, Chapter 12)
(6) Serves as an organizational rallying point and an accelerator of consumer values (for example, Chapter 13)
(7) Leads thanks to passionate CEO editorship and control of its dramatic script (for example, Chapter 14)

Support of this sort of brand requires a system of organization completely different from the classical brand management system.

We believe that many marketing people of the late 1980s and early 1990s have been working harder and harder. But they have been working within an organizational structure – the classical brand management system – which did not facilitate learning on the job. It ended up causing people to look backwards rather than forwards; to be political rather than team networkers; to spend extraordinary amounts of time controlling the uncontrollable. You might make a list of other historical curiosities of this outdated system of corporately branded government. Brand organizations of the future will selectively choose opposite sorts of characteristics.

Box 10.2 Extracts from BBC for Business video 'Branding — the Marketing Advantage'

You need to get the balance right between obviously living today (making the short-term numbers) and having a medium-term future. Brand planning of the classical sort drowned foresightful thinking in numbers. Informative thinking got knotted in unwritten assumptions of quantitative modellers and bureaucrats with particular professional persuasions. In many cases, it stopped looking after the medium-term future in any added-value way whatsoever.

Ninety per cent of marketing think time went on some sort of middle management thinking or day-to-day competitive firefighting. Whereas 90% of what really adds value is either about customer service or thinking about the structure embedded in a few leading brands: how do you create a few-added value superhighways to direct rather than 1,000 channels to manage?

With hindsight you know there are a lot of changes that you could have foreseen if you'd been smart enough, and you know senior management's job is to be smart, so it's definitely a worthwhile challenge to lay down.

We can imagine a day in brand organizations of the future when Brand Chartering will be a much easier job with many fewer questions than appear in this book. Then it will simply get on with editing the brand's living script in a world where consumer-focused structures enable added-value company learning.

Today's challenges are extraordinary, perhaps without precedent in the history of mass marketing. So Brand Chartering is also being used as a Trojan horse for changing a company's 'architecture' at branded, strategic and organizational levels. Moreover, we must all leverage change as the world leaves the semi-intelligent information era of televised one-way relationships and enters the smart era of computer-integrated multimedia-facilitated learning. Today's business teams are the transformation generation. They will find the next decade to be the best of times and the worst of times. Leading change is exciting but jolly hard work. Having your company killed off or relegated to somebody else's added-value chain is depressing and – as the Japanese would say – not so good fortune.

Box 10.3 Opening extract from BBC for BUSINESS video 'Branding — the Marketing Advantage'

If you're going down the branded route, you have two or three years to start building the right foundations. Otherwise some branded companies or retailers or other competitors will eventually extinguish your organization.

However, we firmly believe that learning companies which start on brand organization today are just in time to profit from 'do now' editing of the future, providing their leaders appreciate strong corporate architecture when they see it and instil organization-wide trust in a forward-looking spirit (Chapters 11–14). Before moving up to the third level of directing corporate architecture you may want to make some notes on:

- connections between the chapters you have read so far;
- other things you feel should have already been covered in the brand's script.

brand Architect

Why directors of intangible assets increasingly need to be architects

The brand architect is concerned with how a company's branding of goodwill is being organized strategically to add value and leverage to corporate advantage. Beyond fragmented management of a portfolio of separated brands, there is a new world of competition in which survival of the fittest ultimately depends on the evolution of a company's brand architecture. How can two brands be presented together in a way which the consumer perceives as offering the best of both brands' worlds?

The construction of brand partnerships within a company raises such issues as: how do we get the most out of linkages between top-level banner/corporate branding and lower-level product sub-branding?

In 1989 Peter Drucker observed that partnership strategy would become increasingly important and would overtake competitive strategy at some time in the 1990s. So a company's brand architects also need to ask: how can we learn the most about partnering brands with other companies?

An external brand partnership is used to cultivate a valuable alliance with another organization. It is vital to plan how to make a win-win game for both organizations, and to foresee what other processes and competences additional to brand identities are actually being connected up. The architect of any valuable union must have a well balanced sense of control and flexibility. Both parties will need this talent to live in harmony and to profit from co-leadership (see Box 11.1)

Box 11.1 When two brand organizations partner, one linkage leads to another

(1) Identifying link
(2) Essence link?
(3) Future news link?
(4) Additive core competence strategy?
(5) Organizational process interfaces and team networking?

Practising brand architects can qualify at two levels of expertise:

- compulsory curriculum for architects – know company's internal brand architecture;
- advanced curriculum for master-architects – lead other companies into brand partnerships through superior understanding of both companies' brand architectures. In this context we can soon see why some brands are multibillion dollar assets, but only when they are directed dynamically by a CEO who believes in architectural learning.

However big the ultimate strategic prizes, brand architects must keep returning to the fundamental question: how can different levels of branding within the company be linked up as partners to create more value than the sum of their existing parts? Learning this procedure helps to clarify issues like that of internal allocation of resources between brands. Best practice architecture of this sort removes the politics which occurs within organizations when rival groups of managers are fighting turf battles to ensure that their branded empires get the most of the company's investments both in monetary terms and in claims to people's time. The good news is that you can take a helicopter ride over a company's brand architecture quite easily. Its primary building blocks (shown in Figure 11.1) should be:

- *levels* of branding from top-level corporate or banner brands to bottom-level product sub-brands;
- *linkages* between brands.

When you decide to navigate through the breadth and depth of a company's brand architecture you need to be prepared for a long journey. Top-level brands work as banner communications processes, connecting up organization, strategy and creative leadership. Harnessing their corporate advantages involves examining how to integrate the full spectrum of marketing capabilities inherently connected with core business processes, including those shown in Box 11.2.

Top level 'banner' brands connect goodwill across market territories. They are processes connecting up organization, strategy and leadership, that is, banner brands work as unique organizing purposes.

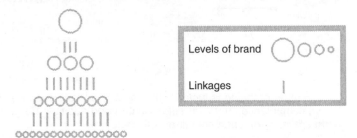

Low level sub-brands target messages within product categories, that is, they may work as unique selling propositions but within a higher level organizational script.

Figure 11.1   Brand architecture 1.

Box 11.2 Exploring architectural connections: brand–organization–strategy

- Leadership of world class quality and value
- Going beyond the classic organizational form of brand management to inter-departmental networking of marketing skills and other added-value schools of thinking, for example innovation
- Banner branding of world class goodwill across marketing territories
- Aligning meanings of leadership for all stakeholders of the company
- Interconnecting specifications of brands, core competences and organizational systems
- Clarifying competition and partnership priorities across added-value chain of sphere of business
- Branding as partnership strategy between different companies

---

As well as being concerned with brand architecture within the company, master architects think in parallel about how to extend the creative arena to that of partnering brands across different companies (see Figure 11.2). This chapter will set out basic rules for understanding the keys to brand architecture. Once these foundations have been

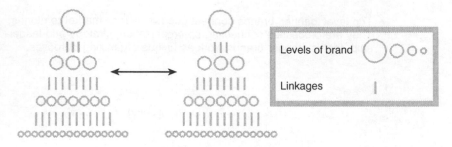

... banner branding is typically the most important level. For win–win, core competences must be differentiated and additive. Be prepared – transparency of leadership is a likely outcome.

Figure 11.2   Brand architecture 2.

established, our travels around a company's brand architecture can help to connect up decision-making at other top-level directions of the business as:

- Strategy Architect (Chapter 12)
- Organization Architect (Chapter 13)
- Drama of Leadership (Chapter 14)

Ownership of Chartering, architecture and brand organization

When a company has tidied up individual Brand Charters and their architectural connections, embarking on a journey around all of a company's goodwill foci will still involve long-distance flying. But concentrating on top-level information structures means that what previously was like going round the world in 80 days in a hot air balloon becomes akin to the astronaut's orbit around the sphere of business.

CEOs do not have time to travel in hot air balloons, so historically critical keys of their companies' brand strategies have often been decentralized. Brand Chartering gives the power back to the central brains of the company, where their input of architectural foresight into leadership systems is needed. It offers an opportunity to go beyond counting up brands as the company's most valuable assets by turning them into core sources of corporate advantage. Brand Chartering, or something similar, is what world class companies need to ensure that their brand communications processes play the lead role in competing for the future.

Two thought experiments illustrate why foresightful management needs to keep asking why a company's brand architecture is the way it is, and how to cultivate investments in it for leveraging the future business.

Experiment 1

Differentiate between two organizational forms of branding: those that brand from the product up and those that evolve from the company brand down. What sorts of generalizations do you associate with these different forms? Some examples are given in Box 11.3.

Box 11.3   Primary investment in branding evolves from . . .

. . .product level (bottom-up)	. . .company level (top-down)
• Classic (fragmented) brand management	• New integrated brand organization process (eg, new Gillette, see Thinkpiece 1)
• Manufacturer-centric	• Service-centric
• Line or business unit performance measurement	• Organization-wide alignment and appraisal
• Short-term is prioritized	• Medium-term is prioritized prioritized
• In-between customers often come first	• End-consumers and employees come first (feedback loop leads each other)
• Core products are today's volume sellers	• Core products are marketing pathways
• Partnership strategies are completely absent in intent or practice	• Partnership strategy has at least as high a priority as competitive strategy
• Western	• Japanese (Asian)

We will show how thought-provoking exercises on brand architecture facilitate a decision-making synthesis between these two organizational forms. Much of our recent work has focused on helping companies transfer branding goodwill historically invested at product levels up to higher-level branding processes. Our empirical evidence would support Mats Urde (1994) in his contention that:

'Today, branding strategies in many companies are inefficient, ineffective, and unnecessarily complicated. This is frequently due to the use of brands being determined by development of the product range. The situation should be the reversed in the brand-orientated company.'

Experiment 2

Consider the following debating case (see Box 11.4) on the fundamental role of brand architecture in influencing what organizational and strategic manoeuvres remain available to the business.

Box 11.4 Future of branding debating case: Heinz UK, 1994

Heinz had for decades (1970s–80s) one of the largest advertising budgets among food products associated with a single brand distributed through British supermarkets. However, investment in its brand architecture was increasingly devoted to fragmented messages in support of its best selling individual lines. With advertising weight often geared to biggest product volumes, sustained campaigning around Beanz Meanz Heinz eventually left many consumers with the reverse impression that Heinz Meanz Beanz.

Heinz (1994–95) deserted advertising for direct marketing as its primary medium. There is a view that suggests Heinz missed an extraordinary broadcasting opportunity. What if Heinz's brand strategy had adopted a change in brand architecture equivalent to that which transformed the meaning of Gillette into the lifestyle 'the best a man can get'?

Example of Heinz-first lifestyle advertising campaign

Create and continuously direct a consumer-exciting script revolving around the brand essence 'Heinz loves families' showing a day in the life of Heinz with:

- babies gurgling over baby food;
- children lapping up beans and nutrition;
- teenagers relishing ketchup;
- adults loving salad cream.

Add to this seasonal episodes such as the family coming home in winter to heart-warming bowls of Heinz soups (possibly served in a co-branded range of uniquely designed soup bowls and mugs); and other integrated PR storylines directing the Heinz banner to be at home with being British consumers' most loved grocery brand.

What might have happened if this brand script had over the years been fully orchestrated with advertising playing the lead role in an

continues

continued

integrated marketing mix? We conclude that there is organizational added value in periodically stepping back to review your brand architecture and, indeed, having one person constantly charged with sifting through the biggest possible ideas involving strategic and organizational perspectives of branding as a core business process. If Heinz is currently missing out on an exciting breadth of consumer relationships, the brand history suggests that the company was not architecturally able to foresee all the creative alternatives that the banner branding of Heinz could offer.

For teams to work with brand architectural design, you need to prepare for two kinds of innovative endeavour. The first involves defining a working language for ways of making brand connections which nobody has yet standardized. The second involves making a collection of the new kinds of questions that different members of a business team need to bring to the table – and creatively develop into an inquisitive agenda – before a considered response on brand architecture can be made. Remember all the while that architectural capabilities offer unique opportunities to connect up, as a virtuous spiral, all the goodwill that a company invests in and earns. These connections can serve to leverage corporately branded credentials across various horizons of doing business such as:

- consumer recognition and extending allegiance across various marketing territories (for example, product category, geographic, generations of human needs);
- forming umbrella partnerships with key contributors to the added-value chain of a sphere of business (for example, partnership strategies which pre-emptively develop allies to your brand that you would not want teamed up under a competitor's umbrella brand);
- pre-marketing leadership credentials (for example, a reputation for having a world leading competence can be leveraged among journalists who look to you as the world's number 1 source of trade news).

Box 11.5 How Macintosh's launch and Apple's architecture 'sneaked' up on IBM

Industry analysts and media representatives were among Apple's most important pre-launch audiences. For them, we put on a series of 'sneaks' (previews) around the country; all told, 60 individual

continues

continued

seven-hour presentations to pave the way for a successful introduction. Not only would the Macintosh product be unveiled at these sessions, but people got to meet creative leaders of Apple's business team including Steve Jobs, myself and members of the design team.

A group of 'luminaries' and key decision makers was also chosen to receive free Apple Macintoshes. Our annual report went on to feature 11 of these 'great imaginations' experimenting with Macintosh: entrepreneur Ted Turner; novelist Kurt Vonnegut; Vietnam Veterans Memorial designer Maya Lin; ballet master Peter Martins; designer Milton Glaser; Muppet creator Jim Henson; San Francisco mayor Dianne Feinstein; composer and lyricist Stephen Sondheim; *Life* magazine's art director Bob Ciano; Lee Iacocca; and David Rockefeller.

(*Source: Odyssey – Pepsi to Apple*, John Sculley)

'First cut' at a terminology for brand architecture

We need to clarify practical meanings for three architectural terms: levels, leagues and linkages.

Levels of branding

These are to do with hierarchy in the brand architecture. You might begin by getting acquainted with five levels of branding:

- corporate or banner brands (for example, Heinz, Gillette, Sony, L'Oréal, McDonald's, Nestlé);
- sub-umbrella of a corporate brand (for example, 'Series' of Gillette, 'Studioline' of L'Oréal);
- product sub-brand (for example, 'Sensor' of Gillette, 'Big Mac or McNuggets' of McDonald's, 'Kit Kat' of Nestlé);
- umbrella but stand-alone (for example, Timotei);
- stand-alone brand (for example, Snickers).

We will see that higher-level branding generates powerful opportunities throughout the architectural chapters of this book. For example, Chapter 12 looks at why the modern strategy gurus Hamel and Prahalad believe that 'any company which fails to take advantage of the logic of global banner branding will find itself at competitive disadvantage'. We have already introduced some of the new rules of umbrella branding in Chapter 9. Add these phenomena together and further reasons why the future of brand management needs more teamworking coordination comes into focus:

- many twentieth-century brands were stand-alones, branded only at one level;
- today most brands already carry more than one name, for example, the product name and the company name (which may or may not be heavily branded);
- tomorrow most brands will learn to make the most of double-branding processes by exploiting the different levels of meaning that each of their names represents.

This irreversible megatrend, whose full impact is yet to come, was already observable in 1990. Getting on to this learning curve early can be very rewarding.

Box 11.6 The way brands were in 1990

'Double-branding' rebuilds corporate brand hierarchies and can be used to evolve internationally recognized brand umbrellas. The ideal of double-branding is to offer a global aspiration with a local touch. Corporate added value is derived from the brand umbrella which translates business leadership into a unique social style.

What's in a name? Sony's Walkman, Schweppes Indian Tonic Water and Ford's Escort illustrate the predominant pattern in branding today – most products are being born with more than one brand name.

An appropriate analogy is to think of brands having surnames and forenames. Typically, the surname depicts the company or the family which the brand belongs to, while the forename identifies the individual product line. Several ideas flow from this analogy:

- The surname should be the constant guarantee of quality, the credentials which a company (or a subsidiary) rallies round. It should epitomize the breadth and depth of tradition that is founded in the interrelationships between the company's expertise and image, and its audiences' demands and expectations. Forenames represent the different product members of the family. They can exhibit their own personalities, functionally and imagewise, so far as they remain loyal to the reputation and sense of style which the family's name evokes.
- Given a choice between a world class surname or forename, the surname will open more doors. As a family name it can be marketed to unite relationships across borders, whereas forenames are more readily positioned for local nicknames.

Historically, the use of branding surnames and forename has often reflected little more than the desire to display who own's whom. As

continues

---

continued

markets converge and world class alliances increasingly make just-in-time business sense, we should expect to see increasingly creative uses of double-branding including arranged marriages of brands. They may literally aim to offer the consumer the best of both their worlds.

Many companies will need to shift allocations of their communications budgets towards family names and away from individual progeny. Or, where the forename has a world class aura, they should consider incorporating it as its own surname subsidiary.

(*Source*: Macrae, 1991)

Companies that cannot be bothered to think through all the organization and strategic purposes of their brand architecture deserve to find themselves at a disadvantage. They are less than the sum of the parts of their brands. In Chapter 1 we argued that it was vital not only that a brand's own essence was fully clarified, but also that its relationships with other brands in the corporate family were properly projected. Think of ways in which a brand's 'selfishness' can damage a company's communications investments:

- By cannibalizing other brands' territories in the company's portfolio, confusion multiplies both in the internal politics of rival brand managers and among retail customers who perceive that the company is unable to empathize with economies of category management which the retailer needs.
- By extending itself too far (for example, downmarket) the brand's dilution of image may spill over to have negative impacts on other levels of brands it is connected to.
- By losing market leadership or in other ways damaging its reputation, spillovers may again damage other brands.
- By claiming too much of a company's promotional resources like Heinz's baked beans, albeit often with the good intent of selling more, a product brand may overwhelm higher-level brands whose meanings are the truly vital strategic properties.

Damaging deviations from a brand's essence of the sorts described are always to someone else's advantage: that is, to the competitor whose brands span an architecture in which each is essential and serves relationships dedicatedly within its own purposeful scope. Once the fit of an individual Brand's Charter is clarified within a company's overall brand architecture, the evolution of brand architecture and individual Brand Charters needs to be synchronized.

3M

SWATCH

Anheuser Busch

BUDWEISER

KODAK

L'Oreal

BRAND
GENL MGMT
TECH

BANNER BRANDS

BRANDING JUNCTIONS

DYNAMICS: • PERCEPTION
• ORG. INPUT
• TIME
• COMPETITI

ESSENCE → 1. MEANINGFUL
2. COMMUNICABLE

LEADERSHIP IS APPARENT
VALUES ADDED ARE SHARED

UNDERSTAND THE FUTURE
OF TECHNOLOGY : IMPLI
-CONVERGENCE

Leagues of branding

These focus the purpose which a particular brand is aiming to fulfil. The structural consistency of Chartering is designed to ensure that all members of a business team are working towards the same goals. Brand leagues aim to clarify information on a brand's purpose and thus prevent different people from making diametrically opposed decisions. Need-to-know examples of what type of league a brand is playing in are as follows:

- If you know that a brand is to be global and local rather than just local you make different decisions.
- The branding goal of being a self-perpetuating fashion rather than a short-term fad calls for different investment decisions.
- The branding goal of having consumer pull requires a different marketing mix from merely clinging to the needs of retail distributors.
- The goals of tactical brands need to be specific and highly disciplined.

Box 11.7 The tactical brand that gets out of its league

Here is a typical case encountered during more client projects than we wish to count. For obvious reasons, we will not cite any branded examples by name.

The brand is conceived for a specific tactical purpose, such as being a value for money offer within the category. Typically, a manufacturer who also owns the brand leader may do this so that the lower added value end of the market is controlled. The tactical brand is then aiming to:

- offer value to consumers who only want to buy on price;
- give retailers a sufficiently good deal that they see no reason to develop their own-label brands;
- contain the size of the value-for-money segment to be no bigger than is necessary to account for these specified consumer and retailer needs.

Over time, these original aims of the brand are forgotten in the organization. This memory lapse often creeps in slowly. Perhaps a new brand manager adds some fancy packaging to make the brand more attractive at point of sale. Perhaps a creative supplier, unaware of the brand's original script, adds some cheerful personality to the brand, with the result that it starts to be marketed as more cheerful than cheap.

Suddenly, the unexpected (or to the Brand Charterer the predictable) happens. A competitor, or a retailer own label, launches

continues

---

continued

into the cheap end of the market. The embarrassing thing is that the tactical brand is no longer competitive because its total offer is no longer low cost to market. It is caught in no-man's land as neither top quality nor top price-fighter. Its share of the market erodes, often irreparably. Worse still the brand leader, which it was devised to protect, has been made highly vulnerable. There is now a live competitor trying to draw everyone it can into the bottom of the market. That is how many strongly branded markets have over time been reduced to little more than commodity status.

None of this needs to happen. The tactical brand is one of the easiest of all to Charter. All its management team needs to do is stay totally focused on its founding aims:

- to ensure that nobody else is lower total cost to market;
- to remain dedicated to the consumer and retailer values that were defined at the brand's conception.

The brand's intended league is a vital part of projecting its essence. Both should be clearly stated in an individual Brand's Charter, and subsequently neither should be adapted without cross-checking the other.

Linkages between brands

A study of linkages between brands involves 'what' identifying components are used to make linkages and 'why' goodwill connections need making.

The 'whats' of linkages include the standard format conventions a company uses in its brand architecture. For example, to retrieve itself from the brink of brand fragmentation (as many as 1,500 were in use in 1990), 3M now specifies that only three options are allowed for every new brand naming decision.

(1) Preferably 3M + generic product name, for example, 3M fire baulk carrier.
(2) 3M + existing sub-brand + description, for example, 3M Scotchmate hook and loop.
(3) New brand name, but this is reserved for very few situations.

The 'whats' of linkages also include how closely consumers are intended to remember linkages between top-level and sub-level brands. For example:

- You probably think of Snickers as a stand-alone brand even if you know it is made by Mars.

- In the case of Studioline from L'Oréal, the link is always clearly presented but you would not speak of the two names as if they were one phrase as you might with Gillette's Sensor.
- There may be designed-in linking codes such as: Mc and Big as used in McDonald's design language; the Nes syllable which connects up many Nestlé brands and the 'Nest' device.

The 'whys' of linkages focus on the next objectives of connecting up goodwill at particular points of time. We will develop this theme later in the chapter but here are two examples:

- In the early 1990s the objective of the temporary use of brand linkages between Philips and Whirlpool was to transfer all the goodwill of Philips relating to its white product division to Whirlpool, which had acquired the division but only a temporary licence to the Philips name. (While Whirlpool's ultimate objective was to have a more competently focused brand process for this sphere of products, it needed to transfer Philips's goodwill first.)
- In the design transformation of the Gillette-Sensor architecture, both brands gained from being linked to each other almost from day one. Gillette paraded the lifestyle message; Sensor provided a flagship product's confirmation of Gillette's leading edge capabilities in razors.

'Take-two' at brand architecture

Many of the greatest creative opportunities will come from the dynamics of reassembling a brand architecture. This is done to fit new competitive or partnering needs, while retaining key connections to your heritage of consumer recognition and reputation. The following dynamic concerns will be reviewed in this section:

- Agreeing your own architectural terminology
- Taking a quantum leap with a brand's level
- Catalogue 'game rules' presenting new architectural styles
- Internalization of new brand architecture is a big change management challenge
- Marrying a brand architecture to partner another company

Agreeing your own architectural terminology

When dealing with dynamic configurations, it is important not to get bogged down with terminology. Nevertheless, a quick recap may be helpful.

- Brands can be classified by levels and leagues; with corresponding investments in essences (Chapter 1) and identifiers (Chapter 2).
- The levels of brands are connected through linkages; identifiers – as designed-in devices consumers associate with a brand – serve specific purposes (one of which may be that of a linkage); other linkages are simple presentational formats like Studioline from L'Oréal.
- Starting with any brand in a company's brand architecture, you can travel up or down a branch through brands that are linked to it; from the consumer's viewpoint this branch may be perceived like a constellation of associations – for example, those starring in McDonald's design language – comprising different levels of branding together with all the identifiers that form each brand's identity system.
- By travelling across branches of brands you can obtain a picture of a company's brand architecture. Higher-level brands may connect up various branches, but even where such branding connections are not explicitly made, some audiences – for example, the retail trade in reviewing what brands a company is offering across its portfolio – will be making their own (dotted line) connections across your brand architecture.
- Ultimately, there is a difference between the brand architecture you present for general awareness, and the much deeper one that opinion (or vested interest) leaders know you by. Henceforth, the most realistic scenario for any globally powerful company is that it is not possible to hide behind brands all the time. For example, if something is perceived by journalists to go importantly wrong with one brand, questions are quite likely to be asked about the whole company's reputation.

This recap provides a reasonable basis for iteratively refining your own terminology. There will always need to be opinion calls for borderline classifications. There is, for example, no harm in treating some elements of a brand's architecture as both brand and identifier.

- Is Ronald an identifier or a sub-brand of McDonald's? You might want to take a hard line and say that he is not a brand because you cannot buy a Ronald (unless you count charitable contributions he sometimes collects); but we would rather treat him as a sub-brand as well because it is valuable to know the 'essence' of Ronald as an integral part of McDonald's cast (and anyway maybe Ronald could or should franchise some wares).
- In Sony's brand architecture is '-man' a linkage-identifier or a banner brand? The argument for regarding -man as a banner brand is that Walkman values, for example, young, hip, street-smart, give -man a differentiated essence, which Sony has conferred as the pivotal part of successive brand names like 'Discman' and 'Watchman'.

To sum up, architectural terminology matters to the Charterer in so far as business teams within a company need it to articulate dynamics of the brand process and to share a deep understanding which consensus-in-action requires.

Taking a quantum leap with a brand's level

A shift from local marketing of products to global marketing of businesses will require quite radical changes in brand architectures. If your company name lacks branded meaning or can never have an essential focus, it may be that some of your big product brands are worth raising to the top level. The BSN corporation recently rechristened itself Danone after its main yogurt and chilled foods business. The strategic logic is irrefutable. Danone is already a world class brand, and BSN is virtually a consumer non-starter.

Opel was reported in 1994 to be the name which will increasingly be used for General Motors' cars in worldwide markets apart from the USA. Radical evolution of a brand's architecture is not a new phenomenon in this early example of a global industry. British Leyland had various famous marques that fell by the wayside over the years, such as Austin and Triumph, but also one that took over all of the corporate reputation as the business converged on being Rover.

Increasingly, companies need to be ruthless with portfolios containing too many fragmented brands, and will make up new brand combos. In the UK the Gibbs of Unilever's personal care subsidiary used to connote toothpaste expertise which until recently remained in a product brand called Gibbs SR now relegated to an SR variant of the Mentadent umbrella. Elida (previously used as a name for the corporate subsidiary Elida Gibbs) is being promoted along with Ponds to a potential consumer banner integrating the 'Institute' form of branding lifestyle that Unilever has recently innovated (see Box 11.8). From 1996, Gibbs disappears from the company name, which becomes Elida Fabergé.

Box 11.8 Elida Gibbs, an organizational revolution: innovation and presentation

In 1991 Elida Gibbs started to change its organizational form. Unilever has gone on to create 'Institute' innovation centres of excellence, such as that for Elida hair products in Paris and those for Ponds and other skin care products in Hamburg and New York.

continues

---

continued

Said Unilever's chairman Sir Michael Perry, 'These innovation centres focus research, development and marketing with a brief to generate things for the whole world. It is a very exciting model that enables you to work much more effectively and much more responsibly.'

To present these foci to consumers, the Institute is evolving within Unilever's brand language. Thus the global roll-out of Unilever's newest shampoo brand features 'Organics from Elida Institute, Paris'. Supporting PR advises cosmopolitan consumers to keep a look out on their travels for Institute showrooms open to consumers like that on Paris's Champs Elysées. Meanwhile, the Ponds Institute is being featured in commercials as the consumer-oriented laboratory source for Ponds expanding range of skin care products. Corresponding PR coverage of this appears in advertorial columns in women's magazines.

Catalogue 'game rules' presenting new architectural styles

It is up to every brand marketer of the future to keep a catalogue of game rules which apply to brand architecture. To date, this is an extraordinarily under-developed area of brand research. One honourable exception, featured in Box 11.9, comes from a quartet of contributors, Farquhar, Han, Herr and Ijiri.

Box 11.9   Think before your brand extensions get out of control

The question of how far to extend a brand overlooks the more fundamental question of how to extend a brand.

Many brand leveraging efforts rely on one strategy: the direct extension of a brand across product categories. This can put valuable brands at risk with the extraordinary strength of an existing brand's association interfering with customers' ability to learn new associations. Instead, marketers can bypass the risk of direct extensions by leveraging brands indirectly across categories. As the following examples show, the marketing key is to link the brand to an association that has enough flexibility to provide a platform for both current positioning and subsequent leveraging.

continues

continued

The new umbrella

In the USA Anheuser-Busch created the Eagle brand for its honey roast peanuts as part of a strategic platform for launching other products. The Eagle banner was easily extendible to a variety of different snack foods. (The Eagle is also a prominent part of Anheuser-Busch's corporate heritage appearing on the corporate crest.)

The renewed umbrella

Aunt Jemima is famous in the USA for its association with pancakes. The company recently began promoting a broader association by moving from a product category, pancakes, to a usage situation, breakfast. This association comes naturally to American consumers (as breakfast is prime time for eating pancakes) and has enabled Aunt Jemima to extend to various breakfast lines.

Sub-branding

Sub- branding can be a key to modifying the meaning of a master brand. It does this by directing attention to the intended new meaning of the master brand in a way that makes it easier for customers to link the master brand with a target category extension.

Modifiers may be phrases not trademarks

The USA's favourite gelatin dessert is Jell-O and this dominant association makes it hard to extend the brand directly to other desserts. In extending the Jell-O brand to fruit-topped cheesecake, the modifier 'No Bake' highlights an alternate association: the customer benefit convenience. This modifier tries to reposition the meaning of Jell-O from a physical product to an intangible benefit for desserts.

Sub-branding devices can upmarket the brand's value range

Holiday Inn has rebranded its top of the market hotels as Holiday Inn Crowne Plaza. Through prominence of the phrase Sony Trinitron, Sony televisions add in their own branded technology. Successive product generations of Procter & Gamble's Ariel brand have progressed through Ariel to Ariel Ultra to Ariel Future (Ultra).

continues

---

continued

Hidden branding

A car brand like Lexus is totally separated as a product and service brand from Toyota, but consumers may still be reassured by the corporate parentage and this seems to be subtly exploited, for example, in the PR of new Lexus models.

(*Source*: Extracted from various works by Peter Farquhar *et al*, including: Strategies for leveraging masterbrands – how to bypass the risks of direct extensions, *Marketing Research*, September 1992)

Synergetically presented multi-brand platforms surround singular brands with a view to overturning their positionings. You can no longer be sure that your brand leader has a right to perpetual existence simply because it is effective at dominating the most important position in a product category.

The multi-brand combination of Colgate (global banner) and Plax (global sub-brand), partnered by local (professional brand) endorsements such as that of the British Dental Association, appears to be extremely confident of winning. To the extent that some UK advertising of Colgate devotes half of its space to the leading rival Listerine (global brand leader of the product category) and Clifford (identifying icon). Conventional advertising effectiveness guidelines do not pay for a competitor to share so much of your copy space. They are apparently being turned upside down by asking the consumer to observe the choice on offer:

- Listerine as recommended by a dragon called Clifford; or
- Colgate Plax as recommended by the British Dental Association.

Brand transfers: corporate reasons why linkages make architectures flexible

One of the most critical of all architectural plans concerns how the diffusion and infusion of branded goodwill between linked brands is to be leveraged.

Permanent double-branded linkages between different levels of brands should be developed so that over time each brand gains from the other's goodwill. Examples are Gillette-Sensor, L'Oreal and its family of sub-brands, Nestlé and its family of sub-brands.

Temporary linkages may deliberately transfuse goodwill from one brand to another (as in the Philips to Whirlpool example cited above), or provide temporary umbrella sponsorship to a new brand launch which may be important to both end-consumer and retail customers. For example, when Kimberly-Clark recently launched its Huggies brand of nappies in the UK, it was presented as Huggies from Kleenex (the company's existing banner brand in the UK). This may be primarily a tactical linkage to get the Huggies brand up and toddling in the fastest possible way.

You may think of other subtle transfers of added value between brands. For example, in the UK two Nestlé coffee brands Nescafe and Nescafe Gold Blend are powder and premium freeze dried alternatives within the instant coffee category. However, these two brands' advertising campaigns appear to endorse each other closely while differentiating popular and prestige coffee-drinking lifestyles. The consumer is effectively allowed to choose which of the branded products to drink and which advertising image to drink. You can enjoy Nescafe Gold Blend's campaigns and still drink Nescafe, or vice versa.

Internalization of a new brand architecture is a big change management challenge

There is nothing new in many branded goods from Western companies carrying a corporate signature as well as the brand name. However, we would cite Gillette's Sensor presentation as a landmark because the double-branding process was explicitly used to re-engineer the interpretation of all that Gillette would stand for. Here are extracts from this corporate transformation. (See ThinkPiece 1 for more about Gillette.)

The consumer story

It is well documented that through most of the 1980s Gillette's advertising of best-selling local products had conveyed an image of cheap, blue and plastic to a generation of consumers. Gillette literally came within a whisker of relegating the shaving category to a commodity one. The new presentation of Gillette scripted the corporate brand's essence as the lifestyle message of 'the best a man can get', and required this to be confirmed by advertising only those product sub-brands like Sensor which were innovative or aspirational. Thus the lifestyle story of Gillette heightened Sensor's leading-edge product story and vice versa. Consumers quickly learned that Gillette products now had doubly leading images.

The corporate story

Gillette's double-branding strategy together with its innovative new products quickly turned a lacklustre in-market corporate performance into a globally winning one. But before this happened internal aspects of the corporate transformation included:

- investment in a lengthy and costly R&D programme whose output was Sensor's world class product;
- a major changeover in responsibilities of global and local marketers, and all the organizational learning that was required to make this happen;
- a totally different resource allocation of advertising spends. This was designed to remove ad spending on local bestsellers (of the cheap, blue and plastic variety) and focus only on Gillette and flagship sub-brands. The new Gillette advertising campaigns were developed as a global communications package which could leverage satellite TV (international advertising) platforms.

We use the term 're-engineering the Gillette brand' advisedly. The problem for brand historians – and all who write up case studies on new brand architecture – is that once a company has successfully transformed the style of its brand architecture, it is easy to see elements of the great new architectural style (the advertising, the brand linkage tactics, the newly exciting composite essence). It is equally easy to forget, or never see, the organizational re-engineering and teamworking which went on behind the scenes before the new architectural style could be consistently served. Two other examples of newly transformed brand architectures (Box 11.10) illustrate:

- how marketers present the achievements of newly transformed brand architectures and the future advantages which they will leverage;
- what happened internally before the architectural transformations could work.

Box 11.10 Double-branding of consumer perceptions at 3M and Nestlé

Here we reproduce interviews recorded on video by BBC for BUSINESS featuring two accounts of how a conscious decision to implement double-branding works to establish leadership perceptions in the minds of consumers. Note how quickly this accelerates trust in the guarantee of the corporate brand, and establishes its own banner credentials to connect up with other brands and products. As Chapter 2 explained, consumers are now highly literate in the multiple ways that they can identify with a brand. A loyal consumer, who recognizes his or her brand through 10 different identifiers, becomes even more delighted if a new identifier turns out to be another famous brand, provided that the new double-branding offer is harmonious and appears to offer the best of both brands' worlds.

continues

---

continued

3M

'One of the issues for 3M in branding is the use of brand of Scotch and 3M. From my perspective being focused on the consumer market, then Scotch brand is the key brand that we advertise. But we do want the name of 3M to be better known. I want people to say yes it's Scotch brand – I'm going to buy that video tape and also to say "Ah and it's by 3M – yes 3M make other products that I like too, like Post-it notes, like adhesives and so on." It's these sorts of connections that I want the consumer to make more strongly. And then I hope in the future they will take the brand either Scotch or 3M and say "Ah that's a Scotch brand, or a 3M brand – all of the products I have tried under that brand have delighted me, they've met my need and served me well, I'll try this one." Because 3M is always going to be bringing out new products.'

Nestlé

'Increasingly more and more branding effort is being put into what Nestlé stands for. Simultaneously, brands bought in business acquisitions – for example, Kit Kat from Rowntree – are re-badged now with Nestlé's name and logo very prominently alongside Kit Kat. The idea is that both brands can contribute to each other. So Kit Kat's leading position in the UK and strong consumer loyalty can rub off on Nestlé, and meanwhile Nestlé can now launch Kit Kat in other parts of Europe where Kit Kat isn't known but Nestlé is.'

(*Source*: Extracted from 'Branding – The Marketing Advantage' © Copyright 1995 BBC for BUSINESS)

The external communications formats of double-branding can look so simple. Indeed, that is how they make their impact on consumers. But before these can work, the internal changes to brand marketing and organization must not be underestimated. There are many reasons why the classical brand management system of junior product managers rotating local brand responsibilities on two-year shifts is passing into history (Low and Fullerton, 1994). But any intent to action double-branding forces the reorganizational issue once and for all. A moment's thought shows that anybody who rushed into imitating the kinds of double-branding strategy described above while keeping junior brand managers in control of the sub-brands would be taking a gamble with the lives of their brands at every level. So what sorts of changes to the structure of brand management were needed before our exemplars of double-branding could externalize their brand new marketing commu-nications? Roughly what we would have seen happening in these organizations if we had re-wound these brand histories back a few years is summarized in Box 11.11.

Box 11.11 Internal brand reorganization prior to externalized double-branding

3M

As recently as 1990 Jean-Noel Kapferer was citing 3M as:

'A typical case illustrating the problems of brand proliferation. Although it ranks 29th in the *Fortune* 500 index and sells 60,000 products worldwide, 3M is rather poorly known with only 25% of people familiar with what 3M does. This poor level of awareness creates a real shortcoming in one of the major roles of a corporate brand: to endorse. 3M does not really act as it should as a power brand. The roots of this situation lie in 3M's brand proliferation policy: 1,500 product brands with each receiving too little financial support to compete properly. Furthermore, the effect is to create a screen, hiding the corporation 3M.'

In the days described by Kapferer, 3M's marketing department was creating as many as 100 new brands a year. First, a virtual moratorium was put on this so that now few if any new brands are created. Second, a lot of product brands were culled, typically by renaming them 3M followed by the generic product descriptor. Third, as part of 3M's continuing reorganization into customer divisions rather than national ones, opportunities have been taken to undepartmentalize marketing. Marketers have increasingly become business managers and vice versa.

Nestlé

In Nestlé's marketing hall of horrors, there is a famous picture of the Kit Kats that were bought when Rowntree was acquired in 1988. Almost every country manager had created his or her own design of Kit Kat. It was not strongly managed international brands that Nestlé bought from Rowntree, but their potential to be reorganized as great international marketing platforms to the corporate advantage of Nestlé's banner brand.

Before Nestlé's double-branding strategy could work it had to converge the designs of Kit Kat; converge local managers' views of

continues

---

continued

what was the essential meaning of Kit Kat; and reorganize ways of working so that national marketing and international branding were harmonious partners. Considering the changes that had to be made, sales of Kit Kat as a European brand have started to boom in a surprisingly short time. Having shown that this could be achieved even with Kit Kat – one of the worst cases of over-localized design interpretation ever perpetrated by a single company across Europe – a similar process has been accelerated with other acquired sub-brands. Over the past few years confirmation of the increased power of Nestlé's corporate brand equity has come from the brand's leap into top 10 rankings of global brand awareness. This is an extraordinary turnround in brand fortune. Not much more than a decade ago, Nestlé's corporate brand had little visibility. Worse still, it had a tarnished image among lobby groups who felt that Nestlé was over-aggressive in its marketing of infant milk formulas in developing countries.

We will consider more practical experiences on changing over to new forms of brand organization in Chapter 13.

Marrying a brand architecture to partner another company

We are old enough still to regard marriage as a strategic partnership and therefore add this to the architect's vocabulary where:

- two brands owned by a company are joined together (starting from apparently equal levels of branding);
- strategic connections are made between architectures owned by different organizations.

(An alternative term, co-branding, has become part of marketing parlance. However, this term seems to be applied to any instance of two brands appearing together from sharing a one night promotional stand to founding a long-term strategic partnership.)

Box 11.12 Who would have thought that American Express and Virgin would co-brand?

Writing in 1995 it is too early to say whether press advertising featuring these brands' combined messages (seen, for example, in *The Times*

continues

continued

newspaper) is a local co-branding affair or the first visible sign of a longer-term business alliance. The immediate consumer proposition is 'Fly free faster – with Membership Rewards (from American Express) and Virgin Freeway'.

What might have seemed totally opposite corporate personalities five years ago find a union in terms of each being a brand whose consumer vitality depends on a 'with-it' platform. Behind the varied lifestyle interpretations of this driving need are service businesses with very different core competences, but that may be how two service businesses can most profitably form a 'glocal' (global and local) network to be more than the sum of their parts.

In the BBC for BUSINESS video 'Branding – the Market Advantage', a detailed journalistic cross-examination of American Express reveals that this brand's mission is to be the number one service brand in the world. The video portrait shows an Amex that is banking on being the first to establish a world class membership club of VIPs (which now appear to be visioned as a global network not just of the wealthy but the entrepreneurial too). To support this infrastructure, Amex will invest whatever it takes in smart cards and technology to customize messages circulated to its club members. It has its own channel for two-way customer relationships through the brand's monthly correspondence, which is set to evolve from being merely 'a bill through the mail' to offering increasingly customized incentives. These currently include:

- the Membership Rewards programme (loyalty points are being transformed into an international currency which, unlike the ecu, can be spent directly on offers of various global service businesses from Virgin's airline network to hotel networks like Forte);
- computerized personal message columns on local happenings activated by an individual member's purchasing history at the stores he or she uses most.

It is fairly clear what Virgin gets from American Express: a foot-in-the-door to a programme which may yet outpace its giant rival's sub-brands Air Miles and Executive Club, loyalty programmes which through 1985–95 have done much to make British Airways the world's favourite airline among many global business travellers. Arguably, Richard Branson ends the 20th century as one of the Western world's most entrepreneurially daring business people. For example, see Chapter 12 for his part in the Virgin-Cott vision to challenge the added-value chains of the world's biggest product brands like Coca-Cola. It may be that a little each-way image investment in leaders who appear to be entrepreneurially redistributing global and local wealth – on top of being the club with status for the established wealthy – is a clever Amex platform for communicating new-millennium values. More simply, if

continues

---

continued

we worked in American Express, we would enjoy being refreshed by having some sort of continuing dialogue with those animating the Virgin way of marketing as well as respecting the more classical American Express disciplines for marketing financial services.

Marrying brands within a company

The wooing and subsequent corporate 'seeding' of Weight Watchers by Heinz is described in ThinkPiece 1. It provides an interesting example of joining two brands to advance each other's added values. Heinz talent spotted an acquisition – Weight Watchers with high image credentials but under-recognized as a commercial branding platform – and carefully extended the business to embrace mass-market products which Heinz wanted to target while retaining the essential values and services of the original Weight Watcher's health club.

We would also expect to see companies becoming more proactive in marrying brands they already own. For example, if a cosmetic company has two famous brands whose category associations are with different grooming functions, and if their categories are increasingly overlapping with 2-in-1 formulations, it is foreseeable that a marriage presented as 'Brand A' tested by the 'Brand B Institute' can offer consumers the opportunity to buy into the best of both brands' worlds.

Marrying brands across companies

Nestlé's brand visions illustrate how a banner corporate brand leverages goodwill of many stakeholders, and not only end-consumers. Typically, Nestlé has leveraged its corporate branding reputation in a Euro-marketing joint venture with General Mills which was happy to join all its American cereals sub-brands, for example, Cheerios, to Nestlé's banner brand and thereby take advantage of Nestlé's distributional reach and the reputation of the Nestlé banner with consumers. (See brand benchmarking of Nestlé's in ThinkPiece 1.)

As we have already speculated, the current co-promotion of American Express and Virgin may mature to be more than a co-branding affair. Certainly, we will see in Chapter 12 that Virgin is an extraordinarily active partnering brand. We will also see that many new markets, for example multimedia, will involve strategic partnerships where it is logical to assume that both partnering brands will want to take the credit for their produce. One confederation of companies has already started to invest in the identity 'General Magic', a sort of cooperative personal entertainment software house for the future.

Credit card brand marriages using one of today's most portable consumer mediums (the wallet/handbag), such as the one between GM and MasterCard, are evolving towards tomorrow's smart card unions.

'Efficient Consumer Response' (ECR) is a world class movement aimed at revolutionising inter-organizational marketing in time for the new millennium. (Refer to MELNET.) Instead of being opposing warriors in the added-value chain, some supermarket retailers and manufacturer brands need to discover intelligent forms of partnership. We have felt recently that consumers have been suffering from the jealousies between these industry types. Partnerships between two organizations do not work unless there is a basis of trust and a genuine search for win-win forms of evolution. Neither trust nor motive other than taking the shortest-term advantage of buyer power is manifest in the following expression of corporate purpose by a buyer in a supermarket chain. Maybe this is only an individual expressing his function in life. But it would be doubly ironical if the current climate of over-accounting means that this was indeed an organizational belief. If the organization concerned fails to realize this consumers may quite soon have no need nor any residual affinity for a brand whose own autobiography is powerful but not smart.

'We are the nation's most powerful brand.
We do not partner suppliers.
Innovation is not our job.
Me-toos of manufacturers' brands gives great value to our customers.
In our service business, front-line employees have no training on what consumer essence we intend to communicate; nor do senior managers share a view on what this is.'

If manufacturers and retailers do not get their acts together as partners, their separate powers will be dwarfed by the newly emerging superpower of multimedia owners. We may be talking about a time horizon of 10–15 years, but world class branding partnerships are now being made precisely because the most significant marketing opportunities are those which prepare to leverage the significance of this sort of business system discontinuity, and to use the 'pre-marketing' time span involved to learn to trust each other.

One more heretical thought is that the world's most valuable brand, as we leave the second millennium, is not owned by a corporation. It is Japan. It comes at the top of the branded architecture to which Sony, Honda, Toyota, Seiko, Toshiba and dozens of other corporate stars are intent on delivering world class quality. This is making the Japanese manufactured product a collector's item in markets whose focus is rapid evolution of consumer-facing technology.

Once upon a time, competitive strategy may have been the only discipline that really counted, but then another – partnership strategy –

came into being. As we will see in later chapters, new strategic architects foresee banner brands being used to unite both of these strategic endeavours.

Summary

If you have too many brands in your portfolio, or want to extend a brand, half an hour invested in reading this chapter may be the best opening investment you have made in branding in recent years. Within one organization, or across companies, when two or more brands partner each other to offer consumers the best of both their worlds, they wipe stand-alone brands off marketing's game board. To do this new kinds of organizational forms of brand management will be needed, but Chapters 12 and 13 show why brand new organization is an urgent priority in many companies.

Until recently, brand management was often operated in fragmented ways through local offices. This is no longer how the marketing process of a world class company adds most value. Major investments in branding purpose and corporate goodwill need to be reflected on iteratively, globally and locally. Real corporate foresight also calls for process insights that must have breadth and depth. Ideas on strategic vision or organizational form are unlikely to confer corporate advantage unless brand architecture is party to the same thinktank sessions. Brands are not a company's greatest assets unless they are directed, and increasingly interconnected, as 'dynamic assets'.

We have discussed a vocabulary for 'brand architecture' including key terms such as levels, leagues and linkages of branding. Refine these as part of a newly fundamental brand marketing vocabulary for your business team, and then build on these dynamic constructs. You will then be able to innovate powerful new game rules for leveraging brand process as a strategy architect (Chapter 12) and as an organization architect (Chapter 13).

References

Kapferer, J. (1992). *Strategic Brand Management*. London: Kogan Page
Low, G. and Fullerton, R. (1994). Brands, brand management, and the brand management system: a critical-historical evaluation, *Journal of Marketing Research*, May
Macrae, C. (1991). *World Class Brands*. Harlow: Addison-Wesley
Urde, M. (1994). Brand orientation – a strategy for survival, *Journal of Consumer Marketing*, **11**(3)

12

brand Strategy Architect

We use the word architect in a general sense to represent strategic and organizational leadership inputs into Brand Chartering for two main reasons.

(1) In Chapter 11 we argued that brand architects who build linkages between levels of branding (for example, corporate branding and product sub-branding) can direct higher-level advantages – integrating a company's total goodwill and leadership capabilities – than those who only have a portfolio of fragmented brands to work with.

(2) A successful architect tries to ensure that everything connects up, for both practical day-to-day operations and long-term qualities like (re)creating robust and flexible environments for people's working lifestyles. Architecture seems a natural metaphor for the new wave of strategic and organizational schools of thinking that companies need to embrace if they are to replace long-term planning by something more proactive in a fast-moving world. At this stage we must defer to Hamel and Prahalad who have pioneered a new school of strategic thinking to get a direct feel for keywords in the new vocabulary of 'strategic architecture' (see Box 12.1).

Box 12.1 Hamel and Prahalad's new strategic lexicon

One doesn't get to the future first by letting someone else blaze the trail. So what is it that compels some companies rather than others to take up the difficult challenge of inventing the future? What allows some companies to create the future despite enormous resource handicaps while others spend billions and come up short? Why do some companies seem to possess over-the-horizon radar while others seem to be walking backwards into the future? In short, what does it take to get to the future first? At a broad level it requires four things:

(1) an understanding of how competition for the future is different;
(2) a process for finding and turning insight into tomorrow's opportunities;
(3) an ability to energize the company top-to-bottom for what may be a long and arduous journey toward the future; and
(4) the capacity to outrun competitors and get to the future first, without taking undue risks.

Implicit here is a view of strategy quite different from that which prevails in many companies. It is a view of strategy that recognizes:

- it is not enough to position optimally within existing markets; the challenge is to pierce the fog of uncertainty and develop great *foresight* into the whereabouts of tomorrow's markets;
- the need for more than an incrementalist, annual planning rain dance; what is needed is a *strategic architecture* that provides a blueprint for building the *core competences* needed to dominate future markets;
- less concern with ensuring a tight fit between goals and resources and more concern with creating *stretch goals* that challenge employees to accomplish the seemingly impossible;
- the quest to overcome resource constraints through a creative and unending pursuit of better *resource leverage*;
- competition often takes place within and between *coalitions* of companies, and not only between individual businesses;
- to capitalize on foresight and core competence leadership, a company must ultimately pre-empt competitors in critical global markets; that the issue is not so much time to market, but time to *global pre-emption*.

(*Source*: Hamel and Prahalad, 1994)

This chapter will suggest ways of exploring how branding processes interconnect with strategic decisions. We will deliberately present some 'far-out' agendas, and stress the need for always distinguishing between 'then' and 'now'. You have to take a view of 'then' in your business and decide which aspects of this require immediate action.

The histories of great brands (see ThinkPiece 1) show that their formative stages benefited from top-level thinking within the company which was intense, iterative and foresightful. Layer upon layer of branding advantage was built up in a process that merited the label of 'founding a leadership system'. Companies with major investments in brand architectures should be inputting top-quality think time into their business processes to perpetuate the roles of brands as leadership systems and as strategic integrators of core competences (that is organization-specific means of adding value). The reality can be different as we shall briefly indicate.

Corporate diversions which undermine brand process and leadership foresight

The following quotation is extracted from a book on business process re-engineering (Johansson *et al*, 1993). Its authors are partners in one of the world's 'Big 6' accountancy firms, Coopers & Lybrand.

> 'There is constant tension between the accountant – valuer of old assets (cash and tangible items) – and the operations executive – the orchestrator that believes he should invest to enhance the value of all his assets. Cutting-edge leaders of business today concentrate more on the new assets (brands, process capabilities, people and know-how) than the old, putting up to five times more effort on the new assets than 10 years ago.'

From time to time arenas of intellectual thinking and organizational functional routine have conspired to relegate the status of the brand below even that of intangible asset, to invisible – and even absent – process. Functional barriers to realizing brands as leadership systems have come from such imposing sources as classical theories of corporate strategy, and valuation procedures tied to preserving the sanctity of the balance sheet.

Michael Porter (1980 and 1985) has made great contributions to corporate strategy and competitive advantage, but early editions of his books did not mention the brand. Porter's frameworks were detailed on how tangible assets evolved competitive advantages, but much more patchy on the practical powers of intangible leadership systems. When the frameworks were conceived today's greatest change forces, such as globalization, affected a minority of branded industries. The cumulative impact of all mass communications was a fraction of what it is now. In the days of tangible asset power, the nearest thing many businesses had to an electronic medium was the telex machine.

Scholars have since begun to recast corporate strategy. From a quantitative analysis of European companies adding most organizational value from 1981 to 1990, Professor Kay identifies the top three capabilities which are sustainable and appropriable within successful companies:

- reputation
- innovation
- architecture (defined by Kay as 'a system of relationships within the firm, or between the firm and its suppliers and customers, or both'). (Kay, 1993)

These capabilities are intimately related to how fast and coherently a company learns. We suggest that the leveraging of all three should be inseparable from the strategic art of branding leadership systems. This appears to be confirmed by evidence from Hamel and Prahalad that winning companies are those that infuse into classical strategic and management frameworks new thinking on banner brand process, core competences and foresightful leadership purpose.

Several human inertias can prevent companies from embarking on new brand strategy thinking. They include the habits of older generations, plus the fact that recent crops of MBAs are too often examined on curricula that do not quickly catch up with revolutionary thinking, particularly where course materials rely heavily on historical case studies.

Nor is the influence of financial analysts likely to have a positive effect on branding's long-term capabilities. In a 1993 MORI survey of top influencers of corporate governance – sampling 97 captains of industry from the UK's 500 top companies, 146 equity fund managers and 34 city editors and broadcasters – British companies were shown to be relatively adept with brands and poor at strategic thinking. Most of the respondents did not make the mental link between branding and strategy.

We also doubt whether foresightful thinking on brand architecture is likely to be enhanced by the relatively new system of brand valuation, which came to prominence in the late 1980s. This system has been devised to comply with accountants' insistence that valuations must be compatible with the balance sheet's founding philosophy, that all figures must be justifiable on the grounds of proven past performance.

This sort of brand valuation may help a company to appraise what it may get if it wants to sell off a brand. It may also indicate the value of brands where these are the company's major resources. By presenting the wealth of the company in a good light, management decision-making need not be put unnecessarily on the defensive, for example, by predators or by bureaucratic rules with arcane effects. (An example of the latter occurs when local accounting regulations require that a board goes back to shareholders for approval if an acquisition exceeds a certain percentage of assets recorded in the balance sheet. In this case, when brands as a company's major assets are excluded from the accountant's reckoning, the board might end up having to spend most of its time convening extraordinary general meetings.)

Balance-sheet aligned techniques of brand valuation cannot help resolve the fundamental paradox of the brand: it is a major corporate asset whose worth is no more than the power of future sources of advantage invested in it.

Navigating leadership systems in times of global revolution

At this turn of the millenium, earth dwellers are living through an era of global revolution in the way that world class businesses operate. The *Financial Times* said on 20 September 1994: 'Companies grown fat on regional dominance now find themselves seventh in a global market where only three will thrive. Big companies, in English-speaking countries at least, are in a Maoist state of permanent revolution.'

Foresight is needed to turn risks, otherwise associated with revolution, into opportunities. Timing is a critical art, especially for the owner of dominant brands whose organization can be lulled into a false sense of security. Forces for global revolution do not materialize overnight; they have been looming for years. In the late 1980s Peter Drucker identified many key forces as megatrends, that is irreversible trends that are already happening but whose impacts are yet to come (see ThinkPiece 5). Earlier, Theodore Levitt foresaw why the globalization of markets would one day herald a revolution in consumer benefits. The sands of time may be fast running out on the locally fragmented ways that branders used to work and profit from.

(Going back to original Levitt papers – and the context he wrote them in – is a delightful experience. In 1960, in *Marketing Myopia*, Levitt was counselling how businesses lose their way whenever they forget to organize marketing as a company learning 'process'. Here is a useful tip regarding Levitt's 1983 paper on globalization. If you encounter a critic of this paper, look first to see if he or she is actually quoting Levitt in context. 'The globalization of markets – companies must learn to operate as if the world were one large market – ignoring superficial regional and national differences.' From the *Harvard Business Review*, May/June 1983.)

All branding and leadership decisions need to be context specific. But if you contribute to branding in a consumer-driven industry, you must be prepared to brainstorm emerging patterns for leveraging global revolution so as to see what learning points may apply to your own leadership systems.

One of the brainstorming questions we use regularly in workshops on strategic architecture is: what can you learn from successful brand franchising models given that some of branding's biggest success stories in recent years – for example, McDonald's, Benetton, Body Shop – have used this evolutionary form?

First, two obvious points are that:

- successful franchising involves making a delivery system competitively strong and then having the capability, if chosen, to replicate it fast and globally;
- in making and renewing process strengths, franchising often capitalizes on having privileged access to both a living distribution system and a consumer laboratory. The franchise founder uses the original franchises as prototypes and role models for testing evolution of the business system, and perfecting consumer values.

Second, two less obvious points are that:

- brand franchising requires you to focus on partnership strategy as well as competitive strategy;
- brand franchising frees you to question what in the total industry chain you need to own. Your aim should be to keep control of the brand's added value, while ensuring that the economics of the whole delivery system are world class. What should you pick from both manufacturing's and retailing's distinctive competences, so that you own branding's added-value leadership rights while giving a fair and secure long-term deal to all your partners?

This process of branding mixes two critical forces for perpetuating brand momentum:

- strong leadership by a brand owner responsible for world class quality and value;
- strong local buy-in and iterative feedback on maximizing the brand's impact in terms of both consumer relationships and business development.

Third a 'case future': a story of two leadership systems which, at time of writing (1995), are evolving in ways that are revolutionary because, on the one hand, we have no idea where these companies will be in 10 years' time. On the other hand, wherever they go, traditional consumer goods competitors are having to reassess the economies of their branding systems. One of the companies in the case future (Cott) has, over a five-year period, multiplied its 1989 turnover of approximately $30 million by a factor of 25, and in the process started to raise questions about the effectiveness of some of the greatest branding systems the world has so far known.

Excerpts from the story of Loblaw's

In 1983, inspired by the innovative foods developed by the British retailer Marks and Spencer for its own brand St Michael, Dave Nichol, director of new product development for the Canadian supermarket retailer Loblaw's, launched his company's own upmarket branding system, President's Choice. All President's Choice lines evolved as super-premium offerings. But at least four types of flagship line served to confirm the fame which President's Choice was designed to cultivate.

- High-quality fresh and chilled food recipes served to make Loblaw's as famous in Canada as Marks and Spencer is in the UK, as a provider of food lines which seem to merge supermarket and delicatessen.
- The President's Choice's 'Memories' Range whose products are both exotic in presentation and convenient to use. They thereby add spice of life to consumers' dinners and make Loblaw's a continuously fashionable talking point. Imagine how two typical lines – President's Choice Memories of Ancient Damascus tangy pomegranate sauce and Szechuan peanut sauce and dressing – convey their own storylines.
- Category best of kinds, for example, a chocolate cookie 'The Decadent' whose loyal fan club claims it to be the world's best manufactured cookie.
- Category emulators, which sought to deliver a taste similar to the big brand leader but at a lower price.

Nichol was proud of his product winners and strongly marketed their exclusive benefits for Loblaw's. 'I have the ultimate retail weapon' he said, referring in 1991 to the Decadent Chocolate Cookie Chip's which had just outsold Canada's erstwhile brand leading cookie. 'Anybody who loves The Decadent Cookie has to shop in my stores.' It soon seemed natural to suggest that retailers outside Canada could benefit from President's Choice as a winning programme of merchandise and Loblaw shops were delighted to be showcased to visiting retailers to prove the point. In its first decade of existence, President's Choice merchandise was evolving into international retailer programmes, including 12 US chains (for example, at the USA's biggest Wal-Mart where the programme was called Sam's American Choice); a Hong Kong chain; K-Mart Australia where the programme was called Australia's Choice.

By then Nichol was convinced that President's Choice had most of the critical elements needed for a world brand. He was close to inventing the one big threat that branded manufacturers had not associated with the concentration of retailer power: the capability to distribute products with proven consumer appeal through a global distribution network. Recently, manufacturers' brands have had to adjust to many reverses at the hands of big retailer chains within national markets, but now it appears that they cannot even rely on transnational marketing as their unique right to brand.

By 1994, Loblaw was buying annually US$7 billion of President's Choice products for its own stores and a similar amount of President's Choice products for its retail customers outside Canada. So exporting the programme doubled Loblaw's buying power, without the company having to make any extra investment in hard assets or inventories.

In Loblaw's we have a retailer which is also working as a virtual supplier to international retailers. A retailer who claims that launching new President's Choice lines is a marginal cost, whereas manufacturer brand line launches in the USA could easily cost $50 million. Big as Loblaw's shock waves have been to some manufacturer's branding systems, they may turn out to be only a scene setter for things to come owing to the evolving ramifications of a second leadership system whose source is attributable to President's Choice's cola. This is Cott Corp.

Excerpts from the story of Cott Corporation

In the words of *Canadian Business Magazine*, Gerry Pencer was in 1989 president of the family's company, 'then a meagre little Montreal bottling outfit called Cott Corp., which sold cheap soda pop under its own label'. In early 1990 Pencer discovered that Loblaw needed a new supplier for its President's Choice cola, met Nichol and was told that what was needed was a cola product as good as Coke or Pepsi but cheaper. Nichol has subsequently confessed that he thought it unlikely he would see Pencer again, but for what actually happened next we return to *Canadian Business Magazine*. 'Pencer was back in Nichol's office within a few weeks, having bought the right to use Royal Crown Cola Inc's recipe. Nichol helped Cott modify RC's cola recipe, and relaunched President's Choice cola in March of 1990. It was an instant hit, and soon accounted for the majority of Loblaw's Ontario cola sales.'

A lot of things happened in the next four years. Cott's production of private-label soft drinks sold in Canada has reached 85%. The company now sells soft drinks to more than 50 retail chains in the USA, including giants such as Wal-Mart and Safeway. Pencer has also developed a growing stable of international clients for his soft drinks business including major retail chains in the UK, Spain and Japan.

Canada may seem to be an unlikely epicentre for an earthquake in world branding, but Canadian Business magazine's reporting of the local scene seems pretty devastating. 'Certainly, the threat of private label is real enough. In Canada, Coca-Cola Beverages lost $143 million in 1993 and closed eight plants – in part because it lost share to private-label brands. Pepsi's new Pepsi Max cola and Nabisco's Chunks Ahoy! cookie probably owe their existence to the private-label threat.' 'Innovation hadn't been there from the national brands,' says Pepsi-Cola Canada Ltd's president, Ron McEachern. 'The growth of premium private label is a wake-up call.'

Cott has also increased its presence and breadth in supporting retail programmes. For example, at Safeway (the second largest supermarket chain in the USA) Cott has helped out with various aspects of the Safeway Select programme including packaging, sourcing and specification of products. To support this process Cott has been buying stakes in suppliers of Loblaw's other President's Choice lines. Then in the middle of 1994 Dave Nichol joined Cott, which has also been attracting other marketing luminaries like Don Watt, whose design work has been key to the presentation of many leading retailer programmes. The strategic intent of Cott is well signposted in Box 12.2.

Box 12.2   Will Cott become a virtual General Foods?

Heather Reisman, Cott's president, says: 'Pencer likes to say let's see if we can create the next General Foods. He's probably projecting a decade, but there is a fundamental transformation taking place in the whole food chain. Who manufactures, how they work with suppliers, how they work with retailers, how the marketing happens. If we understand that change, we could build a giant company.'

What this means is that Pencer thinks he's figured out how to use other companies' manufacturing facilities and expertise to build his own conglomerate. For instance, when faced with making soft drinks for an exploding market, Pencer negotiated 'co-packing' deals that saw existing bottlers use their excess capacity to pump out his product. Pencer has bought three bottling plants in the US and is building a new

continues

continued

Montreal facility, but he relies heavily on co-packing deals with a network of Royal Crown bottlers in the US. In Europe, he is expanding through similar arrangements with Benjamin Shaw and sons in the UK and Cadbury Schweppes on the continent.

Now Pencer wants to catapult from soda pop into a full range of products and services, replicating the operating philosophy of his soft-drink business as he goes. As Reisman explains it, private-label soft drinks sell better when they are part of a comprehensive, well merchandised programme. The company will create packaging for a retail programme and help locate suppliers. It will refine recipes and develop the products themselves. All of this Cott will do, ostensibly free of charge, in the belief that it promotes the company's core business.

Cott plans eventually to spread the costs of these services over as many as six or seven categories. All must be high-volume, high-profile products that currently do not return enough profit to the retailers. They must all, in other words, resemble the soft-drink category of a few years back. Pet food is one promising category. Snack foods, beer (including non-alcoholic beer) and juice-based drinks may prove to be others. Cott is buying into these President's Choice supplier companies in order to gain expertise in their product categories, and to test the vision.

If more opportunities become available and other product categories fit the bill, Cott is 'definitely open' to further investments says Reisman. The plan is to negotiate more excess capacity deals, manage more relationships and leverage Cott's intellectual capital. 'I'm not saying we don't have to own anything,' says Reisman, 'but we don't have to own things, in the way the old world did, in order to create value. If we wrap our ingenuity around someone else's bricks and mortar, we add value and make money. It's not so much a "new-age General Foods" as a kind of "virtual" General Foods.'

(*Source*: Extracted from an article by Stevenson, 1994)

As with all brainstorming exercises, you will need to come to your own context-specific conclusions as to what threats and opportunities could result from somebody doing a Cott to your industry's added-value chain.

In brief, Cott appears to be in the business of identifying world class product formulae and then franchising these products through developing partnerships with countries' existing retail chains. So far Cott has shown amazing adaptability in establishing its beach-head in different country's added-value distribution chains.

- In Canada its entry point was into and then learning from the President's Choice retail programme.
- In the USA most retail chains are regional and not nationwide competitors. This allowed Cott to start by offering many retailers an

exclusive advantage – the promise of a world class retail programme – within their region.
- In the UK the market is dominated by a handful of major
  supermarket retailers. Cott has exploited the country's comparatively
  lax visual identity laws to convince retailers that they will all be
  missing out if they do not exploit their opportunity to develop
  'lookalike' brands to the full. So designer-red American cola
  formulations are, as of early 1995, produced by Cott as Sainsbury's
  classic cola, Safeway's select Cola, Woolworth's American diner cola,
  and (in an extraordinary three-way partnership) cola produced by
  Cott, branded by Virgin, and premiering in Tesco supermarkets.

It would be wise not to underestimate the confederation of
entrepreneurs which seem to be a core part of Cott's strategy. For
example, Cott seems to be replicating its networking pattern through
like-minded partners, as revealed by the following extracts from UK
press coverage.

'Retailer Nick Kirkbride has joined the Virgin Cola Company as
its new managing director. The Virgin Cola Company is a joint
venture between Virgin and the European subsidiary of the Cott
Corporation. It oversees Virgin's soft drinks business, including
its own-brand cola and forthcoming energy drink, understood to
be called Pure Virgin Energy.

'Kirkbride has also spent five years at management consultancy McKinsey. His connection with Virgin goes back six
years, when he worked at Cadbury Schweppes alongside Simon
Lester, who is now managing director of Virgin partner Cott
Europe.

(*Marketing Week*, 24 February 1995)

'Branson is leading the chase in the cola market. In line with his
taste for David-and-Goliath battles, Branson has pumped up his
ambitions since launching Virgin cola in November 1994; now
his ultimate goal is for his cola to be the number one brand.

'In his 50/50 venture with Cott, he hopes to capitalize on the
Virgin brand name and launch the drink this year in Asia,
continental Europe and the central battlefield of the cola war –
America. Branson accepts that it may take him the rest of his life
to knock Coca-Cola from the top spot, but believes he has the
brand and product to do it. "We have come up with a drink that
people prefer to Coke that is also much cheaper." Branson
believes that there is room for three main global cola companies.
"I hope the market will support three," he says. "I would
certainly hate Coke to go bust."'

(*Sunday Times*, 5 March 1995)

Ironically, Cott's strategy appears to be targeting brands that have built individual product categories, such as colas, into fashions that are on the world's shopping lists. In brainstorming mode, you now need to consider questions that old branders still feel to be heretical.

- Has Coca-Cola invested in an essence that was too big for a single product compass?
- What is it about Coca-Cola's brand architecture that has stopped the world's most refreshing and friendly drinks going beyond colas?
- At some stage, could not Sprite and Fanta have been interweaved more closely into Coca-Cola's mental tapestry without prejudicing the company's goal of maximizing cola's share of the global stomach?
- Is it not slightly strange that Coca-Cola now markets Nestea (under Nestlé's brand architecture) instead of Co-tea?
- Will the strategies of Cott and worldwide retail franchisees mean that high added-value global fashions associated with singular product categories become a thing of our passing millennium?
- What categories offer continuous scope for product innovation, or other fast-evolving capabilities, to secure their manufacturers' right to brand?

We asked a senior figure in the soft drinks industry to bring his own sense of balance to this debate (see Box 12.3).

Box 12.3   Leaders find their own way to go closest to consumer needs

(1) What is noteworthy about Cott and Virgin is that basically they use the resources of others. This has to be the best way to avoid risk and achieve good margins. If Virgin cola flops, there appears to be no real loss to Branson. Putting the package together (as bankers once did) has to be sound strategy.

(2) Consumers are discriminating and long-run success depends on taste. The first test for any cola will in the end be do you want to drink it day in, day out? For example, even though Pepsi often wins in a blind test (ie, a one-off serving), it does not seem historically to have achieved the same permanent drinkability as Coke.

(3) The big markets for these brands are turning to Africa, India, China and the rest of Asia. The lion's share of the cola market will go, as the market develops, to Coke and Pepsi. Competing entries will come in after the markets are established.

(4) Remember that even in the UK, a hot summer may produce an impulse market of $500,000 million of colas not easily tapped by

continues

continued

Sainsbury, Cott, Virgin, *et al*. This is bought from non-grocery outlets. The key, as always, is whether the product is within easy reach when you feel thirsty. This is where Coke scores with its distribution and merchandising systems.

(5) The end position will come when you can make decent drinks in your own home. You are then likely to want to drink the brand leaders, who will presumably patent their cartridges so that outsiders cannot use their system.

We also surveyed (in 1995) 30 marketing directors in the UK focusing on the question: could an added-value chain of any of your core businesses be at risk to somebody perpetrating a 'Cott-Virgin' attack on it? To our surprise, over 90% said yes.

Survival qualities of brand leadership systems

In competing for the future, models of brand leadership will be far more diverse than twentieth-century branders have been accustomed to. Some brand leadership systems will continue to be configured around advertising-led investments. Some, like President's Choice and Cott, will involve investments that are virtually advertising free (at least at the high-risk stage of product launch), which gives huge cost savings. Companies will need to foresee how characteristics of specific product categories will determine what kinds of marketing investments you need for the architecture of your branding system to be fit to lead.

When an industry's product processes reach a plateau of maturity – as appears to be the case in products Cott is targeting – the needs of retailing channels cannot be expected to coincide with those of the manufacturer's brand. Products that are apparently easy to copy are fodder for retailers' own brands.

The opposite business context involves production processes and product categories that are themselves in a fast-moving stage of evolution. In this case the architect of a brand leadership system needs to prioritize:

• making a realistic vision of the future the company's own business case;
• helping stakeholders to see its part in this future; and

- moving consumer aspirations towards new products even if the company has selectively to focus its own business competences and technological partnerships to deliver the new added values.

Consider future markets for multimedia products as the emerging technological pioneers of digital communications space. Companies' right to compete in this environment already involves forging corporately suitable branded joint ventures and so on in the evolutionary race of 'pre-marketing' digital industry. Arguably, brand leadership reputation within the industry as the leading player in particular core competences is currently even more important than consumer reputation in transient product markets (assuming, of course, that you are not doing anything reckless with in-market reputation among consumers).

Alternative perspectives on the value of the IBM brand

How would you evaluate the real worth of the IBM brand today? Unlike the position advocated in Box 12.4, we would not dwell too much on current in-market consumer shares.

Box 12.4   Our tip: no better buy in the world at around this price!

The American magazine *Financial World* has a paid circulation of over 500,000 readers. On 2 August 1994 it reported results of a brand valuation survey carried out by FW staff.

'Here's a shock: The IBM brand name is now worthless. That's just one thing we discovered in valuing 290 of the world's most popular brands.

'Of the 290 brands surveyed, 14 had negative or zero value . . . . In such cases, a competing generic product could have generated high profits on the same level of sales.'

'IBM is in trouble because, while pouring millions into its mainframe business, it neglected the general switch into personal computers. And as PCs became more and more of a commodity, they began selling more and more on price. Now, thanks to low-cost producers like Dell, IBM is a big loser.'

'If nothing else,' says Raymond Perrier of Interbrand 'what brand valuation does is to get marketing and financial people to talk to each other in the same language – the language of brand value, because it involves every part of the business.'

We do not know what to make of a valuation of the IBM brand on the basis of past performance in the personal computer market. If asked to evaluate the IBM brand, we would concentrate on examining the foresight with which the company is leveraging and confirming its pre-marketing reputation as a world class leader of core competences. Would you prefer to partner or to compete against IBM as various multimedia markets evolve? We would bet that IBM will take first pick of partners needed to develop many of these markets of the future.

Taking a fresh look at whether branding processes are as robust as leadership systems

In branding a leadership system which is strategically robust, the architect must concentrate on owning the added-value chain of a company's sphere of business by serving:

- the changing needs of consumers; and
- the dynamic interests of other stakeholders in the company or between the company and its consumer franchise; and
- the evolution of the company's core competences and partnerships as profitable marketplaces change in substance or in focus.

With many new forces of change emerging and interacting with each other, we suggest that all companies need to conduct regular topline reviews into the robustness of their branding processes and overall strategic architecture. Note, for example, how viciously a brand leader's audiences can interact to the detriment of its reputation.

Box 12.5   How great is the knock-on effect of any stakeholder on the relationships of all other stakeholders?

In 1989 we advised branders to think through the magnifying impacts that journalists would increasingly have on world class brands.

'Fame and the high international standards expected of world class brands make them natural candidates for global news

continues

continued

headlines. Like superstars, megabrands own the hallmarks which journalists revel in:

- They have differentiated themselves as the world's number one in something
- They offer stereotyped images which can be used in international copy with few words of introduction to the reader
- As celebrities they are fair play for public scrutiny where the ground rules of the popular media are passive adoration of success and 'rottweiler' investigation into failure. Branded contradictions will prove to be as naggingly self-destructive as human scandals.

World class brands as the most public faces of international corporations are drawing an increasing share of media attention. This trend will accelerate as parochial news barons are being replaced by transnational news merchandisers. All of this puts a premium on a corporate appetite for what-iffing alternative future scenarios in relation to their impacts on brand processes.'

Since making this observation, we wonder whether we understated the case given the following examples.

- 1993: Marlboro receives globally critical publicity over a local pricing manoeuvre. As the shares of an increasing number of brand owners suffer, Wall Street christens the day of the price cut as Marlboro Friday. We doubt whether Marlboro's marketing tactic would have made any global headlines in earlier years before it became the world champion of all brands with a reported valuation of over $30 billion of goodwill.
- 1994: Unilever starts European detergent 'Power' wars. In 1994 Unilever brought PR into its branding mix in a big way offering leading European newspapers exclusives on one of the company's biggest ever new product launches featuring the 'power' of an aluminium detergent catalyst, to be launched simultaneously across Europe as the culmination of a 10-year R&D programme. PR boomerangs back in an even bigger way when you find out in the marketplace that there has been a product slip-up somewhere between R&D and marketing.
- 1994: Intel's overt branding of the chip's importance inside the PC added-value chain was a strongly executed strategy apart from one side-effect. It became too much for IBM which, as manufacturer, customer and rival producer of chips, was prepared to join in a global PR war over a technical and very infrequently experienced imperfection in the Intel Pentium. Part of IBM's purpose in this was to redress the balance of global perceptions as to whose brand contributes most as a quality guarantee to the end-consumer of personal computers, and presumably future products which include computer chips in their ingredients.

Before discussing some exercises for interrogating brands from a variety of strategic perspectives, we present an unusual definition of branding a leadership system. It can be used as a road test to ensure that a company does not have any fundamental organizational barriers to developing a harmonious architecture between strategy and brand process.

Definition of branding a leadership system

Try defining branding as the business process of developing relationships which makes people act, feel, or look smart. Take a mental time-out to get a feeling of why branding, directed in this way, acts like the 'DNA' of competitive business strategy.

(1) Ask yourself about the ways in which company staff act smart, feel smart, or look smart. You will start to develop a list of subtle insights into how companies create and accumulate value. *This is vital when brand's raison d'etre is service-oriented or built on core competences involving accumulation of human know-how.*

(2) Make consumers the subject of these questions and your list will be reflecting components of human value judgements – rational and emotional – which are made by purchasers and end-consumers. This is vital for brands which involve end-user fashions and culturally reinforced consumption beliefs

(3) Next ask yourself who else you should apply these questions to; for example, partners which the company needs in its marketing channels; retailers; sourcing partners; suppliers; journalists; management consultants; business analysts; governments; society; and so on. This is vital for re-examining wider roles of branding such as:

- influence over total added-value chain, for example, getting a fair share of industry surplus;
- gaining geographic privileges, for example, ultimately being the kind of global insider where every country competes to host parts of your organization;
- leveraging goodwill which can spiral virtuously or viciously through media circles and/or across stakeholders.

(4) Finally, ask whether the profit-seeking objectives of a company's business relationships in a specific marketplace are short-term or long-term. Business teams really do need to know where they stand, otherwise internal market championing within an organization can go wildly askew. A notorious example is a bank which makes decisions on which of its businesses are 'core' every six months. A business unit manager newly accorded core status frankly admitted his plan was to put his business unit's logo on every piece of

corporate literature he could get his brand on as a means of staying core. This was apparently the way to build an internal empire irrespective of corporate costs or consumer needs.

Although the smart relationship definition of branding may sound quite simple, we have often found that it can save a lot of time. If a company has no consistent owner of strategic investments and/or no owner of brand processes, it is best to face up to this from the start.

In the rest of this chapter we summarize some precepts (listed below) from new strategy and branding schools of thought which we find useful in brainstorming how to brand corporate leadership systems which exploit foresightful contributions from across the organization. This is not an exhaustive list of the interconnections between strategic thinking and branding process. The strategy architect will need to supplement it with context-specific brainstorming.

- Strategic architecture and foresight
- Keys for the brand architect: banner brands, core competences
- Re-engineering accounting
- The added-value chain and industry surplus: alternative models of branding
- Change mastery
- Why brand?

Strategic architecture and foresight

Foresight, strategic intent and architecture are some of the outstanding contributions to organizational exploration of strategic leadership made by Hamel and Prahalad in *Competing for the future*. The extracts from their book, featured in Box 12.6, have been chosen to give an impression of why a networking spirit of management has an increasingly critical role to play in forming an integrated and continuously actionable corporate strategy.

Box 12.6   New architects for old planners

'Not only must the future be imagined, it must be built; hence our term "strategic architecture". An architect must be capable of

continues

---

continued

dreaming of things not yet created – a cathedral where there is only a dusty plain, or an elegant span across a chasm that hasn't yet been crossed. But an architect must also be capable of producing a blueprint for how to turn the dream into reality. An architect is both a dreamer and a draughtsman. An architect marries art with structural engineering.

'To build a strategic architecture top management must have a point of view on which new benefits or "functionalities" will be offered customers over the next decade or so, on what new competences will be needed to create those benefits, and on how the customer interface will need to change to allow customers to access those benefits most effectively. Strategic architecture is basically a high-level blueprint for the deployment of new functionalities, the acquisition of new competences and the reconfiguring of the interface with the customer.

'Strategic architecture is not a detailed plan. It identifies the major capabilities to be built, but doesn't specify exactly how they are to be built. Try a cartographic analogy: strategic architecture is a high level map of interstate highways, not a detailed map of city streets. It is specific enough to provide a general sense of direction.

'Creating a detailed plan for a 10- or 15-year competitive quest is impossible. Planning assumes a degree of exactitude (which price points, which channels, where to source from, what merchandising strategy, what exact product features) that is impossible to achieve when one looks out beyond the next two or three years. Insisting on such exactitude before embarking on a new strategic direction is a recipe for inertia and incrementalism. Luckily, it is possible to create a broad agenda for functionality deployment and competence acquisition.'

(*Source*: Hamel and Prahalad, 1994)

Hamel and Prahalad stress that the architectural leader determines how the company's business evolves through clarification of strategic intent in ways that everyone in the organization can action. Figure 12.1 lists some of the primary distinctions they aim to harness in crafting a strategic architecture instead of operating strategic planning the way that (Western) companies have often done.

A user's view of how these contrasts play out in organizational practice is summarized in Figure 12.2. It is part of the EIU's research library and was originally compiled by Geoff Dance from his experiences in the late 1980s as vice-president of strategic planning at Colgate-Palmolive, when the firm used the approach of strategic intent to help bring a unity of purpose across its far-flung operations.

Strategic planning	Crafting strategic architecture
Goal:	Goal:
• Incremental improvement in market share and position	• Rewriting industry rules and creating new competitive space
Process:	Process:
• formulaic and ritualistic	• exploratory and open-ended
• existing industry and market structure as the base line	• an understanding of discontinuities and competences in the base line
• industry structure analysis (eg segmentation analysis, competitive benchmarking . . .)	• a search for new functionalities or new ways of delivering traditional functionalities
• tests for fit between resources and plans	• enlarging opportunity horizons; tests for significance/timeliness of new opportunities
• capital budgeting and allocation of resources among competing projects	• development of plans for competence acquisition and migration
• individual businesses as units of analysis	• the corporation as unit of analysis
Resources:	Resources:
• business unit executives	• many managers
• few experts	• the collective wisdom of the company
• staff driven	• line and staff driven

Renewing resource leverage
* building consensus on strategic goals
* specifying precise improvement goals
* emphasizing high-value activities
* fully using the brain of every employee
* accessing resources of partners
* combining skills in new ways
* securing critical complementary resources
* reusing skills and resources
* finding common causes with others
* shielding resources from competitors
* minimizing time to payback

Figure 12.1   Strategic architecture: the new style rules.
(*Source*: Hamel and Prahalad, 1994)

Factor	Before Core Competence Conventional Planning Environment	After Core Competence Strategic Intent Environment
Business Organization	Strategic business unit; decentralized	Centralized; can afford to invest in core competences
Management	Mobile: financial orientation	Experienced in the business, much 'value added'
Focus of Top Management	Attainment of profit/ROI goals; 'denominator management'	Attainment of long-term vision or strategic intent
Visions or Goals	Often in terms of financial results (ROI, profits, shareholder value)	A broader purpose, a general area of business endeavor, to be or to remain the 'best' and the market leader worldwide
Time Span	One to five years, redirected at the beginning of each planning period; rigid short-term plan	Constancy of intent over 10 to 20 years with 'built-in' flexibility of execution
Focus of Strategist	Present resources, competitors and problems: how to react in this environment	The future: a 10 to 20-year vision of what the company is to become (which lies outside the realm of planning). Focus on competition and patterns of industry evolution
Effects of the Process	Acts as a 'feasibility sieve' – strategies are accepted or discarded based on what is 'possible' here and now	Clear about ultimate goal while providing a process within the organization for all to improve short-term actions
Competitive Innovation	Shows the 'strategic fit' between resources and current opportunities or the industry structure	Shows the extreme misfit of 'gaps' between resources and long-term ambitions. Short-term 'themes' to focus efforts of the entire organization to close the gaps
Executional Emphasis	Limited by four basic financial strategies: Invest, hold, harvest, divest	Fostered by: building layers of advantage, searching for loose bricks, changing the terms of engagement, competing through collaboration
Goals for Employees	Economy of scale	Economy of scope as well as scale
Ownership	Often financial-shareholder value/return	To remain the 'best'; to unseat the 'best' worldwide
	Top management formulates strategy; lower levels execute	Top management sets the challenge through the vision; all levels share in setting short-term goals and actions, thereby creating a reciprocal responsibility for competitiveness. Management provides tools and process

Figure 12.2 Contrast: conventional planning vs strategic intent. (*Source:* Geoff Dance, Colgate-Palmolive)

Keys for the brand architect: banner brands

Banner brands serve to connect up the goodwill that a company has won in a variety of its market territories: across nations, across product categories and over time. They are the highest-level brands that a company directs as leadership systems and are therefore most strategically capable of linking up the goodwill of all a company's stakeholders.

A company name – when it is branded – is a banner brand. Thus Sony brands its corporate meaning on every product and in the process offers consumers the ultimate guarantee (connecting the product to all the goodwill that is Sony's) as well as a visible confirmation to the world of its evolving breadth of core competences. Other banner brands evolve in a variety of forms to flag up goodwill which an organization interfaces with multiple marketplaces. For example:

- in Sony's case '-man' connects up a lot of markets with a hip sense of style which goes beyond what Sony by itself conveys;
- in the L'Oréal portfolio of cosmetics, the fashion strategy of Laboratoire Garnier is used as a distinctively different banner for product sub-brands than those that are presented as L'Oréal's own produce.

Banner brands may not have been needed in bygone days when local marketing segmentations were a highly profitable tactic of competitive marketing. But the tide is turning – or has already turned – wherever the primary advantages of business competition are international, or consumers demand that their brands visibly deliver world class quality and value. In the heyday of multinational operations – probably the 1960s and 1970s – organizations like Unilever and Procter & Gamble assigned brand managers to what were effectively thousands of different targeting devices throughout the world. International organizations can no longer profit from such fragmented brand management systems (see Chapter 13). Strategically, these classical brand-manufacturing organizations need to transfer a lot of goodwill residing at local-product levels to higher levels of their brand architectures (for example, by presenting products as sub-brands to suitably developed banner branding systems; see brand benchmarking of Nestlé and Gillette in ThinkPiece 1).

Thoughtful companies need not wait to be struck by a 'future shock of consumerism'. It is already evident that consumers with access to global information prefer branding systems that deliver experiences of the world's best quality and value. They do not need unnecessary local presentations whose additional organizational complexity benefits nobody (apart from providing work for mountains of brand managers). Between branding's local and global extremes, there is a proper branding balance to be practised. In part this involves organized mixing of the best of global and local marketing activities; usually it implies that other organizational processes must also be reconfigured.

To start to (re)focus on this issue in a brainstorming session for your own sphere of business, ask the following questions:

- What new critical success criteria apply to world class marketing? In particular, how do they reverse success criteria where local (geographical, product or business unit, short-term) marketing operations once came first?
- How do banner brands leverage the new critical success criteria? There are some crucial points to note.

Banner brand momentum offers global strategic economies in accommodating new products

A strong banner brand addresses two primary needs of competing in global markets:

- The race to global market. If you have developed a world class product you want to get it to all markets fast, before a competitor copies it and benefits from your innovation.
- Cost to communicate to global market. A new line, sponsored by a banner brand which already has an appropriate global awareness, can incur communications costs which are only marginal. Compare this with the cost of going global with a new brand estimated by advertisers today as involving a cool $1 billion or more.

(It is remarkable that some companies are still embarking on the route of developing new global brands with advertising of very narrowly scoped product domains. Business historians will look back on this as one of the great strategic wastes of the late 20th century.)

Modern consumers look to the company banner behind the brand

Box 12.7   Serve and serve again

'Virtually everything we buy is a combination of product and service. For a brand to be successful, the service element will have to become more dominant.

continues

continued

'This fact in turn will imply, in an era of technological leapfrog, that the company brand will become the main discriminator. That is, consumer's choice of what they buy will depend less on an evaluation of the functional benefits to them of a product or service, but rather more on the assessment of the people in the company behind it, their skills, attitudes, behaviour, design, style, language, greenism, altruism, modes of communication, speed of response, and so on – the whole company culture, in fact.'

(*Source*: Extracted from an article by King, 1991)

Take some phrases, whether from consumer-speak or strategy-speak, and dig deep.

Core competences

Increasingly consumers hunt these out and are prepared to see banner brands for their service competences first and their products second. For example, one of the UK's biggest grocery brands is Sainsbury's merchandising competence encapsulated in the slogan 'everyone's favourite ingredient'. This is portrayed by advertising campaigns featuring celebrities' favourite cooking recipes made out of Sainsbury's banner-branded produce, and retailed through nationwide stores offering a good balance between quality and value for money. Also it is no longer just engineering freaks who talk of Honda as being world class in engine technology. We doubt whether those who have heard this word-of-mouth support can have this impression overwritten by any amount of advertising by a competitive car model which chooses to campaign on this USP.

The company behind the brand

You increasingly hear this phrase used by consumers, either in disappointment when a brand appears disassociated from its maker ('you wonder if there's something wrong with it if they will not put their name on it'), or because of the immediacy of a strong corporate reputation ('if they make it, it must be good').

The highest form of guarantee

In the authors' personal experiences and in research of consumers' anticipations, there is widespread confirmation that consumers tend to get much better service – or indeed compensation – if a banner branded product fails than if products branded at a lower level of goodwill go wrong.

The lifetime relationship

Do not underestimate the human capacity, where delighted by a product, to return for more from the same company. Banner branding makes it easy for customers to become loyal to you if your range of produce is world class. Fragmented branding does not. Consumers sometimes seem to be ahead of manufacturers in deducing that if a company is proud that all its products are world class it will banner brand them. If it is not, it will not.

Box 12.8   Trust and satisfaction

Regarding consumers' relationships with corporate brands, two vital components of successful positive relationships are: **trust** in the brand and consumer **satisfaction** with the brand.

Trust in a brand has been defined by Eric Baron as:

TRUST = (1/RISK)*CREDIBILITY*INTIMCACY

Many corporations act as if only credibility counts. They act as if producing good quality products and services, which gives the corporation a good image for dependability and reliability, is sufficient to gain the consumer's trust. They forget two other critical factors. First, the greater the level of risk consumers perceive, the less likely they are to place their trust in the brand. Second, the degree of intimacy is a measure of a brand's success in creating a personal link with the individual consumer. It means showing that the brand knows the consumer.

SATISFACTION = PROACTIVE + SUPPORTIVE

People want to deal with companies which they see as innovative, ambitious to succeed, ingenious in the development of new ideas and hardworking. In image terms, this can be summarized by the term proactive. However, all this proactivity comes down to aggressive salesmanship unless customers perceive this energy as being as a response to and in support of their needs. So supportiveness communicates to the customer that a company listens and responds appropriately.

(*Source*: Extracted from an article by Blackston, 1993)

Banner branding of multiple stakeholder relationships

As a process which is directed as a unique organizing purpose, the banner brand goes far beyond mere consumer communications of a product's unique selling proposition. The organizing opportunity involves cultivating the goodwill of many audiences at the same time. In Chapter 3 we noted how many audiences McDonald's reached through the act of opening its Moscow business. As another example of relevance to any service industry, consider 'Roverization', a process instigated by Sir Graham Day on his appointment as Chairman of Rover Group in 1986. As authors Hankinson and Cowking (1993) have observed, Day instilled real meaning in the process of moving from a product-orientation to a consumer-orientation with one of his favourite sayings: 'If you love the consumer to death, you can't go far wrong'. One of the key factors in Rover's remarkable progress over the last decade was the adoption of this attitude in everything that Rover people do and represent, from factory workers' enthusiastic pursuit of quality production to Rover dealerships which represent the service interface of Rover with the consumer. The company's two British advertising tag lines are: Above All, it's a Rover; and Above All, we're Rover Dealers. These have become integrated banner meanings for quality expectations associated with Rover's whole range of cars and customer services.

Banner branding of organization-wide involvement

In *World Class Brands*, we wrote:

'Much has been written about Japanese corporate man, his practice of consensus and the importance of the company to his way of life. At work, the Sony man simply wouldn't do anything that was unSony-like. Sony quality becomes a matter of the care you take if you see yourself as part of the Sony family. This is the company working as the brand at its most powerful. The bond between the company and the outside world, through employee-product-service-trade-consumer-society, is communicated, almost ritually, by means of the corporate symbol. Product lines are seldom advertised on Japanese television without clear identification of the corporate symbols which warrants them. Almost subliminally, the Japanese consumer vets new products for their corporate status. Reciprocally, the esteem in which the corporate badge is held throughout the community returns to the pride of the individual employee.'

Research by Hamel and Prahalad confirms that the basic stocks in trade of the banner brand's goodwill are reputation, recognition, affinity and domain. Intuitively, wherever these four communications properties of banner brands are concerned, there should be opportunities for almost every department of the organization to contribute actively to the brand's purpose. Note that purposeful leadership systems are continuously rewarded by higher levels of employee motivation and cooperation than those that are not part of an organization-wide culture or whose goals are couched only in terms of financial goals (see Chapter 14).

Experiences of Brand Chartering have been structured as a call to action for these four communications property rights of banner branding in every department of an organization, and indeed to evolve a form of organization where networking is encouraged and departmental barriers are dissolved. We can search out and accumulate these components of a brand's power at every practical level of brand process: creating, managing, directing. For example, from our opening chapters on creative sub-processes we were particularly concerned with:

- projecting a brand's domain in Chapter 1;
- maximizing a brand's recognition power in Chapter 2;
- reviewing how a brand's reputation and affinity evolves with corporate culture and values in Chapter 3.

Keys for the brand architect: core competences

Core competences are a good strategic concept as long as you are prepared to question iteratively what these really mean for your corporate purpose. Gary Hamel suggests starting with three questions:

- Does this process make a disproportionate contribution to customer value?
- Does it offer the opportunity to build competitive distinction?
- Is it applicable in other businesses, locations or products?

We find that a core competence search has particular values in its own right. It can mix strategic and organizational thinking and implementation in ways that previous corporate procedures have often failed to do. For example, by looking beyond any single departmentalized perspective, the competence quest can be used to facilitate real teamworking in organizations that are not well practised in this. Indeed, it can be a Trojan horse for developing a networking style of organization instead of a departmentalized or hierarchical one.

A new focus for an organization's priorities is cultivated both in the final recognition of a core competence in itself and by sifting through the kind of values that the core competence embodies. Ask teamworkers to hunt out for competence winning values in their own words such as:

- nobody can do this better, cheaper, quicker;
- they create value (that customers can recognize) and fit the company's core business visions;
- they can be flexibly configured into a total market leadership delivery system either through the firm's own resources or in partnership with other firms;

- they are sustainable and differentiated processes which can give their firm unique advantages;
- they accelerate our learning.

It is clear that meaningful core competences often revolve around long-term acquisition of people skills and motivation, such as Honda's engineering; Marks and Spencer's relationships with suppliers and consumers; American Express's transaction systems and evolution of club relationships. Delight in the fact that brand leadership of world class quality and value often depends on organization-wide learning of core competences and the focused sustenance of this through a relevantly exciting vision. Western leaders will need to overrule short-term financial analysts and reinvent the Japanese-style notion that the goodwill invested in a company's brands is the organization's primary commercial licence to promote long-term inspiration over short-term expediency.

Conversely, the thorough and honest appraisal of core competences can help a company to realize that it cannot do without either forming compatible and long-term partnerships with other organizations; or re-engineering processes whose economies 'or ways of working', while once conventionally wise, are foreseen to be redundant in a world class environment or which will become liabilities on foresightful under-standing of trends that are already happening.

In these kinds of ways the hunt for core competences can be viewed as an activity which integrates vital service characteristics such as:

- teamworking
- internal marketing
- the learning company
- employees' motivation to stretch themselves and each other (for example, by recognizing that each is an internal customer of another)
- change leadership.

Master players at the core competence game go on to institutionalize this as an ongoing activity. Japanese companies have invented various ways of doing this. One is Hoshin planning (or literally planning planning) described in Chapter 14.

Another way is to publish a list of forthcoming market opportunities and to get individuals to compete as to which new development network they wish to join. Team leaders become more like football coaches than managers in their motives for transferring people in and out. In part they are aiming to match the best people with the most important projects, but they are also configuring teams so that they can learn from each other. By creating some form of internal bidding system which respects both employees' proven talents and their personal learning choices, business unit directors have an incentive to ensure that their key people are being rewarded with the most interesting challenges. This is a very different dynamic from those old-style Western hierarchies where departments had bosses with their own political agendas. It is not only in London's Downing Street that the prime minister has been known to place a personal priority on ensuring that his seat is beyond the reach of any rising talent.

The discipline of a focused search for core competences can also assist a company's understanding of which stakeholders it must bring on board in branding a leadership system. Hundreds of millions of consumers need not always be the world class marketer's direct focus. Earlier in this chapter we saw that Cott's virtuosity involves supporting the world's leading retailers with products it believes are near to perfection, in the sense that further innovation is superfluous. Conversely, if your sphere of business leadership involves a fast-moving component technology whose evolutionary applications are sustainable and varied, you may foresee brand leadership, as Sharp does with its world of liquid crystal displays (LCDs) in Figure 12.3, as primarily revolving around partnerships formed to develop other companies' markets.

Sharp pioneered commercial applications for LCDs over 20 years ago. The company projects (or brands) its future visions with ambassadorial vigour and enthusiasm. For example, Sharp foresees that the LCD is an ideal candidate for the man-machine interface of the future; it is already being used for both output and input functions. In the car of the future, Sharp foresees drivers checking their positions on an LCD map on the dashboard.

In combination the concepts of banner brands and core competences are likely to take on ever increasing importance in global markets. As Hamel and Prahalad observe, 'being first from concept to market is no longer enough; the real winners are those companies who individually or as players in a partnership are first to global market'. If you extend the development chain backwards you may see that competence acquisition often precedes product concept. So does learning faster than competitors where the heart of future consumer demand actually lies.

We suggest one more way of interpreting Hamel and Prahalad's vision of banner brands as a company's roof and core competences as its floor. The company which Charters both brands and competences empowers teams to focus on the two most productive streams of questions that a learning company can ask. These integrate the capability to add value by brand organization and through strategic implementation. We would bet heavily on any CEO who continuously has both of these up-to-date scripts on hand beating any competitive CEO who does not.

(For further experiences with core competences see ThinkPiece 6.)

Re-engineering accounting: the case for debate

Core competences and banner branding are the kinds of flexible concepts we will all need as witnesses of two revolutions in the environment which face world class companies. These are:

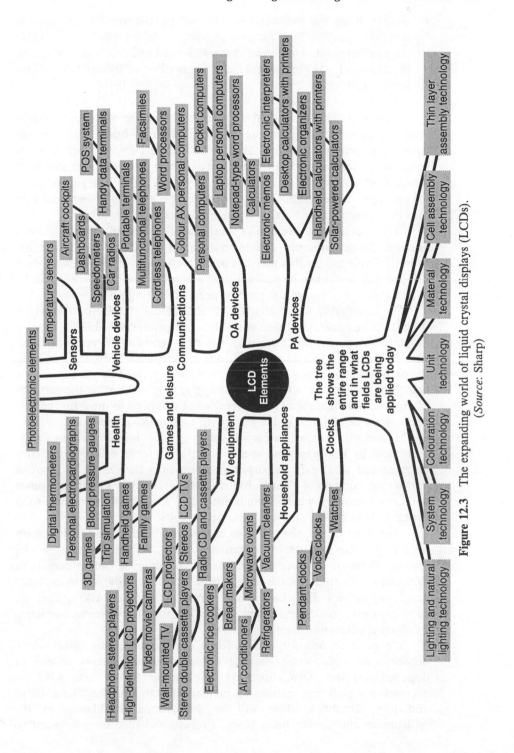

Figure 12.3 The expanding world of liquid crystal displays (LCDs). (*Source*: Sharp)

- change from the industrial era to the post-industrial information era;
- change from competing in markets with hard and fast local borders to the ultimately far greater and freer competition of 'glocal' (global and local) marketing.

Accountants have hindered the great brand changeover from product branding to banner branding by trying to count up brand worth on the basis of proven past performance, when almost every other kind of business person can see that meaningful brand leaders are dynamic assets. Fortunately, accountants have not yet got round to trying to value the other great intangible – core competences – and it is to be hoped that they do not until they have re-engineered their own profession.

Who said that the strength or weaknesses of a world class company's horizons-for-performance could be counted up every three months? Indeed, if you can do this why not audit a company's results every day? Then all the world can be accountants, and all wealth production can be counted precisely and in the process precisely extinguished.

The new reality which Hamel and Prahalad's architectural school is forcing us to confront is that world-leading products will often involve longer development processes than the new products of recent decades. They will require greater combinations of resources brought to bear in the pre-marketing phase than products which survived because they only had to be locally competitive. Increasingly, they will not be the produce of one company's stock of competences but will need to draw on the best networking capabilities which groups of companies could offer.

Henceforth, business units will need to plan how to delight future customers by knowing what specific corporate focus of excellence they leverage and what gaps in corporate know-how they must fill through partnering companies. They should not be isolated counting houses within a company whose foundations and managers' incentives (and careers) stand or fall on every quarter's results.

Like most things, the practices envisioned here sound revolutionary only if you are not already organizing them. A primary reason why leading Japanese and Asian companies continue to outperform their Western counterparts is the longer time horizons they use to evaluate marketing success. They have found forms of financial back-up that are consistent with world class intent and realization. They are not burdened by short-termism and over-accounting.

We have argued for a new form of marketing discipline which networks its added-value learning across the organization instead of departmentalizing itself. Similarly, we argue for a new kind of accountancy skill that teamworks instead of acting as short-term judge and jury. Doubtless there will be professional backlashes as the millennium changeover takes place. Professional luddites who want to talk themselves out of participating in world class business have that right individually. But societies will not thank them if they sacrifice the competitive advantages that nations and regions would otherwise have enjoyed by co-hosting the greatest wealth-producing companies and added-value spheres of business the world will come to know.

In *World Class Brands*, published in 1991, we argued that the greatest threat to world class marketing as companies entered the 1990s was overbranding. Writing in the mid-1990s, we now argue that one of the greatest threats to rising communal prosperity occurs in those regions of the world where companies are subject to the extraordinary false precisions in business thinking caused, directly and indirectly, by over-accounting.

Karl Watkin is a rare species. He is British and an entrepreneur who has made his millions from manufacturing during the recession of the early 1990s. He deserves an audience.

Box 12.9

'Over the past 30 years the UK has systematically destroyed its manufacturing base, losing 50% of its share of world manufacturing trade. Time after time, we have allowed strategic industries to be sold overseas.

'We are involved in a third world war, a war of economies which we are losing. The fact of the matter is business leaders don't know there is a war – the "what war" attitude, born of complacency. We need to change the whole business culture of the UK. Why, for example, do we need 20 times more accountants per head than either Germany or Japan?

'Teamwork amongst members of the EC is a crucial element. We should play to the combined strengths of the team rather than drag it down to the lowest common denominator. Members including the UK have much to learn from the manufacturing strengths of each other. Germany, for example, with its high level of support for manufacturing quality and design. Italy, with its emphasis on its network of subtractors.'

(*Source*: *Business Life*, April 1995)

The added-value chain and industry surplus: alternative models of branding

Who controls the added-value chain and profits most from a sphere of business?

- In diet soft drinks, is it Nutrasweet as patented owner of the lead ingredient? Is it the branded manufacturers of diet drinks? Is it the retailers who present the merchandise to consumers?
- In personal computers, is it the manufacturer of the computer chip? The brander of the computer box which consumers physically interface with? Or the brander of the software which consumers mentally interface with?

There are no easy answers, but recently many branded manufacturers could have benefited from doing more scenario building on the strategic logic of promoting somebody else's branded component without at least securing a partnership deal or favourable terms over the long-run.

This issue will grow more pertinent as technologies and competences continue to overlap. If and when a market's produce promotes itself through the home shopping capabilities of multimedia highways, who other than the media owner will gain from the integration of communications and distribution channels? We can see in Box 12.10 why McKinsey advocates that branders can no longer afford to assess their progress on market share alone.

Box 12.10   Winning the right to brand

Focusing on market share seems to concentrate attention on competing manufacturers, when perhaps the key need today is to understand the total system in which a company operates. Adopting a total system perspective is critical in a world where suppliers and customers are more sophisticated, always seeking to shift the balance of power and gain profit at the expense of each other. Market share, we would therefore argue – if taken as the primary aim – is fundamentally misleading.

In fact, marketing should be measured against market surplus. By market surplus we mean simply the difference between the price paid by the consumer and total industry costs – ie the total profit earned by suppliers, by manufacturers and retailers. This new measure introduces two critical changes in perspectives: it focuses on profit rather than simply on income or revenue (hence capturing the different profitabilities of brands and channels) and it focuses on the total system and the profits earned by everyone within it. It stimulates concentration not

continues

---

continued

only on grabbing share from direct competitors, but by exploring how total industry surplus might be increased (through adding extra value for the consumer), or how industry costs can be cut through increased supply chain efficiency and it focuses attention on whether supplier, manufacturer or retailer is strategically secure in retaining its share of the total profit pie.

The right to brand will tend to go to the company that, other things being equal, meets three criteria:

- it is part of a winning value proposition
- it controls the core assets to deliver the value
- it owns the consumer relationship in the most efficient way.

(*Source*: *Winning the right to brand.* McKinsey, 1994)

Change mastery

Make a list of some of the main trends encountered so far in this chapter:

- The strategic need to focus more of the brand architecture on higher-level branding.
- The interconnections between core competences and the branded delivery of world class quality and value.
- The need to partner as well as compete.
- The need to pre-market and post-market as well as market.

These trends point in one common direction. Major brands and business strategies must now be directed hand-in-hand as unique and total business strategies. In other words, there is no longer an automatic model for operating brands successfully; enduring models of branding will need to be business-strategy specific. In directing brand processes of this nature, everyone in a branded business team should take Kenichi Ohmae's advice to heart (see Box 12.11).

Box 12.11   The discernible sequential pattern in consistently successful, foresighted decision-making

The business domain must be clearly defined.

The forces at work in the business environment must be extrapolated into the future on the basis of cause and effect, and a logical hypothesis on the most likely scenario must be stated simply and succinctly.

Of the many strategic options open to the business, only a few may be chosen. Once the choice is made, people, technology and money must be deployed very boldly and aggressively. By concentrating more resources in support of fewer options, the company gains a bigger edge over its competitors in those businesses and thereby improves its success rate. This is why successful and unsuccessful companies diverge so greatly over time.

The company must pace its strategy according to its resources rather than going all out to achieve too much too soon. It must guard against overreaching itself.

Management must adhere to the basic assumptions underlying its original strategic choice as long as those assumptions hold. But if changed conditions demand it, they must be prepared to change even the basic direction of the business.

(*Source*: Ohmae, 1992)

The branding of leadership systems in the future will need to be a highly proactive process. An enthusiastic appetite for asking 'what if' of change scenarios will be vital. ThinkPiece 3 provides a general list of change factors. You should selectively brainstorm which of these need priority attention in your business environment and foresee how branding processes can take advantage of them.

Why brand?

How do core relationship foci evolve in branding leadership systems? Some of the best training exercises for strategists involve thinking the unthinkable. Occasionally, it will be worth going back to the beginning and asking: do we really need to brand and why?

We suggest two reasons for believing the question 'why brand?' is not as naïve as it might appear. (There are certainly other reasons which you may also brainstorm.)

First, a sea-change is under way in the economies of branding processes which suggest that future efficiencies in mass marketing will pay little respect to the ways and means that have evolved in the 20th century. Do the 2010 test now:

- Do you believe that in 2010 the main consumer medium (and therefore the main economic means of brand communications) will still be television broadcasting (one way, national not international, and disintegrated from buying and communications processes)?
- Will the consumer 'point of sales' environment in 2010 for your sphere of business resemble today's?
- What will be the extremes of world class quality and generic pricing points in your markets?
- What form of organizational network will be your biggest single competitor (allowing for your base scenario on globalization trends in your sphere of business)?

Remember Cott, at least as a warning. We suspect that evolution of the manufacturing-retail hybrid or partnership team has a lot further to go in packaged goods markets. Some of the rifts between manufacturers and retail chains today will look pretty costly when consumers have more global information on what world class quality and value can deliver.

Second, Figure 12.4, based on preliminary research from the University of Bradford's Management Centre, serves to illustrate that branding processes do have different foci. Questions about 'why' and 'on whom' deserve different answers for different products. We need tracking devices to help illuminate areas where brand processes have previously relied on blind leaps of faith.

- Do all managers believe that the purpose of their branding process has the same relative investment foci?
- Are investments of branding resources actually controlled to fit with these relative priorities?
- Do the diamond-shaped forms evolve in different patterns that can be explained by: sphere of business; over time; between winning and losing organizations?
- Are there other identities such as countries and cities which would benefit from a structural clarity of purpose related to which stakeholders' needs they are intent on being closest to and why?

Research of this sort is in its infancy. This is surprising when you consider that we are talking about processes whose evolutionary forms are now quite commonly valued as multi-billion dollar assets. In certain senses they are both the main engines of corporate strategy and the most valuable property rights the world has ever invented.

- Branding translates the social visibility of our products into consumer lifestyles
- Branding can play a key role in motivating a company's staff
- Branding helps us to access joint ventures with the most suitable partners
- Branding commits us to providing customers with a seamless service across our SBUs
- Branding provides the focus for continuously improving the customer offer
- Powerful branding is the critical sucess factor in maintaining the goodwill of a strong network of business partners/suppliers
- Branding policy and corporate vision/mission should feed on each other
- Flexibility (in organizing our capabilities) is critical for our company to live up to our world class image for innovation

+ 40 others...

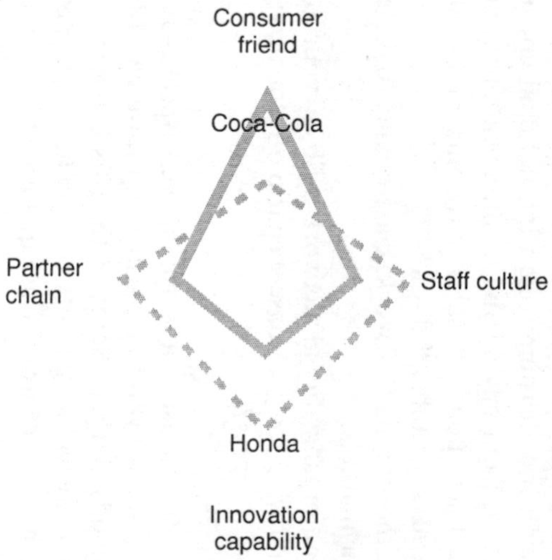

Figure 12.4 Project Diamond: cluster-mapping CEOs' perspectives on branding process.

(*Source:* doctoral research, Janette Sheerman. Contact Dr Sheerman at MELNET http://www.brad.ac.uk/branding/.)

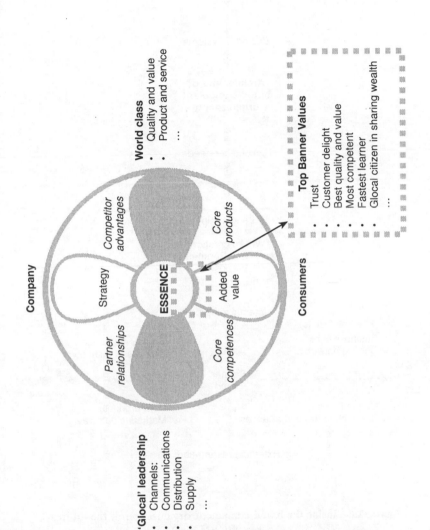

Figure 12.5 The powerful banner brand. (*Source:* WCBN files)

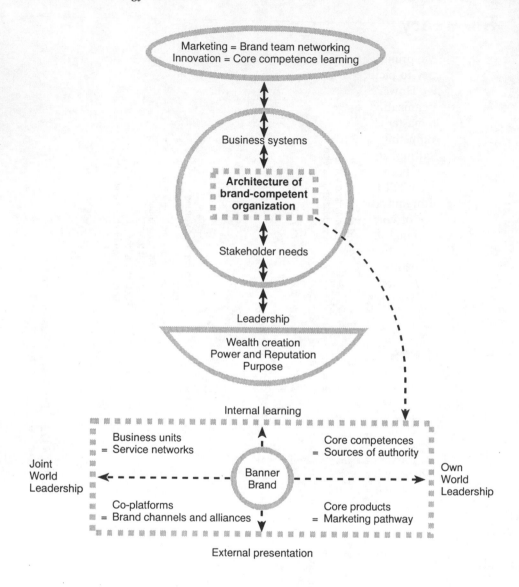

Figure 12.6   Inside the brand competent organization of the future.
(*Source*: WCBN files)

Summary

The primary strategic features of a powerful banner brand are relatively easy to picture (see, for example, Figure 12.5).

However, the supporting corporate architecture – of strategy, organization and brands – requires an increasingly integrated approach to master change and to balance such opposite needs as global and local, competing and partnering. Foresightful exercises and attitudes for crafting strategic architectures and interconnecting brand processes have been discussed in this chapter.

What Peter Drucker once called the only two added-value functions of organizations – marketing and innovation – may in a future vocabulary of corporate leadership be called 'the two added-value schools of thinking'. If you prefer to emphasize a process vocabulary, read 'brand team networking' for marketing, and 'core competence learning' for innovation. The strategic architect must champion appreciation of these values across departments of an old company until the departments disappear and the new company is a network.

References

Blackston, M. (1993). Beyond brand personality. In *Brand Equity and Advertising* (Aaker, D. and Biel, A., eds). LEA Publishers

Freeling, A. (McKinsey). 'Winning the right to brand', speech at the Marketing Forum on the Canberra, 1994

Hamel, G. and Prahalad, C.K. (1994). *Competing for the future*. Harvard: Harvard Business School Press

Hankinson, G. and Cowking, P. (1993). *Branding in action: cases and strategies for profitable brand management*. London: McGraw Hill

Johansson, H., McHugh, P., Pendlebury, J. and Wheeler W. (Coopers & Lybrand) (1993). *Business Process Re-engineering*. New York: Wiley

Kay, J. (1993). *Foundations of corporate success – how business strategies add value*. Oxford: Oxford University Press

King, W. (1991). Brand building in the 1990s, *The Journal of Consumer Marketing*, **8**(4)

Ohmae, K. (1982). *The mind of the strategist – the art of Japanese business*. New York: McGraw Hill

Macrae, C. (1991). *World Class Brands*. Harlow: Addison-Wesley

Porter, M. (1980). *Competitive Strategy*. New York: Free Press

Porter, M. (1985) *Competitive Advantage. New York: Free Press*

Stevenson, M. (1994). The Hired Hand Waves Goodbye, *Canadian Business*, August

13

brand Organization Architect

Strong brands have always been those which have proved themselves capable of taking advantage of change. Until recently, the required level of change seldom had an impact on the form of the organization itself. Now it does.

Keywords can help leaders communicate a change culture. 'Architecture', 'glocalization' and 'team networking' reverberate through Brand Chartering in general, as they must through the mind of the organization architect in particular. However, in this chapter we will use the word globalization more often than glocalization. A semantic reason for this is that globalization is the term on most organizations' minds. A practical reason is that many companies now have a lot to learn about focusing global leadership competences and their organizational connections with brand marketing.

We do not believe that an international business can afford the classic brand management system any more. With hindsight the number of local and fragmented biasses imposed on a company by this organizational system are alarming. Equally, a company courts disaster if it leaps to the opposite extreme of a pure global brand system in which consumers are not permitted to interpret the brand through locally designed identifiers or sub-brands, and local marketers are not encouraged to discuss with headquarters their intuitive feel for and informed monitoring of local competitive conditions.

In this regard, we often advise that pilot Chartering of an intended global brand system should start with draft scripts contributed by teams from both headquarters and local units. We can then work on whatever degree of synthesis is needed. The true art of brand organization concerns balance: globally and locally; medium-term and short-term; partner and competitor; plus any other areas you can think of.

To ensure that top-level brands serve as Unique Organizing Purposes, be prepared to think in general organizational terms as well as those of brand process. For example, in *Competing for the Future* Hamel and Prahalad recommend steering towards such organizational 'syntheses' as:

- collective, to balance centralized and decentralized;
- directed, to balance bureaucratic and empowered;
- benefits-led, to balance technology-led and customer-led;
- core competence, to balance diversified and core business.

This chapter asks you to:

- consider why global branding is likely to require an organizational form which places new emphasis on integration of marketing process and networking culture;
- explore practitioners' visions of top-level organizational meanings of global/corporate (banner) branding;
- review why making changes to brand marketing process – inside and outside an organization – can involve bigger challenges than many companies realize;
- share in principles and practices which can be used to lead the organization beyond classic brand management.

Global branding: facilitating networking process and organizing systems

There have been many attempts in marketing and academic literature to define global branding. Most of them are confusingly precise. They departmentalize a concept whose essence is organizational integration. Distractions involve meaningless agendas (unless you have a vested interest in supplying some fragmented component of branding), such as whether the brand has to have a global advertising campaign before it is accredited with belonging to the global species.

In refining what global brands need to revolve round, we suggest a particular starting point. What are the organizational implications of globalization? Make a list of the most fundamental organizational requirements first. Some examples are given in Box 13.1.

Box 13.1   Mosaic of organization meanings conveyed by globalization

'Globalization means a greater need to coordinate management services over wider expanses of distance and time.'

(Shocker, Srivastava and Ruekert, 1994)

'Globalization has created the new critical success factor of organizational foresight – wherein managers spend less time worrying about how to position the firm in existing "competitive space", and more time creating fundamentally new competitive space.'

(Hamel and Prahalad, 1994)

'Different cultural preferences, international tastes and standards, and business institutions are vestiges of the past . . . I do not advocate the systematic disregard of local or national differences, but a company's sensitivity to such differences does not require that it ignore the possibilities of doing things differently or better.'

(Levitt, 1983)

'The global corporation will serve its key customers in all key markets with equal dedication. Its value system will be universal and apply everywhere. In an information-linked world where consumers, no matter where they live, know which products are the best and cheapest, the power to choose or refuse lies in their hands, not in the back pockets of sleepy, privileged monopolies like the earlier multinationals.'

(Ohmae, 1990)

'The business world is going international rather than insular. So, big regional companies which have grown fairly fat are now finding that they are only seventh in a world where only the top three will survive.'

(©BBC for BUSINESS video, 'Branding – the Marketing Advantage', 1995)

Add to this your simplest conceptual statement of the ingredients of a strong global brand. As an illustration we will try out the following:

STRONG GLOBAL BRAND = organizational network which interfaces two global good marketing fortunes

(1) Marketing system. Owns highly selective competences and team networking culture capable of sustaining world beating integration of:

- product offers; and
- distribution systems through to end-consumers.

(2) Marketing communications: owns categories whose essence can always be represented by an exciting communications platform to the world at large. Examples of 'exciting' are the mass fashion images of the twentieth-century and soon those human needs, eg medicines, where 1:1 information support systems will be most relevant.

Try out your definition (or ours) on, say, four currently strong global brands to decide whether it works for you in balancing architectural simplicity and completeness. An example is given in Box 13.2.

Box 13.2   Four strong global brands

marketing	GILLETTE	NESTLÉ
fortune	razors and male toiletries	family menu of packaged foods
systems	Re-engineered brand marketing architecture: moved from locally operated marketing to global orchestration; for example, satellite advertising campaigns, flagship product sub-brands (such as Sensor)	Structured banner brand and 'global' management system around portfolio of category leaders. These gain from and add to corporate banner of being the world class foods company
	Male fashion theme lifts product category above competitive renderings and fits programme (for example, sports, music TV) material most capable of reaching out to global audiences	Global use of 'Nest' icon connects: • intricately smart execution of a global quality marque • simple theme fitting wide range of category leaders in family-hoarded foods
marketing	WALLS	PAMPERS
fortune	+ Unilever's other ice cream companies	nappies
systems	Globally Unilever has installed more company-owned freezers for distributing ice cream than any rival company	P&G scale & commitment to constant innovation of world class technology relevant to product category

continues

continued		
platform	Ice cream advertising easily communicates: ● impact on hot day ● impulse (immediate self-gratification from one of 'life's little luxuries')	Human emotional high ground: ● spokesbaby works universally as most powerful TV ad announcer ● natural upmarket category – in some developing countries we've seen residents flying in with Pampers instead of 'duty free'!

These are not intended to be comprehensive brand portraits. But they do provide a window for exploring two of the most basic truths of global marketing, even for packaged goods manufacturers' brands (where some commentators argue, misleadingly in our view, that organizations have a lot more time to accommodate globalization forces than nearly global categories such as electronics, cars, fashion goods, and so on).

(1)   Survival of the fittest depends on harmonizing product offers ahead of competitors so that world class standards of quality and value are delivered, and non-essential local variations in every country are streamlined out of business processes.

Box 13.3   Just one Cornetto

Unilever was surprised to discover recently that it was making Cornetto ice creams – supposedly a standardized Euro-product – in 15 different cone shapes.

Only a few years ago, this kind of disparity would have gone unchallenged, and probably unnoticed. However, the focus of the single European market and fiercer competition have forced Unilever to ask whether it needs – or can afford – such diversity. In many cases, the answer is no. Indeed, the company has concluded that its product range has often evolved less in response to vagaries in consumer taste than because each of its traditionally autonomous national subsidiaries had been left to do things in its own way.

(*Source*: *Financial Times*, 28 October 1991)

(2) Global branding is not sustainable just because of world class products; brands represent specifically focused business systems and uniquely economic communications platforms. These are keys to an organization's ability to perpetuate sustainable advantage and communicate added value. Reciprocally, a selective focus is necessary on product categories which have globally brandable characteristics either individually or as a collection of categories.

What made the above categories natural candidates for global branding?

Interestingly, the category territories of Gillette and Nestlé were not originally conceived as profitable global categories. Major reorganization was required to change profitable ways of operating in an era of multi-local marketing which had become inappropriate organizational forms for doing global business. (See ThinkPiece 1, and Nestlé's transformation of Kit Kat later in this chapter)

In the case of babies' nappies, the category fits a global communications theme 'baby-love' as naturally as it fitted local ones. It also has a marketing pattern that fits Procter & Gamble's quintessential operating culture: scope for perpetual product innovation; world scale and ever increasing market size; and consumer need where demonstration of product superiority is integral to branded emotional platform.

In the case of ice cream, ownership of freezer systems has been a competitive advantage (making it difficult for new competitors to gain distribution in as economical a way) that has historically allowed Unilever to move at its own multinational pace even when challenged by more globally fast-run competitors such as Mars. Unilever's organization is apparently most at ease with a pace of change which is relatively slow by some global standards. Typically, Magnum (choc ice stick bar), Cornetto (packaged ice cream cone) and Vienetta (ice cream meringue pudding) have had time to shape up to be three popular reference points of consumer ice cream menus. Merchandised side by side in the company's dedicated freezers, these product flagships are designed to form a strong global collection whether their local corporate name is Walls or Igloo or Ola.

Visioning new organizational meanings in global brands

Box 13.4 contains a selection of quotes, primarily from practitioners, reflecting on how visions of global branding tend to unify strategic leadership meanings and operational practices.

Box 13.4 Global branding: strategic meanings and organizational practices

'The 3M logo is the primary symbolic representation of 3M's people, products and values. It is also the most valuable property we own.'

(3M corporate brochure)

'Global brands are emerging because companies that make and market them are becoming global organizations . . . The brand is a by-product of organizational experience and business systems (which is what we truly leverage rather than some catchy name) . . . So why do organizations, including my own, continue to strive for worldwide brands? I believe that they are rallying points or symbols for the organization itself, for the experience and knowledge it brings to the marketing of soft drinks, cigarettes or beer'

(Michael Jordon, former president of PepsiCo,
now CEO Westinghouse)

'Successful companies will be market-driven by adapting their products to their customers' strategies. New marketing will be orientated towards creating rather than controlling a market; it will be based on developmental education, incremental improvement, and ongoing process rather than simple market-share tactics, raw sales and one-time events. Most important, it will draw on the base of knowledge and experience that exists in the organization.'

(McKenna, 1991)

'The dominant associations that produce a master brand also reflect the core competences of a company. In particular, brand competences are those marketing activities that give a brand meaning and provide its added value to products. To protect brand competences from erosion many brand decisions are now being made by senior managers instead of category managers and brand teams. One result is a much tighter focus on the brand's distinctive competences.'

(Farquhar, Han, Herr and Ijiri, *Marketing Research*, September 1992)

continues

continued

'In the old days, it was up to the worldwide business manager to make the case that a new product was right for local markets. Now it is up to the local manager to demonstrate that it is not going to fly locally. Our expectation is that every new product will find a global market.'
(Anonymous US executive quoted in
Hamel and Prahalad, 1994)

'To compete internationally a company cannot afford to be in the second division of a branded marketplace. Being one of the leaders matters. It gives you the credentials to invest in the latest technology, to continue to attract the best teams of people, to deal as an equal with the trade, to be respected for independent corporate values in the joint ventures you enter . . .'
(Sir Adrian Cadbury quoted in Macrae, 1991)

'To me a global brand is a product or service that has a consistent worldwide identity and a consistent message and a consistency in terms of price, value and performance. Your identity must be clear, credible, and relevant. If you want to own this globally, you are going to have to transport your culture, your vision, your way of doing business to marketplaces where you are dealing with foreign nationals. If you are going to partner with these people, you have to find the right partners, establish the right deal, and if these people are strong and entrepreneurial business people they will want to share your vision and work with you on it.'
(Alan Siegel, chairman of Siegel & Gale, in BBC for
BUSINESS video 'Branding – the Marketing Advantage')

'A global brand is a brand where people around the world share the same vision of that brand.'
(John Hegarty, Bartle Bogle Hegarty, in BBC for
BUSINESS video 'Branding – the Marketing Advantage')

'In effect, Europe marketing (at Häagen-Dazs) works with the local teams in order to be able to meld what is European about the brand with the local components. I have to say it's not always the easiest thing for us because we're all individuals with different opinions. We have a lot of debates before we actually deliver or execute in the

continues

continued

marketplace, but I think that's healthy, actually very positive because it brings people together against the same objective.'

(Claire Watson, European marketing director,
Häagen-Dazs, in © BBC for BUSINESS video
'Branding – the Marketing Advantage')

'As a global brand we have a real challenge in terms of ensuring consistency in our advertising message. We want to come across as a global business as well as making sure that people think of us as a local business. One way we have succeeded in this is our testimonial format of advertising. If you go to Germany or Italy or Japan or Mexico you will see a similar type of advertising on the television. You may not understand the language the person is speaking but the style, the approach, the endorsement from the service establishment featured in any one of those markets comes through and says this is an American Express ad. So we have a global approach to advertising but we really try and localize it which helps us to make it much more relevant to the customer in any given market.'

(Russ Shaw, American Express, in © BBC for BUSINESS
video 'Branding – the Marketing Advantage')

As Box 13.4 demonstrates, it should increasingly be impossible to separate strategic meanings of global brands from organizational practices. We would go further and say that if this separation is apparent in a global brand, then the brand is a weak one.

We can now refine our earlier concept of a global brand. The organization architect may wish to use the following perspective:

'A strong global brand embodies a total organizational system for managing its service raison d'etre (or essence) to its own uniquely orientated advantage wherever primary value forces are foreseen to be global in nature; the weak global brand either does not have such an internal (ie organizational) support system or has one which is not continuously being tuned to its own proactive needs.' Weak global brands either have to be made strong as a matter of urgency, or the free forces of market globalization will kill them off.

(Composite view from International Branding Workshop,
Kuala Lumpur, 1995)

We would urge you to put this into your own words. It should take you to the organizational heart of why strong global branding is a vital leadership endeavour.

Ask yourself and then everyone around you whether an international manufacturing company's processes should be directed towards providing solutions to consumers' needs that are the best quality and value in the world, or whether the extra cost of multiple and fragmented processes should be taken on in the name of local customization. The latter approach has persisted until very recently in various companies – even as other aspects of the business were going global – because built in to marketing departments' functions was the organizational belief that they, on the company's behalf, could profitably manage up to 1,000 different branded devices for targeting local market segments. Divided to conquer, brands often became disconnected enterprises; brand planning often meant internal warfare between managers of brands over allocations of the company's resources of time and money. This is not to argue against suitable local customization, but you do not need – and cannot any longer afford – to divide and multiply your branding process into fragmented brands at every decision-making junction of the brand organization.

The classical brand management system encouraged companies to brand products. Recently it has become far more important to brand businesses instead. Almost every change factor with an influence on the future economies of branding processes points to this trend being irreversible. And, we repeat, you can always sub-brand products for point-of-sales impact.

The integrated characteristics which make global brand processes powerful require continuous organizational learning to be an accomplished player. No decade in business history will be more timely than the 1990s for an exchange of working precepts between companies which are learning about globally integrated brand organization.

There are three stages of evolution of international companies with significant investments in brands.

(1) The company whose business is globalizing but whose brands are operated by local managers.
(2) The company which has formed global brand and business teams but is only a few years into the cultural evolution that this entails.
(3) The company whose global branding process has robustly led its sphere(s) of business over a significant period of time. Ten years is typically a minimum period to demonstrate that the process achieves a suitable balance between such subtle cultural characteristics as consistency, flexibility, quality, being value driven, and being globally and locally meaningful.

In the mid-1990s the evolutionary spread of these companies is as follows:

- Most are at stage 2, having departed from local systems of branding and being intent on discovering a form of world class branding which uniquely suits their corporate purpose. Employees of these companies are usually quite open in admitting that the company is learning anew about brand organization.
- Relatively few are as yet culturally proven at stage 3, and most of these are Japanese.
- Some are stuck at stage 1.

Changing marketing process from a departmental to an organizational function

We would advise you not to underestimate the sizeable and varied organization challenges that are involved in making the change from stage 1 to stage 3. There is a world of difference between fragmented local brands and branding the company so that everyone in the organization's network understands the subtle contributions they can make to its fitness as a glocal competitor (that is global and local in action and in thinking).

Box 13.5 contains a landmark article from *The Economist* of 9 April 1994. It is cited by a wide variety of people as a turning point. The need to go organizationally beyond the classic brand management system is no longer something that business people talk about behind closed doors.

Box 13.5   Death of the brand manager

One year after Marlboro Friday, brands are still alive. But keeping them so may mean killing off the marketing department.

At the start of this year Unilever's British soap arm, Lever Brothers, abolished the job of marketing director. A year earlier, Elida Gibbs, the Anglo-Dutch conglomerate's personal-products division, had done the same. Though the details vary slightly, both companies have squashed together what they used to call the 'marketing' and 'sales' departments, and then reorganized them as a series of 'business groups' focusing on consumer research and product development. Both also set up a separate 'customer development' team, responsible for relations with retailers across all the companies' brands.

continues

---

continued

At Pillsbury, the American food subsidiary of Britain's Grand Metropolitan, the old-style marketing department has been replaced by multi-disciplinary teams, each gathered around a product group, such as pizza snacks. Each team involves managers from production and sales as well as marketing. 'In the past if anything went wrong, Marketing would blame Sales and Sales would blame Operations,' says Paul Walsh, Pillsbury's chief executive. Under the new system, the aim is to make everyone – not just those who might have carried a marketing label – 'the champion of the brand'.

Ever since the 1950s, when they were developed by American manufacturers of fast moving consumer goods (FMCG), marketing departments have revolved round brand managers. Companies such as Procter & Gamble developed brands that divided markets into ever-narrower segments (not just shampoo but anti-dandruff shampoo). Each brand manager was responsible for a single brand in a single country, handling matters such as advertising and packaging. A separate sales department was responsible for getting the products on the shelves.

This time-tested structure is now facing unprecedented questioning in FMCG heartland. A recent study of American consumer goods companies by the Boston Consulting Group found that 90% of those surveyed claimed to have restructured their marketing departments. 'Every company is debating this internally right now, but they are making changes without big announcements,' says Ray Goldberg of the Harvard Business School.

Some of the marketers' woes stem simply from the recession in the rich countries. Most of the so-called FMCG companies have been on a cost-cutting drive. In the past year, Procter & Gamble, Philip Morris and Unilever have all announced plans to close plants and sack thousands of workers. Yet the pains of the FMCG manufacturers are also linked to two more permanent changes in the pattern of shopping. Neither trend is new. Indeed, FMCG firms have spent a decade busily denying that they matter. Only now have they begun to admit that the danger is real.

The first trend is that people increasingly buy goods on price, not because they carry a famous name. This was driven home to advertising men on April 2nd 1993, when Philip Morris announced that it would slash the price of Marlboro cigarettes to defend the much-advertised brand from cheap, generic rivals whose share of America's cigarette market had jumped to 36% from 28% in nine months. 'Marlboro Friday' prompted some analysts to proclaim the death of brands, though it may be that Philip Morris had simply pushed up the price of Marlboro too far. Marlboro's market share had recovered to 27% in December 1993, up from 22% in March 1993 (though Philip Morris's American tobacco profits fell by almost half last year).

continues

continued

The second trend is the shift in power from manufacturers to retailers. Investment in new shops and information technology, and the weakening power of brands, have helped retailers to exploit their proximity to the consumer and dictate terms to their suppliers sales of own-label goods continue to rise, pushing branded goods from the shelves, especially if they are not leaders in their category.

In Britain, own-label sales take 36% of the grocery market. In America, where own-label brands still have a cheaper image, sales of own-label goods at supermarkets rose from 22% of their total grocery sales in 1990 to 23.5% last year. By 2000, the figure will be 27%, according to a study by J.P. Morgan, a New York bank. Even mighty Coca-Cola is not immune. In the past three years, Cott Corporation, which bottles private-label colas, has grabbed about 20% of the cola market in Canada and 2% of America's. Coca-Cola's Canadian operation lost C$143m ($111m) in the year to January and closed half of its 16 plants. Cott is now discussing the launch of an own-label cola in Britain with J. Sainsbury, a supermarket chain.

Although manufacturers continue to scoff at the own-label threat in public, in private they are bending over backwards to be nice to retailers. In 1992 America's Grocery Manufacturers Association joined the Food Marketing Institute (representing the supermarkets) to launch an 'Efficient Consumer Response' programme aimed at cutting costs and eliminating $130 billion in excess inventory carried by food retailers.

Has all this made marketing too important to be left to the marketing department? A recent study by the London branch of Coopers & Lybrand, an accountancy firm, concluded that 'marketing as a discipline is more vital than ever before' but that the marketing department itself is 'critically ill'. And in an essay last year, consultants at McKinsey argued that large marketing departments are 'often a millstone around an organization's neck'. Many companies that have 're-engineered' their production departments are now applying the same process-driven logic to their marketing department.

Even without pressure from retailers, internationalization and the rise of global brands had weakened the autonomy of the traditional national brand manager. To respond better to retailers, Procter & Gamble has switched to 'category' rather than brand management. It now manages all disposable nappies (diapers) or shampoos as a unit, rather than just Pampers or Pantene separately. Both P&G and Unilever are dropping lesser brand names and concentrating on wider 'umbrella' brands.

Meanwhile senior brand managers have taken over control of pricing and promotions from marketing departments. This was prompted, in part, by the mistakes marketing departments made during the recession. In America, brand managers had embarked on a suicidal orgy of trade promotions and coupon offers. Grocery-coupon

continues

continued

redemption doubled between 1985 and 1992, to $4.6 billion, and 60% of breakfast cereals are now bought on promotions. All this merely helped to undermine brand loyalty. And trade promotions encouraged retailers to bunch their orders, playing havoc with manufacturers' production schedules.

In 1991 Procter & Gamble introduced 'everyday low pricing': it has switched to lower stable prices, scaling back promotions. P&G has since gained sales volume, and even – thanks to its cost-cutting efforts – posted higher profits. General Mills, a breakfast-cereal maker, announced a similar move this week. It is cutting list prices and withdrawing 30% of its promotions.

Changes like these are destroying the traditional brand manager's role. But, says Chris Macrae of Coopers & Lybrand, companies have found it easier to pull apart an outdated marketing department than to decide what to put in its place. Even when the reorganizations seem to work (Pillsbury claims that its shake-up has cut product-development time by 30%) they hardly constitute a universal model for how firms should approach marketing.

Instead, FMCG chieftains talk mistily about 'evolution'. Through the mist, two contradictory ideas are emerging. One is that manufacturers must move closer to retailers. 'Marketing departments will have to get rid of their arrogance and go and ask retailers how they can make money together,' argues David Nicol, a campaigner for own-label and a consultant to Cott. That means shared computing and, maybe, shared research. To many manufacturers, this spells an unglorious future as sub-contractors.

An alternative idea is to focus more on the consumer. Don Leemon of the Boston Consulting Group points out that some FMCG have created geographical teams that include people from marketing, sales, finance and production. Their job is to keep retailers happy. It would be better, Mr Leemon says, if they revamped arguably the most important marketing function of all: developing new products that consumers want. That means yet more expensive research and even quicker ways to rush new products to market in the hope of inventing a new Coca-Cola. The odds against that speak for themselves. Marketing's mid-life crisis is far from over.

Amen to the death of the brand manager, but long live the brand. Throughout the history of brand management systems (Low and Fullerton, 1994), since their emergence with manufacturers' investments in the televisual age of mass broadcasting, common organizational problems can be detected.

- **A non-entrepreneurial bias**. Over time managers learn the art of contracting out risk decision-making, for example, by passing the buck to creative suppliers, unless some additional element of the organization's culture specifically overrides this system defect.

- **A tendency towards proliferation of brands**. Since managers like to have their own power bases and both they and their suppliers, from creatives to market researchers, get more work from having more brands.
- **The spawning of complex political power battles** as managers battle over resources for each brand; a problem which companies compound when they fail continuously to ensure essential differentiation between their brands.
- **The value destroying syndrome**. By apparently delegating brand decisions to junior and rotating brand managers, the system starts to lack continuity of know-how and soon becomes the antithesis of a process which engages genuinely innovative teamwork.

Worse still, there have been an extraordinary number of major branding investments this century which have had no strategy to speak of owing to the absence of a strategic owner of the branding process (Urde, 1994).

Our one quibble with *The Economist*'s challenging piece would be with the journalist's reference to evolution of brand organization as 'misty'. It should be anything but. Chieftains cannot buy or sell world class branding competence. They must visibly lead it, dramatizing the need for interpersonal motivations which appeal to both the sprinter's energy and the marathon runner's stamina. They need to balance conflicts of change and to overcome the internal politics which can fester in every department or business unit that interacts with branding to a greater extent than occurs with any other kind of corporate competence.

On which brands should the company selectively focus resources in competing for the future? Why? Who should be in strategic control of these brands? Who contributes most to their practical realization? How will factors associated with world class branding redefine job roles and responsibilities? How can world class branding serve to enhance teamwork, break down departmental barriers and give the brand organization the power of united purpose?

An organization needs to be thoroughly prepared for global marketing. Your people will face new kinds of marketing warfare. Global brand launches will be exposed to heightened forms of interrogation by opinion leaders such as journalists, technical experts and other experts who may also have commercial or amateur vested interests in what world class standards are judged by. All departments of the organization need to know how to coherently service the brand promises you are making. Mistakes, even if they are only perceived to be organizationally clumsy, may pierce the heart of corporate goodwill not just some local loyalty to a product brand. Brainstorm a detailed risk list by extrapolating this paragraph's headlines to the context-specific environment of your marketing organization.

Before leaving this discussion on the dangers of being ill prepared for global marketing, Box 13.6 provides one more journalistic warning of the dimensions of the issue (extracted from the *Financial Times*).

Box 13.6   Global marketing wars in chips and suds

Intel (chips)

- In 1993 the American accountancy magazine, *Financial World*, declared that advertising campaigning on 'Intel Inside' had resulted in the 'year's biggest increase in brand value, up a staggering 107% to $17.8 billion'. Then, a little over a year later, we have Intel CEO Andrew Grove quoted thus: 'This is a very important moment in Intel history as we continue to evolve into a consumer technology company. The company is learning some painful lessons about how to deal with the concerns of the buying public. The Pentium is the most tested microprocessor that has ever been manufactured in the world, but there is no such thing as a perfect microprocessor. We are anxious to have this event behind us, but given this has become a major event in the mass media, involving people who are not accustomed to dealing with sophisticated terms like random divides, operands and floating points, quite frankly we do not know what to do.'

(*Financial Times*, 14 December 1994)

Unilever (suds)

Two retailers' verdicts sum up why Unilever needs to learn fast from its 1994 'Power failures' in European detergents markets:

- 'We know Unilever well. Normally, they are a class act but they don't look too clever now'
- 'The whole detergents sector is drowning in over-claiming and publicity which leaves consumers confused.'

(*Financial Times*, 21 December 1994)

continues

continued

Editorial

1994 will go down as the year when the gloves came off in international businesses. The fact is that markets for goods and services are becoming fiercer as they become global. The year's two great marketing struggles – the 'soap war' over Unilever's Power detergent, and the dispute between Intel and IBM – also offer broader lessons:

- Global marketing is uniquely challenging. Launching a product more or less simultaneously across a continent, or the world, as is increasingly the trend in consumer markets, demands that companies attain a flexibility and focus that few have yet achieved. If something goes wrong in one national market, the chances are that the problem will spread rapidly as Unilever has found to its cost.
- Technology can be a marketing curse as well as a blessing. Companies seize on technological innovations as a unique selling point. Yet unless they subject their new products to the most rigorous testing – looking, as Unilever patently did not in the case of Power detergents, for flaws that a ruthless competitor might expose – the invention may blow up in their faces.
- Even where technology is the only obvious selling point, as with Pentium chips, there is a risk that over-ambitious marketing claims, without adequate information, will simply confuse the consumer. How many PC users had worried about possible flaws in the inner workings of their computers until Intel started trumpeting Pentium? How many users of soap powder noticed that washing damaged their clothes before Power came along?
- Companies like Unilever and P&G have learned in recent months that they can no longer hide behind the carefully manipulated image of their (product) brands; they have to explain themselves and their activities more effectively to consumers and a wider public. Consumers are more demanding than ever before – and competitors more ruthless. The manufacturer that fails to appreciate these facts will go to the wall.

(*Financial Times*, 21 December 1994)

Global brand organization: transition in practice

Evolving Kit Kat as a global brand within Nestlé

In the decade before 1994, Kit Kat's role was part of three different brand organizations.

- Rowntree mark 1: country managers across Europe free to run their own businesses provided objectives for the business unit were met.
- Rowntree mark 2: outside the UK, regional responsibilities amalgamated to be Rowntree Continental Europe.
- Nestlé: a brand organization which by 1994 was close to being glocal thanks to sustained evolutionary efforts for more than a decade.

With hindsight, two points can be made about the part played by Kit Kat within Rowntree. First, the orientation of Rowntree mark 1 was short-termist. Country managers added nothing to the overall organization and Kit Kat was effectively ignored outside the UK. Second, while Rowntree mark 2 was constituted to gain from development of organizational systems and learning across continental Europe, this did not benefit Kit Kat which was launched as a multi-local brand. Kit Kat was a brand which had led chocolate bar and biscuit markets in the UK for many decades, but was in the 1980s being newly launched into Europe. Rowntree's local market research suggested that almost every aspect of Kit Kat's UK brand mix needed customization. The name reminded some Europeans of a cat food brand. The pack's bold red and white colours were regarded as unfamiliar and drew a cold Euro-response. It was said that Kit Kat's UK advertising slogan 'have a break, have a Kit Kat' meant nothing to Europeans, because only the British were lazy enough to institutionalize the tea or coffee break at work.

When Nestlé acquired the Rowntree brands – at the epoch-making price of £2.3 billion – it was not because of the performance which Rowntree had achieved with the brands. It was because of the worth that Nestlé could turn them into. Kit Kat was focused on as a flagship example of how to turn a multi-local brand into a global one.

At Nestlé, brands have strategic elements that are not negotiable across countries. It was decided that 'have a break, have a Kit Kat' was essential to the brand, and henceforth all advertising campaigns had to focus this message. It did not have to be a coffee break. Continental Europeans could, for example, empathize with a car driver being transported mentally by Kit Kat away from the gloom of being caught in a traffic jam. This was an early example of how Nestlé's European managers worked collaboratively to converge Kit Kat's multi-local branding back to a singular European one on all strategic elements of the brand. Five years into this process:

- Kit Kat's sales in continental Europe have more than doubled;
- Kit Kat has become a flagship brand of the Nestlé organization's brand architecture. The linkage of 'Kit Kat from Nestlé' has become strong enough for each brand to add to the other's reputation;
- Kit Kat has evolved from being a learning experience to being proof that Nestlé's business teams have the collaborative know-how to evolve the support systems a global brand needs, even from the most multi-local starting positions. They are thinking and acting glocally to meet a fulfilling marketing challenge.

Drawing more generally from the Kit Kat experience, Nestlé has stated some of its conclusions (for confectionery brands in Europe) as follows.

- 'The future will be in the hands of the mega brands whose manufacturers have understood and managed the "virtuous circle"

CONFECTIONERY'S VIRTUOUS CIRCLE

value for money
+
strong advertising support
=
high volume
=
manufacturing efficiencies

- The future will be in the hands of the lowest cost producer
- Single production units supplying multiple markets require the harmonization of strategy
- It will no longer be valid to argue that "my market is different"
- Kit Kat's experience has shown that there are more significant similarities than differences
- Kit Kat's experience has shown that if managements are prepared to work together towards common goals with common strategies, mutual benefits will be realized'

Figure 13.1 shows some of the challenges which Kit Kat has met across the different branding junctions of Brand Chartering.

The world of Guinness

This global brand is coordinated round the world by a ring of seven regional marketing directors, who meet at least four times a year. After 10 years' experience of knowing each other and having often done each other's jobs, they have managed to refine a working consensus on global strategy for the branding process.

The emergent brand strategy revolves round the idea that every country should have one core reference point for buying into Guinness. This reference point varies from country to country. Guinness aims to provide every country's consumers with the reference to Guinness which is the best competitive quality/value point for their needs.

Thus in Nigeria, which is Guinness's third biggest market, and many other developing countries, 'Extra Stout' is brewed locally and is the consumers' local beer. In confirming this position, Guinness seeks to be unbeatable on price. Local production ensures that no import tax is due. While much of the Guinness identity systems employed in these countries would be recognized by international visitors, the local perception of Guinness has little or nothing to do with Ireland.

In most of Europe and the USA another image is studiously cultivated to support Guinness's premium positioning. Guinness is Ireland's leading brand. More than that the company is delighted to franchise the Irish drinking experience and bonhomie wherever demand can be created. It owns a company that will build an Irish pub for entrepreneur and would-be landlords around the world. As well as offering a choice of five typical 'Irish-designer pub formats', Guinness provides the brand paraphernalia and recruitment services placing Irish bar staff (and access to Irish musicians, including Irish bands on tours which Guinness orchestrates).

The Irish card provides global staging opportunities for the country's leading brand ambassador. Thus Guinness staged 6,000 parties on nights when Jack Charlton's team were playing in the 1994 football World Cup, as well as being closely associated with Big Jack's press conferences. Guinness regarded the relaying of this sporting celebration around the world as 'a great event for pulling our organization and our people together'.

Another PR platform, which puts Guinness in the news just before the festive season, is the year's *Guinness Book of Records*. This shows how a book can turn out to be a world class sponsorship platform.

The support systems for premium quality Guinness are probably unrivalled anywhere in the world of serving a drinking experience. Pub staff are educated in rituals for serving Guinness, and rewarded with mystery shopper competitions – where market researchers are employed to observe the perfect pint of Guiness which bartenders serve. The Guinness which is exported around the world is subject to elaborate quality tests to ensure consistency of taste.

Guinness's strategy also involves offering a complementary portfolio to most of the world's brewers of blond lager. Guinness aims to be the ideal partner with a major brand in every distinct sector. So Guinness stout is accompanied by the red beer Kilkenny from Guinness, and non-alcoholic lagers such as Kaliber by Guinness.

ESSENCE	IDENTITY	HERITAGE/FRIENDSHIP	FUTURE NEWS	OTHER CREATIVE
Psychology of 'Have a break, have a Kit Kat' is its core (global branding property (not the product *per se*)	The opportunity to persevere and become a forceful and inimitable global eccentric is real and more appropriate than promoting an abundance of locally mutated forms 'Break' is an universal 'calendar of mind' identifier	If a brand has led a highly competitive market for many decades, it is likely to comprise some strategic elements which should be non-negotiable in any international translation of the brand		
MASTERBRIEFING	QUALITY AND	FLOW/TEAM VALUE	UMBRELLA CONNECTIONS	OTHER MANAGE
Kit Kat: evolution of many aspects of mix needed direct and evolutionary coordination to turn local leader into Eurobrand	In the long term the costs of not turning Kit Kat European would probably have made the product too costly for everyone	'It was necessary to recognize and formalize interdependence' Examples: • country managers to work together • lead ad agency had to be appointed to focus core meaning • market researchers had to be taught to put global interpretation before local accentuation		

Figure 13.1   Kit Kat: why going glocal is the ultimate competitive advantage of branding; and why getting there is so hard organizationally

BRAND ARCHITECT	STRATEGY ARCHITECT	ORGANIZATION ARCHITECT	DRAMA OF LEADERSHIP	OTHER DIRECT
As global brands Nestlé and Kit Kat add to each other's reputations at corporate and product levels	Worth of brand was in its competitive future as a global, not its past performance as a local Combination of brand scale and personality make it very unlikely that own-label could ever beat this brand 'The future (of confectionery) will be in the hands of megabrands whose manufacturers have understood and managed the 'virtuous circle' (of world class quality and value)	• mix elements/production had to be progressively harmonized Central strategic ownership with negotiable implementation essential to developing Kit Kat as successful Eurobrand Rowntree's experience with Kit Kat suggest that this company was not in a fit organizational form to compete in a globalizing business world	The success of Kit Kat has provided Nestlé organization with inspiration that act global and local is the company's future of branding	

Figure 13.1 continued.

Guinness has an unquenchable appetite for vital strands of branding such as:

- innovation, for example, draft in the can;
- sampling and other trial inducing activities;
- visible point-of-sales material, placing the unique appearances of its flagship products centre stage wherever they are consumed.

Integrated presentation of the mix is taken seriously globally and locally. Guinness people keep at their fingertips a comprehensive bible on every major branding process (called the brand equity benchmark).

Seven marketing directors with ultimate responsibility for the branding world of Guinness is – we are told – close to being the ideal size for Guinness's top marketing team. With fewer it would be hard to keep locally in touch with the world; with more it would be hard to forge the collaborative instinct of what strategically important details need continuous circulation to be within fingertip reach of everyone who contributes to the brands.

A group financial director asked why recent global launches seem to have been relatively poor performers. The marketing team was able to show that in fact every meaningful worldwide business in Guinness history had taken 10 years to cultivate, and recent launches were just as much on track as any historical initiative. The lesson that world brand businesses can take 10 years to substantiate is one many other organizations never get the opportunity to learn. They are beaten by short-term pressures and the vicious circle of lack of marketing confidence that comes from:

- diffuse and disorganized records on the historical drivers of their brands;
- lack of stability among pivotal marketing personnel and the lost learning opportunities associated with such branding disorganization;
- an organizational culture that fails actively to support medium-term brand developments that are vital to leading the quality standard.

All that Guinness's marketing people would claim is:

- the bottom line is that our brand organization is working for us;
- Guinness is the most profitable brewer per hectolitre in the world;
- globalization forces mean that there is lots more growth potential to come on tap for Guinness.

The new horizons of branding at SmithKline Beecham

SmithKline and Beecham merged to be a worldwide company. Outside ethical pharmaceuticals, the new organization elected to focus on six consumer branded categories. These are the principles that they say 'we' at Smithkline Beecham are putting into practice.

- Our purpose in each category is to focus on innovations with worldwide potential. Gone are the days when innovation was locally driven and meant little more than a 10th flavour for a Ribena drink or a 15th perfume for Bodymist deodorant.
- We need few failures; real competitive advantages; and real returns from investments whether these are R&D or media.
  - Our goal is to maximize resources on a global basis and so gain competitive advantage.
  - Our attitude has become more long term; more oriented to the big idea or project.
  - Designated key categories are: oral health, nutritional drinks and over-the-counter pharmaceuticals (gastro/intestinal, upper respiratory, dermatology, analgesics).

- Members of our category innovation teams are multifunctional, drawn from around the world. They are charged with searching out and conceptualizing the best innovation ideas from across the organization. These are then independently evaluated, and we aim to make the whole process transparent to all involved. We communicate our criteria for selecting new product developments within categories as simply as possible. For example, this two by two matrix represents our lead criteria in prioritizing practical business opportunities.

	commercial potential	
	LOW	HIGH
HIGH	Bread & Butter	Pearls
LOW	White Elephants	Oysters

Likelihood of technological success

- Obviously we aim to avoid White Elephants and push up Oysters into Pearls wherever possible. We are focusing on time to develop, R&D costs, competitive scenarios, pricing, positioning, market growth, product life cycle.
- We want to avoid the brand management syndrome; it was a real menace with everyone wanting to make their mark in the two years they were assigned to a particular brand. And we want to move faster than competitors on winning ideas.
- On 'go' projects, we provide local markets with a complete 'franchise' kit on how to market; changes can be made but only with proven

evidence. Since adopting Category Management, international consumer research has shown that strong concepts generate much more commonality of consumer appeal than had previously been realized.

- We insist that winning concepts are rolled round the world fast, for example, in under one year rather than the five years it used to take. The way we have organized Category Management aligns people to feel part of world teams that win.
- We are organizing Category Management so that everybody pulls together globally and locally. This did not happen before.

When an organization is committed to international teamworking, it needs to be sure that all managers adopt the same ways of working. The extract in Box 13.7 comes from the EIU's *Transforming the global corporation*.

Box 13.7   Nine Statements of Leadership Practices

SmithKline Beecham articulates precisely what it expects of leadership within the organization. The company's Nine Statements of Leadership Practices are well known within the industry. SKB managers know fully well they are expected to do the following:

(1) Find opportunities for constantly challenging and improving his/her personal performance

(2) Work with his/her people individually and as a team to determine new targets and to develop programmes to achieve these higher standards of performance

(3) Identify and continuously implement improved ways to anticipate, serve and satisfy internal and external customer needs

(4) Stress the importance of developing and implementing more effective and efficient ways to improve SKB procedures, products and services through quality analysis

(5) Initiate and display a willingness to change in order to obtain and sustain a competitive advantage

(6) Reward and celebrate significant creative achievements

(7) Develop and appoint high-performing and high-potential people to key positions

(8) Help all employees achieve their full potential by matching talents with the jobs to be done and through quality performance feedback and coaching

(9) Communicate with all constituents openly, honestly, interactively and on a timely basis

(*Source*: EIU Report *Transforming the global corporation*)

Lessons from being less than global and local in thought and action

There are many pitfalls to avoid on the way to going global with your branding process. Today's 'organizing architects' look for lessons in other company's mistakes. But they realize it is essential to globalize now – in spite of all the lurking dangers – because the spectator never wins a competition.

Here are some practical pitfalls which have been experienced by companies embarking on global branding processes. For obvious reasons we have disguised our sources.

- Some companies race into a global branding process so fast that they forget to integrate the global elements of their brands' communications and fail to encourage their local marketers to maintain the local vitality of the brand mix. For example, a London advertising agency was commissioned to develop a global advertising campaign, while a New York designer was commissioned to develop the brand's packaging. Problems arose in consumers' recognition and understanding of this brand's presentation, because neither creative agency had been shown the other's brief. At a local level, the need in many countries for extensive point-of-sales materials was not only overlooked by a company's headquarters marketing strategists, but also subsequently discouraged in spite of strong representation by local marketers that the brand's impact would be adversely effected.

- A company developed a novel way of extending a brand's range in the USA, which relied heavily on PR, word-of-mouth and building up a fashionable reputation for frequent additions to the range. Within this mix, the role of advertising was to generate PR, advertorials, word-of-mouth and direct response mechanisms around the appearance of each new line. After two years of hard and intensive marketing, the brand's success in the USA was such that (re)launch of the business was made a top global priority across the company. Unfortunately, this was despatched to marketers around the world with very little supporting information on how to maintain PR and word-of-mouth appeal. Instead of producing 'a franchise kit' of the US experience – most of which had a generalizable fashion appeal – countries were largely left to themselves to create, interact with and sustain PR, consumer word-of-mouth and database marketing. This was not something that many of the company's local marketers had ever done before and consequently the brand was underperforming in many local markets.

- A company informed its R&D people of a new product development (NPD) policy: future products must have Europe-wide markets. However, the performance objectives of local business units were left unaltered. R&D people were not empowered to gain the simultaneous commitment of all local marketers to refining NPD concepts or to buy into a consensus of what quality/value points particular brands should stand for. Very little real innovation has resulted in the three years since the European product policy was instigated.

Other R&D people report why the kind of teamworking that gurus stress is vital for NPD often does not sit comfortably with the way people in a company organize themselves:

- 'R&D information is released to people in our company on a "need-to-know basis". The last people with whom I would regularly network are the brand managers. Many of them are only here for two years, and they will move on to a competitor next.'
- 'Almost all really useful innovations for our industry have been invented by independent research laboratories. Leading-edge R&D is too specialized these days for any manufacturer to expect to create much of it. If our company really wanted to turn R&D into a competitive advantage, it should partner world class companies in non-competitive industries, for example cement, and sponsor world class research institutes in specifically designated areas where leading-edge innovations would be an advantage to all of the corporate partners.'

Box 13.8   Straight talk

'We're all familiar with the innovation blockers: top management isolation, conformism, bureaucracy, fear of change, short-term vision. They're particularly prevalent in large, well-established, structured 'we-know-it-all' organizations like mine. Most of us work for companies that innovate all the time. But most of these innovations are small, predictable, imitative and won't last.'

(*Source*: Andrew Seth while managing director Lever Brothers UK and member of Lever Europe board, November 1994)

Is your system of brand organization proactive?

The acid test for any brand organization is to make a shortlist of change factors which will impact branding across your sphere of business over the next 10 years. These may include globalization, new and fragmented media, innovation partnerships, and so on (see ThinkPiece 3 for a selection). Now ask for each change factor: does the way we organize our branding process help everyone to respond proactively to change?

With the benefit of hindsight, we can look back at many local branding processes and see how inertia ridden they often were. Not only did different organizational departments have different perspectives on what branding did, but many people also had vested interests in preserving the status quo:

- Brand managers, advertising and other creative suppliers, and market researchers gained from 'the more brands the better syndrome'. Their job empires depended on it.
- Financial directors were persuaded that brands should be valued according to balance sheet criteria, that is proven past performance.
- Perhaps marketing directors should have fought the opposite corner 'that brands are actually worth no more than the future advantages invested in them'. But in practice corporate operating environments have stacked up ever increasing short-term pressures against making a stand for the future (see Box 13.9).
- Country or strategic business unit managers have often been charged to 'do your own thing provided you meet your revenue targets'.
- Brand managers have often wanted to make their individual mark while on particular two-year tours of duty.
- Sales directors and sales people have often been left with the impression that they are out there doing the day-to-day fire fighting; and the conflicting signals coming from brand managers and marketers just add to the smoke.
- Strategists, economists, quality controllers and product innovators did not appear to recognize the organizational interconnections between their disciplines and brand processes. They may often have felt that the brand was about advertising, and therefore failed to appreciate that a brand's orientation should positively interact with the whole of the business process.

Box 13.9 Increasing patterns of short-term influence over 1980s – 90s organizations

- Ad hoc management consultants (and their products selling instant results: benchmarking, re-engineering, downsizing, activity-based costing).
- City analyst pressures (punter capitalists on stocks, for example Survey on capitalism, Rupert Pennant-Rea, *The Economist*, 5 May 1990; short-term reward schemes for CEOs; ever-increasing analytic focus on last three months' performance).
- IT models (more data on measuring the recent past).
- Appraisal/reward schemes geared only to recent sales.
- A corporate belief system biased towards competitive response, and away from leadership of the company's own standards.

At some stage when evolving away from the politics of local brand processes, shock tactics may be necessary for an organization to demonstrate that it is serious about change management and re-engineering its brand processes. But we are keen to stress that teamwork stems from the architect's leadership ability to refocus attitudes and unite people round competence-building goals. Recognize that old branding systems were at fault in being organizationally divisive in a myriad of different ways. Get key people from functions together in pairs, for example, marketing and finance, and use humour to start up a fresh debate on how each other's talents can support brand organization. Changing a brand organization is a cultural matter. Finding the right kind of human touch to launch this promotional enterprise internally requires as much creativity as developing a great advertising campaign. (See also Chapter 14.)

Above all, organization architects should recognize that all corporate decision-making involves continuing balancing acts between growing businesses up and cutting them down. But leading brand organizations are dedicated to the spirit of actively exploring every valuable means of growing and evolving before they think of cutting. Directed and practised in this way, the branding of leadership systems is the most vital organizational competence of all. It depends on the foresight and networking skills which the organization architect musters across the company and is intent on enhancing through the perpetual emotion of branding.

Experience the raw, gut-wrenching drama of human conflict through ACCOUNTING

Preparing to do battle   The thrill of victory   The agony of defeat

Leo Burnett Brand Consultancy

Understanding Marketing People

People enter the marketing profession after they realize they have grown up without any particular skills

I say we should listen to the customers and give them what they want

They want better products for free

Oh... then let's just sell them what we've got and call it a strategy

Leo Burnett Brand Consultancy

Figure 13.2   (*Source*: Leo Burnett Brand Consultancy)

Summary

Strong brands take advantage of change, including the structural change in the ways that the marketing process is organized in a new informational world of glocal partnerships and competition. Making the changeover to glocal marketing requires that the organizing architect:

* evolves a networking form of organization;
* foresees the full nature of the challenges this involves.

We have illustrated the risks involved and examined detailed experiences of companies whose organization of global marketing is being transformed.

Doing nothing is the biggest risk of all. The way that twentieth-century marketing functions were executed to target local markets does not provide a fit organizational form for a future where the brand organization's processes – as systems and communications platforms – must be capable of delivering world class quality and value, globally and locally.

In parallel, the corporate architect must foresee how to leverage changes relating to internal company learning, information systems, external media and glocal stakeholder relationships.

Top level banner brands embody Unique Oganizing Purposes; they determine what organizational goals and strategic visions are realizable and vice versa. Direction given from this integrated perspective is what makes global branding succeed.

In the future, the claim that branding is a corporate core competence will mean that two organizational feedback loops are continuously working to perpetuate a company's leadership of a sphere of business.

* Banner brands must shine out from a company's brand architecture as reference points of the total brand equity and leadership.
* Banner brands as unique organizing purposes must be aligned with the company's ways of focusing core competences. Through this means, everything that employees learn and action can serve to confirm the company's right to lead.

(See also ThinkPiece 4 on 'flexible' companies.)

References

Hamel, G. and Prahalad, C.K. (1994). *Competing for the future*. Harvard: Harvard Business School Press

Levitt, T. (1983). The Globalisation of markets, *Harvard Business Review*, May/June

Low, G. and Fullerton, R. (1994). Brands, brand management and the brand management system: a critical-historical evaluation, *Journal of Marketing Research*, May

McKenna, R. (1991). Marketing is everything. *Harvard Business Review*, Jan/Feb

Ohmae, K. (1990). *The borderless world*. London: Collins

Shocker, A., Srivastava, R. and Ruekert, R. (1994). Challenges and opportunities facing brand management, *Journal of Marketing Research*, May

Urde, M. (1994). Brand orientation – a strategy for survival, *Journal of Consumer Marketing*, **11**(3)

14

brand Drama of Leadership

In a Japanese internal communications process called Hoshin Planning, the CEO regularly (for example annually) writes to all employees (or team leaders) clarifying corporate strategic intent and issuing the next improvement challenge that the company must implement. Employees (or team leaders) are required to reply in terms of what contributions they will make to this challenge and how performance improvements can best be measured. Note that a reply such as 'none' is acceptable if employee and CEO agree, but the communications gap needs to be narrowed if their conception of potential actions varies. The Japanese CEO delights in identifying communications gaps as learning opportunities for improving organizational alignment and not as faults of individuals.

The Japanese say that great challenges concentrate the organization's minds wonderfully. Learning companies need the best of teams and the best of individuals. A culture which gets the best of one but not the other will not serve to lead.

Why not go one better than the Japanese? Do something similar to what they do with core competences, but script it for brands too. Thus you could have a customer leading service culture; a lot of flexibility in focusing learning; and an organization in which everyone is aligned to prioritized leadership goals and confident enough to keep on asking questions.

If you want this it must be promoted by cross-functional leaders at the top of the organization, starting with the CEO. But then the Japanese say 'leadership is about showing people what they are achieving and what they can achieve'. So Charterers say 'how can we dramatize brand and corporate leadership as inseparable allies in the art of propagating added value purpose?'

Box 14.1   A Declaration of Interdependence for Brand Leadership

- WE believe that strong brand processes are never managed, always led.

- WE believe that meaningful brands are service visions whose purpose is to accelerate the future.

- WE believe that brands are often a company's only commercial licence to invest in medium-term foresight.

- WE believe that brands have rights. Leaders must develop proactive organizational cultures specific to a brand's needs.

- WE believe that Brand Chartering can keep the brand's accumulation of service know-how top of mind across the business team.

- WE believe that stewardship of corporate reputation must be culturally embedded as the responsibility of one and all.

- WE believe that the entirety of a company's brand architecture is appropriately thought of as a megaprocess, that is one which interconnects all of the company's other core business processes.

- WE believe that future wealth creation resides in strong brand leadership.

We believe that the CEO in every company whose main assets are brands should have a Declaration of Interdependence. He or she should tailor it to the company, and then ensure it is enacted throughout the organization. This declaration must be ripe for its time and that future horizon which the CEO sees as his or her responsibility to direct. Our Declaration is meant to be ripe just in time for the new millennium.

So where do the inspirations of our Declaration come from? And what meanings need to be read between the lines of the Declaration of Interdependence?

Strong brands are never managed, always led

Look at any period of sustained brand growth and you will see that there was strong organizational leadership. The following brand benchmarking examples are explored in ThinkPiece 1:

- Gillette's re-engineering of the marketing process which now propagates its global lifestyle image as 'the best a man can get'.
- British Airways' renewed service mission to be the world's favourite.
- Coca-Cola's drive during the second quarter of the 20th century to be 'within arm's reach of desire' around the globe. As part of this process, its successful advocacy to the USA's War Office that Coke should be adopted as the GI's mascot for the duration of the second world war.
- Sony's determination to overrule market research findings that the Walkman did not have a market.
- Shiseido's enduring perspective regarding cultivation of 'glocal' beauty.

Strong leaders propagate their foresight for the brand, make symbolic leadership gestures and are prepared to involve their businesses in acts of world statesmanship that go beyond the short term, and therefore require the total organizational commitment that only the CEO can lead. Consider a symbolic and a statesmanship episode in the life of McDonald's (Box 14.2).

Box 14.2 Ray Kroc, founder of McDonald's franchising, demonstrating his shared vision of cleanliness

'On his way back to the office from an important lunch in the best place in town, Ray Kroc asked his driver to pass through several McDonald's parking lots. In one parking lot he spots papers caught up in the windscreen of shrubs along the outer fence. He goes to the nearest payphone and calls the office, gets the name of the local manager, and calls the manager to offer to help him pick up the trash in the parking lot. Both Ray Kroc, the owner of the McDonald's chain (in his expensive business suit), and the young manager of the

continues

continued

store meet in the parking lot and get on their hands and knees to pick up the paper.'

This story is told and retold thousands of times within McDonald's to emphasize the importance of the shared vision of cleanliness. In short your actions in living your vision will motivate your employees to use the vision.

(*Source*: Belasco, 1990)

The costs and the time-consuming process of meaningful global PR can be immense. Are we getting to the stage where globally branded companies, like nations, may best be served by two sorts of governing bodies: executive managers in charge of business operations and elder statesmen with the status and the time to engage in ambassadorial missions for the company? Consider how *The Economist* observed McDonald's Moscow opening in Box 14.3.

Box 14.3   McDonald's: nature of organizational investment of being an ambassador to Moscow

True the symbolism is irresistible: the epitome of capitalist consumerism come to the citadel of world communism. But note the extraordinary lengths to which McDonald's has had to go to open its Moscow outlet.

Although the food and drink served by the Moscow restaurant are indistinguishable from that served in McDonald's restaurants from Peoria to Tokyo, the company has had to alter radically the way it does business in order to achieve this feat. Rather than buying from local suppliers, as it does everywhere else, it has been forced to integrate vertically through the local food industry on a heroic scale, importing potato seeds and bull semen and indirectly managing dairy farms, cattle ranches and vegetable plots. It has had to construct the world's largest food processing plant, the size of five soccer pitches, at a cost of $40m. The restaurant itself cost a mere $4.5m. . . .

Worse it has taken McDonald's 14 years of relentless effort to open its first restaurant. In 1976 the company began talks aimed at opening a restaurant at the 1980 Olympic Games in Moscow. That

continues

continued

prospect died when western countries boycotted the games after the Soviet Union's invasion of Afghanistan. McDonald's hopes only managed to survive by a fluke; the Moscow McDonald's is being operated not by the American parent but by its Canadian subsidiary. When the deal died in 1980, the Soviet ambassador in Canada was Mr Alexander Yakovlev, a would-be reformer whom Leonid Brezhnev had dispatched into diplomatic exile. Mr Yakovlev told Mr George Cohon, the head of the Canadian operation: 'Don't lose heart. At the moment this is ideologically impossible. One day you will be able to do it.' Patience was to have its reward when Mr Yakovlev became a sidekick of Mr Mikhail Gorbachev and, for a time, one of the most influential figures in the Soviet Union.

Restarted in earnest after Russia's first joint-venture law in 1987, negotiations for this one $50m deal have taken about half of Mr Cohon's time, a huge commitment for a man running a $1 billion-a-year business. If Soviet leaders think that all chief executives can spend this amount of time on a single deal, they will be sorely disappointed.'

(*Source*: *The Economist*, 3 February 1990)

Meaningful brands are service visions for accelerating the future

Leo Burnett put the essence of service leadership brilliantly. 'When you reach for the stars you may not quite get one, but you won't come up with a handful of mud either.' Branding offers a unique process for facilitating this. Leaders employ the high visibility of branding to reach for the stars with their company's services in front of all their publics.

Two ramifications of this should not be underestimated by those wanting to exploit the breadth and depth of meanings communicated by strong brand processes:

- All brands are services
- The leader's purpose of investing in communications is to accelerate the future

Brands are services

Even when a brand is manifest by some product of the moment, the consumer's own buying agenda is there to be served. You can reinterpret

'Shall I buy this product?' as 'Will this brand meet my need?' People make purchases to solve problems which they prioritize as instantaneously at the top of their personal agendas.

The brander's service purpose here is primarily twofold:

- *to guarantee* – continuously to do everything in the company's power to ensure the purchaser will not be disappointed, and will indeed be delighted;
- *to befriend* – to be constantly perceived as serving the human need in the most friendly way by integrating product functions and the human interpretations which are most relevant to the roles people play in purchasing a brand, consuming it, or witnessing consumption of it. In other words: fulfilling needs

If a Brand Charter ensures that everyone who serves a business shares the same purchasing agenda as the brand's most loyal consumers, a valuable job will have been done. As Judy Lannon says: 'think of brands as consumers' editors of choice' and you will start to feel what great service responsibilities pass through your reporting desk.

Box 14.4   IKEA's leaders: meet the coach, not the boss

IKEA's no-frills management seeks to coach, not boss. Talking with Goran Carstedt, president and CEO of IKEA North America, is to experience management by realism. His office is in a sprawling IKEA store in Pennsylvania, so that he can stay close to employees, customers and products of the world's largest retailer of home furnishings. Mr Carstedt greets guests in an open-plan office, and thinks he is failing at his job if he senses employees are nervous when he eats in the IKEA cafeteria or walks around the store.

For all its financial success, Mr Carstedt stresses that IKEA's philosophy remains low cost, high value – with management practising what it preaches in its everyday dealings. 'The mission for IKEA founded several decades ago by Ingvar Kamprad is "to create a better everyday life for the majority of the people" by offering high quality furnishings to the masses. 'Much is made of the fact that at IKEA there are few titles, no executive parking spaces, and business travel is economy-class airfares and $60 per-night hotels. The reason for this is simple: a low cost structure enables us to provide our customers with the best value. We cannot provide good design at good prices if management costs are high. As managers, we must set good examples

continues

continued

and are constantly asking ourselves, "How do we cut costs that do not add value for the customer?"

'We at IKEA are radically decentralized. We are less of a hierarchy than an organization in which authoritative information can enter the system from one of several points. Our Los Angeles store, for example, could give the lead to the entire global system if an initiative originating there was found to have system-wide appeal. Each co-worker is invited to try new solutions. To increase speed, we have replaced instructions from headquarters with general guidelines on how to recognize out-standing opportunities. By substituting a general strategic direction for specific goals, we give local store managers the power and freedom to recognize stepping-stones that lead in desired directions.

'IKEA's corporate structure should be looked upon as a reverse hierarchy. Customers stand on the top rung, supported by local stores who serve them. The stores in turn are supported by regional organizations. Finally, at the bottom – and I mean the bottom – is IKEA's headquarters. This includes me.

'Managers should first learn to be servants. This is how I see my role in the organization: helping the employee who has the most contact with customers to do the best job possible.

'Like most people, I read what I like to read and I see what I want to see. In terms of management theories, the one I find most true to corporate life is the learning organization. You can score in the short-term or make some achievement without being one. But I think to be truly successful, the organization has to learn and adapt to changes in society. I can give you a few examples of how we have acted upon what we have learned about our customers:

- At IKEA, we have learnt that shopping is now an activity families do together, because both parents work and there generally seems to be less time for families to be together these days. So we set out to make the shopping experience something all family members can enjoy: for example, supervised child-care and playgrounds, wheel-chairs for the elderly, restaurants and cafeterias to relax in.
- Some customers want to do more for themselves so that they can save money. We offer them instructions on setting up their own furniture. But for those customers who want to buy assembled pieces and have them delivered, we provide those services as well. We constantly ask our customers to tell us what they need, how they want to buy it, how much they want to do for themselves, how much they want us to do for them. IKEA's vision of communication is that it must be straight-forward, informal, authentic and where possible, face-to-face.

'We see a historical role for ourselves within the industry and the market in which we operate. In many ways we think we are creating the

continues

continued

company of the future, and this is very exciting for all involved. This sense of mission enables our employees to transcend the day-to-day details of often mundane work and to see themselves as making a contribution to the wider society. Retailing involves massive attention to detail, to control of inventories, to timely re-ordering, to spotting trends. With so vast an array of numbers, our errors and omissions pass before our eyes in an endless stream. But all we ask is our employees learn from their mistakes. We can all too easily drown in statistics, and so it is vital to share corporate values and to agree on what feedback means about the fulfilment of those values. Only if you are committed to improving trends are statistics meaningful.'

Source: Extract from EIU Report *The successful corporation of the year 2000*

Leaders invest in communications to accelerate the future

This is where the essence of leadership and the essence of investing in mass media coalesce. Unless a company's brand architecture is being used to cultivate this sense of purpose, leaders and mass media risk being conduits for squandering enormous resources in terms of money, and people's time, energy and working purpose.

On a first visit to Japan, more than a decade ago, we recall what then felt like a future shock of being told by a Japanese electronics company that they were proud to be giving fast moving goods a new meaning: that of marketing products with less than six months' life cycle and having the capability, if competitively necessary, to leapfrog four product generations ahead with their market offer.

A similar drive to revitalize is seen in:

- fashion markets where leaders action plan many seasons ahead;
- toys, where, for example, Lego remains competitive against more high tech toys because 'Lego theme' years are already planned beyond 2000;
- packaged foods, where the added value is increasingly found in acting as an early passport to exotic taste sensations inspired from all corners of the world;
- Disney, where anniversary celebrations are used to plot the history of the future. As far back as 1990, Disney's CEO, Michael Eisner, explained the company's future-now culture like this:

'I've probably thought through every year through the turn of the century. Things take so long to do, you have to plant your flag and build your company around it.

'An anniversary forces you to reanalyse your life. It forces you to recommit yourself to your vows and forces you to finish all your projects on time to get them done by the anniversary. . . . Deadlines are probably the strongest creative tools I know of. You've got to do it. You have to get your act together. The anniversary philosophy is much more than marketing.'

In *Competing for the Future* Hamel and Prahalad add to marketing's old four Ps (Product, Price, Promotion and Position) its new four Ps:

- Global Pre-emption, for example, suitably foreseen core competences.
- Predisposition, for example, global consumer awareness from banner branding.
- Proximity, for example, global access to national distribution channels.
- Propagation, for example, fast global roll-out of any new world class product offer.

Our ninth P for Purpose reminds us that world class employees need highly motivated stamina. Constantly reaching out for the stars is a peculiarly tiring thing to do unless you have pride in the mission.

We predict that the big losers of the next 10 years will be branded companies which go global but whose leaders forget their employees' need for purpose and the need to foresee what accelerating the future means in their sphere of business, globally and locally.

Too many Western corporate leaders in the last decade seem to have lost the lust for ensuring that their companies purposefully take advantage of change. Bartlett and Ghoshal (Box 14.5) explain that organizational danger signals are currently widespread.

Box 14.5 Whose purpose is being served?

Structure follows strategy, and systems support structure. Few aphorisms have penetrated Western business thinking as deeply as these two. Yet they and the management doctrine they have given rise to are no longer up to the job.

Neither the valueless quantitative terms of most planning and control processes nor the mechanical formulas of leveraged incentive systems nurture employees' commitment or motivation.

In most corporations today, people no longer know – or even

continues

---

continued

care – what or why their companies are. In such an environment, leaders have an urgent role to play. Obviously they must retain control over the processes that frame the company's strategic priorities. But strategies can engender strong enduring emotional attachments only when they are embedded in a broader organizational purpose. This means creating an organization in which members can identify, in which they share a sense of pride, and to which they are willing to commit.

(*Source*: Bartlett and Ghoshal, 1994)

Avoid a stagnating state of affairs by adopting cultural priorities like those of Nestlé's Helmut Maucher, profiled in the EIU Report *Winning in the global marketplace*:

'The common thread that binds Maucher's Nestlé together is a reliance on management style that is more product and people oriented than systems oriented. "Personnel policy is the key to all else," Maucher says. "Ultimately it is a question of character, sense of responsibility and moral integrity." He has articulated these concepts in the following "six qualities of corporate leadership":

(1) Courage, good nerves and composure;
(2) The ability to learn, an open mind, perceptiveness and vision;
(3) The ability to communicate and motivate;
(4) The ability to create an innovative climate
(5) Thinking in context
(6) Credibility – practising what you preach

'The creation of advantage at Nestlé has come about through its identification and adaption to the mentality, habits and situations in the countries where it operates "with of course a dash of the Swiss virtues", Maucher adds, "and the Nestlé spirit of mutual cooperation". He tries to combat complacency. "Although Nestlé is a successful company, it worries me sometimes," he says "We have seen many companies go under through overconfidence. If people are overconfident and contented, they have a tendency to think they know all the answers. They are no longer conscious of the changes which are taking place in the world. So my main job is to keep alert and achieve the right balance between contentment and awareness of change."' (See also brand benchmarking of Nestlé in ThinkPiece 1.)

Once you realize that global branding works at the highest level by combining the service esprit de corps and accelerating the future, you can appreciate what a brilliant idea United Airlines is executing in Box 14.6. It is extracted from one of the company's inflight magazines, which reaches both staff and customers. As an approach for aligning the cultural values of United, it makes basic Hoshin planning look like a somewhat primitive tool.

Box 14.6   In the company of warriors

Circumstances compelled me to view my co-workers' jobs through their eyes, their minds, their hands. And through this perspective, I glimpsed not only my own future, but the future of United Airlines.

I've watched a hundred sunsets from the cockpit, gazed at a thousand contrails, crossed a million miles of ocean, cruised beneath a billion stars, always musing, pondering how privileged I am to fly these magnificent jets, always thankful for the most fabulous of jobs, with the most esteemed of corporations. But my most profound comprehension of what this job is all about came when I turned my attention backward, into the cabin on a dark lonely night in Nashville, after all the passengers had left.

I must admit it wasn't the sort of lofty ideals of teamwork, loyalty. or even compassion that motivated me to do it. I was commuting back home from Chicago at the end of a four-day trip – I wanted to get home. But my car was having troubles, and I had accepted an offer for a ride home from one of the three ground service personnel who was cleaning the Boeing 737 for its nightly bed-down. My motive was clear: the sooner they got done, the sooner I got home. I did the unthinkable. I – a pilot – rolled up my sleeves and grabbed a dust cloth.

The work was harder and longer that I anticipated. My workmates eagerly supervised my efforts to gather the trash, clean the overhead bins, and wipe the tray tables. They were fussy over the haphazard way I arranged the seat belts. Not neat enough. I had to redo several rows.

Throughout 20 years of military and commercial flying, I've always been meticulously concerned with an aircraft's mechanical condition, but this was something totally new. And if the job was subordinate to the maintenance of the plane's engines and engineering systems, you could never convince my workmates of it.

Yet what impressed me the most were the subjects of their constant bantering as they worked. Rarely had they spoken with a pilot. They peppered me with questions about flying and the mysterious workings in the cockpit, which they had often marvelled at during the still hours of the night shift. But most fervently, they wanted to know how 'we' were doing.

continues

continued

'We?' I asked.

'Yeah, you know – the company,' one of them clarified. 'Do you think we're doing as well as they say?'

I wasn't sure what she meant by 'they'. Probably company news releases or the news media. I guess to them I was like a soldier returning from the front. 'We're doing great,' I assured them.

And we are. We're part of a grand experiment, the economists say – the largest employee-owned corporation in history. But to the ground service crew and me, this is not an experiment, this is life. We will live it and make it work. Together.

I had always tried to maintain a proper perspective for my job by being constantly mindful of the lives and trust of those customers seated in the cabin behind me. But from that point on, I resolved to add another dimension to that awareness. I'll always recall the grinning faces that I worked with that night and how they were every bit as essential to United Airlines' success as we pilots are.

We finished our work and shut the power off. As we walked toward the employee bus stop, I saw them taking a last glance at their airplane – the sleeping Boeing, glistening in the moonlight. Then I realized how arrogant I had been in presuming to be the soldier returning from the front. The front was there. And I was in the company of gentle, but determined, warriors.

(Alan Cockrell, United Airlines First Officer, published in United Airlines in-flight magazine, Hemispheres, February 1995)

Brands are a company's commercial licence to invest in medium-term foresight

In a business world populated by short-term consultants and reporting pressures, branding should harness the organization's cultural motivation for investing in medium-term foresight. The leader must spot what an insult badly executed brand valuation is. Valuation may be fair game when deployed for some tactical margin for manoeuvre owing to some financial technicality. But when technocrats suggest that they have some magic all-embracing algorithm for calculating the strengths of your marketing process, the quality of your organizational culture and the foresightfulness of your investments in core competences, it is time to free yourself from such shackles. Any accountant who believes that competing for the future can be reduced to a set of numbers is overstepping the profession's hallmark of prudence by a long way.

Wherever brands are in crisis, leadership is in crisis. Ironically, a company with a large investment in brands that are losing their purpose will often remain highly profitable in the short-term. But in the medium-term its future is bleak because somewhere around the world a company will be investing in accelerating the future. One of this competitor's purposes is to create a discontinuity in the added-value chain of the sphere of business and to accelerate this future shock to the particular disadvantage of competitors with a weaker sense of purpose.

In our era of global communications, the essence of powerful leadership is to establish a cultural climate and organizing sense of purpose which prioritizes confidence in accelerating the medium-term future and perceives brand organization as the integral means for achieving this.

Brand rights

Core corporate or banner brands ought to have rights which are given organization-wide respect. After the apparent debacle of new Coke in 1985, there was widespread acknowledgement of the irony that while brand marketers are mortal, great brands need not be. But this hides a greater irony: organizations can kill off their greatest brands if they do nothing about major environmental trends.

The leader must detect potential killer trends and ensure that overall organizational culture and specific systems of brand management are taking proactive steps to ensure the brand's right to at least survive, and preferably to use the trend to its own advantage. In our view, there is not an important brand process in the world that can afford to dismiss all four of these potential killer trends.

(1) Globalization in all its forms.
(2) New configurations of partnerships across the added-value chain, for example, Cott Corporation.
(3) New media economies and integrated models for the brand mix.
(4) New technologies and communities of learning owing to computers in communications.

Leaders should be constantly carrying out this acid test. Prioritize potential killer trends for every core branded business, and then ask: does the way in which the company organizes its brand process encourage employees in all departments to help the company to respond to this particular change?

Once the leader has identified key cultural challenges, a constructive way forward is to prioritize one as the year's challenge. By the means of Hoshin Planning invite everyone (or every departmental head) to respond in one-to-one correspondence designed to elicit:

- What will you personally be doing about this challenge?
- Is there anything within the organization which is impeding you from taking other constructive actions?
- How will you measure the process effects of your intended actions?

Hoshin planning is an organizing process for practising the dynamic style rules of leadership which Bartlett and Ghoshal have summarized (Box 14.7).

Box 14.7   Leadership sense and system

Leaders embed clearly articulated, well-defined ambition in the thinking of every individual while giving each person the freedom to interpret the company's broad objectives creatively. Specifically:

- they articulate corporate ambition in terms designed to capture employees' attention and interest them rather than in terms related to strategic or financial goals
- they engage the organization in developing, refining and renewing the ambition.
- they ensure it is translated into measurable activities to provide a benchmark for achievement and a sense of momentum

(*Source*: Bartlett and Ghoshal, 1994)

Through iterative tuning of the Hoshin planning dialogue, such as seeing what expected answers are not volunteered, the leader can decide what can be left to departments of the organization and what needs interdepartmental leadership. Also cultural operating rules can be adjusted. For example, consider these two opposite corporate views:

- We seek partnerships with select demanding customers whose opinions are central in influencing product development.
- This company does not, as a matter of policy, involve customers in new product development because if they get wind of something new then they stop buying our existing products.

You can tell which organization subscribes to Hoshin planning, and you can imagine what the destiny of the other company will be.

Brand Chartering: top-of-mind brand know-how

A brand is much more powerful if everyone who contributes to its added value is working with the same script. We cannot think of a Brand Chartering project where members of the business team have started with the same script in mind. There is a mathematical reason for this. The case study in Chapter 16 produced a relatively short Brand Charter, involving six essential keyword meanings of the brand and about 10 lead thoughts (as well as indexing to more detailed company systems). Combinatorial logic suggests that the likelihood of two people having the same 16 lead ideas is remote unless you have teamworked to achieve a consensus. As a business team usually comprises more than two people, it becomes clear why the most wasteful forms of brand warfare are those fought within an organization.

The importance of having these top 16 brand codes as the common starting point in the minds of all members of the business team cannot be overstressed. This empowered them to utilize the same leadership perspective in contributing to subtle decision-making on evolving the brand's vitality in consumers' minds. One of the workshop sessions during the early stages of the Chartering project was provocatively titled 'we've come to bury ABC brand or to praise her'. Somewhere between global and local marketing, there is a real danger of missing out on understanding real consumers. This potentially deadly communications gap is resolved not by adding an extra regional layer of marketing but by Chartering a living script for the brand which integrates the best of global and local understanding as well as the best of interdepartmental know-how.

Like the best film scripts, the Charter as a brand's living script must be edited by a person of empowering vision and authority. He or she will need to make leadership calls but these decisions should be formed in a way that enables teamworking to gel and recognizes who in the business team is closest to specific elements of the service objective of the brand for each of its evolving marketplaces.

Brand reputation

Leaders are also responsible for the protective role of caring for a company's reputation. When we say that branding is concerned with leveraging high visibility, we are assuming that it is a consciously chosen strategy to magnify the opportunities and risks associated with claiming a leader's reputation. It is vital to propagate an organization-wide awareness that the substance of reputation may only be as strong as your weakest link. This is summarized in the review in Box 14.8.

Box 14.8   Reputation: king piece in boardroom chess

Suppose that we are playing chess with the pieces of goodwill that a company owns. Corporate reputation is always your king. In many cases where the company's name is also synonymous with its biggest brand (for example, Sony) or visibly marketed as the corporate sponsor of product sub-brands (for example, Nestlé's Kit Kat), corporate reputation is also your queen.

The most naïve kind of move endangers both king and queen, through failure to understand the human dynamics of communications. Not only does every corporate stakeholder (or audience) have a view of the company's reputation. A performance conceived with only one stakeholder group in mind may instigate a chain reaction that endangers the quality of your reputation with all stakeholders.

To the British reader, the most quotable example of such a chain reaction was Gerald Ratner's quip that the durability of some of his company's jewellery had a consumer shelf-life on a par with a Marks and Spencer prawn sandwich. Although this joke about the crap segment of the jewellery market was made to an audience of city analysts, it was pounced on by tabloid journalists. The chain reaction quickly handed on to Ratner's erstwhile consumers – and prospective gift-givers – was that of the emotional let-down which humans feel when a relationship publicly crashes from smart to crap.

Progressing beyond the naive, watch out next for reactive moves and others which exhibit less than complete awareness of the symmetries of the reputation game. These too will often put your king and queen in check as Grahame Dowling's book on corporate reputations from an Australian perspective reveals through a variety of valuable citations, including the following:

- **The Westpac Letters Affair** in which a disgruntled employee (of Australia's second largest retail bank) leaked some confidential letters showing that some of the bank's advice to customers on certain types of foreign currency loans was questionable. The gut reaction of the bank's public affairs unit – legally exact but communications insensitive – was to hand the matter over to the lawyers. Although the court finally ruled in favour of the bank against the employee's

continues

continued

actions, the impact on the reputation of the bank held by journalists and customers was negative to the point that it contributed to the resignation of the bank's then managing director.

- **Thinking big for whom**. 'During the 1980s, Australian steel and resource company BHP called itself "The Big Australian". Its management, employees and shareholders liked being associated with Australia's biggest company. Also, the company's public relations group thought that reminding politicians and public servants that BHP was a big contributor to the country's economy was a good idea. For customers of the company's steel products, however, being reminded that BHP was The Big Australian was not highly valued. It just reminded them of the power the company used when allocating its steel production to subservient customers.'

If combining your king and queen can result in such exposed positions, why do it? The reasons range from the statesmanship status that is accorded to a company which knows its integrated values so well that it can even initiate best practice responses while in the midst of a crisis, to potential problems besetting companies which consciously or subconsciously appear to hide behind their brands.

A classic case of corporately branded statesmanship relates to Johnson & Johnson's Tylenol, when this top-selling American analgesic was contaminated with cyanide by an unknown person. Johnson & Johnson's response to this crisis was immediate nationwide product withdrawal, total corporate sincerity and refusal to relaunch the product until a tamper-proof package had been innovated. This response is now regarded as textbook corporate management of a crisis. Here was grandmastership of corporate reputation in action, confirmed philosophically by J&J chairman Jim Burke's summing up:

'The reputation of the corporation which has been carefully built over 90 years, provided a reservoir of goodwill among the public, the people in the regulatory agencies, and the media, which was of incalculable value in helping to restore the brand.'

The result was that Johnson & Johnson's reputation grew out of its handling of the crisis. As noted in Dowling's book, there is something to learn from the fact that the Chinese characters for crisis denote two words: danger and opportunity.

Organizations which do not use the company name publicly (that is where king and queen are not combined) are more prone to neglect corporate reputation. This occurs wherever nobody has integrated charge of corporate reputation, and no measurements of corporate reputation are being monitored across the different stakeholder groups.

continues

> *continued*
>
> Such lack of process leaves you uninsured against two main kinds of eventuality:
>
> - overcoming disadvantages at times of crisis;
> - taking advantage of any trend among consumers or other stakeholders of wanting to know more about the company behind the products.

We suggest that the most natural form of the global branding process – for would-be disciples to learn from – begins and ends with the reputation of world class companies. Human beings expect that such organizations will behave with equal levels of care and attention across all their market borders. Where they do not live up to this, damage limitation is a misleading term because it suggests that image control can mask reality. New dynamics of globalization and openness in communications reveal that damage transfer can cross the borders of the world class company's reputation at something approaching the speed of light. In *The Borderless World* Kenichi Ohmae said:

> 'People are global when as consumers they have access to information about goods and services from around the world.'

Brand architecture is the megaprocess of business

A company's brand architecture interconnects with all other core business processes. Consequently, Chapter 11 proposed that the CEO must be able to take a top-level view of brand architecture. He or she needs enough information to gauge whether the investment foci of the brand architecture matches with his or her strategic intent in matters such as core competence building. Unless this happens the company will be giving signals to the outside world that are not in line with where it wants to go. Mix this with increasing confusion inside the organization's departments and the result might be described as a vicious circle of mis-intent. As Akio Morita of Sony said:

> 'Only truly global companies can achieve "global localization", that is, be as much of an insider as a local company but still accomplish benefits of world-scale operations.'

A well ordered brand architecture gives rise to the evolutionary form of the global networking organization. This can harness such newly critical survival characteristics as flexibility, flat management structure, competent people and purposefully aligned competences.

It is time to reconsider the question of who should be in charge of a business megaprocess. We believe that top-level brands in a company's brand architecture need to be perceived as at least quasi-corporate. In some companies there may be only one top company brand, in others there could be 10 in some kind of confederation that network into the organization's core competences. This makes good sense because internal partnerships can be more secure than external ones. The important thing is that any quasi-corporate brand has its own CEO, by which we mean a person whose decisions cannot be overtrumped by someone else higher up the organization. There are two reasons for this.

(1) For the brand to be a megaprocess, the CEO as architect of the networking organization must ultimately call decisions relating to how those responsible for specific processes/competences cooperate together. In some cases this may be the power to flatten the organization if necessary; in others the leader's ability may be manifest in inspiring an integrated service culture rather than an operation of functional hierarchies.

(2) The health of the top-level brand cannot be measured simply in yearly financial instalments. The most powerful brands are multi-faceted investment channels. It may be that Wall Street will always call for yearly reports on financial performance, but this art must be blended with more realistic facets of brands as megaprocesses such as:

- reputation, where one wrong act can sow a cancer in a corporate brand (killing off goodwill in the long term, even when the immediate prognosis appears to be no damage done);
- core competence building and pre-marketing investments, which are bound to involve longer-term paybacks if a company is competing to develop world class produce;
- service motivation/stamina/focus/know-how of employees which often involves getting onto a learning curve whose dividend shape is purposefully exponential;
- long-term robustness of the company brand's channels and presence of preference in front of consumers and other stakeholders;
- taking just-in-time advantage of fundamental discontinuities in added-value chains (this book has suggested that megatrends such as globalization mean that now more than ever before hugely significant opportunities exist and require urgent leveraging by the truly foresightful corporate leader).

It may not be entirely an accident that some of the world's most dynamic companies – ranging from employee-owned United Airlines, to Richard Branson's rendering of Virgin lifestyles, to Levi's global business enterprise – have recently unravelled their ownership structures from Wall Street's punter capitalists (Pennant-Rea, 1990) and/or those bankers who seem themselves to have lost touch with medium-term realities. (We write this in mid-1995 when such famous banking brands as Baring's and Crédit Lyonnais seem to have been something less than world class in either control or vision.)

We are not saying that confederations of CEOs may always find it easy to work with each other. On the soft side of being mutually accountable, they will need all the leadership graces of trust in each other's shared visions. On the hard side of accounting, their plans will need to be synchronized so that cash is flowing from some while investment building is occurring in others. As indicated, they may have to make the company private if they feel threatened by too many 'punter capitalists'. Or a company may need to decide that, after all, branding is not a competence it can manage. However, since we believe that we developed the term World Class Brands before anyone else in the West, we have a right to foresee what we mean by this as a core competence. The vision that we have just outlined is close to what we think the term possessing world class branding competence will mean to companies in a decade from now.

Future wealth creation resides in strong brand leadership

In his prescient paper, Stephen Parkinson (1991) provides evidence on how critical branding decisions have repeatedly created and destroyed great companies and national industries. At that time, as marketing professor at the Management Centre of the University of Bradford, he was well situated to catalogue evidence on the importance of brand leadership spanning over 130 years. His first citation involved the death of the local worsted industry reported by the *Bradford Observer* of 1868:

'The time has gone by when England possessed so many political, geographic, natural and artificial advantages over other nations that she had only to ask for a clear field and no favours to be sure of outdistancing her competitors. Roubaix attracts our buyers of fancy goods and Belgium undersells us in worsteds abroad. It is neither wise nor right to deceive ourselves that while some of our neighbours have advanced we have, in some departments, stood still and in others moved more slowly.'

Parkinson concludes that world class marketing has six foundation stones:

(1) Vision and leadership
(2) Understanding the customer
(3) Recruitment training and motivation of employees
(4) Developing a total quality operation
(5) Innovation
(6) Branding: and this is the keystone.

Those who travelled behind the Iron Curtain in the late 1970s or early 1980s could see a system where brands were as conspicuously absent as the cultural lack of market competition. Strong brands, flourishing media, free competitive markets and wealth creation go together. In 1983 the author contributed to a future history book (Macrae, 1984) which foresaw that wealth creation in the USSR was so visibly not happening that the system would fail, the Iron Curtain would come down and free-market structures would start to be built. We did not intend to forecast dates exactly, and indeed the Berlin Wall fell a few weeks before the date predicted in *The 2024 Report*. It is as evident to us today that what used to be a strong organizational model for branding in days when companies could profit from segmenting local markets cannot be a strong model for globalizing businesses competing in future markets.

Corporate systems are prone to developing a lot of built-in inertias at interpersonal levels which only corporate leaders can change. Today, in making the following exhortation, we are as confident in its forecast as we were when writing in 1983: the CEO of any company that is highly invested in brands who does not believe that responsibility for the drama of brand leadership needs to be near the top of his or her personal agenda will have abrogated his or her company's right to brand early in the new millennium.

Summary

World class marketing involves organizational learning of the highest order regarding service process and leadership purpose. The CEO needs to clarify a Declaration of Interdependence for Brand Leadership and his or her part in orchestrating organization-wide commitment to this. Culturally relevant beliefs for such a declaration have been listed.

Brand architecture must be aligned to core competence acquisition, organization structure and strategic intent. The CEO can give the lead by ensuring clarity of purpose is propagated throughout the organization. We have recommended circulating know-how round a feedback loop which makes integrated use of five toolkits for company learning:

(1) Strategic foresight (focus sphere of business and core competences)
(2) Hoshin planning
(3) Brand architecture
(4) Brand Chartering
(5) Refine ownership and monitoring roles vis-à-vis brand process and corporate reputation.

Future wealth creation depends on leadership of strong brand organizations. Brands, if you invest them, must interrelate with every employee's working vision of winning for consumers and customers.

References

Bartlett, C.A. and Ghoshal, S. (1994). Beyond strategy to purpose, *Harvard Business Review*, Nov/Dec

Belasco, J. (1990). *Teaching the elephant to dance – empowering change in your organisation*. London: Century Business.

Dowling, G. (1994). *Corporate Reputations*, London: Kogan Page

Hamel, G. and Prahalad, C.K. (1994). *Competing for the Future*. Harvard: Harvard Business School Press

Macrae, N. (1984). *The 2024 Report – a concise history of the future*. London: Sidgwick & Jackson

Ohmai, K. (1990). *The Borderless World*. London: Collins

Pennant-Rea, R. Punters or Proprietors? (a survey on capitalism), *The Economist*, 5 May 1990

Parkinson, S. (1991). World Class Marketing – from lost empires to the image men, *Journal of Marketing Management*, 7

15

brand Other Direct

We are nearing the end of this attempt to explain and explore Brand Chartering. This is a good reason for starting a second lap, and then a third, and so on, because we all have a lot to learn. One way to do this is to access MELNET's worldwide web site at http://www.brad.ac.uk/branding/ where Brand Charterers are continuously exchanging experiences and updating Think Paths.

Or you may want to start Chartering in practice with a brand you know. Chapter 16 describes how one brand scriptwriter started.

You may like to reflect on a few of this book's ThinkPieces, which follow Chapter 16. Some relate directly to one junction of Brand Chartering; some are there just to stimulate some timely mental connections. Which ThinkPieces would you add to this book to ensure that a first exploration of Brand Chartering trawls for all kinds of employees' brainwaves on brand organization?

Many of our ThinkPieces can also be adapted as training exercises for exchanging ideas on brand processes.

We suggest that it is a bad idea to define brand process in one way. You can always vote for one definition as being most important in any specific context. Allow people in a team to vote for their own current top of the pops from a collection which the company values. This chapter concludes with a ThinkPiece on this topic.

Some alternative definitions relating to brand organization

Exercise: please add your own favourites. The best definition for a multifaceted process, like brand organization, is the one that is user-friendly in your own context and vaguely right for all those with whom you team, network or share in brand organizing.

- Brands are not a company's most valuable assets unless they are organized as dynamic assets.
- Branding is about partnership strategy as well as competitive strategy. This determines organizational form and strategic realization as well as vice versa.
- Branding global awareness but only one kind of product may seem increasingly to be a waste of resources.
- Products are now best regarded as sub-brands. They may be linked to brands as added-value pathways which go beyond the product life cycle or the meaning of one market segment. These pathways lead a sphere of business by connecting up systems/investments pre-market and post-market, as well as in-market.
- Brand process involves the organization-wide discipline of talking across purposes until you have a competent consensus on how to lead. (Once you have achieved this, be prepared to start again.)
- A company's collection of powerful brands can become highly political unless their architecture is cultivated with care, foresight and integrity.
- Since trust is the primary key to corporate reputation, the CEO who is not involved with his or her brand architecture is not in command of the company.
- Brand organizations aim to be one giant feedback loop between employees and consumers, not forgetting the partnership rights and competitive interests of in-between audiences (and channels). Employees must be sufficiently interested in leadership of consumer/customer rights to run a marathon, win it, pick themselves up from the winning line, and prepare for running the next one.
- Branding is the business process of continuously making smart relationships with everyone you need. The brand organization must create, communicate and learn, because no other business process is responsible for integrating these roles.
- Some goals of branding emphasize short-term needs; others must make a stand for investing in medium-term vitality. Unless your organization measures both in simple-to-communicate but cleverly sensitive ways – this includes tailoring reward systems appropriately – you cannot expect to earn the right to brand. Hostile climates, for

example over-accounting, must be removed for world class leadership to be sustainable.

- Brand lifestyles consistently influence the pride and passions of everyone connected to the brand's club whether as a server of the Charter, fee-paying member or honoured guest.
- The ultimate banner brand is so sure of its own core competence leadership and its democratic building of shared wealth that it is prepared to make its strategy transparent to everybody. In this way the banner gets, and is recognized for getting, all the best partners in building 'glocal' added-value chains. This is truly valuable leadership.
- Brands which do not incorporate the indomitable spirit of purposefully accelerating change deserve to die. Corporate leaders have to take full responsibility for the implications of this if their declared strategy includes investing in brand process as a core competence. The same applies for anybody in charge of great identities, such as celebrities, nations, regions, cities, charities, business schools: you name it.
- A brand's living script should focus on 'editing the future now' in the integrated way which only essential leaders know how, and keep on learning to be.

16

Brand Chartering case study: glocal branding process

This case shows how action-oriented teamworking takes place once a suitable Brand Charter starts to evolve. For reasons of confidentiality some elements of the Brand Charter have been disguised, but you will be able to perceive the real decision-making challenges involved.

We were working for a local subsidiary of one of the world's top 10 packaged goods manufacturers. The country involved is not currently one of the top dozen contributors to global revenue but is forecast to be so by 2005. The local subsidiary had three main divisions and we were asked to review all brands maintained by one of these divisions (call it XYZ). It was anticipated that brand rationalization would need to take place because the division was operating around 20 separate brands in seven product categories. This lack of focus compared with rivals whose brand architecture employed umbrella and banner branding was one of the reasons why the division was underperforming.

We reviewed the essences of all 20 brands looking for those with big idea potential. We asked the business team to think about one brand at a time and consider, if it was the only brand, what they could make out of it. One brand – call it ABC – stood out as by far the the most valuable brand in the portfolio. Local marketers' eyes lit up when discussing what they would do if this was the company brand. Sales people said that this was the national company's most important brand; all three divisions had leveraged its goodwill with retailers to get other brands stocked on favourable terms. Financial data revealed that some of the division's other brands had been allocated bigger marketing budgets in recent years but ABC was contributing half of the division's profits.

A natural starting point for our Charter was to expand the local perspective of how big the brand could be. We could then test this local vision through international levels of the organization's hierarchy to understand why this brand appeared not to be getting its fair share of resources in terms of promotional money and people's time and attention. We chose to start our Charter from branding junctions:

- Essence
- Quality and Value
- Heritage/Friends
- Future (product evolution/brand) News

ABC essence

To dramatize the importance of the brand we asked what consumers and the company's shareholders would really miss if it ceased to exist. After a lot of debate involving departments across the local division, we achieved a consensus that six keywords summed up the brand.

ABC's consumer essence is:

- **leader of the biggest end-benefit banner meaning** that consumers would associate with all product categories served by XYZ division;
- **pre-empting brand icon** (like Marlboro's cowboy this brand's essence is portrayed by a human icon that pre-empts its leadership meaning and gives this to consumers as an image to wear);
- **trust** (our favourite keyword for brand equity to own though we had not mentioned this to the team);
- **value**;
- **a functional property** of ABC products;
- **joy of use**.

This list may be too long, but ABC is surely a brand any business team would be proud of. So what would company shareholders miss if this brand did not exist? ABC's shareholder essence included being:

- **the national company's most famous brand and one of the country's top 10 brands;**
- the division's primary source of profits;
- according to some reports, the international company's most famous semi-global brand (in the sense of being a more famous name in more countries than any other single brand).

At this stage the experienced Brand Charterer double-checks whether the brand is really this big and starts to tune into the politics of the organization (for example, apparent loss of a marketing opportunity as big as this one is usually something to do with globalization).

For now, we proceed with the first draft of the Brand Charter, scripting it in the way that the local team would like to rally round the brand. This 'draft' can then be used to explore where potential global marketing conflicts lie.

ABC quality

Regarding brand quality Charterers sometimes insert a standard paragraph and then ask the business team to tone it down if necessary Thus:

Our quality commitment to ABC is where we (and the brand) will thrive or die

Declaration: we, the business team, must continuously improve ABC in the light of product-quality standards which (name world class competitor) would launch if they only had the channels and operating advantages that are currently ours. We must resist all accountants' and so on ideas for cost-cutting of product quality where consumers might notice these either short-term (for example, because of a different feeling of product usage), or long-term (because cutting quality in an imperceptible sequence of 'salami-cuts' might open the door to a future competitor launching an offer whose quality feels a quantum leap better).

This opened up several interesting lines of discussion. For example, some consumer research on a cheaper product formulation was just being reported as no consumer difference; but on closer inspection the ingredient that was being reduced was a key property in distinguishing the essential joy of use. More extensive research of consumer perceptions was carried out and a different conclusion was reached. Also, how were we going to Charter the value balance of ABC which is of particular importance to its essence? We decided to leave this in the margin of the draft Charter while more consumer research was done on the value/ quality balance of ABC leadership.

ABC heritage

Consumer **perceptions anchored ABC in one product category** which it dominated. (New categories had been entered but with only partial success.)

The main element of the marketing mix was internationally conceived advertising. Some queries on mix related to consistency of support and local marketing effectiveness vis a vis competitors, for example, at point of sales.

ABC future

There were plans for entry into several new categories, one of which was imminent. The team was particularly concerned about an international competitor whose essence was thought to be less popular but more upmarket; some concepts were being tested which appeared to communicate more of the competitor's essence and less of ABC'S.

The primary agenda was how to transform ABC from a product to a business umbrella leader

We needed to adjourn. The team needed to do some more thinking (and the Chartering consultant needed to understand some organizational constraints) but we tabled some 'do now' questions which this first Brand Chartering workshop had stimulated. These included the following:

- What emotional bridge can we use to get consumers to translate the relevance of ABC to other product confirmations of its essence?
- Is local awareness/impact of the brand optimal? (For example, has the brand been supported enough and does the international TV script communicate all we need to?)
- As a strong umbrella brand develops, how do we rotate which products to feature in television advertising? (For example, should our bias be away from our best-selling product and towards (which) new categories?)
- Does our essence need to be moved, and how do we deal with the upmarket competitive threat?

In passing we noted that the brand's identity was blessed with a **highly impactful name** and various representations of the brand's essential icon. In other respects, brand identity system had not been a consistent focus of the brand's marketing history.

Our next steps were largely to check out our Chartering beliefs and questions. We set out to collect opinions from the various people that we could network with across the organization and with others such as creative suppliers. In particular, the Charterer was concerned with testing out whether there were any flaws in the glocal format, that is were local consumers failing to make important interpretations of the brand? A specific context for this concern was the umbrella transformation of ABC which was urgently needed to maximize local consumer response, and which might not have been anticipated by marketing communicators concerned with global common denominators.

With television advertising, it is a good idea to distinguish between subtle messages which only consumer research can quantify and other more top-line connections whose presence or absence can be checked in more qualitative ways. These include:

- demanding to see the source brief which the advertising agency has been executing;
- watching a reel of advertising campaigns and making your own top-level interpretations;
- asking somebody who is totally independent to give you their feedback on watching this reel of advertising prompted by a sensitively designed mini-questionnaire.

In this case, the minimum advertising research was necessary to establish two things. First, **the structural format of the advertising campaigns was great for re-establishing the brand's icon, but it was not a good vehicle for highlighting various products**. (The product only got a brief close-up way into the advertisement's storyline which meant that consumers used to following the campaign story would be unlikely to be paying much attention to a brief appearance by new product at that stage.) Second, being a global campaign, nobody had briefed the advertisement's scriptwriter that there was a critical need to write in an emotional bridge which enabled local consumers to start thinking of ABC in umbrella terms.

Initial soundings taken among international managers revealed why they had different agendas from the one which would have optimally fitted ABC locally. A manager had just been given regional responsibility for the brand. His initial attitude was that other local subsidiaries had no criticisms of the global television advertising so it would not be changing. His suggestion was: do what you like with local advertising in other media provided you do not take away any budget from the global TV advertising, and you will be fully responsible for your actions. Back at global headquarters, two things were conditioning an agenda far removed from our local one for ABC:

- The global product development for future ABC was prioritizing a much higher added-value positioning. The implication was that this premium range ABC would eventually need to be launched alongside basic ABC.
- There was currently more global push behind a new brand which had, in fact, been grabbing the lion's share of the local budget (partly explaining why ABCs recent budgets had been undersupported).

There is a Catch 22 here. Chartering has been designed so that organizational conflicts of this sort do not arise. But the first time a company uses Chartering, it is precisely these kinds of conflicts that are most likely to be prevalent. In our case, the aspiring global brand soon started to fail badly in the locality and most of the region, which from ABC's point of view was fortunate as it was now able to retrieve a bit of its local marketing budget.

By the time the local business team reconvened for a second Chartering workshop, the group consensus was that we had learned quite a lot in terms of both our 'do now margins for manoeuvre' and being closer to consumer feelings for ABC brand.

We knew it was up to us locally to help consumers translate umbrella meaning for the brand. Local consumers knew where the brand had come from better than any (global) marketer, but we wanted to help them interpret where the brand was going to. We felt this immediate communications agenda involved two creative keys:

- The need to bridge the way consumers perceived the functional element of ABC's essence away from association with a single product and towards an occasion of use that was in everyone's diary.
- A newsline for announcing that ABC was an umbrella brand with lots of good lines to its name.

We had some local promotional budget and the team had unfettered authority to pilot a press or poster advertising campaign. We meditated over the six keywords that we all now felt to be the brand's essence and in particular the one which represented the functional property. Instead of looking at this word in terms of what ABC products were conceived functionally to do, was there something to communicate about occasions of use of ABC products? Could we highlight this as a favourite time in every consumer's day? There we were working in the humid local climate – unlike a global coordinator sitting in New York, London, Cincinnati or wherever – and the key emotional interpretation of ABCs function was staring us in the face. For most consumers, the usage occasion common to all ABC's products was indeed one of the great relaxations after a day at work. So the **bridge to ABC's essence was functional property < - > ***time**. The client executive of the local advertising agency jotted down the creative ingredients for one press campaign there and then:

picture = brand icon enjoying ***time
slogan: ***time = ABCtime

This could confirm the essence of ABC. Specifically it would be the essence of the emotional bridge between ABC as a product function to usage of each and every product in the ABC umbrella as being a favourite event in the consumer's 'diary of the mind'.

Press is probably a more friendly medium for communicating a brand range than television, at least for the creative artist. This is because the products can be arranged to stand to attention on one of the borders of the largely pictorial copy in a way that adds to rather than detracts from evoking the overall joy of the moment and correspondingly the essential product of the moment. We foresaw that a similar press advertising format could be key to a second, **'teaser' campaign**. In periods prior to the television launch of a new ABC product, we could use the same pictorial format but temporarily change the textual focus to something like: **'How many ways do you know to be ABC ***time?'** . . . **Watch out for the new ABC product that consumers have told us they want next'**. As you can see we were not trying to write the advertising copy there and then, but we wanted the essence of our advertising brief to marry everything we believed about the essence of ABC with the two key newslines that we wanted ABC consumers to interpret for themselves.

We have subsequently played on these keynotes in other local media including posters and radio in our campaign to develop and pre-empt ABC s umbrella meaning.

Our Chartering workshop had another brainteaser to focus on. We had found out more on what ABC's 'good value' meant to local consumers. Historically ABC had been many local consumers' first affordable invitation to experience the fashion values and qualities of an international brand. Although much of this happened a generation ago, the brand was trusted by a wide range of age groups for being that good first friend who had elevated their expectations above what local manufacturers could offer. The brand's icon had maintained the brand's relevance as passport to a wider world of cosmopolitan aspirations. All this had been delivered through a product category which had a relatively small price per unit, notwithstanding the fact that ABC as a brand leader commanded a premium price over competing products. So in Chatering brand essence **Value < - > Affordable first international friend < - > Trust and Contemporary Icon.**

These dotted line confirmations between elements of the brand's essence are a good sign that our convergence and focus on essential keywords was indeed pretty close to the core of the brand's meaning. However, this deeper understanding of what ABC's 'value' meant to consumers brought us good, puzzling and bad news.

The good and the puzzling news

Knowing that ABC's good value was because we were one of the country's most trusted brands was in itself great news. We would cite Nivea's recent wealth of extensions as evidence that in terms of brand equity's role as a relationship maintainer and maker, trust is one of the biggest property rights that a brand's core can reflect. It adds value to the products you sell today and gives a flying start to the brand's extension to new products.

In some ways this magnified the puzzle of our jigsaw pieces regarding the extension of ABC. We knew that headquarters would always back the globally executed TV commercial with the majority of the marketing budget, and while it was good at reconfirming the brand's iconography it was not a vehicle for reinforcing ABC as an umbrella brand with an expanding range of winning products. We also knew that, unlike Nivea with its uniform blue looks, when you put ABC's brand lines side by side, the uniformity of their visual language was pretty mediocre. (The second press campaign had helped the marketing team to figure this out for themselves more clearly than before, but as a teaser campaign we kept on voting for it.) But our soul searching over brand identity was being magnified by another factor. As part of our research between the Chartering sessions, we had examined how smart city retailers preferred to arrange their shelf facings. This resulted in another local shock to the global marketer's system. Retailers preferred to merchandise range lines of major umbrella brands together in one visual unit. Locally most major brands took advantage of this format, which has very different implications from the assumption that products in the same category will be arranged side by side. ABC was missing out on local merchandising displays in two major ways:

- Without a coherent range, its products were often sidelined to appear among a jumble of the remaining category offers (usually small brands given the least visible shelf spacing).
- When current and planned ABC lines were put together the impact relative to competitors could be described as visual disharmony.

The bad news

More information had come through on the headquarters vision for the new globally premium range of ABC. It had a totally new identity system, so much so that one of the company's local marketers quipped jokingly (but seriously): 'That's OK then, consumers will think that this is some other company's brand of ABC.'

The new premium range was an eclectic mixture of new products that ABC had never been associated with, and some of these were clearly attempting to invade the pitch of the aforementioned 'rival' international brand. Also planned was a line in ABCs existing core category. This new premium line, in. keeping with the global upmarket intent, was to be offered locally at nearly three times the cost of the current ABC line.

Learning

As this case study illustrates, in a glocally organized company Brand Chartering soon needs to be conducted from both the global perspective and the local perspective. This is now taking place, and it would be inappropriate to anticipate global strategic judgements, let alone the focused enthusiasm that the local business team will need to continuously dedicate to the brand's consumer momentum. But subjectively the Charterer knows that the brand is big enough to get back on global and local track (with a little bit of navigational assistance from Brand Chartering's evolutionary focusing and experience-based checklists compiled from previous Chartering research).

Take a second look at this case study and ask yourself how many branding junctions the Charterer used as he navigated his way through different people's perspectives of the ABC brand process. The fact is that all 15 branding junctions were referred to for practical analogy-based support as the business team brainstormed how the ABC brand worked as a core business process and what the next challenges to this brand leadership process would be.

You can reconstruct something like our current draft of the local Brand Charter using the bold typeface in the text and a little polishing of your own. No one had this view in mind before the Chartering process began. Everyone in the local team came to a consensus that their Charter summarizes the key strengths of the brand and the critical challenges it needs to overcome. The Charterer had made five days of inputs in two different sessions. The team had spent a lot more time than this, but it was essential brand development work of the sort that does not concertedly take place in the marketing BC (Before Chartering) organization.

ThinkPiece 1

Brand Benchmarking

Exercises in Brand Benchmarking aim to illuminate practical learning points through such procedures as:

- debating what particularly powerful brands do best;
- searching for both generalizations and differences among powerful models of branding. Out of context, imitating one brand's best practice can sometimes make for an ineffective contribution within a different model of branding.

Also a collection of benchmarked brands is a resource bank for easy reference. We have repeatedly referred to this section of the book so that specific brand citations can also be viewed in their integrated contexts.

The main criteria for choosing the dozen brands in this benchmarking bank were variety and recent proof of at least semi-global success. This means that not all of the brands discussed are the biggest in their sectors, though many are. Also we have omitted classic retailers whose competences are undoubtedly world class but whose fame or operations are often more regional. (Semi-global retail contenders such as Loblaw, Marks and Spencer and IKEA have already featured prominently in this book. If you do start collecting your own bank of benchmarked brands, you should also add some highly efficient local brands.)

Our benchmarking bank of a dozen brands is divided into four different investment models of the brand as a business process.

(1) **Advertising of focal image**
Coca-Cola
Gillette

(2) **Franchising** (see pages 84–87)
   McDonald's
   Benetton
   Body Shop
(3) **Company-wide communicators**
   Sony
   Nestlé
   British Airways
   Shiseido
   Singapore
(4) **Seeding** (see page 81)
   Häagen-Dazs
   Weight Watchers (Heinz)

These are not intended to be hard and fast classifications of our nominated brands. But they confirm that there is no such thing as one investment model for branding. Brand-oriented investments evolve subtly different competitive forms. This should be a matter of conscious strategic and organizational choice. As you explore the benchmarking bank you might like to ask yourself some questions. Taking the advertising image model as a base mark:

• How is the company-wide communicator model similar, different?
• How is the franchise model similar, different?
• How is the seeding model similar, different?

Interpret 'differences' in such ways as:

• How do investment inputs vary?
• How do goals determining corporate advantages vary?
• Which models have most to gain or lose from globalization trends discussed in this book?

Throughout the exploration process, note any creative discoveries you make. Examples may include the following:

• Franchising and seeding models have featured prominently among successful global brand expansions over the last 15 years.
• Even a classical model such as advertising may be leveraged in new forms; for example, Gillette's satellite form, or the new standard of global advertising that British Airways pioneered with the help of world class film directors.
• Seeding is a model that many brands have used to get a highly fashionable start in a new marketing territory, both deliberately (for example, Häagen-Dazs) and accidentally (for example, Coca-Cola prior to 1910).
• Gillette and Nestlé have made particular use of the game rules of brand architecture catalogued in Chapter 11; many brands have

exploited the new competitive rationales of global banner branding discussed in Chapter 12.

Strong as these brands have proved to be in recent years, which would you be most confident to work for over the next five years? And the next 10 years?

Figure T1.1 classifies outstanding elements of the marketing mix to look out for in our benchmarked brands. You may wish to make some adjustments to our judgements, but it becomes clear that strong brand processes exhibit:

- exceptionally strong practices on lead elements of their marketing mix;
- integration of these lead components;
- patterns of investments in lead components which are often unique as a branding process.

Keys to the Coca-Cola process

Brief history of Coca-Cola

1886	Founded by the pharmacist John Pemberton; nurtured by industrialist Asa Candler; mentored for most of 20th century by Robert Woodruff
1911	Annual advertising budget exceeds $1 million
1915	Coca-Cola's designer bottle is launched
1919	The USA's favourite soft drink finds new meaning as prohibition starts (and continues to this day for under 21s)
1928	Coca-Cola's first sponsorship of the Olympics
1990s	Reported to be world's number 1 brand in terms of awareness and reputation; one of the world's top brands in monetary value

To be a legend

Legend has it that as recently as 1930 Father Christmas had no uniform. His image, grey and ghostly, was in need of a boost. Then Santa's fortunes changed. He met an agent who wanted no money for designing the smart suit which is universally recognized today as Father Christmas's own. The agent was the Coca-Cola company which talent-spotted Santa for the feature role in the company's Christmas cards, calendars and yuletide advertising. In the new presentation of Father Christmas a star was born. The main condition of Santa's contract was

	Coca-Cola	Gillette	Sony	Nestlé	British Airways	Shiseido	Singapore	McDonald's	Benetton	Body Shop	Häagen-Dazs	Weight Watchers
Advertising	•	•			•	•	•	•				
Identity system			•	•		•	•	•				
Legend building	•		•					•		•	•	
Slogans	•	•	•		•		•	•				
Visible consumption	•		•	•	•		•	•	•	•	•	
World stage sponsor (eg, sports)	•							•				
Double-branding			•	•	•			•				•
Pioneering products		•	•			•	•	•			•	
General PR	•		•		•		•	•	•	•	•	

Figure T1.1 Best practice foci of benchmarked brands

	Coca-Cola	Gillette	Sony	Nestlé	British Airways	Shiseido	Singapore	McDonald's	Benetton	Body Shop	Häagen-Dazs	Weight Watchers
Ad exploitation of PR									•		•	
Partners of brand			•	•			•					•
Service leadership					•		•	•				
Loyalty scheme					•							
Name			•									
Sampling			•								•	•
Word-of-mouth (opinion leading consumers)									•	•	•	•
'Glocal' culture			•	•		•						

Figure T1.1 *continued*

that he should always be dressed in the company's red and white livery. This has proved to be a smart way of perpetuating the twin legends of company branding and universal folk hero.

In the book *World Class Brands*, we argued that: 'Every quest for identity is about tradition in the making. There is a fact and a fiction in every great communal inspiration of man because that is the way legends humanly circulate.' Coca-Cola's ability to build legends is second to none. Even the product formulation has been made the stuff of legends as evidenced by the long-running mythology of the original secret recipe locked away in an Atlanta bank vault and the world's most extraordinary centennial celebration of a product. The latter attracted global news coverage when it appeared that an American referendum was being staged to choose between a new Coke and the old one for the brand's second century. The result, after 40 days of forced abstinence from the real thing, was that the American public voted overwhelmingly for Classic Coca-Cola's return to the shops. What may have begun as one of marketing's biggest mistakes was transformed through a magical piece of theatre into one of the most globally efficient ways of dealing with a competitor's comparative challenge ever seen.

The seeding accident: born to be fashionable

Coca-Cola enjoyed the good fortune of being born in 1886 into the right social circles. While Victorian Britons had their teahouses and the French had their cafes, American society had soda fountains. Coca-Cola soon became the standard drink of the soda fountain set. Until Coca-Cola was in its teens as a product, the only way to participate in the Coca-Cola experience was by sharing it in such genteel company.

In 1899 Asa Candler, proprietor of Coca-Cola, was approached by two young men, Thomas and Whitehead, who wanted the concession to bottle Coca-Cola. The idea seemed distant from the core business that Candler had nurtured. He surrendered the right to bottle Coca-Cola in the USA for the peppercorn royalty of $1.

To make the most of product visibility

Coca-Cola has consistently positioned itself as the world's friendliest drink. The creative hypothesis is that the biggest platform for a drink is social visibility. Correspondingly, the role of the world's number 1 branding is to evoke friendship in the sense of being perceived as the point of contact where friends meet up and where friendships are made.

To be an ambassador to the world

Historically, being a founding icon of the American Dream has been one of Coca-Cola's main routes to achieving superstar status around the world. The most amazing distribution coup ever made on behalf of a brand came with the USA's entry into the second world war. Robert Woodruff, who was the brand's mentor for most of the 20th century, declared that regardless of cost to the company, Coca-Cola would go wherever American GIs went at a price of 5 cents a bottle. Woodruff was so convincing about Coca-Cola's powers as a morale booster that the USA's war office contributed to the investment in bottling plants that Coca-Cola needed to be the GIs' mascot (which also helped Coca-Cola to double the size of its geographic empire during the 1940s).

More recently Coca-Cola has been prepared to make its own contribution to popular history. By 1970 the damage of Vietnam was such that being part of the American Dream was becoming an international liability. Coke's response was to declare a peace treaty in a way that no American president ever could. In 1971 the famous 'Hill Top' advertisement became a forerunner of global advertising. It pictured a world without frontiers, with young people dressed in national costumes of 30 countries, congregated on a hillside singing 'I'd like to buy the world a home, and furnish it with love, grow apple trees and honey bees and snow white turtle doves'. Not for eight lines was Coca-Cola mentioned: 'I'd like to buy the world a Coke'. The song was then licensed to the New Seekers to render a non-commercial version which hit the top of the pops and whose royalties were donated to UNICEF.

In 1989, as the Berlin Wall crumbled, Coke made sure it was the first brand to be sampled by East German border crossers. At one early checkpoint cans were given out at the rate of 10,000 an hour. Handing out product to over 150 people per minute called for almost military precision, but of an altogether more friendly kind than generations of Berliners could remember.

Double reminders

Coca-Cola stands for tradition, Coke pronounces modernity; linkages between the two names are continually made to portray the best of both worlds. Coca-Cola also sails as close to the wind as a brand name dares. One letter away from being the double generic of the product category makes it impossible to think of colas without Coca-Cola coming first to mind.

Doubling up is also apparent in other aspects of the brand's identity system such as the brand's two character fonts and more recently two versions of the famous bottle. Note that the original bottle put packaging on the branding agenda when the company decided in 1913 that a designer bottle would differentiate its product from any other. The design brief was announced in the form of a competition 'to find a bottle that anyone would recognize even in the dark; a bottle unique in all the world'.

Branding slogans as a cultural form and a company's sense of direction.

Here are just a few of these ageless scripts. (Some of their decoded meanings appear in parentheses, but like any good art form they can be interpreted in many ways.)

- *The world's friendliest drink* (represents the number 1 added value of the social visibility of the product).
- *The pause that refreshes* (used to persuade employers of the 1920s and 1930s that workers deserved a vending break; subsequently enhanced Coca-Cola's claim to be the appropriate morale booster for GIs)
- *The Real Thing* (a consumer nickname; the means of ensuring that Coca-Cola goes beyond being perceived as the reference point for a product category to being a category of its own; a reminder to the company that its branding should always be above the temptation of comparative advertising)
- *Always Coca-Cola* (in a world where change is accelerating, best friends offer the promise of constancy). It is also reputed to be the first global advertising campaign planned with an opening series of over 20 different executions, synchronized to target consumers' different lifestyle or consumption situations. Two of our favourite sightings so far are polar bears as cool Coca-Cola spokesmen during winter in the UK; and 'Always Springtime' at end of a hot day's skiing in Austria. Which are yours?

Keys to the re-engineered Gillette process

Re-engineered history of Gillette

Born again in 1987, Gillette has rapidly become best-in-class as a newly relaunched global lifestyle brand which is mainstream, ad-led and pitched at the level of corporate brand linked to product sub-brands.

Central orchestration of the global lifestyle components of the brand's equity

Pre-1987 Gillette learned all about the risks of being typecast to a market's lower added-value products – through local fragmented advertising campaigns focusing on best selling products – Gillette's global common denominator had become the lowest one of cheap, blue and plastic among a young generation of target consumers. Galvanized by the shock of coming within a whisker of turning its market into a commodity one, and committed to the big idea of orchestrating a global lifestyle, Gillette took the brave but necessary step of ensuring that the global branding of Gillette was coherently produced and directed by a centralized team of marketers.

A big idea for universal communications

The big idea is to aim to be the world's number 1 representation of the faces of manhood. Specifically, the brand dares to portray a tapestry of every major male lifestyle: father (family man); business man (team-man); sex object (play-man); sportsman (competition-man). The common thread used to knit this into one coherent image is the interestingly ambiguous 'best a man can get'. Is this referring to Gillette's products or the goals men can be witnessed to set themselves? (Bear in mind that women remain both the main purchasers for and witnesses of Gillette's consumers and products.) The ad-led marketing mix is only efficient because the idea is a big one and benefits from the economy of scale execution of a single global advertising campaign. Arguably, Gillette is the only brand yet conceived to work as effectively on satellite TV as it does on terrestrial TV. Its execution ensures global comprehension by being primarily visual. Gillette's target consumers fit well with the audiences of such staples of satellite programming as sports and pop videos.

Exploiting the double-branding linkages between corporate lifestyle banner and product sub-brand

Only flagship product sub-brands, for example Sensor and Series, would be featured in advertising Gillette's produce. The idea was to play on their aspirational qualities even if they were not initially best-selling lines. Through such linkages to the company brand, a double-branding campaign could evolve with lifestyle story and product stories leading each other. Competitors with a product brand would find it very hard to compete at this double level of lifestyling and product excellence.

Keys to the Sony process

Brief history of Sony

1950s	Sony trademark replaces 1946 corporate tongue twister (Tokyo Tsushin Kogyo Kabushiki Kaisha); developed world's smallest transistor radio
1960s	Built world class image in TVs through strong branding, quality, and technological competences, for example, transistorized TV sets and Trinitron technology
1970s	Continuously invested over 6% of sales in product R&D. Innovated a myriad of new electronics products including Walkman and the 3.5 inch computer diskette
1980s	Major investments in entertainment software, for example music companies and film studios
1990s	Regarded as a pivotal player in multimedia; likely to start the third millennium as the world's most valuable brand

A brand at one with its corporate purpose

Sony is a brand whose extendibility looks second to none. It must seem like a giant space invader to established industry leaders when they are first confronted by a Sony entrant into their category, mobile telecoms handsets being a recent example. Sony's image, which roughly speaking is 'global-state-of-the-art in anything electronic and consumable' might be described as osmotic rather than stretchable. No company has been smarter than Sony in directing branding as a business process. We can learn from Sony how to spin a virtuous spiral out of the three consumer pull properties which are the unique property rights of branding: world class leadership, identity and image.

To be a world class leader

As Jean-Noel Kapferer points out in his excellent book *Strategic Brand Management*, corporate branding is really about communicating a direction as uniquely yours. Your 'essence' should integrate vision, values and corporate culture into a mission which continuously answers the question: what would consumers be missing if this company brand did not exist? A feeling of Sony's sense of direction is obtained by understanding where the company brand comes from and what the strategic intent is. Sony's birthmark derives from a founder's statement in 1946:

'If it were possible to establish conditions where persons could become united with a firm spirit of teamwork and exercise to their hearts' desire their technological capacity, then such an organization could bring untold pleasure and untold benefits.'

This was harnessed to an epoch in which Emperor Showa established the post-war vision that Japanese pride would henceforth be channelled into productive excellence.

Akio Morita, who has personified Sony leadership during the company's first half century, explains the importance of employee creativity like this:

'What is the secret behind the success of Japanese companies? It is very simple. The human infant is born curious, but natural curiosity drains away with age. It's my job to nurture the curiosity of people I work with. At Sony, we know that a terrific new idea is more likely to happen in an open, free and trusting atmosphere.'

Sony's proud and global vision today is to strive for world-leading capabilities at the two consumable ends of multimedia products (but not the in-between communications pipelines) as clarified in a recent issue of Forbes (20 December 1993):

'Sony has skilfully positioned itself as a leader in blending under one roof both the machines that carry the information/ entertainment into homes and the entertainment/information itself. There are bigger companies on the hardware side and bigger companies on the software side, but none has gone so far in integrating the medium and the message.'

Propagating global awareness of Sony's 'one and only' identity

Identity's contribution to branding's virtuous spiral is about every way that the brand makes its design language – products, logos, symbols – visible and keeps it uniquely that way by efficient selection of all kinds of different communications media. The identity system aims to jog human minds to recall Sony first at any time, place, product or experience which is, in David Ogilvy's phrase, 'the fabric-of-life' of being Sony. Here are three snapshots from the Sony family album of identity-building.

(1) I used to think from its first day in TV sets, Sony had designed its logo so that you could not watch a Sony TV without the logo being part of your visual landscape. Then I met a Sony engineer who said his own criterion was that I shouldn't fail to notice a Sony TV even

when it appeared only fleetingly as a prop in a Hollywood film! In those days Sony was adept at media planning of this sort of product placement; today, of course, it also owns a few movie studios including Columbia in the heart of Hollywood.

(2)   Some of the best media opportunities come from cultivating VIP consumers and their word-of-mouth, since all sorts of new electronic products are naturally high visibility categories among them. The precedent for using this kind of medium can be seen in a favourite corporate legend from Akio Morita's autobiography of Sony *Made in Japan*:

> 'The Prince of Wales was coming to Expo '70 in Tokyo and the British ambassador had asked me to install Sony TV sets in the Prince's suite at the Embassy. Later at a reception, I was introduced to the Prince who thanked me for the TV sets and then asked if Sony had any intention of building plant in the UK. I told him we didn't have plans as yet and he replied with a smile "well if one day you do, don't forget my territory". Later, we did choose Wales for our first UK factory. . . . A few years after that, Queen Elizabeth made an official visit to Japan and I had the honour of meeting her at a reception at the British Embassy. She asked me whether the story about Prince Charles's recommendation for the plant's site was true. I said it was a true story and she was very pleased.'

Incidentally, co-branding endorsements of Wales and Sony remain a prominent feature to this day as can be seen from most copy issued by the Welsh Board for Business Development.

(3)   In addition to being a revenue earner, the Walkman must have done as much for global awareness of a company as any single product ever has. Interestingly, market research forecast that there would not be a market for Walkmans. So the Walkman was born out of the Sony philosophy of leading the public with new products rather than asking the public what kind of new product it wanted. To which we might also add Akio Morita's foresight on the kind of visibility this product would have: 'Of course from the start we hired young couples to stroll through the Tokyo Ginza's "Pedestrian Paradise" on Sundays listening to their Walkmans and showing them off.'

Bonding image: smart company, smart consumers

Image shares the smart identity of a company/product with consumers who feel smart when purchasing the world leader, and then 'wear the image' when consuming – and being witnessed to consume – the smartest brand. Yet the process of the virtual spiral of branding is more subtle than that. Because of the combination of global awareness of Sony as state-of-the-art and the company's speed in covering competitors' initiatives, on occasions when Sony is not the first to innovate a new product feature – for example, the ear-to-mouth sized mobile telecoms handset – most consumers will come to believe that such a smart new feature was invented by Sony. Since Sony is prepared to be judged by the leader's quality standard on every product marketed, the most consistent way to express this faith is the company as the brand, which is then further connected to every product sub-brand (for example Walkman). Because of the consumer pull properties of identity, image and world class leadership, the branding is the core business process in what is ultimately a very tangible sense. From company through industry channels to consumers, the branded property rights of being Sony give the company first choice of such important market-builders as joint venture partners and smart employees.

Akio Morita's conclusion is:

> 'The stiffest global market competition is local. To win in each market, product R&D and manufacturing must be customer-driven, as must marketing. Sony must be a "glocal" citizen'.

Keys to refocusing brand architecture on the top-level Nestlé banner

Recent history of Nestlé

1988	Price paid in acquisition of Rowntree Company regarded as a landmark tribute to the value of the branded asset
1990	Leaped into Landor Associates' list of the world's 10 ten brands (whose representatives in foods had previously been confined to the Cola companies)
1990s	Power of Nestlé brand attracts worldwide joint ventures, for example, with General Mills in cereal market

Valuing brand equity as a portfolio approach to business partnerships over and above the consumer franchises of separate brands

Nestlé's consistent use of the 'Nes' syllable has served to connect the identities of indigenous brands such as Nestlé (chocolate), Nescafé (coffee), Nestea (tea) and Nesquik (milk shakes) creating an umbrella reputation over a wider range of categories than any other foods manufacturer. When Nestlé acquires 'power brands' (that is ones supermarkets would prefer not to go without), for example Kit Kat, they are quickly endorsed as produce of the Nestlé company thereby strengthening the breadth of the Nestlé portfolio. This portfolio approach helps the company to negotiate with supermarket chains as an equal and so maintain its strategy of 'every year marketing value' (long before P&G's recent declaration that every day 'value pricing' was preferable to promoting peaks and troughs into every separately branded line).

Stability of purpose is a hallmark which Nestlé strives for in all of its business relationships; note, for example, the company's long-term sourcing contracts for core product ingredients. By combining the power of the Nestlé brand and the company's reputation for long-term partnerships, Nestlé has leveraged some of the most interesting global joint ventures made by packaged goods companies: Cereal Partners Worldwide, in which General Mills provides product sub-brands which are marketed under the Nestlé corporate brand; the joint venture with Coca-Cola to market ready-to-drink Nescafé and Nestea brands which was described by Coca-Cola's chairman as 'having the potential to combine some of the world's most admired and recognized trademarks with a distribution system of unparalleled reach and efficiency'.

Working the internal partnership of a global-local management culture

Global strategic framework, local operating freedom: world class brands are managed to thrive on this creative tension (think of Coca-Cola and its bottlers or McDonald's and its franchisees). A brand has a global heart when its presentation across national borders shares a common name, visual look and price-positioning strategy, all of which should be integrated to the world class company's quality standard and customer-oriented service culture. When this framework is in place local faces of a brand can be designed to represent the transient ways in which consumers at any particular time or place like to feel involved in reflecting their own lifestyles on a global institution. Nestlé asks local managers to search for cosmopolitan commonalities of approach before detailing insurmountable local differences. This attitude of mind has grown naturally in Nestlé (a transnational business headquartered in Switzerland) because the corporate culture and brand portfolio have never been burdened by a domestic bias. Characteristic elements of Nestlé's business culture in the eyes of top management, quoted in *The Marketing Challenge* (Mazur and Hogg, 1993), are as follows:

- Informal communication at the top
- Quick decision-making

- Anti-paper, anti-bureaucratic systems
- Strong cynicism towards projected figures – 'they are always wrong'
- Pragmatism
- An emphasis on long-term directional planning as the basis for all decisions
- Avoiding the use of market research as a crutch and the sole basis of decisions.

Visual communications as the global fabric of life

Design, wherein the powers of corporate identity and branding are made to coalesce, is the universal language spoken by global brand strategists. Thus Nestlé's visual communications team translates the headquarters strategic framework and regional offices' local product presentations. It also builds on the internal and external lifestyles signified by corporate devices like Nestlé's mother's nest logo. When you come to think of it, the term 'nestkeeper' is a better one than 'gatekeeper' for perpetuating the vision of the end-customer that everyone in a packaged foods consumer-led company is trying to serve.

A Nestlé visionary

Leadership credit at Nestlé goes to Helmut Maucher who took over as managing director in 1981 and is widely recognized as having revitalized the once 'quiet giant'. According to Maucher 'Nestlé must be present in all major markets around the world'. One advantage of global presence is the ability to cross-pollinate successful food products from native markets to growing markets around the world. The company strives to be an 'insider' in all markets and is willing to be patient to attain that goal. This patience is bolstered by great faith in the future. 'The ability to continuously adapt to altered circumstances and efficient management of change are as important as development of long-term plans and concepts.' Maucher believes that Nestlé's long-term licence to operate comes from being able to supply consumers with food and beverage products that are attractive in terms of quality, service, variety and price. As a result, Nestlé's marketing, research and product development are closely attuned for taking advantage of change through modification or renovation of products.

To Maucher, one of the more dubious business theories of recent times is product life cycles. There is no reason for a basic food product, once a 'star', to become a 'dog'. 'For me, product renovation is an important aspect of innovation. You can do a lot to maintain many areas . . . if you stick with existing products and ask "What has changed, what can we offer in technology, in more convenience, in another taste?" We revive classic products just by not giving up . . . and using our brains.'

Product passion

An extract from *European Advertising Strategies* by Rein Rijkens:

> 'In 1989, I asked Nestlé's CEO for the three factors that contributed most to the success of Nescafé. He asked those directly responsible for the product to answer. After deliberation, they attributed its success to:
>
> * the fact that the product had been developed at the right moment – brand launch 1938 – and had benefited for a long time from the novelty of instant coffee;
> * Nescafé consistent and superior quality "We've always been very good at taking water out of something";
> * the quality of the communications used to support the product, the scope of its geographical presence and the dedication of all at Nestlé and their long familiarity with Nescafé, which have created what almost amounts to a Nescafé culture.'

Keys to the re-engineered British Airways process

Recent history of British Airways

1980   Prior to privatization consumers joked that 'BA is Bloody Awful'. Today's word-of-mouth is 'BA is Best of All'

1993   Rolling out in Club World are packages of all the best features benchmarked from other airlines, for example, personal videos, four-course meals . . . plus BA's own innovations such as 'Well-being in the Air', a keep-fit programme at 30,000 feet.

Above all, the image of the 'World's Favourite Airline' coalesces reality because branding and staff communications lead each other around the virtuous spiral of 'Winning for the Customer'.

The learning organization

The Japanese explain their ideal concept of a company as one giant feedback loop which continually joins up the identification of consumer needs and the satisfying of them. Transplanting this objective into the heart of a company's culture and committing to the ritual of continually measuring yourself against world class standards are two of the most vital acts of branding a service company which lives for its customers. One nomination for the global service company whose staff have made the most dramatic achievements in adding value for customers over the last decade is British Airways (BA). Judge for yourself what companies can learn when branding is directed towards building a global stage and creating the expectation of world class performances; and how the latent capabilities of the business – for example, routes and hub needed for a profitable global network, highly qualified engineering staff – were invisible to customers until the brand process was re-engineered.

Global advertising used as a leader's declaration of intent

Legend has it that BA dared Saatchi and Saatchi to invent the genre of global advertising. The big idea was that if one visual experience was going to be shown in 29 countries simultaneously then BA would make a big enough budget available to bring cinematic effects to the television commercial break. The result was Manhattan Island being 'flown' across the Atlantic to appear over the heads of puzzled British villagers using sci-fi effects which even dwarfed those of the movie 'ET'. This had a breathtaking impact while working by creating images and feelings that are so plain that they can readily be absorbed in any number of countries and across different cultures. Because no words were needed to describe this experience, the words declaring the brand's new slogan – British Airways: The World's Favourite Airline – had the stage to themselves. To consumers, what mattered most about the slogan was not whether BA could immediately verify its assertion, but that the company was issuing a global declaration of what it would try harder to be. To staff, it was the start of a never-ending journey towards an ideal to live up to.

'To fly to serve': interweaving advertising and customer service training programmes

The public launch of the world's favourite airline was orchestrated to coincide with a stepping up of staff training programmes built around the company's motto 'to fly to serve'. Just as the advertising slogan of the World's Favourite Airline loops round to an image for staff to live up to, the company motto 'to fly to serve' revolves round to remind customers of their rights in expecting superb service prompted by the motto's designed-in appearance on flight menus, staff uniforms and other BA signage. Progressively, BA's research has uncovered facts such as it was costing six times more to obtain a new customer than to retain an old one. Thus BA has even managed to win over its accountants to the idea that everyone in a service company is also in marketing. Hence a staff training programme 'winning for the customer' has been developed in which all 48,000 BA staff participate. This focuses on such clear messages as 'customer retention is about service delivery, that is getting it right the first time and for those few (but inevitable occasions) when things don't go to plan, service recovery'.

Air Miles and Executive Club: world class customer loyalty schemes

As sub-brands of BA, these loyalty schemes have quickly become phenomena in their own right. Air Miles – co-sponsored by such diverse businesses as oil companies, supermarkets, credit cards and news-papers – conveys the message of the excitement of air travel with a ubiquitous visibility which advertising alone could never muster. Executive Club is a prime example of what a leader can do when it reinvests in its heavier customers. A recurring pattern from research into customer loyalty schemes is that leaders who design schemes in their own image (that is first, best and biggest) win a pre-emptive marketing advantage which leverages their economy of scale. Research also reveals that customer loyalty schemes amplify customer feedback, especially those involving customer complaints. True service competence is about turning this into an advantage.

The global brand equity of 'to fly to serve to smile'

To complete the 'giant feedback loop', BA's global advertising campaign has evolved towards making a big smile the company's trademark with staff and customers alike 'it's the way we make you feel which makes us the World's Favourite Airline'. The executions of this theme – from Hugh Hudson's 'global face' (a bird's-eye view of a smile portrayed by an animated human sculpture involving a cast of thousands) to the recent 'fantasia' on smiles – are masterpieces. Nonetheless, some people may be tempted to dismiss the theme as a corny commercial strategy, whereas we would categorize it as an audacious one. It doubles up the ideals for staff to live up to in trying harder not only to deliver world class standards efficiently, but also to display a corporate body language of warmth and friendliness which is particularly welcome when you are travelling in foreign lands.

A continuing last word

This should go to Liam Strong who for many years was in the thick of the transformation of BA in his dual role as marketing director/employee manager.

> 'The challenge from our point of view is to keep people surprised. You have to give them more than they thought they were going to get. If people are going to notice that the service is good – when they are already expecting that to be the case – it's up to us to surprise them, to make them say "Oh, that's interesting" or "Oh, that's nice".'

In short, the airline's customers have got used to a high level of service and expect BA to continue to deliver it, and more.

Keys to the Shiseido process

Brief history of Shiseido

1872   Founded in Tokyo's Ginza district by Yushin Fukuhara with the original inspiration of giving Japan a Western-style pharmacy emphasizing the latest in foreign technology and remedies.

1900   Inspired by a visit to the USA, Fukuhara features elements of the American drugstore. His shop becomes a place to rendezvous and his decorative cosmetic products revered both as artistic symbols and as the progress of science towards beauty

1990s   Japan's leading cosmetics company and one of the world's top five.

(A primary research source for this brand is the EIU's *Going local: how global companies become market insiders.*)

Where East meets West

In 1908 the founder's son Shinzo left Japan to read pharmacology at Columbia University (New York) and to tour Europe where Paris's artistic culture made a fundamental impression. Soon after returning to Tokyo, Shinzo took over as head of Shiseido. The credo which he put into practice was that business and culture should not be two separate domains foreign to one another. He saw them as twins which grow only through mutual interaction. Under Shinzo's direction a design department was created within Shiseido, consisting of an elite mix of artists, writers and researchers. It was their responsibility to develop promotional materials for the company's products. One of the first fruits of these labours was the sign of the camellia to be branded on all Shiseido's products, a trademark which the company still uses today. More remarkably, Shinzo's cultural aspirations for Shiseido live on. For example, the brand's vision defined by today's CEO, Yoshiharu Fukuhara, the founder's grandson, is: 'Our fundamental objective is to enhance customers' beauty and well-being by synthesizing the most beneficial features of Eastern and Western culture and technology. Our very corporate culture is a hybrid of East and West.'

The artistic heritage of Shiseido is reflected today in the work of the company and the art of its foremost commercial designer, a Frenchman, Serge Lutens. Lutens' work is regularly awarded prizes by juries at international advertising congresses. It often pays to be cynical about the selling power of arty advertising, but this does not apply to Shiseido where artistic merit is the living part of the product. Shiseido has an ethereal sense of femineity nurtured on the coalescence of Eastern and Western imaginations. We cannot think of another company that would sum up a public retrospective of the company's century of advertising with these words in the exhibition catalogue. The name of Shiseido has a particular sense. It signifies 'the house which contributes to and facilitates a human way of living', and this finds its essence in a famous Japanese poem from the book on divine virtues by Ekikyo Kohka:

> 'The virtue of the earth which we inherit is incomparable. This
> virtue of the earth combines with the virtue of the sky to collapse
> the boundary between what we do and what we imagine.'

CEO Fukuhara translates the artistic into a cultural perspective. 'Our advertisements have a significance beyond their immediate utility; since we can trace the changes in popular attitude to feminine beauty, they are a valuable social statement.'

Glocalizing culture

Global business at Shiseido involves the art of the long view. As head of international business, Matsuda explains: 'It is not only sales that are important in our marketing effort but laying the ground for selling our products. We've got to become an entity that pleases all the citizens in the local markets.' For example, in 1991 Shiseido completed its first European factory in Giens in France's Loire valley. This was the culmination of an 11-year effort for Shiseido to align itself with a country synonymous with beauty. First came a joint venture: 'We wanted to capitalize on the enormous experiences of French people themselves, running our business under the guidance of French leadership and personnel.' Second, five years of 'mood image building for Shiseido' deemed worthwhile because 'now Shiseido's image in Europe is a

Japanese company in France with high quality product'. Third, diligent cooperation with local people to ensure that the Giens factory suited the natural landscape in an effort to 'become harmoniously integrated with the local community'.

Matsuda notes 'there are two methods for a company to become international:

- muscle, in which an attempt is made to build market share quickly;
- spirit, the way we use to persuade and convince people of our meaning. It is more important to us to win reputation, prestige and consumers satisfied in using our products than to increase sales volume rapidly.'

State-of-the-art product

Shinzo also believed that every Shiseido product should improve the image of the business. Through his expert scientific knowledge, Shiseido products have always prioritized leading-edge quality. Today, the company invests heavily in the beauty sciences of dermatology, ageing and the like. In Japan, Shiseido helped to found a collaboration called The Advance Skin Research Inc (partnered by Chugai Pharmaceuticals, Nippon Oils and Fats and the Ministry of Health and Welfare). In the USA, its relationship with Harvard Medical School (HMS) goes back over 20 years when a joint study on melanin was initiated. In its latest project, Shiseido has joined up with HMS and Massachusetts General Hospital to establish the world's first comprehensive dermatology centre called The Cutaneous Biology Research Centre. This is bringing together leading scientists from around the world in the fields of biology, immunology, cell biology and molecular biology. This entity will own the patents to any discoveries, but as Fukuhara is quick to point out 'Shiseido has priority to license and use the technology'.

Keys to the modern Singapore process

Brief history of Singapore

1330s   The sleepy fishing village of Temasek was renamed Singa Pura 'Lion City' by a visiting Srivijayan prince who saw an animal he believed to be a lion

1819   Modern Singapore was born when British East India Company official, Sir Stamford Raffle, claimed Singapore as a base. Its fine natural harbour, favourable location and free trading policy attracted merchants and migrants from Malaya, Indonesia, China, India, the Middle East and even Europe

1955   Progressed from being a crown colony to self-government

1963   Federation with Malaya

1965   Emergence of Singapore as independent republic.

Singapore's independent essence

'From the earliest days of the country's independence, Singapore's mission was to satisfy foreign customers. Just as many big cities had previously grown up around their trading links as ports, Singapore deserves the credit for aiming singlemindedly to be the world's most attractive airport destination. Singapore's original communications strategy, using its national airline as its commercial flagship, is a long-running example of branded excellence. The slogan "Singapore girl – you're a great way to fly" is legendary. It has provided the image for a tourist and businessmen's centre of gravity in the Far East around which servicing infrastructure has been relentlessly built. For example, Singapore innovated the idea that an airport should be an attractive place for customers and had the confidence to charge them for this privilege. Now Singapore has become Asia's late 20th century New York, giving its citizens every bit as much pride in what they have built as New Yorkers must have had in the 1920s.

'Some people are tempted to look down on Singapore's image-building by querying its sexism. They should answer two questions. Do they think that Singaporeans would enjoy the advantages they now have if their airline had been marketed like Aeroflot? What right do they have to criticize an emblem of hope and beauty which was designed as a statue of liberty in our mass-communications age?'

Customer satisfaction on the most surprising tropical isle on earth

I had never felt what the word exotic meant until I visited South East Asia – the colours, the smells, the street-life celebrations which Singaporeans call 'the love of socializing'. Here is a visual vocabulary which many advertisers would give their eye teeth for and which Singapore advertising campaigns blend skilfully. Where in the world do you find: . . . ten year old boys walking 8 feet tall? or dragons chasing lions down the street? Singapore may not be my favourite destination after decades of exploring South East Asia, but it certainly deserves its reputation as a reference point for its welcome to newcomers to the region. Do you know of any other country publishing an official tourist guide which includes a section on 'errant retailers'? These are shops which you are recommended to avoid because of recent 'malpractices'. With such detailed attention to customer values, it is not surprising that Singapore has now been voted Asia's number 1 convention centre for six consecutive years.

An organized mission

Singapore organizes its people, probably more bossily than a country should. On my first visit, I was quite startled to be told that if a Singaporean's hair was as long as mine, he would be relegated to the back of the queue in post offices and other public institutions. It was explained to me that if Singapore's mission was to consistently attract the highest added-value service businesses within its reach, then every member of the community was expected to live a lifestyle compatible with this goal.

A self-portrait

Returning to its self-vision as centreport to the skies, here is a typical tourist script as only Singapore can tell it.

Surprising Singapore

Strategically poised at the tip of the Malaysian peninsula, just over 1 degree north of the equator, lies Singapore, the dynamic crossroads of East and West. Clean, modern and efficient, Singapore's sophisticated skyline is set off by lush gardens, vivid orchids and tree-lined avenues. Luxurious hotels, among the world's finest, offer excellent service at unbeatable prices. Gleaming shopping centres, brimful of bargain buys.

An amazing amalgam of Chinese, Malay, Indian and Western cultures, Singapore is a tropical isle of fascinating festivals, traditions and exotic cuisines. At the numerous restaurants and food centres, the cost of sumptuous seafood and tropical fruit is delightfully modest. A constant round of surprises awaits the Singapore visitor. A fortune-telling parrot in 'Little India'. The colour of a classical Chinese opera. Bargaining for batik and baskets, while the muezzin calls the faithful to prayer from the nearby mosque. A sunset cruise on a Chinese junk. Having tea with a well-mannered orang utan. Or travelling by trishaw through Chinatown.

After Singapore, further adventures await just a few hours away. Bali with its mystical temple rituals and dances. Java where the mighty Buddhist stupa of Borobodur lies near an active volcano. Sumatra, home of the fathomless mystery of Lake Toba. Sarawak, where rushing rivers and jungle paths lead to Iban longhouses. Sabah, the mountain home of the Kadazan tribes' ancestral spirits.

Just a short drive away, in Peninsular Malaysia, stands historical Malacca with its ruins of the Portuguese and Dutch eras; Penang's Reclining Buddha and the sun-warmed islands of the South China Sea. Surprising Singapore's exciting neighbours.

Keys to the McDonald's process

Brief history of McDonald's

1937	First McDonald's restaurant opens in Pasadena; 17 years of continuous improvement of fast food service
1954	Ray Kroc buys company; brands the franchise of homely values and consistent quality across USA (growing from two to 200 outlets by as early as 1961)
1970s	Building of global brand accelerates
1995	14,000 branches in 70 countries. Reportedly second most recognized brand in the world after Coca-Cola

A 3-stage process on the road to McPerfection

In future, it is a fair bet that most big new branded successes in a convergent world marketplace will employ more of the franchiser's mechanisms of timely growth and less of the classical brander's all-or-nothing launches. Franchisers have the advantage of testing their markets as they go; they get feedbacks on improvements from traders which have their interests at heart. The business has more opportunity to evolve at the brand's natural rate of growth.

The improvement of McDonald's to the state we know today involved three broad stages of development. The first was the working definition of a single fast food site to customers' satisfaction which the McDonald's family had clearly engineered by 1954. The second was the business genius of Ray Kroc in expanding the franchise throughout the

USA over the next quarter of a century. The third was fine-tuning of an image to international consumption.

While the McDonald clearly pioneered the fast food product, they did not in our book invent the brand. A world of communications separates a popular local emporium from a chain store image capable of supporting hundreds of outlets. What Ray Kroc identified was the emotional need for a consistently homely offering across the length and breadth of the USA's highways. The kind of place that a stranger to town could take his family to in complete confidence. McDonald's began to export its family-peace-of-mind successfully in the 1970s. By this time a significant proportion of city dwellers everywhere found mobile mealtimes were part of their personal calendars. Not necessarily competing with a real meal, nor often the proper time for a meal break, but the relaxing experience of sitting down to a table or picnicking nonetheless.

Directing a service brand as a staff lifestyle and a consumer lifestyle

With a daily customer base of 23 million people, McDonald's is a pioneer of the arrival of the factory floor at the point of mass consumption. Everything depends on making a staff ritual out of those minimum standards of consistency that customers have a right to expect, day-in day-out, from branch to branch across the globe. The friendly faces which the young crews at McDonald's bring to this repetitive exercise is a remarkable compliment to the culture of the brand and their sense of pride. In an organization whose training is achieved with world class efficiency, there is something to learn at every level from the symbolic motivation of attending a management course at Hamburger University, to the teamwork prizes which make crews compete to be the branch which offers the best customer service, to the values expressed in the handbook which every crew member reads beginning with the words: 'Cleanliness is like a magnet drawing customers to McDonald's. Our restaurants must be spotless at all times both inside and out.' Moreover, the McDonald's tradition of keeping close to customer needs is celebrated annually on Founder's Day when everyone from the chief executive down becomes a crew member for the day.

Investing in the visibility of an internationalized design language

Unlike the branding of a unique selling point, a strong umbrella brand knits together a design language in order to portray a multidimensional personality which competitors cannot replicate. This is achieved by connecting up corporate values with product sub-brands (which may be targeted at different audiences and occasions of use) and branding symbols (which may make most efficient use of different communications pitches and create a tapestry of awareness for the brand).

It is also interesting to see how sub-brands and symbols can then become stars in their own right. In the USA Ronald is second only to Mickey Mouse in his commercial rapport with children; in the world of business, the pricing of Big Macs has become *The Economist*'s regular alternative measurement system for monitoring currency exchange rates; and M's role as probably the most powerful single letter logo in the world has transcended such uses as being the motorist's signpost to McDonald's restaurants, to its consumer nickname as the golden arches, to its use as a corporate badge on crews' uniforms, to its newly tilted use in spelling out where personal sized pizzas are now available.

A world class citizen produced with global heart and local faces

One of the most poignant souvenirs of the late 20th century was captured in a globally syndicated newspaper photograph of McDonald's Moscow opening. On the kitchen side of the counter was a crew of young Muscovites busily serving and smiling radiantly at their first customers: members of the KGB looking hungry and bemused. A local journalist summed up this bemusement: 'It will be harder for the old guard to penetrate the secret of this dazzling palace than it would be to penetrate that of the B2 bomber.' Companies intent on being global ambassadors for their markets need to be prepared to allocate some of their promotional and advertising budgets to more concrete investments of faith like McDonald's Moscow opening. Moreover, it would be difficult to over-estimate the long-term local goodwill created by McDonald's as Brian Moynahan's recent report on the world's busiest restaurant explains:

> 'Though not the largest joint venture with the West, McDonald's is in terms of public awareness the country's Number One joint venture. That is psychologically important, for the Russians crave concrete signs of cooperation with the West as they try to navigate a rising tide of troubles . . .. McDonald's has also dispelled the fear that Russians cannot be trained to work in the service sector. Only seven expatriates remain to supervise the 2000-employee operation.'

Keys to the Benetton process

Brief history of Benetton

1960s	Family company formed in northern Italy: sister designed colourful woollens, brothers added commercial flair
1970s	Visioned international franchise from fourth retail outlet. Integrated marketing built on vision of the United Colours of Benetton and flexible architecture of supply chain and customer channels
1980s	The second most successful European owned company in terms of creating added value for its owners. Probably the brand recording the most bans of individual poster campaigns in different countries. Established a loyal and cosmopolitan consumer culture appealing to youthful values
1990s	Over 6,000 retail outlets in over 80 countries.

Brand essence and bridging

In the late 1950s Giuliana Benetton developed a taste for knitting colourful jumpers. This was the source of an identity that would later be the essence of the branding of 'The United Colours of Benetton'. A supportive family, and brother Luciano in particular, resulted in the formation of the Benetton company in 1965. Soon three stores in northern Italy were experiments for franchising a retail format. Unlike most franchisers (for example McDonald's) who spent decades perfecting a national format, Luciano decided that the company's fourth store would signal his intent to be an international franchiser. Soon Luciano was inspired to take an extraordinary creative leap: the branding of multiracial harmony as a suitable image for connecting colourful products, youthful markets and cosmopolitan vision. As Luciano later explained, this integrating image established consumer pull and attracted franchise partners because of its globally relevant theme. He who dared to build this bridge between product lines, consumer lifestyle and corporate mission found it quite natural to direct that the company would subsequently embrace the controversy of multiracial harmony and then the controversy of controversy.

Added value

The objective of a commercially branded organization is to add value for its stakeholders. In this respect Benetton's success has been outstanding. According to Professor John Kay's analysis in *Foundations of corporate success – how businesses add value*, Benetton was the second most successful company in Europe in adding value for its owners through the 1980s (only Glaxo did better).

Benetton is a brand designed to segment opinion in the strongest possible way. You love it or you hate it, but either way you are aware of the brand. Benetton's consumers get a very effective promotional deal every time the company gains 20 units of free press coverage to one unit of advertising. This clearly occurred when the UK's Advertising Standards Authority unilaterally decided to ban Benetton's poster of an umbilical baby. Interestingly, when I asked my niece what she thought of Benetton at the time, she gave me the politically correct answer of 'I don't like their advertising but I like their clothes'. And? 'Oh yeah – you know that wearing Benetton is always going to be a talking point.' In effect, she was translating for me why controversy is the primary added value that a marketer can choose to design into products for young people to wear.

Context specific marketing and the art of the possible

Guerrilla marketing, particularly the form of this which actively offends some audiences to attract alternative ones, is not a suitable practice for every company. However, note two points:

- For a new company in a heavily branded market controlled by big manufacturers and retailers, authors like the Americans Trout and Ries argue that this can be the only practical form of marketing.
- Every marketer needs to be able to understand the workings of guerrilla marketers wherever they may be competitors or prospective partners. A favourite parable of mine is the brief co-branding affair of Benetton and Barbie. The co-branding logic, as far as it went, was that Barbie dolls dressed in Benetton colours would benefit from additional seasonal purchasing, while Benetton would benefit as girls transferred their attachment to smart clothes from their dolls to themselves. Of course the essences of the two brands were entirely different. Unsurprisingly, in PR terms the guerrilla gained what the innocent lost.

Will Benetton's advertising continue to have the last laugh?

Here are some further points that are worth debating:

- Three of the ways that advertising works, which some less savvy than Benetton overlook, are adding a value that's not in the product itself; overcoming cultural lags (relevant in positioning to youth in their increasingly cosmopolitan world); and keeping a company in the news.

- It is interesting that the Benetton poster campaigns which evoke the most outrage vary from country to country. For example, the baby which outraged the UK establishment induced barely a ripple of reaction in the rest of Europe. I can imagine that a future doctoral thesis will measure specific national prejudices by analysing responses to Benetton's cosmopolitan history of campaigns!

- Does anyone have evidence to prove that Benetton's recent Aids-tattooed torso campaign is a less effective social service than government sponsored advertisements campaigning to contain Aids? The reason for asking this question is that the Benetton family argue that they are interested in a social agenda of concerns confronting young people and that some of their company's advertising campaigns are designed to serve this purpose.

- A recent issue of *Marketing*, a British trade journal, made the point that the images which Benetton uses to promote woollens are frequently similar to those used by magazine covers and other broadcasters from CNN to the BBC to sell their services. What images are proper for whom to sponsor? This is not an easy question to answer, particularly now that Benetton's Colours magazine is developing a sincere readership among Benetton's consumer club. Sample this, and you may not need to be part of Benetton's clan to agree that this magazine's editorials have a cosmopolitan and constructive purpose, which shows up some established broadcasters' jingoistic news coverage in a surprisingly poor light.

Keys to The Body Shop process

Brief history of The Body Shop

1976   Born in Brighton where the first shop was opened by Anita Roddick with a £14,000 loan from her bank

1990s   Retail network of outlets now extends to over 40 countries.

Designing a global network

The Body Shop shows us how to turn a retail format into a global news and product network. Franchised outlets in shopping centres around the world provide stages for synchronized merchandising presentations themed to the cultural mission which The Body Shop leads. 'To be a success in business, be daring, be first, be different' is a guiding principle of Anita Roddick, the founder of The Body Shop. Here is Anita on The Body Shop's corporate tone of voice:

> 'Being successful doesn't mean that you have to be soulless. . . . We will work on the "feminine principles, putting our love where our labour is". We will do this, and still open up 1,000 shops, still produce new products and retail concepts that will leave the High Street reeling. We will carry this through with a sense of enthusiasm, joy, magic and theatre which have always been our essential qualities. But when faced by copycats we defend the visual image of The Body Shop like a lioness defends her cubs.'

Communications as a process of dialogue, and learning

According to a company brochure: 'Consumers are not passive; they are educated, articulate and informed. They demand information. They can effect change. The four specific topics of mutual interest to us and our customers are:

- The use of animals by the cosmetics industry, for testing and ingredients, and the alternatives – as practised by The Body Shop
- The hype and hard-sell of advertising and packaging in the cosmetics industry
- Our responsibilities to the environment and the community
- The Body Shop itself – its ideals in practice.'

The process which The Body Shop represents is that of branding a cultural movement, involving all of the company's audiences: customers, staff and trading partners.

> 'The Body Shop's frontline are our staff. Most businesses focus all the time on profits. I think that is deeply boring. I want to create an electricity and passion which bonds people to the company. Especially with young people, you have to find ways to grab their imagination. You want them to feel they are doing something important. I'd never get that kind of motivation if we were just selling shampoo and body lotion.'

New product domains, such as those of aromatherapy and aloe vera, come from Anita's worldwide mission to rediscover 'natural cosmetics'. 'We are happy to reach into the past and look to the practices of other cultures'. Above all: 'While others (in cosmetics businesses) are talking in terms of "beauty", we've eliminated that word because we want to align ourselves with the health industry.'

Playing David against Goliath

Anita knows that the rewards for playing David's role can include global press coverage supporting your cause. What could be more fittingly newsworthy than pitting the soul of The Body Shop against the bureaucratic excesses of the EU? This giant has probably never had to retract a draft directive more quickly than when it sought to impose that all cosmetics sold in Europe should be animal-tested. It took The Body Shop's network only a few days to win the battle by means of a petition signed by hundreds of thousands of Europeans.

In *World Class Brands* I have argued that 'if your brand is to perform in a global theatre, it must have an enduring sense of character. Shakespeare knew how to create immortal characters. Is it unrealistic to expect that World Class branders should apply a similar know-how to their craft? After all, they are creating character scripts involving millions of consumer rehearsals every day.' Anita's sense of theatre deserves a standing ovation for developing The Body Shop into an epic global brand.

Keys to the local seeding process of Häagen-Dazs

Brief history of Häagen-Dazs

1961   Born in New York. Communications were entirely word-of-mouth through the 1960s and 1970s

1989   International transfer of brand equity has accelerated since 1989 when Grand Metropolitan acquired Pilsbury. Retrospectively, Häagen-Dazs has been called 'the hidden jewel in the crown' of the Pilsbury portfolio of brands.

Introducing 'seeding'

World class branding involves several added-value communications processes which have yet to be documented in classical marketing text books. One of these, which we call 'brand seeding', uses an alternative launch plan to that of the advertising burst; indeed many brand seeders go further and say that advertising too early will destroy the legend of the brand which must be cultivated and diffused through opinion leaders.

The European entry strategy of Häagen-Dazs puts it in the grand master's league of brand seeding. Members of this elite group are traditionally populated by haute couture fashion 'marqués' which have always sensed that premium pricing, quality product and jetsetters' word-of-mouth bless a brand's image with a certain '*Je ne sais quoi*'. Alcohol spirit brands are another category which are mostly seeded, seldom launched. But adopting a wider perspective, semi-global brands are increasingly seeking to trail their cosmopolitan heritages in the run-up to penetrating new national markets. For the purpose of this benchmarking masterclass, our primary focus is the UK launch of Häagen-Dazs.

A name which invented a tradition

If you are going to exploit word-of-mouth, there is no better starting place than a great name. Opinion leaders like to make impressions on people and what can be more effective than their endorsements of a brand's name transferring its own message in the process. Häagen-Dazs works for the branding – down to its strategically placed umlaut – to convey an exotic Danish image. Arguably, the naming of Häagen-Dazs invented the concept of conferring the stereotype of a national identity on a brand to launch it as a cosmopolitan lifestyle.

Setting a fashionable trail

The UK launch began in 1989 with distribution in a single outlet: Harrods. Next came Häagen-Dazs On The Square, an ice cream parlour in Leicester Square where theatregoers could see that the longest queue that summer was to get into Häagen-Dazs. Then Häagen-Dazs appeared on selected hotel menus, for example the Hilton, but only when hotels agreed to 'list' the brand name on the menu.

In parallel, sampling was conducted through Häagen-Dazs ice cream parlours and from a specially designed 'brandwagon'. Selected venues – polo tournaments, sailing regatta, grand slam tennis tournaments – were the kind where debutantes 'come out' and jetsetters 'mingle'. Another sampling coup (or should it be coupe?) was the Conservative Party ball with a write-up in the next day's *Daily Telegraph*.

Orchestrating word-of-mouth diffusion

The fashion trail had been planned as studiously for opinion leader ratings as any conventional media plan for TVRs. Moreover, branded PR was carefully orchestrated. Typically, journalists were supplied with 'brand biographies' and the trade was reassured about the brand's premium pricing with the briefing that it was only natural for fresh cream ice cream to cost up to seven times that of ice cream which had never seen a cow.

Consumption of a premium product can be its own best PR. Befitting the yuletide season of gastronomic indulgence, Häagen-Dazs sponsored London's Capital Radio over a Christmas period ensuring that all DJs had unlimited supplies of Häagen-Dazs to snack on. The festive spirit was returned with almost hourly free mentions ('Jocktorials') of Häagen-Dazs.

When the time had come . . . to speak of cabbages and kings

Timing when a seeding strategy is ripe for mass-market expansion calls for all a marketer's finesse. In early 1992, after more than three years of seeding, Häagen-Dazs wanted to blossom as a mass-market brand. Two barriers needed to be side-stepped. First, Häagen-Dazs needed super-market listings, but the big British supermarket chains demand that brands must be advertised. Second, there was the prospect of an ice-cream war with the transatlantic arrival of the Clarke family and their declaration of the launch of their premium brand in the summer of 1992 with a multimillion pound advertising budget. Characteristically, Häagen-Dazs met these challenges with a creative solution. The plan was to go for 40% share of noise with an advertising budget representing 2% share of voice. This was achieved through an investment in a press and poster campaign whose returns included 19-fold free news coverage. The Häagen-Dazs advertising brief – one of the most effective in branded history – is revealing: 'Use the style rules of haute couture perfume branding to propagate the feeling that Häagen-Dazs is the second most pleasurable personal indulgence after the 'O-word'.'

The brand marriage of Heinz with Weight Watchers

Brief history

1978   Heinz CEO, Tony O'Reilly, acquires Weight Watchers Interna-
        tional (WWI)

1980s   Building of WWI into the largest weight control company in the
        world lays claim to the universal high ground of healthy diets,

healthy lifestyles, health foods. Starting in the USA, processed foods businesses suiting Heinz and Weight Watchers are developed

1991   UK launch of Weight Watchers products from Heinz.

Marrying into a World Class image

Could a world-leading position in healthy foods have been cultivated in any more efficient way? Note the following steps in the execution of this added value strategy.

- Heinz acquired Weight Watchers at a reasonable price, before anyone else had the vision that this business was a world class branding platform.
- Heinz groomed the Weight Watchers brand – in similar ways to the seeding of Häagen-Dazs – to ensure that the goodwill of the brand's opinion leaders was enhanced before mass marketing was consummated.
- Weight Watchers' staff were encouraged to preserve strict quality controls on the development of new products to ensure that they lived up to the company's name. The style rule of their branding process is: the credibility of Weight Watchers' clubs depends on their reputation for teaching members to replace bad eating habits with healthy eating habits for life.

Exploiting global and local media platforms

Being the world's largest weight control company is a newsworthy positioning. Staff from the original Weight Watchers company take every opportunity to point out to journalists that: 'Heinz really has improved the quality of both Weight Watchers brand foods and programmes we offer through the weight loss meetings. Moreover, the company has such a good name that when customers hear that we are owned by Heinz, they are really impressed.' Word-of-mouth of this sort shows how effectively the Heinz and Weight Watchers brands are being orchestrated to feed on mutual endorsement of each other's qualities.

Weight Watchers also thrives on grassroots appeal propagated by loyal members of the weight control clubs. Through these champions the brand utilizes such impressive direct marketing media as networks of office workers who circulate to each other news of the club's latest programmes.

References

Kay, J. *Foundations of corporate success – how businesses add value.*

Kapferer, J. (1992). *Strategic Brand Management.* Kogan Page

Macrae, C. (1991). *World Class Brands.* Harlow: Addison-Wesley

Mazur, L. and Hogg, A. (1993). *The Marketing Challenge.* Harlow: Addison-Wesley

Morita, A. *Made in Japan (Sony).* E P Dutton

ThinkPiece 2

Workshop formats
for Brand Chartering

Most of Chartering's 'branding junctions' featured in the chapters of this book are easily transformed into workshop formats. We include some examples here to illustrate:

- practical inputs and outputs involved in business team workshops;
- how simply chapters of this book can be transformed into workshop formats.

A few notes on workshop practices

Typically, we view workshops as means for facilitating both brainstorming and consensus-building. They may also be used for training purposes.

It is not a good idea to rush into a workshop format without considering how much ground is to be covered. A meaningful Brand Charter will often need to be cultivated from a series of workshops. There are various practical reasons for this.

- Exploratory phases of Brand Chartering where questions raised may be more important than driving out answers (for example, if the questions suggest that some specific consumer research is needed to resolve either a new issue or one on which the team has alternative views).

- Some of the tools of Brand Chartering require deeper or broader thinking on brand processes than may be anticipated by participants who have not previously been asked to examine the varied perspectives of a 'branding junction'.
- Thinking time between workshops to allow individuals and teams to regroup their ideas is important, particularly where views formed from considering a specific branding junction in isolation can be expected to be modified by considering connections between branding junctions as the integrated perspective of brand organization develops.

In forming workshop procedures and groupings of participants, it helps to foresee whether opposing agendas – either openly expressed or hidden – are likely to dominate individual participants' contributions. For example, if one of the reasons for a specific Brand Chartering project is to converge two fundamentally conflicting points of view, it may be appropriate to convene workshops between teams with the similar perspective first, before attempting alignment.

It is often a good idea to pilot Chartering of a branding junction on a competitive brand or other brand that the team knows well but has no vested interest in. In particular, this applies if subsequent Chartering on your own brand is expected to flush out that the brand has (unexpectedly) weak spots at this junction (which may or may not be of some embarrassment to particular members of the team).

Each workshop agenda described below comprises several parts which the facilitator should integrate as the flow of the workshop moves to a consensus conclusion.

Essence expert (from Chapter 1)

(1)   Heritage searches

- Look at briefs issued at critical periods of time (for example, by brand's founder, at times when brand was in a strong growth period).
- Look at brand guidelines HQ gives to local operations and then at local briefs.
- Listen to why consumers say brand is unique (particularly in businesses endorsed by the brand which have strong upward momentum).
- Do a quasi-corporate identity audit of everywhere the brand appears. Where is it visible (independently of media promotions)? What meanings does its signage convey? Who are opinion leaders in the

brand's sphere of business; among whom does it get first endorsement? How newsworthy is the brand's business per se and how additionally newsworthy is the brand's unique essence?

- Are there any biographies on the brand?
- Pinpoint the most popular brand campaigns in the history of the brand. How did they present the brand's essence?
- Look at global and local stereotypes associated with the brand. How does company vision/mission/culture interact (if at all) with the brand (for example, what makes Shell-man different from Esso-man?). How is R&D/NPD innovation shaped by being your company rather than being any other competitor?

(2) Workshop probes

What would consumer, company or other audiences (for example staff/ channels) really miss if the brand did not exist? The Leo Burnett Brand Consultancy (LBBC) four-corner analysis of brand essence (see page 33):

- 1: usage meanings
- 2: performance differentiation
- 3: source/platform of values owned
- 4: personality/image representing smart consumer identity

+ Is this essence the biggest motivator in the categories in which the brand competes?

Which categories is the brand anchored in? Which categories do we need to evolve towards?

How does essence cross-check (that is integrate with):

- positioning of every product line;
- priority of investments in identities/consumer awareness codes;
- all aspects of Brand Charter;
- linkages with other brands (in corporate hierarchy)?

(3) Cross-validation of essence as best communications investment

- Does it have long-term validity? Does it match our heritage and our future?
- Does it help 'seed' the most newsworthy platforms for us?
- Does it have biggest emotive (for example, purchasing-consuming-witnessing) meaning?

- Will it support the most vibrant organizational vision/culture? Is it the right vision/mission/culture for added value in our sphere of business? Does it match our world class competences? Is it what leadership (being number 1) means to our company? Does it encapsulate why our company is unique and is worthwhile (to, for example, our stakeholders) preserving as an independent identity?
- Will it make others want to partner us rather than compete against us? Does it help us to control the added-value chain of our sphere of business?
- Does this brand have any essential market 'presences' – countries, products, channels – which are outside of our organizational resources? Are these urgent enough to require corporate partners?
- Can branding language pre-empt this essence as uniquely ours? Can this essence be communicated cost-effectively?
- Is it rich in production/direction opportunities affording a consistent variety of consumer-exciting executions?
- If we had to compete against this essence, are there weaknesses in it which we would exploit?
- What style rules does this essence imply on every way we communicate?
- What are the different essence perspectives (for example, among consumers, journalists, channels, staff)? Ask representatives of every corporate function to:

  – imagineer what contributions they can make to essence?;
  – risk-analyse activities they undertake which could peculiarly damage perceptions of essence?

Identity expert (from Chapter 2)

(1) What?

What brand identifiers (for example, colours, symbols, stereotypes, slogans, platforms, famous moments in brand's history, product features, design icons, other appeals to senses, and so on) are in the minds of your consumers?

Begin by compiling a broad inventory of the brand's identifiers. Use a mixture of consumer research, brand team expertise and detailed search of brand communications (packaging, advertising, and so on). Where identifiers are similar, cluster these and highlight a leading representative (for example, the one with the most communications impact).

Add to your broad identity inventory by probing into meanings/information which your identities are built to represent as the brand's own. Typically:

- unique features identifying the products of the brand;
- usage occasions which the brand's identifiers are designed to own (for example, which usages would you expect your brand to be recalled first in mind for?);
- images designed by the brand for your consumer club to 'wear';
- word-of-mouth colloquialisms;
- stereotypes that are identified as part of the brand's heritage;
- values/feelings which are designed into the essence of the brand;
- visions identified by your brand as to why it is number 1 (the leader) of its sphere of business.

Within the broad inventory, parenthesize identities that have low uniqueness or low awareness (for example, those which most consumers of the brand would not recognize as uniquely yours).

Put to the top of your inventory those identities which you value most as part of the brand's equity (and which have been a significant part of your total communications investment in the brand). Get each member of the brand team to make a personal inventory before compiling a communal inventory. For example, identifiers top of Budweiser's USA inventory include:

- Clydesdales (shire horses)
- 'This Bud's for you'
- Red, white and blue
- (American) eagle logo
- Beechwood ageing
- Genuine article

(2)   How?

Strong brands use identifiers to work in many ways. How? Make a list of all the ways in which your brand's identity system must compete for consumer attention, for example:

- General recall of brand as top of mind
- Specific recall of brand as top of mind (for example, occasion of use, calendar of mind)
- Multi-position brand (for example, Coke is modernity, Coca-Cola is classic)
- Badge brand as image to wear
- Seed a brand's cachet

- Identify a brand as a source of PR
- Endow a brand with a stereotype bringing instant cosmopolitan appeal
- Local buy-in to a globally branded phenomenon
- General reminder of brand essence
- Pre-emptive (for example, symbolic) ownership of brand essence Souvenir of brand essence (or other empathy translator)
- Translate essence into lifestyle or service guarantee
- Heighten visibility/recognition of brand (for example, impact in a specific media or own a new platform)
- Transition brand umbrella (for example, to incorporate new products)
- Connect up values of flagship products to other umbrella products
- Connect brand to other portfolio brands (for example, corporate brand and product sub-brand)

(3) Why?

Do the following workshop exercise to explain why specific identifiers are vital to the brand. List the 'what' identifiers down a page; list the 'how' identifiers across the page. Use this matrix to tick off why your identifiers are important.

- Are there any identifiers which you need to phase out (for example, because they no longer distinguish the brand's future values)?
- Are there any identifiers you need to phase in (for example, to support new products or because your identity system is not working on some important hows)?
- Is your brand underperforming for some markets' consumers because of a lack of awareness of a specific identifier? In building new geographical markets, does the brand's identity building need to be sequenced in a certain order?
- Do your communications investments emphasize all your key identities in an orchestrated manner? Is your marketing mix totally integrated? Which product lines should you advertise when to identify your brand's umbrella essence as being most relevant to consumers' diaries of life?
- Are any of your identities weak in the sense of being easily imitated or spoiled by competitors? How can these weaknesses be repaired? Are there any new identities or stereotypes which you must stop competitors from establishing?
- Does your identity system reconfirm your brand essence for every audience? Does your identity system work the way you want it to in every consumer locality?

- What connections are there between the brand's identity system and other brands in the corporate portfolio?
- Does every branded product and service have a coordinated visual look? If your brand is offering different value points, are these visually coded in a way which enhances (rather than confuses) consumer choice?
- What tone of voice are you communicating?

Masterbriefing expert (from Chapter 6)

(1)   Big purposes of the brand platform

Prioritize the top two or three 'continuous big purposes' of branded communications process. For example:

- Keeping the brand in the news
- Consistently adding real value
- Bonding smart 'two-way' relationships (for example, not only your perception of brand but brand's perception of you)
- Sell more

Brainstorm examples of 'ways' branding can work on a specified purpose. For example, what keeping in the 'news' can do for a mass market brand:

- Convey a popular image of the brand (that is one that a consumer expects everyone to see in the brand)
- Make a declaration in public, such as a guarantee
- Applaud loyal consumers (most consumers like to see their brand in the news and, apparently, winning against competitive brands)
- Make news items – reported by journalists
- Make a brand into a celebrity whose ownership transfers some of its celebrity status
- Capture and symbolize a mood of the times
- Establish the brand as a reference point, against which other brands are compared by critics and public
- Make brand a topic of social conversation
- Make brand famous; endorsed by opinion leaders
- 'Multi-audiencing' (for example, sharing news with trade channels and with consumers)

Across 'purposes' and 'ways' prioritize three groups:

- We need to 'do now'
- We should aim to include these ways soon
- We do not need these for this brand process

(2) Integrating communications

Make two matrices. Across each matrix (columns) are those 'ways' you have prioritized as 'do nows'.

- Down the first matrix are elements of the marketing communications mix such as: advertising, packaging/design, PR, direct marketing, point-of-sales materials, franchising, price cutting, own promotional stage (for example, Beaujolais' birthday party).
- For each 'do now', tick communications elements which could efficiently contribute. Discuss whether these elements would work in isolation or interactively. If interactively, ensure that the 'masterbrief' clarifies focal points where creative executions will need to interact.
- Across the 'do nows', ensure that the 'masterbrief' includes sufficient detailing of how the 'do nows' work together for the big purposes.
- Down the second matrix (rows) are possible audiences of brand marketing and communications. Include, for example, consumers, channels, staff, journalists, other consumer opinion leaders, business partners. Is each 'do now' a single audience process or a multi-audience process? If a multi-audience process:

    – to whom do you need to communicate and in what order?
    – revisit whether multi-audiencing has any extra implications for your 'masterbrief'.

- Does multi-audiencing prompt us to think of any additional 'do nows'?

(3) Iteration and fine tuning

Which 'continuing purposes' of the brand are most efficiently communicated by broadcasting media (for example advertising) and which by narrowcasting media (for example direct marketing)? What should be the lead medium for the brand and how will contributions of secondary media be integrated?

Develop a format for 'masterbriefing'. Is this making fully integrated use of brand essence? And proactive use of brand identity? (References: Essence and Identity Experts, earlier in this ThinkPiece)

If you own a portfolio of brands, do an early piloting of the differences which should exist in masterbriefs for different leagues of brands (for example, the one product brand, the umbrella-but-not-corporate brand, the corporate brand).

Best practice for a global and local branding process:

- First, let teams do their own integration and masterbriefing workshop from both ends (global, local) of the brand process.

- Second, use the workshops' outputs to build consensus on similarities and learn from differences (work from both ends to ensure global brands keep on adding value locally).

Sequencing of branding activities has an impact on how consumers identify with a brand's evolution. Variations, for example by national marketplace, should be recorded. Accordingly, masterbriefings must be easy to fine-tune/update and supportive of:

- actioning local 'do nows' within a consistent framework;
- quick over-reviews anticipating competitive moves or environmental changes.

Is the brand process smart in making two-way relationships? For example, for corporate brands, is full use being made of Blackston's two primary relationship factors which consumers want from brand:

- trust = credibility*intimacy/risk
- satisfaction = proactive + supportive?

Do not underestimate possible inertias (from different internal functions and external agencies); find some quick wins; encourage everyone to observe examples of competitive brands that are dying because their processes are not integrated.

Leadership expert

(1) Marketing/organizational visions

Make a list of marketing/organizational visions which appear to be connected with creating significant added-value momentum. Are there parallels for your company? Also rehearse the relevance to you of some of the following examples.

- Anniversary marketing (big creative service goals, deadlines, integrated marketing ideas). For example, at Disney, Eisner's brand planners are committed to turning every year into birthday celebrations. Hence Snow White's 50th was followed by Mickey's 60th, and so on.
- British Airways: (1) Slogan as a declaration of intent, that is a service goal and a consumer right of expectation (World's favourite airline); (2) Loyalty clubs designed to understand how heavy users' needs are evolving (for example, Executive Club + Air Miles).
- World class response to consumer complaints (for example, Marks & Spencer gift vouchers worth many times the faulty merchandise; Nordstrom).

- McDonald's: (1) Training prizes (Hamburger University; awards to franchiser's crews); (2) Mc-language: McDonald's, Big Mac, McNuggets; (3) Go where you're really needed (profit from goodwill building before you do in monetary terms, for example, McDonald's in Moscow).
- Turning product exhibitions into themed family entertainments (for example, Lego toylands).
- Franchise/format enjoyable aspects of a national culture (for example, Club Med, Guinness).
- Establish network of celebrity connections (for example, Hard Rock Cafe).
- Build your own media (for example, Beaujolais' global birthday party)
- In branding smart relationships with everyone keep up an active search for what will excite passionate responses from: external audiences (for example, consumers, channels, journalists); internal audiences (for example, staff generally, every functional expert specifically).
- Sony-Walkman leadership credo overriding negative market research: we know what is possible, the public does not. Plus Sony-founder's corporate mission statement: 'If it were possible to establish conditions where persons could become united with a firm spirit of teamwork and exercise to their hearts' desire their technological capacity, then such an organization could bring untold pleasure and untold benefits.'
- Honda legend: global race (going public on staff challenge; we need world class engineers as our core competence) from 1950s 'to win the TT race' to 1980s 'to win the Formula 1 championship'.
- Xerox revitalization story (benchmark stretch goals and backward engineer competitors, for example, Canon's photocopiers).
- 3M culture (steal some innovation time).
- Be first; be biggest; be within mind's and arm's reach of desire (Coca-Cola).
- Seed the top of the market. Fashion meaning-leading values as your own. (For example, Häagen-Dazs British market seeding of the second most pleasurable thing that an adult can do; Japanese popular slogan: Shall we Häagen-Dazs tonight?)
- Acquire a high-image business in a limited or unbranded market. Then marry it into a mass market business. For example, Weight Watchers and Heinz.

Architecture agenda

Describe (up to) five most essential relationships between company and end-consumers from the consumer viewpoint. Identify for each relationship, the biggest historical leap forward (event/process) in advancing the relationship and describe corresponding unique values to the consumer: internally produced (for example, product/service characteristics); externally built (for example, superior communications or distribution channel). Pinpoint who developed this big idea and how the company's essence or vision empowered them to implement this. Is anything in the company's current organization/visioning likely to contribute a similar quantum leap forward in the next three years?

(If instead of leaps forward you associate your essential added-value relationships with continuous development over time, state what were the most important factors underpinning this continuous development. Will these factors continue to be as important in developing consumer added value? If so, how do the organization's culture and systems work to safeguard these 'investments' over short-term measurements such as those of financial performance?)

Do the same exercise for other non-consumer audiences; for example, staff, customers (channels). To what extent are value advances in these essential relationships interdependent and how do they differ? Discuss how all the above is interconnected with:

- the way the company's portfolio of brands is structured;
- the clarity/motivation that exists across the organization in terms of strategic concepts such as goals, vision, mission, values, core competences.

Make a list of some organizations which you regard as very competitive. How does their organizational architecture (see Thinkpiece 4 on flexible companies) vary from yours? Is their brand architecture more focused? Is everyone in the company more aligned to a leadership mission? Do their core competences combine to add unique value?

Ask this question at every strategic or tactical opportunity: could we engineer a more efficient branding architecture for communicating perceived quality as the passion underlying everyone's smart relationship with the company and the hallmark of everything which the company does or will want to do?

Does everybody in the company have two jobs: doing the job, and learning to do a better job? Are the internal marketing communications of the company geared to evolving individual and collective competences?

ThinkPiece 3

A change list for the future marketing environment compiled by professor Michael Thomas

Whither brand management?

I would like to pose a few questions about the future marketing environment. (I am paid to think about post-millennial times!)

The first set of questions relate directly to customers, and are of obvious importance to the custodians of brands. The remaining sets are more broadly focused, but it does not take a great leap of the imagination to connect them to brand management. The last group of questions relate to the current wave of questions about marketing itself.

Customers

This refers to both consumers, business end-users, and distributors.

(1) How do customers define value and satisfaction? Does one have access to any methodology that really explores these issues?
(2) From what base does one build customer loyalty?
(3) How do customers trade off quality and price?
(4) Can one any longer reach customers by mass advertising?
(5) What implications does globalization have for local identity – does local identity have any meaning in a world of global brands?

Markets

(1) Have we begun to understand the implications for markets of the information-based, post-industrial society?

(2) Market saturation is a common characteristic of Western developed economies with too many goods and services chasing too few discretionary spending customers – can marketers find a solution to this problem?

(3) Too few discretionary spending customers – is this the beginnings of bipolar society, with high-income knowledge workers a small minority, surrounded by a low-income proletariat?

(4) If markets are dominated by global producers and/or distributors, will there be any space for small and medium-sized enterprises?

Technology

Will the convergence of computing and telecommunications lead to:

(1) the dominance of direct marketing at the expense of national advertising?

(2) efficiency drives in producing companies so that real time productivity analysis will expose unprofitable products, customers and outlets? Will outlets quickly delist unprofitable brands?

(3) customer-based market analysis with redundancy risk for data-based analysis (based on aggregate Census data)? Will lifestyle analysis come to dominate consumer market analysis?

(4) reduction of the distance between suppliers and their customers by way of electronic data interchanges, electronic mail, voice mail, video conferencing and videophone? Who will become the communicators?

(5) interactive marketing? If cable reaches 25% of the estimated 50% of all UK households with satellite/cable (expected by the year 2000), then interactive marketing, voting, home shopping and game playing will touch a significant proportion of all householders. Who will be the interaction managers?

(6) new product development and testing based on new interactive/response mechanisms? What are the implications for co-designing and co-makership and where does marketing fit in?

Communications

Technology is already revolutionising both information access and communications. What are the marketing implications of the following factors?

(1) Interactive marketing – dealing directly with the human face of the customer? Multimedia is the human face of electronic information!
(2) An advertising industry showing the same globalizing tendencies as is manufacturing. What are the implications for marketing of a global oligopoly in advertising – eight or 10 conglomerate communications companies?

Distribution

The concentration of ownership in UK distribution raises a number of questions:

(1) Has the rise of retailer power begun the process of destroying national brands? Is brand management, which in the past has been the apprenticeship route of many marketing directors, coming to the end of its life?
(2) Will competitive advantage lie with those marketing organizations that are really close to the customer, ie retailers?
(3) Will retailer brands and corporate brands dominate markets?

Marketing organization

Is the current criticism of marketing due to all (or some) of the following factors?

(1) A failure to distinguish between the marketing concept and the marketing function.
(2) A failure to decide whether marketing is a holistic or a specialist subject.
(3) A failure to see that the only thing that really matters is that strategic thinking is dominated by marketing imperatives.
(4) A failure to match the claims of finance and manufacturing/ engineering/research and development in respect of sovereignty over boardroom decision making.
(5) A failure to discern that marketing and sales are inseparable.
(6) A failure to understand that internal marketing must precede external marketing.
(7) A failure to realize/understand that the marketing concept is the only strategic vision that can forge value-added relationships with customers, employees and suppliers.

But what about the answers? I have views about most of them, do you?

(*Source*: Editorial contributed by Professor Michael Thomas (1994), *Journal of Brand Management*, 2(2). London: Henry Stewart Publications)

ThinkPiece 4

Flexible companies (organizational structure for flexing change)

20 questions for the organization architecture

	From rules to goals	From product to market	From hierarchy to network	From compliance to alliance
Customer-driven	Have you found catalysts for the 'customer reorientation'?	Have you identified your true customers?	Have you built organizational support for customer focus?	Are you building and managing customer partnership?
Quality-driven	Have you adopted and understood Quality language?	Have you formalized agreement with customer?	Have you disseminated but not bureaucratized Quality?	Do you insist on Quality partnerships, internally and externally?
Flat	Is corporate structure matched to customer strategy?	Do you delegate authority to respond to customers?	Can you balance decentralization and identity?	Have you built a corporate structure which responds to collaborate instead of command?
Fast	Are you fostering fast management processes?	Are you building fast development processes?	Have you absorbed networking technologies?	Are you achieving better collaboration through fast technologies?

continues

continued				
Alliance	Do you identify strategic goals beyond corporate boundaries?	Do you seek alliance partners in the market?	Can you manage your alliance partners?	Can you extend collaborative culture beyond the company?

(*Source: Building flexible companies.* EIU)

The Stockade

Defensive structure – product focus

The Stockade is a series of functional hierarchies. Resources are limited and must be defended; all products will find a market.

The Matrix

Defensive structure – market focus

The Matrix is the stockade adapted. A more demanding market forces corporate functions to begin cross-reporting for better response. But the matrix may only bring inherent power conflicts out into the open.

The Collaborative Circle

Collaborative structure – market focus

The Collaborative Circle reverses the assumption of the stockade. The company is focused on the outside world – its customers instead of on its products. It draws customers into the corporate process.

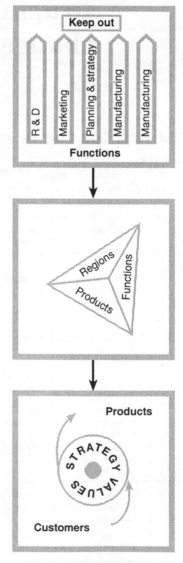

Figure T4.1   From confrontation to collaboration

The slow-development hierarchy

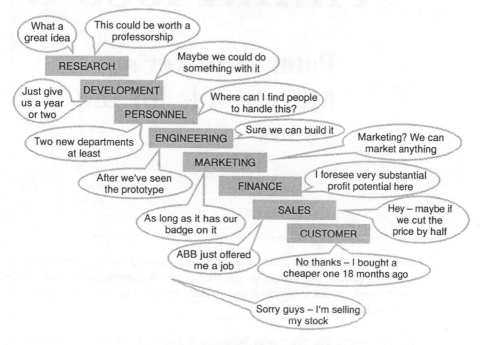

Simultaneous Development Processes

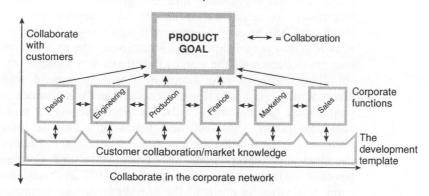

Figure T4.2   Who integrates wins

ThinkPiece 5

Peter Drucker's Megatrends for the 1990s

(The remarkable thing about Drucker's megatrends is that they seem to be just as salient every time you revisit them. We included the following in our previous book *World Class Brands* (1991), but make no apologies for repeating them.)

(1) The world economy will be quite different from that businessmen, politicians and economists take for granted. The trend towards reciprocity as a central principle of international economic integration has by now become well-nigh irreversible whether one likes it or not (and I don't). ... Reciprocity can easily disintegrate into protectionism of the worst kind (that's why I dislike it). But it could be fashioned into a powerful tool to expand trade and investment, if – but only if – governments and businessmen act with imagination and courage. ... In the past whenever a new major economic power appeared, new forms of economic integration followed (eg the multinational which was invented in the middle of the nineteenth century when the United States and Germany first emerged as major economic powers; by 1913 multinationals had come to control as much of the world's industrial output, maybe more, as they do now). Reciprocity is the way, for better or worse, to integrate a modern but proudly non-Western country such as Japan into a West-dominated world economy.

(2) Businesses will integrate themselves into the world economy through alliances; minority participations, joint ventures, research and marketing consortia, partnerships in subsidiaries in special projects, cross-licensing and so on. The dynamics of economic integration are shifting rapidly to partnerships based neither on the nexus of trade

nor on the power nexus of multinational ownership for several reasons:

- Many middle-sized and even small businesses will have to become active in the world economy. To maintain leadership in one developed market, a company increasingly has to have a strong presence in all such markets worldwide. But middle-sized and small companies rarely have the financial or managerial resources to build subsidiaries abroad or acquire them.

- Financially, only the Japanese can still afford to go multi-national. Their capital costs them around 5% or so. In contrast, European or American companies now pay up to 20% for money.

- The major driving forces behind the trend towards alliances are technology and markets. In the past technologies overlapped little. . . . Today there is hardly any field in which this is still the case. Not even a big company can any longer get from its research laboratories all, or even most, of the technology it needs. Conversely, a good lab now produces results in many more areas than can interest even a big and diversified company. The need for alliances is the greater the faster a technology grows. . . . Markets similarly are rapidly changing, merging, criss-crossing and overlapping each other. They too are no longer separate and distinct.

(3) Businesses will undergo more and more radical structuring in the 1990s than at any time since the corporate organisation first evolved in the 1920s. Businesses tomorrow will follow two new rules. One: to move work where people are, rather than people to where work is. Two: to farm out activities that do not offer opportunities for advancement into fairly senior management and professional positions (eg clerical work, maintenance, the medical man in the hospital) to an outside contractor. The corporation in stockmarket jargon will become unbundled. . . . Underlying this trend is the growing need for productivity in service work done largely by people without much education or skill. This almost requires that the work be lodged in a separate, outside organisation with its own career ladders. Otherwise, it will be given neither enough attention nor importance to ensure the hard work that is needed not just on quality and training, but on work-study, work-flow and tools. . . . Corporate size will by the end of the 1990s have become a strategic decision. Neither 'big is better' nor 'small is beautiful' makes much sense.

(4) The shift of ownership in the large, publicly held corporation to representatives of the employee class – ie pension funds and unit trusts – constitutes a fundamental change in the locus and character

of ownership. It is therefore bound to have a profound impact, especially on the governance of companies; above all to challenge the doctrine developed since the second world war of the self-perpetuating professional management in the big company; and to raise new questions regarding the accountability and legitimacy of big company management. . . . Hostile takeovers have been one early symptom of this. They work primarily because pension funds are 'investors' not owners in their legal obligations, their interests and their mentality. The raiders are surely right to assert that a company must be run for performance rather than for the benefit of management. They are, however, surely wrong in defining 'performance' as nothing but immediate, short-term gains for shareholders. They are also wrong because immediate stockholder gains do not, as has been amply proven, optimise the creation of wealth. That requires a balance between the short term and the long term, which is precisely what management is supposed to provide and get paid for.

(*Source*: *The Economist*, 21 October 1989)

ThinkPiece 6

Core competences: belief and practice

(1) Five business trends which are making core competences vital

1.1 Barriers to open competition are breaking down

As the marketplace becomes increasingly global, companies no longer enjoy home-turf advantages. In addition, regulatory barriers are crumbling. Companies must compete on their capabilities.

1.2 Command-and-control planning and management styles arebecoming unwieldy

Companies are better able to set a course for the future by focusing employees on competences. Products and markets will come and go, but competences provide a stable base on which to build the future.

1.3 Wooing customers has become tougher than ever

For many companies, quality and cost are no longer reliable sources of competitiveness. Instead, they are the basic requirements of doing business. A company's unique competences are potentially the wellspring for the development of new products and services that can both captivate consumers and create new markets.

1.4 Highly diversified corporations need new organizing principles to leverage their resources

Today many corporations have divided themselves into SBUs. However, the same internal competition that can rejuvenate business units sabotages the sharing of corporate resources across SBUs. An emphasis on the competences that underlie several SBUs promotes broader vision and cooperation.

1.5 A new mood of caution guides merger-and-acquisition activity

Core competences offer an internal logic for diversification, thereby helping employees and consumers appreciate why the company is in certain businesses.

(2)   The benefits of a core competence approach

2.1 Spurs innovation

Innovative products that create new markets overnight are becoming increasingly important to the profitability of global companies. The persistent cultivation of a core competence, sometimes for a decade or more, often leads to breakthrough products.

2.2 Prevents bad divestitures

A working knowledge of its core competences helps a company avoid making unsound divestment decisions. Companies that divest themselves of businesses in mature or overtly competitive markets may find that they have significantly reduced the prospects of entering new and lucrative markets. For example, when GTE sold Sylvania and left the TV business, it unknowingly gave up participating in the profitable VCR market of the future. The core competence approach is a gateway to a set of opportunities. If you jettison a business or a product, you may also forgo future profits from the underlying skills developed in support of that discarded activity.

2.3 Guides diversification

Core competences allow a company to 'stick to the knitting even while reaching into new markets'. The bridge between the successes of the past and the new products and services of the future is a firm's core competences. In embarking on new ventures, firms can manage risk by bringing their core skills to their future enterprises.

2.4 Aids globalization

Colgate-Palmolive was fragmented into 62 operating subsidiaries with 42 product lines before it was reorganized in the late 1980s around five core global businesses in five regions. It used the concept of core competence to unite its far flung operations. Emphasizing the skills that subsidiaries share is one way companies can break down the encapsulating walls between units and bring focus to a global operation.

2.5 Chooses strategic alliances

To thrive and even survive, companies will have to forge key strategic alliances. When Polaroid began to leverage its instant-imaging technology into new markets, it chose not to build all the required new components and products in-house. Instead, the firm carefully chose partners based on a methodological mapping of the potential partner's competences.

(3) Guidelines for selecting the right core competences

3.1 Forge a clear link between strategy and skills

Strategy drives skills. If this linkage is missed, your company may end up doing some things well, but not doing the right things right.

3.2 Look at what is happening in the marketplace

Some companies assemble all their engineers to discuss core competences and will forget that effective debate on the subject requires more than technical people alone. Managements must include sales and marketing viewpoints. Core competences mediate and integrate technology and market needs.

3.3 Clarify the implications for pivotal jobs

In a department store that has identified the types of customer service it wants to develop, the store needs to create a list of skills and qualifications for pivotal jobs. What kinds of people should be hired? What kind of training and coaching should they receive? How should they be rewarded and motivated? All too often, companies define areas in which they wish to excel in general terms and then stop short. They fail to take the time to drive those critical conclusions through to mesh with key job implications.

3.4 Determine future needs

In assessing a company's core competences, it is important to project into the future and determine which skills and capabilities will be necessary for effective competition in the medium and long term. Executives and others involved in the process need to develop a point of view about the future and what core competences are shaping it. Executives must look at corporate development priorities and future growth opportunities. Then, they should come away with an implementable conviction that the company can control its own destiny with its strategic competences.

(4) Guidelines for integrating core competences into the life-blood of your organization

4.1 Provide leadership from the top

The single most powerful discriminating factor between success and failure in building core skills is the commitment of top leadership to the effort. Managements need to reinforce consistently and continuously the importance and value of building core skills. Over-communicate to your superiors, your subordinates, your customers and – especially – your pivotal job holders. Talk and write frequently about your skill-building programme. Here are some of the successful programme's features to trumpet: the skills you are trying to build, why they are critical, early wins, heroes, lessons learned from failures and milestones achieved.

4.2 Empower the organization to learn

Managements need to sketch out the boundaries of the employees' playing field by defining core skill strategy – the skills the firm is trying to build, the pivotal job behaviours it is seeking and the convictions the company wants its employees to hold. But within these boundaries, employees should be given plenty of room to manoeuvre – to try things, to succeed, to fail and hence to learn for themselves what works and what does not. This will allow them to experience lessons that could never have been taught academically or simply delivered from above.

4.3 Set high goals

Core competences are the muscles of an organization; they make it possible to accomplish much of the day's work. However, as any marathoner knows, muscles alone are not enough to win the race. High aspirations are also necessary for notable achievements.

4.4 Maintain a clear vision

An inspiring corporate vision can also mobilize a firm's people and resources. As a Colgate-Palmolive executive says: 'If you focus only on the execution of small things, you only use a small part of people's talents. If you focus on concepts, you use the larger part of people's talents; you tap into the totality of their personality.'

4.5 Communicate values

Values provide moral, as opposed to commercial reasons for behaviour and thus have a more powerful influence. When values and strategy match up, they offer more than twice the rationale for a standard of behaviour. Strong shared values provide individuals with a healthy regard for their colleagues, subordinates and superiors. Such shared values also instil a sense of success, fulfilment, and increased vitality in their work and lives.

(*Source:Best Practices:Management.(1993). The Economist Intelligence Unit.*)

ThinkPiece 7

Beyond departmental marketing

Here two authors give examples of the problems that occur in companies which organize brand marketing as something less than an organization-wide process. Their contributions are followed by comments on changing brand management extracted from the BBC for BUSINESS video 'Branding – the Marketing Advantage'.

Moving into the third dimension

Increasingly merger and acquisition activity revolves around brands. Brand portfolios in 1995 are being reshuffled as never before. In recent months, Quaker has snapped up Snapple, Cadbury has swallowed Dr Pepper, Glaxo has taken over Wellcome, Dalgety has gobbled up Felix and other Quaker pet food brands, while Colgate has acquired American Home Products' Kolynos (a huge Latin American oral care company), Grand Met's El Paso, and KKR's Borden Foods.

The pace seems to be quickening. So much so that a large part of many divisional senior marketers' time is spent trying to persuade the board that their particular brands deserve investment, while other divisions' brands are not core to the business.

Understandably, the headlines are made by the hunt for the branded jewels and the disposals of the branded dogs. But behind the corporate to-ing and fro-ing there's a crucial marketing question: what is the fundamental difference between a dog and a jewel? And can dogs be turned into jewels?

Here is one possible answer. Faced with the growth of retailer power and media inflation/fragmentation, it's not just individual brands that are being found wanting but a whole model of brand management.

This model is taught in nearly every modern textbook. It revolves around the view of a brand as a sort of target. The bull's eye in the middle is the core product. The concentric rings around it encompass added attributes such as added-value service elements, positioning, image and emotional attributes. A nice-to-look at two-dimensional picture of the brand.

However, companies are now realizing there's a third dimension that really counts. The demands of modern branding must reach further and further back through the company into its organizational structure, culture and 'core competences' – even into its purchasing policies and the development of proprietary technologies. They also accept that it reaches forward to the distribution channel and the consumer's total brand experience, including where and how it is shopped and consumed.

If all these factors are aligned and integrated, the various parts of the two-dimensional brand model can begin to shine. If not, it's on its way to dogdom. Turning a dog into a jewel is not a matter of a clever TV commercial, new product launch or even an integrated marketing campaign. The secret is the culture and the organizational structure of the company behind it.

Suddenly, all sorts of people are making this point in different ways. Kevin Thompson at marketing consultancy MCA, for example, points out that leading-edge companies are realizing that continuous improvement, internal communications and marketing are all aspects of the same thing: the delivery of the brand promise.

Co-workers at the World Class Branding network argue that brands have become more than unique selling propositions. They are now also unique organizing purposes around which a company needs to organize all its processes and resources. If it doesn't, its brand management becomes disorganized – and dysfunctional.

Meanwhile, McKinsey's suggests that marketing is moving beyond brand and market share wars to a struggle for 'the right to brand itself'. Brands are not only the key to establishing relationships with consumers. Those who win the right to brand gain a pivotal position of power – and therefore profitability – within the supply chain as a whole.

The common thread? That to survive in today's environment, brand management has to become a three-dimensional activity; one that involves the entire company. This shift lies behind marketing's current identity crisis, in particular the growing debate about whether marketing is a function or a pan-company process.

When brand management is too important to be left to marketing departments alone, what future for marketing professionals? Judging by some of the radical experiments under way, where strategic marketing integrators are being separated from true specialists (whose job is to be at the cutting-edge of a sub-discipline such as marketing research, direct marketing or advertising), many marketers may feel that their horizons are being narrowed rather than broadened. But then, working for a diamond mine is infinitely preferable to being part of a dog that's about to be put down.

(*Source*: Extracted from an article by Alan Mitchell in *Marketing Week*, 24 February 1995)

What future for marketing in the financial services revolution?

Marketing, in my view, is at the strategic heart and mind of the business. It therefore has a special responsibility. To recognize its challenges. To face up to the disaffected. To offer, promote and engage others in the way forward. As marketing in financial services reaches a cross-roads, how do we go forward?

Can we any longer look to our icons, our points of reference in fast moving consumer goods, to show us the way forward? Broadly, in a current sense, I do not believe so. Unilever with its Lever Brothers division recently seemed to subsume marketing within 'commercial director' activities and functions. Could this have been a contributory reason to what many see as the Persil Power debacle? Could short-term commercial imperatives and technical research and development people have overridden marketing's passion for the consumer? Marketing's responsibility for holding on to the chalice of the brand and what it stands for? Wasn't Persil all about care? Did care square with a manganese accelerator? Was this forgotten about and lost through the ascendancy of commercial and 'technical performance' interest? Well, I don't know and I don't want to just dump on others. I want to start focusing on us: financial services.

My opening assertion is that marketing – old age marketing – has failed in financial services. We must not be blinkered by the past. If we continue as we are there is no future.

One failure has been of an over-concentration on advertising. Marketing in the financial services hasn't managed advertising. We've presented our customers with too many advertising tag solutions, and not enough core service solutions. What went wrong in financial services is that the client and the agency believed that the solution to the business problem was the advertising. That advertising of itself could solve the problem. Market research was used. Creative ideas and solutions were presented. TV story boards of mock commercials showed the problem solved. The client was happy and spent the money. On average a customer is showered with over 1,000 financial services ads a week. Advertising in this era of marketing literate consumers is not seen as a fact. Even if you say you are best, customers don't believe it. They see it as a promise that you want to be best for them. And they test that promise. And if you don't deliver, you fail. With failure, comes the internal assumption within a company that it is the advertising that has failed. So marketing embarks on another adventure into uncharted territory with another new advertising agency, which changes the advertising and develops a further hollow promise which compounds the error.

We have challenged in NatWest our own tag line 'We're here to make life easier'. It is in my view an excellent internal one liner in helping describe what we are trying to do for our customers. Possibly better than a mission statement. However, I don't believe it has the same potency externally. I believe, in the current world, that customers are not interested in what we say we do for them. They are interested in what they want us to do for them.

We live in an era of rampant consumer disbelief. We have allowed our love and joy of things creative to cloud our judgement. We have continued to promote the misconception that advertising is communication and that advertising communication is persuasion. It isn't. We have to jolt ourselves. And remind ourselves that communication is by definition two-way. But in doing so we have to be wary of the latest buzz words based on technology such as 'interactive media'. Customers are only interested in technologically driven distribution methods when they deliver clear added-value benefits, and are easy to use.

Beware. Over 75% of customers still choose their bank on the basis of branch and cash machine convenience. And hang about, we can do interactive communication now. Staff in branches can ask customers questions like 'How was it for you?' Now. Perhaps too often we seek for customers' feedback through market research.

Marketing has failed in its championship of the customer. It has not yet become the internal customer activist in getting staff in a company to think and respond to those who pay the wages.

Can we find a new age for marketing? Let's think more, understand more, value more, our brands. Is your chief executive your ultimate brand manager? What is and how would you express your brand's character? Building, enhancing a brand should be at the core of marketing. Not exploiting it for short-term gain. Why not turn on its head the way we used to think about the hierarchy of communications?

Let's build not from our advertising but from our staff. How they speak, write, behave. People are our business. Our ability to build on our people. To value them. Understanding their roles and contributions to serving customers – to marketing.

I see people as our brand ambassadors. In this arena where trust is so critical, a brand is a signpost, is a source of reassurance. A brand built and actively managed on the values, beliefs and integrity of people within a company engenders confidence and trust. A brand can be an external manifestation of its people, its values. What is difficult to copy is another company's values, its beliefs, its proper confidence in what they do right for their customers. This is when a brand becomes a source of competitive advantage. A badge of pride for those who work for the company. A way of standing out in a crowded market.

We have a role as brand designers, not just of the pictures, but of the organization. Working with other functions, not just sales and service areas but functions such as personnel areas to create new alignments of understanding.

What is a brand? I believe that our brand is our people. The brand experience is through people. Trust is earned by people and given to people. In NatWest, we have a brand that touches customers 900 million times a year. 900 million times a year our customers seek us out or we provide service to them. Brand moments. A task of active brand management is to recognize these. And where appropriate give extra dimensions of understanding and meaning to them – through our people.

We have to wake up to the real world. We have to understand that customers do not, on a day-to-day basis, get excited about, for example, their bank accounts. They expect them to work – like turning on an electric light switch. But they get very excited when they don't work, or go wrong.

Marketing. We need to steer the people within our business. We need to set the ice on fire. To the service of our customers. So that we get it right for them. We need to actively manage what we are – and how we express it through our brands. As they say in McDonald's, 'popularity doesn't happen by accident'.

(*Source*: Extracted from a speech given by Raoul Pinnell, director of marketing, NatWest Bank. NatWest is the leading clearing bank in the UK. This speech was given as The Marketer's City Lecture in the City of London, March 1995)

Leading the organization beyond brand management

'The idea of the classical brand management system was that you would have in a relatively junior role someone who would champion a product as brand within the company. But as soon as you get umbrella branding, this becomes a terrible political system because the real purpose of brands these days is to extend across territories – whether they are product territories or national territories. Instead you end up with a system where fairly junior managers are trying to save their job or save their brand; you end up with just a sea of politics, and a lot of internal brands fighting with each other, and a lot of internal departments fighting with each other.'

'An old idea that a brand was its name, logo and message is one of the most dangerous statements ever to have circulated about branding. Winning brand processes are really about managing the whole set of relationships with customers, and everything that has an impact in the system. This can be very complex indeed.'

'You don't need a marketing department any more. What you do need is a very powerful marketing voice within the company to make sure that the company focuses on the customer right through all the stages and processes in which it operates.'

'The main theme of our recent reorganization was focus. We've set up key dimensions in our marketing team; for example, one is customer loyalty, another is new customer marketing. We want our marketing process to operate along the line of key customer processes rather than specific functions. The customer used to start at point A and move through several departments. In other words, the customer moves through horizontally whereas we were organized vertically. We have had to relearn marketing. We are not yet there 100%, but it's been a real revolution for us thinking about how you walk through with the customer in every process.'

'Added value is something which uniquely you can continue to do, and which as you evolve through it, is something which is always worth the money to consumers. It's really a pathway where you can improve the quality of the offer through a long series of steps.'

'Most brands including product brands are now more or less service brands and they really have to be delivered, irritatingly, by things that walk around on two legs. It has to happen – it's a human thing and you know humans have to be motivated in order to perform at a high level. The key cornerstone of a brand is consistent performance at a high level.'

Source: Comments extracted from BBC for BUSINESS video 'Branding – the Marketing Advantage', 1995)

ThinkPiece 8

Strong views

'There is only one boss. The customer. And (s)he can fire everybody in the company, from chairman on down, simply by spending money somewhere else.'

(Sam Walton, founder, Wal-Mart Stores)

'Financial accounting's assertion that it is capable of faithfully representing reality has been shown as susceptible to challenge on both political and epistemological grounds. The accounting profession does not accept this, however, and seeks to preserve its status as arbiter of the truth by requiring "objective verification" to counteract uncertainties. This was apparent in the prescriptive nature of the accounting reasoning applied to brands. By keeping brands off the balance sheet and dismissing claims of marketing concerning the fruits of its labour, the accounting profession succeeds in preserving its own reputation for integrity, at the expense of the integrity of marketing. It would be naive to see this in terms of deliberate conspiracy. Effective regulation depends on reliable information, and in this accounting is inevitably constrained by the uncertainties of the world which it represents. But perhaps it does illustrate how accounting can misuse the power it gains from the control of financial reporting, when the recognition tests which it applies are too restrictive.'

(David Oldroyd, School of Business Management,

University of Newcastle upon Tyne. Accounting and marketing rationale: the juxtaposition within brands, *International Marketing Review*, **11**(2) 1994)

'When measuring advertising effectiveness the primary focus should be on the brand not the ad. What should be measured is the consumer-brand relationship. The way this is done should be strategy-specific, not generic.'

(Malcolm Law, Haylen Research Centre, Auckland
Is research ruining good advertising? *Ad Media*, July 1994)

The necessary activities of product innovation do not fit into the institutionalized practices in large old firms. These activities either violate the existing systems of thought and action, or fall into a vacuum where no shared understandings exist to make them meaningful. Therefore, while managers may support "innovation" in general, product innovation is in fact illegitimate at the level of everyday thought and action.'

(Deborah Dougherty, McGill University, Quebec, and Trudy Heller, The Wharton School, University of Pennsylvania. The illegitimacy of successful product innovation in established firms, *Organization Science*, **5**(2) 1994)

'There is evidence to suggest that many organizations are currently floundering because they are operating systems, structures and processes which reflect yesterday's certainties and yesterday's realities and, in particular, show an ignorance of the power of information technology to revolutionize the ways in which organizations can operate. In a world which increasingly demands agility, flexibility and responsiveness from organizations, it has become clear that a vital source of strategic capability and competitiveness may well reside in process.'

(James Lynch, University of Leeds. Only connect: the role of marketing and strategic management in the modern organization, *Journal of Marketing Management*, **10**, 1994)

'Collective myopia is especially prevalent within organizations that carefully segment their activities and keep functions separate and distinct in the belief that problems are best solved by breaking them into pieces for assignment to specialists working in isolation. Even when employees emerge from their isolated activities and attempt to work in teams, their collective interpretations may still be myopic because of unexamined differences in their "thought worlds". Each "thought world" offers an internally consistent view of the team project or assignment even though it is skewed or limited.'

(George S. Day. Continuous learning about markets, *California Management Review*, Summer 1994)

ThinkPiece 9

BBC World Series articles on brand process

World Series articles were created as a forum for debating the lessons that can be learned from watching the BBC for Business video 'Branding – the Marketing Advantage'. The contributors of these articles are volunteers in two senses of the word:

- no pay for the contribution;
- article can be republished anywhere with reference to the BBC's video but without any other copyright restrictions.

Two early contributions to the World Series are included in this ThinkPiece.

World Series – Integrated communications for brands

Broadly consistent messages to all your target audiences will help your brand to flourish. Prof Mark Uncles explains why

Central to modern marketing management is the concept of *Integrated Marketing Communications* (IMC); the planning and execution of all types of communication to meet a common set of objectives for the brand. In particular, the aim is to support a single positioning for the brand. Thus, the positioning of **McDonald's** as a family-appeal company is supported by advertising in 'safe' media, by gaining image-appropriate PR coverage for its investment in children's activities, and by co-branding with like-minded companies in the soft drinks and children's entertainment markets.

An implication is that the marketing manager ought to take an holistic view of communications. The company that uses above-the-line media advertising and direct marketing needs to ensure that these various types of communication support a single positioning. If there was a compartmentalised view of the communications mix in the past, this needs to be reviewed. If organisational walls have been erected between one element of the mix and another, these need to be sealed, if not breached.

To some extent the pace of innovation and technological change is such that a more holistic view is being imposed on both receptive and reluctant managers alike. The existence of thousands of direct-response adverts in print media – with their reply coupons and 0800 numbers – highlights the desire to shift mass market advertising away from talking at consumers, to interacting with consumers. In the UK, **Tango**'s 'Apple Seduction' campaign has shown the sceptics that for a leading brand direct-response advertising can work even on television (over a million phonecalls were received within the first few weeks of the ad being shown).

Another way of saying that an holistic view should be pursued is to stress the importance of consistency in marketing planning and execution. This is not to say that there must be one rigid, omnipotent message, rather it is to suggest that the messages conveyed by different types of communication need to interconnect. They all need to tell broadly the same story.

There is nothing to be gained from promising one thing in your advertising, and not being able to deliver at the point-of-sale. That is a sure route to customer dissatisfaction, resentment and frustration. By all means say "we're the friendly brand . . . the listening service . . . the company to talk to" if you can match the promise, but think twice if these values are not evident at the point-of-sale, and in the packaging, and in your publicity. Since privatisation **BT** is one company that has made a bold attempt to face up to this challenge; so far **British Gas** has yet to learn the lesson.

'The brand' lies at the heart of IMC, in the sense that the different types of communication are used to support a single positioning for the brand. 'The brand' itself is the constellation of functional attributes and emotional associations that define a product, service or company. At its simplest, the object itself communicates these attributes and associations: the **Pears** name embossed into soap and the Golden Arches of McDonald's. Typically a mix of other communication types is employed, as shown in Figure T9.1.

Figure T9.1 Integrated marketing communications and 'the brand'.

The concept of IMC has a bearing on at least three aspects of brand communications:

(1) The messages that we wish to convey are usually targeted at different audiences living in different 'spaces'.
(2) Broadly consistent messages need to be sent to the different audiences.
(3) Broadly consistent messages need to be sent to the different 'spaces'.

The background is that brands are becoming transnational, modern markets are becoming more open and transparent, and as a consequence communications aimed at one audience are increasingly seeping out into the spheres of other audiences. **Shell**, **BP**, **Castrol**, **Esso** have all had to standardise their corporate images on a global scale; it is no longer acceptable to have Shell petrol stations in Nigeria wearing a facia that could be confused with BP. Prior to the **Nestlé** takeover of **Rowntree** 'the' **Kit Kat** was an assemblage of local varieties; subsequently it became clear that this was an untenable situation, and today we see a more consistent approach.

The words 'different audiences' and 'different spaces' need to be explained because they are open to mis-interpretation. The conventional view is that buyers and users of a brand can be grouped into segments. At a product category level this agrees with our intuition (baby foods are bought for babies!), but it is less apparent at a brand level (why should one group of babies systematically prefer **Farley's**, **SMA**, **Cow & Gate**, or **Boots** private label?).

One response is to think of 'different audiences' in two ways:

(a) We can envisage truly different people making brand purchases.
(b) Or we can think of the same people making brand purchases at different times and in different 'spaces'.

The latter is more likely, especially for brand choice (as against product buying). This is almost an inevitable consequence of brands becoming transnational and modern markets becoming more open and transparent. The executive traveller flying with **BA** to New York is also the family man who flies on holiday to Spain – does he then choose BA? The habitual drinker of **Nescafé** might well buy **Lavazza** if he is expecting guests for dinner, and undoubtedly he will gulp espresso when visiting Italy: the person is the same, but the roles and mental states vary. Wendy Gordon, chairman of **The Research Business**, dubs this Needs States. The inclusion of mental states alerts us to the possibility that even 'sub-culture brands' (like Tango and **Pot Noodles**) will be bought by people who move in and out of the sub-culture (a 16-year-old Tango drinker at school may be a coffee drinker at home).

This view of 'different audiences', in combination with our earlier discussion of IMC, has major implications for brand management. Reconsider the case of British Gas: as a user I welcome its commitment to customer care, but as a small shareholder I am unimpressed with the messages coming from the board, and as an employee I would be concerned about the closure of gas showrooms. There are two things to note here: the communications messages are inconsistent (which is worrying enough), and the recipient of these messages might be the same person in multiple roles (which is doubly worrying).

All these concepts are pulled together in Figure T9.2. 'The brand' resides at the centre. Earlier this was defined as the constellation of functional attributes and emotional associations that define a product, service or company. These attributes may be tangible or intangible, or more likely, a combination of the two.

In recent times we have seen greater emphasis being given to corporate or banner brands. Thus, the **Nestlé** name is given greater prominence on packaging, and **Penguin** is explicitly badged with other **McVitie's** brands on the covers of 14-bar packs. This suggest that 'the brand' is becoming the most visible and coherent expression of a company's values and vision, and it is something that demands senior management attention, if not input from the main board. Hamel and Prahalad, writing in Competing for the Future, stress this 'visioning' role for brands.

Around the centre are perceptual filters. We can think of these as lenses through which audiences interpret the communications which help to position the brand. The exact content and language of these

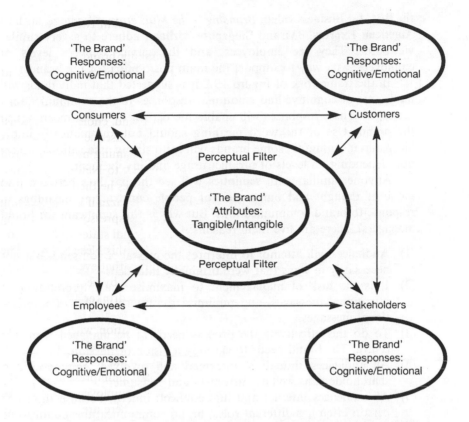

Figure T9.2   Integration of 'the brand' across different audiences.

communications will differ, depending on the audience that is being addressed, but the aim is to convey broadly consistent messages.

There are four main audiences: customers (the trade), consumers (final buyers and users), employees (actual and potential), and shareholders (both private and institutional). The significance of our earlier discussion is that it would be misleading to think of these as islands – as isolated and mutually exclusive groups. The quarter million people who work for BT are going to be phone users and subscribers, some of those who are no longer direct employees may continue to act a third-party contractors, and many will be private shareholders.

Arguably, as much attention should be given to 'managing the employee brand' as to the consumer brand. Employees are the most direct link between the brand and the customer. The agency **Macmillan Davies** point out that thousands of consumers might see and react to a recruitment advert, and while only a few of them will be recruited, many will remain as consumers. Significantly, several of the cases described in the **BBC for Business** video, *Branding – the Marketing Advantage*, such as **American Express**, **3M** and **Singapore Airlines**, adhere to a very similar viewpoint. They see employees, and the service delivery levels of employees, as a way to support the main positioning for the brand.

In the framework of Figure T9.2 it is suggested that individuals will have a set of cognitive and emotional responses to the communications messages. These responses will enable the person to attach meanings to the brand. Use of the word meaning should not automatically imply 'deep and meaningful'; some brands will instil strong associations, others not, depending on levels of product usage and involvement.

Anyone familiar with semiotics will see the parallels between that mode of thought and our notion of people constructing meanings in response to brand communications. But why is this significant for brand managers? There are five main reasons:

(1) Audiences will attempt to interpret the messages you send, but not necessarily in ways that were originally intended.
(2) It is the task of management to maximise the interpretation of intentional messages, and minimise the interpretation of unintentional messages.
(3) To do this effectively the process needs to be managed from the centre. The brand needs to embody a vision or mission.
(4) All audiences should be informed and involved: employees and shareholders, as well as customers and consumers.
(5) All audiences interact and interconnect; indeed, because the same person often has different roles, brand communications ought to be broadly consistent across these audiences.

These five points should serve as a checklist for anyone charged with the difficult and challenging job of integrating brand communications.

World Series –
The brand's right to survive depends on a dynamic organizational process

Melanie Cocks and Chris Macrae attend 'The Branding Forum' and learn what makes companies such as 3M so successful

This year's Marketing Education Group (MEG) conference held at Bradford University hosted a new event – The Branding Forum. A variety of two minute video clips were extracted from the BBC for Business video 'Branding – the Marketing Advantage' as platforms for debating key issues on branding.

A recurring theme of the Forum was that the brand's only right to survive is as a dynamic organisational process. Long term business performance depends on an ongoing balance between:

- Essential strategic elements which differentiate the brand as a leader
- Serving quality and value to local customers. Personal relevance ultimately depends on enabling every consumer to leverage his or her own sense of added value

So if the heart of brand process is this simple, why did 50 academics spend 90 minutes debating it? The complexity is in the organisational details – the dramatic growth of conflicting pressures which practitioners bring to life through the unique medium of the BBC video (see table below).

For example, consider current misunderstandings caused by those who sought a perfect definition of brand equity: in Professor Barwise's words a "snark or boojum" quest to cage corporate intangibles in a zoo for financial audiences. If a ceo believes that brand valuation is all he needs to know about brand equity, then in the words of another Professor "it's as if the company's senior job spec is for a historian whose only duty is to look back at the past".

As Hamel and Prahalad have cautioned, this is not the way to compete for the future. Enter here an up-to-date reading of Britain's corporate pulse measured by Professor Parkinson's benchmarking of marketing process, commisioned by the CIM, and endorsed by no less than Michael Heseltine.

The findings sound alarm bells for us all: most British manufacturing companies fail to get pass marks at marketing process in general and brand process in particular. Unless an urgent sense of marketing leadership is restored at the top of the company, organisations will quite simply become the prisoners of other companies' added value chains.

Those of us who believe in brand marketing as the process which is totally interconnected with the growth of a company's added value relationships need all the sources of practical inspiration we can find, like those which BBC for Business has spotlighted. Here are some of the quotes from the video which were used to open our academic eyes to the urgent challenges of making brand process happen in a fully integrated way.

Total brand organizing at Singapore Airlines (Sim Kay Wee)

"We don't have positions like brand managers or just marketing managers. The people who are running each of the countries we fly to are called general managers. If we had called them brand managers then the focus would be just one sided. And because they are general

	BBC – running agendas on brand change/conflict
brand EQUITY	How to iteratively plan and focus marketing advantages invested in a brand system; how to rehearse scenarios of discontinuity threats to brand equity; how to narrow the gap between marketing and financial assessment of equity; how to align measurement and performance time frames
GLOBAL branding	Balancing HQ and local roles and information leads; how to beat locally targeted brands; how models of external and internal priorities differs from local era branding
WORLD CLASS culture	World number 1 culture for serving essence of brand – how to sustain and how not to lose; stakeholder priorities as global citizens; specific clarification of right to lead (eg visionary capabilities); manoeuvring corporate environment – eg abolishing over-accounting
'GLOCAL' added value WELFARE	Market-partnership networks configured to glocally overthrow classic added value chains; principles of 'holonic' organisations (beyond process re-engineering)
SEEDED marketing CHANNELS	New brand targeting of opinion leaders before mass marketing consumers; global and local transfer tactics of haute couture goodwill; co-developiing new channels
SERVICE SMART integration	Consumer relationships smarts of 1:1 and broadcast media: eg lifetime focus, two-way feedback loops; employees empowered to delight (through super-motivation and communal learning mechanisms)
brand ARCHITECTURE	Brand partnership strategy: new rules for externalising and internalising linkages between brands; exploiting reputation, top level values etc of banner brands; culling or refocusing brand equity in an 'overbranded' company; leverage of change through synthesis of alternate frames of reference
brand ORGANIZING	Brand scripting and teamworking tools, eg Chartering; transformation from marketing department to network which learns how to create, manage, and direct brand as process; integration of strategy frames for leveraging brand and other intangibles (eg competences); restoring CEO lead in connecting brand organization and architecture

managers, the loyalty to the brand is subtly understood by everybody in the country, so that there is pride in ensuring the integrity of the brand while they are doing their various activities be it reservations or sales or ticketing, the consciousness of contributing to the quality of the brand is there.''

Channel partnership foresight at Häagen Dazs (Claire Watson)

"There's no doubt about it that as retailers become more concentrated, they do have a impact on brands which they feature in their stores. They themselves are building their Sainsbury's brand, or their Tescos brand, and therefore they're very selective about their ranges that they put in their stores in order to be able to communicate the values that they want to communicate about their brand. So inevitably they can be difficult partners for us to deal with because sometimes their agenda is different form our agenda. Furthermore, what they obviously want to be able to do is establish a long term relationship with their consumers with their brands, and often what they tend to do is use supplier brands or manufacturer brands to establish new categories in order that they can then prepare and develop their own version of that particular brand. So they do tend to put pressure on both ends. They have a direct relationship with our consumer and then furthermore they have the potential effectively to attack our brand with their own label."

On global branding with Professor Quelch

"The big question from my point of view is what is the added value to a consumer in France from knowing that when he or she buys Häagen-Dazs, that Häagen-Dazs is a global brand? I think the first essential is that you ahve a clear concept of what differential attributes are, the differential equities of your brand in the marketplaces in which you are currently selling."

"The second is do you have an understanding of the transferability of these attributes, of these equities to other markets. Have you done research that proves these equities are transferable? And then thirdly assuming the research is positive and suggests that they are transferable, the next step is to sort out the degree to which the customer is going to be benefitted by the application of a global brand strategy to the service or the product that you're trying to sell on a worldwide basis."

Brand architecture at 3M (Christopher Hobbs)

"One of the issues for 3M in terms of branding is the use of the Scotch and 3M brands. From my perspective being focused on the consumer market, the Scotch brand is the key brand that we advertise. But we do want the name of the 3M brand to be better known. I want people to say yes it's a Scotch brand – I'm going to buy that videotape and also to say "Ah and it's by 3M – yes 3M makes other products I like too, like Post-It notes, adhesives and so on.". It's those sorts of connections I want consumers to make more strongly. And then I hope in the future they will take the brand of either Scotch or 3M and say "Ah that's a Scotch brand, or a 3M brand – all of the products I've tried under that brand have delighted me, they've met my need, and served me well, I'll try this one. Because 3M's always going to be bringing out new products."

The organisational process which 3M had to put into place before offering consumers the best of both brands' worlds is instructive. The following extract is from our research paper on "Brand Architecture" with Mark Uncles, (The Journal of Brand Management, October 1995, 3(2)).

"As recently as 1990, 3M's marketing department was creating as many as 100 new brands a year. This had to change. First a virtual moratorium was put on the creation of new brands. Second, a lot of product brands were culled – typically by renaming them with 3M followed by the generic product descriptor. Third, as part of 3M's continuing re-organisation towards customer divisions and away from national ones, opportunities have been taken to integrate marketing and general business management.

Through this process, 3M's banner branded architecture is being set to make the most of such top level branding powers as trust, transference of goodwill, greater integration and transparency of leadership."

After the Forum, we discovered several people in the audience had been struck by a discomforting thought. Most textbooks dwell on the external presentation power of the brand, the ways its Unique Selling Proposition are manifest outside the company. But what about the internal marketing of the brand? In how many companies do employees really share the same balanced perspective on the brand's essence and its local customisation? Furthermore, how do they take advantage of increasing change forces such a globalisation whilst staying organisationally at one with the brand's value added?

The consensus of our Forum delegates was that Singapore Airlines, Häagen-Dazs and 3M are exceptionally strong marketing companies, yet even their marketing people seemed to be saying that they had still a lot to learn about brand marketing as the integrating process of business. This seemed like a valuable message for all of us to take away from Bradford.

ThinkPiece 10

CEO audit of brand equity responsibilities

Chartering's five-point audit for examining whether anybody is in charge of a company's brand equity is listed below. Accompanying alarm signals are provided for the CEO who wants to do a quick check of the system.

(1) Start with your most important brand. Who is the brand equity director of this in terms of total organization-wide responsibility for leading the brand process?
(Alarm 1: no single person identifiable

(2) Can the brand equity director answer a generalized version of 'Chartering's Mastermind' quiz on the brand process with near zero errors or omissions?
(Alarm 2: no)

(3) Does the brand equity director circulate a one-page up-to-date Charter (living script of the brand) as the first reference point for everybody who makes valuable contributions to the process?
(Alarm 3: no)

(4) Does the brand equity director keep challenging the Charter, both to update it and to foresee major change discontinuities that will require new organizational competences to perpetuate the brand's added value?
(Alarm 4: no)

(5) Do the brand equity director and the CEO regularly discuss the fit of the brand:

    (a) within the architecture of the company in terms of organization, strategy and other brands?,

    (b) in terms of interaction with other learning processes/competences of the business?

(Alarm 5 – no to either question)

ThinkPiece 11

MELNET
http://www.brad.ac.
uk/branding/

'A worldwide web site and a NETwork for Marketing Export Learning'

MELNET has been created by co-workers of WCBN who wanted to pursue the following objectives:

- Continuous improvement of Brand Chartering.
- Development of other learning systems relating to the architectural connections between branding, organization (implementation/culture etc), strategy (thinking/foresight etc) or any discipline that consistently adds value
- Exploring how to use internet-styles of thinking in coaching marketing pupils whether these perceive themselves as first year marketing students or final year CEOs.

The evolution of internet-styles of thinking fascinates MELNET co-workers, who are thinking of the interconnecting possibilities. These include facilitating:

- debates between marketing beginners and experts;
- forums for global and local participation;
- interdepartmental teamworking through pooling of perspectives and creating knowledge;
- interaction in terms of asking all user-members to help create and update learning materials;

- interaction in the sense that at the click of a mouse two ideas can be connected together which one person will find to be like mixing chalk and cheese, while another discovers it to be the missing link in his/her (or their brand's) learning process.

The following extract from an article written in early 1995 explains our original reasons for getting together to assemble MELNET.

Reengineering management thinking with the help of the internet

(Chris Macrae, Professor Stephen Parkinson and Professor Mark Uncles, 1995)

'Two years ago, we three marketing people – a consultant and two professors – discovered that our favourite topic of conversation coincided. How was it that Business Process Reengineering (BPR) had taken less than three years to become a billion dollar consultancy product? And if this was so important to the business world, why were few, if any, applications being made to the most valuable process of all – the way senior managers leveraged marketing process in general, and branding assets in particular?

'In 1995, it emerged from James Champy, one of the co-authors who coined BPR as a best-seller that "Reengineering is in trouble". Reengineering of management thinking processes does need to happen first. While James Champy has written a follow-up book on this, our parallel focus has evolved into testing how the internet's capabilities can be exploited as a media for continuous learning.

'In one respect, we have modelled MELNET, our new management thinking club, on Club Med. Namely the Club's Gentil Officers and Gentil Members. Our Network comprises co-workers and user-members. Co-workers tend to come from business schools, advertising agencies and management consultants. Typically, user-members are managers, marketing practitioners and students, but as membership is free and on the internet, our club is for anybody who wants to keep on questioning whether the organization of marketing is delivering quality and value. Specifically, do companies connect up all the talents of their employees through marketing process and in the brands they serve?

'You will find MELNET at http://www.brad.ac.uk/branding/

'Because there are so many different ways-in to thinking about marketing we are developing about 30 different display boards. Start with any one you like, but use the computerized media to play the game of connecting up as many different perspectives on marketing that you can. Don't be afraid of the choice. We know of no company that needs to integrate all 30 playing fields, but we also second a conclusion of an editorial in the *Financial Times* (21 December 1994) 'Global marketing is uniquely challenging . . . it demands that companies attain a flexibility and focus that few have yet achieved . . . manufacturers who do not appreciate this will go to the wall'. Everybody in business needs to relearn marketing if a sustainable added-value culture is to be networked across a company's people, globally and locally.

'If you type your way into MELNET, you can quickly choose to start from any display board. As an example, here is part of the display board on brand equity, followed by what you would have seen on an early version of MELNET if you had clicked down to the first ThinkPath.

Box 1.1   Brand equity

'Brand equity management has to be more than asset manipulation: it has to be an activity that involves the whole firm.' Alan Mitchell.
Running agendas include how to:

- narrow gap between marketing and financial assessment of equity
- align measurement and performance time frames for evaluating brand health
- connect external presentation of the brand with organization's internal competences
- share the brand relationship with consumers and other stakeholders
- iteratively plan and focus marketing advantages invested in brand system
- rehearse scenarios of discontinuity threats to brand equity
- clarify leadership and teamworking responsibilities for brand equity.

MELNET ThinkPaths on Brand Equity

1.1.1   Brand Equity: snark or boojum? Barwise P, London Business School, (1993)

1.1.2   Brand wars – Accounting versus marketing, Oldroyd D, Newcastle University, (1994)

1.1.3   Goodbye British Marketing, The Economist (1995)

1.1.4   Winning the right to brand, McKinsey & Co, (1994)

1.1.5   "What is your brand equity about? . . . ", BBC for BUSINESS video (1995)

1.1.6   CEO audit of brand equity responsibilities, Brand Chartering Handbook, Macrae C and WCBN co-workers, Addison-Wesley/EIU (1996)

continues

---

continued

1.1.1 Brand Equity: snark or boojum? Barwise P, International Journal of Research in Marketing, 10(1) (1993)

In Lewis Carroll's poem, the hunting of the snark was literally a matter of life and death. If the supposed snark, once finally encountered, turned out instead to be a boojum, its pursuer would 'softly and suddenly vanish away, and never be met again'.

In branding's context, the big boojum is to believe that research will one day improve techniques for defining and measuring brand equity so that brand valuation becomes both valid and objective. It will never be possible to find a single all-embracing measure of brand equity, because the value of the brand is not in practice separable from the value of the product and (leadership qualities invested in) the rest of the firm.

Barwise's paper chronicles how brand equity became a much abused concept in the late eighties and early nineties as various researchers and consultants aimed to coin their own over-simplified measurement algorithms. Following Barwise's lead, the useful way to think of brand equity is as the ultimate value adding process of business. The one whose value added connections with other corporate competences/ processes need to be continuously foreseen, and consistently organized and directed.

'But please do not make a snap judgement on what you see. We invite all user-members to help us continuously improve the ThinkPaths displayed. We will also cull those ThinkPaths which draw no browsers and leverage other dynamics that the internet's interactive media allows. In other words, the MELNET mission is to explore both internet technology applied to team thinking, and the meaning of the reengineering of marketing. And everybody is invited to join the search party.

'The essence of MELNET is a universal laboratory for test marketing what thinking adds value, to whom, when, why and where.'

MELNET master-menus and Brand Chartering updates

For the 1996 version of MELNET, our 30 odd display boards have been virtually grouped into three MELNET master-menus. These are shown in the MELNET reference sheet (Figure T11.1). Brand Chartering is represented by MELNET2 and its display boards 2.1 to 2.15, corresponding to the chapters of this book. This enables Brand Charterers to swap practical experiences and WCBN to provide you with continuous updating of this Handbook.

We call these master-menus virtual to remind ourselves that:

- they are all interconnected to one overall directory of learning modules. You do not have to be thinking about Brand Chartering (or even to be aware of its structural purpose) to access a learning module even though a co-worker may have originally prepared it with the intention of illuminating practical aspects of Chartering;
- there are no limits to continuously improving master-menu structures as these are crafted by co-workers, or user-members who download their favourite learning modules.

You will find that MELNET learning modules employ a variety of styles.

Below, we have clicked through some prototype MELNET ThinkPaths to illustrate some of these styles. Written down, the juxtaposition of these ideas may seem odd. In internet thought-flux, the interactive user chooses between off-piste flows of thoughts and guided tours through structured mental scenery.

< 1: General review style from MELNET3.6 >

Manufacturing – the marketing solution. Alias – benchmarking marketing's contribution to competitive manufacturing, Parkinson S, Chartered Institute of Marketing (1995)

Here are three kinds of introductions to this report so you can decide whether you need to read it.

(1) Extract from Foreword by Rt Hon. Michael Heseltine MP (while President of the (British) Board of Trade)

'I warmly welcome this new benchmarking report from the Chartered Institute of Marketing which represents a major milestone in the need to objectively measure and monitor this key sector.

'It serves to highlight marketing's pervasive and influential role throughout an organization where the focus of fulfilling customer needs effectively, efficiently and profitably requires every activity in the "value adding chain" to be regarded as a marketing process.

'Its practical approach to self-diagnosis and strategic response will ensure that we will have many more "winners" in the future.'

MELNET1 TEAM AGENDAS FOR BRAND CHANGE	MELNET3 LEARNING TO ORGANIZE NEW ADDED VALUE ENVIRONMENTS
• Junction approach based on BBC Brand Change Agendas • MELNET1 'menu' of ThinkPaths corresponds to Figure 8.1, pages 147–8	• Network information to connect best thinking of 'old world' and 'new world' Junctions: THESIS = 'OLD WORLD' ↔ ANTITHESIS = 'NEW WORLD' 3.1 Product sub-brand ↔ Company banner brand 3.2 Competitive strategy ↔ Partner strategy 3.3 Broadcast media ↔ 1:1 Multimedia 3.4 Local first ↔ Global first 3.5 Departmental organization ↔ Networking organization 3.6 Top CEO mindset: financial ↔ Top CEO mindset: brand marketing 3.7 Brand's outward manifestation ↔ Brand's internal learning culture 3.8 Business unit: product selling ↔ Business unit: customer service/process consultant 3.9 Stakeholder bias ↔ Stakeholder balance 3.10 Product: in-market ↔ Product : pre-, post- and in-market 3.11 Culture measures past performance ↔ Culture supports competence growth
MELNET2 BRAND CHARTERING	
• 15 Junction approach corresponds to chapters of this Handbook • MELNET2 'menu' of ThinkPaths corresponds to Figure 0.1 on page 21	

Figure T11.1 MELNET-based project reference sheet.

(2) The research methodology identifies seven interconnecting processes of marketing and 123 questions ('performance dimensions') for a complete benchmarking examination of the breadth and depth of best organizational practice. This interrogative approach ensures that an implementation audit occurs which brings the following terms alive:

- Marketing strategy
- Quality strategy
- Brand organization
- Product innovation
- Customer development
- Supply chain management
- Manufacturing strategy

(3) If you're a typical British manufacturer examination results of 1995 contain:

- Bad news – most companies fail this total marketing process test by wide margins. Worst of the interconnecting process performances is brand organization where two out of three companies get the bottom mark (ie, 1 out of 5).
- Good news – there is a lot of competitive improvement to go for, and much of this involves organizational investment in soft items like thinking/teamworking as opposed to hard cash.

(Note: Professor Parkinson's research for this report was carried out while at Bradford Management Centre. He is now head of the Business School of the University of Ulster. 1995/96 applications of this 'benchmarking of marketing' methodology are taking place in other sectors, eg, service industries.)

< 2: Quotation style from MELNET1.1 >

'What is your brand equity about? . . .', Extracted from BBC for BUSINESS video 'Branding – the Marketing Advantage', 1995

Impromptu replies from marketers at:

- American Express: 'We think of the green plastic card, but originally it started as a piece of purple cardboard, so things have evolved and transformed over time, and today we're sitting with some very interesting brand equity – obviously we've retained some things about globalness and travelness, but we've also included some things about prestige, and I think that comes largely from the travel card.'

- 3M Audio and Video: 'Our brand equity is very simple. We produce a product which we guarantee for a lifetime of re-recording, so that it will always be as good as the first recording that's ever made.'
- Club Med: 'It's difficult to put the term into the Club Med context, but let's just say that the equity we have with Club Med is an offer that combines different percentages of emotion and rational, where the emotion is probably 95% and the rational is probably 5%.'

< 3: Composite brand case style from MELNET2.7 >

Marks & Spencer – were Japan Inc's quality standards made in Britain? WCBN file (1995)

Organizational process

M&S chooses the focus for the next improvement of every supplier's line, namely better quality or better price. In this way M&S ensures it is always a quality step ahead of its competitors.

M&S accelerates innovation in all the product categories it merchandises. At the same time, its consumer guarantees ensure that strict quality controls must be forever present. Since the 1920s M&S has invented many operational systems of this kind before the world came to think of this as Japanese organizational philosophy. (Also indirectly M&S inspired the marketer of the global retail program 'President's Choice' whence also came the phenomenon of Cott Corp.)

Value adding roles

Suppliers continuously asked for improvements.

Consumers perceive all St Michael merchandise as leading quality standards: a British institution that has won the world's respect.

Whereas 'own labelling' of over 30% of stores' lines is often perceived by consumers as restricting their lifestyles, St Michael (close to 100% own label) merchandise avoids this impression. Consumers go to M&S for the total service relationship. For example, if M&S makes a mistake, the compensation offered is outstanding.

Brand learning

A strong branded culture sets the quality/value standard. This becomes the corporate guarantee; the basis of consumer trust; indeed the brand becomes the consumers' editor of choice; often that highest level of brand loyalty: a lifetime relationship.

Provided every new product delights on quality, the M&S umbrella can be used to endorse almost anything the company chooses to market.

The M&S brand relationship seems to be equally well balanced with all key stakeholders:

- employees
- consumers
- preferred suppliers
- investor relations.

The brand is seen as a long-term investment. M&S does not milk the brand by rushing into new areas. It learns how to focus the competences of its network carefully, before replicating new formats, etc. By using pilot shops as experimental laboratories, it can gauge which new lines will be mass market successes at the earliest possible moment.

< 4: Challenge style from MELNET2.7 >

This MELNET challenge comes in two parts. A summary of an article published by the London trade magazine *Marketing Week* (16 June 1995) and an invitation to explore possible lessons for companies whose marketing purpose is dedicated to adding sustainable value.

Summary of 'No value in image over innovation' by Alan Mitchell

Advertising agencies do their profession endless harm when they propagate the following heresy: in a world where product replication is often quickly achieved, a brand's lasting source of differentiation can be through advertising alone.

Alan examined the 1992 IPA Advertising Awards Effectiveness Paper on the British brand Andrex (which dominates the British category for toilet paper and is a brand owned by Scott whose leading international brand of toilet paper is Scottex).

Andrex had won first prize for longer and broader effects (associated with the much loved puppy advertising campaigns). In proving advertising effectiveness the case revealed the brand's heritage as indicating:

- relatively little innovation;
- unconvincing performances in blind product tests of consumer preference;
- low retailer margins;
- price realization (from consumers) 'higher than any other toilet tissue market in the world'.

In the past few years, Andrex's market leading share has been falling, arguably its just desserts for heretical marketing. After all, in what way has Andrex's marketing and advertising benefited consumers? In Alan's eyes and words 'the core of modern branding is about delivering continuous improvement in both price and quality to consumers'.

Lessons for ongoing debate

MELNET co-workers would like an e-mail from you if you have alternative views to these provisional lessons from the article by Alan Mitchell:

- Ad agencies must pursue excellence in copy for clients. Their industry bodies are right to champion the power of advertising particularly in view of its shamefully low share of some 1990s marketing (read selling) budgets. But these professionals must also help diffuse the view that if a brand's only means of support is great presentation it is not a great brand. (Possible exception: some fashion markets where consumers are consciously paying for image to wear.)

- Marketers who scope their job as merely unique sell propositioning — without integrating unique organization purpose – have no (world class) future. However, corporate strategy – thinking and implementing – is where all marketing sins begin and end. World class strategists, that is CEOs who want their companies to lead their spheres of business, now need to ask whether their own language is divisive organizationally, for example the seeking of cash cows with marketplaces to milk. One way round this is a corporate mission statement-and-culture which enshrines the vision of fair returns for all stakeholders. As day follows night, this leads to re-training city analysts and many other experts wherever their functional views support short-termism or strange extrapolations (as recently as 1993 market share measurers A C Nielsen were predicting Andrex would be the UK's top brand in the year 2000).

- Our favourite lesson comes from Japanese consumers. They insist that product brands are inferior – not worth consideration – unless they visibly carry the corporate brand's guarantee. We understood this sophisticated consumer logic to mean: if a company is not proud enough to endorse a product maybe there is something risky about it. Or is it that the Japanese already see through the brand that is advertising-led rather than organization-led?

< 5: Question hunt style from MELNET2.7 >

Chartering's Mastermind Quiz – global and local update of popular questions on balancing quality and value

Original suggestions from The Brand Chartering Handbook, Macrae, C. and WCBN co-workers, Addison-Wesley/EIU (1996):

- How do we get perceived quality and value consistently right for every customer and consumer with every product and service directed in the brand's name?
- How do we set goals and measure performance?

List of alternative questions (please 'internet in' your favourite suggestions):

- What discontinuity scenarios could cause our brand's delivery to get competitively out of touch with:

    (1) low cost
    (2) new quality standards?

- Do these discontinuity scenarios fully reflect environmental changes to our value-added network, globally and locally?

Merging Oriental and Western thinking

To close this ThinkPiece and the book, it seems appropriate to conclude with a final twinning of oriental and western thinking. The oriental contribution is one of MELNET's most popular reviews of 1995; the western contribution is in the form of a parable.

MELNET3.11.1: *The Knowledge-Creating Company – How Japanese companies create the dynamics of innovation*

The overall importance of this book can be judged from its endorsement by Kenichi Ohmae as the being 'the most creative book on management to have come out of Japan'.

Why have Japanese companies become successful? This book offers a new explanation. It is argued that the success of Japanese companies is not due to manufacturing prowess; access to cheap capital; close and cooperative relationships with customers, suppliers and government agencies; or lifetime employment and other human resources management practices, although all of these factors are important. Instead the claim is made that Japanese companies have been successful because of their skills and expertise at 'organizational knowledge creation'. This term is defined as the capability of the company as a whole to create new knowledge, disseminate it throughout the organization, and embody it in products, services and systems.

The book's case studies demonstrate that this is the golden key to the distinctive ways that Japanese companies innovate continuously, incrementally and spirally.

Rugby football provides a metaphor for the speed and flexibility with which Japanese companies develop new products: as in rugby, the ball gets passed within the team as it moves up the field as a unit. The ball being passed around in the team contains a shared understanding of what the company stands for, where it is going, what kind of a world it wants to live in and how to make that world a reality. Highly subjective insights, intuitions and hunches are also embraced. This is what the ball contains, namely ideals, values and emotions.

Ball movement in rugby comes from the team members' interplay on the field. It is determined on the spot ('here and now'), based on direct experience and trial and error. It requires an intensive and laborious interaction among members of the team. This interactive process is analogous to how total knowledge is created organizationally.

This book calls for a fundamental shift in thinking about what the business organization does with knowledge. Two kinds of human knowledge are distinguished. One is 'explicit knowledge', which can be articulated in formal language including mathematical expressions and manuals. It can be transmitted formally and easily among individuals and has been the dominant kind of knowledge in the western philosophical tradition. The Japanese company adds a second type of knowledge, 'tacit knowledge', which is hard to articulate in formal language. This more personal form of knowledge is embedded in individual experience and involves intangible factors such as personal belief, perspective and the value system. In the West, tacit knowledge has been overlooked as a critical component of collective human behaviour. In contrast, tacit knowledge, and diffusion of learning from individual to team to organization, is a critical source of Japanese companies' competitiveness. Unless you understand this, Japanese management – and the way they win the business team game – will remain an enigma.

A western parable

Two friends were having lunch, one ex-Procter & Gamble but nowadays a consultant, the other still a P&G man. The consultant tried to explain Brand Chartering as 15 expert sets of questions for determining whether a branding process is fully integrated. The P&G man said: 'You are beginning to sound like a consultant trying to proposition me with a mega-project.'

The friend replied: 'Not really. Let me have one more go at explaining why I like Brand Chartering. The brand you work on is about P&G's fifth most important brand worldwide. In addition to you, there are about four other people in P&G who study that brand and its business all the time. But in the world of P&G, hundreds of employees contribute to the development of that brand. What if they all understood its essential (organizational/cultural) meanings as well as you did?'

There was a pause (quite a short one relatively speaking) before the P&G man said: 'Oh. That might be a big idea. I will need to go away and think about that.'

Reference

Nonaka, I. and Takeuchi, H. (1995) *The Knowledge-Creating Company – How Japanese companies create the dynamics of innovation.* Oxford: Oxford University Press

Top 10 ThinkPaths at MELNET as at January 1996

15 years of consistent leadership at Coca-Cola company < MEL2.14.3 >
Ambler's relationship paradigm of branding < MEL1.1.17 >
Branson's teamworking spirit at Virgin companies < MEL2.8.1 >
Drucker: Who are leading enterprises being organized for? < MEL2.14.2 >
Efficient Consumer Response – European terms of engagement < MEL2.8.2 >
Mitchell's systemic failure of late 20th-century marketing and financial functions
      < MEL2.8.3 >
Senge's Learning Organizations and Systems Archetypes < MEL3.11.2 >
The knowledge creating company of Nonaka and Takeuchi < MEL3.11.1 >
The Economist's 'death of the brand manager' < MEL2.13.5 >
The brand architecture school – founding thoughts < MEL2.11.1 >

Au revoir

We aim to answer all constructive questions internetted to us by MELNET's Gentil Members. However, as an owner of this first edition of The Brand Chartering Handbook, please mention the password WCBN999 to prioritize response to any questions you may want to ask.

Additional references to those cited in chapters

Additional references to those cited in chapters

Adweek (1995). *Inside Coke*, 6 November

Ambler, T. (1992). *Need-to-know marketing*, London: Century Business

Ambler, T. (1994). Marketing's third paradigm: Guanxi. *Business Strategy Review*, **5**(4)

Ambler, T. (1995). Building brand relationships. Part 6 of Series on Mastering Management. *The Financial Times*, 1 December

Argyris, C. (1992). *On organisational learning*, Cambridge, MA: Blackwell

Bernstein, D. (1984). *Corporate image and reality*, London: Casswell

Berry, N. (1988). Revitalising brands. *Journal of Consumer Marketing*, **5**(3)

Berwick, P., Godfrey, A. and Roessmer, J. (1990). *Curing healthcare*, Jossey-Bass

Boze, B. and Patton, C. (1995). The future of consumer branding as seen from the picture today, *Journal of Consumer Marketing*, **12**(4)

Broadbent, S. (1992). Using data better, *ADMAP*, January

Broadbent, S. (1995). Best practice in campaign evaluation, *IPA*, London

Burnett, Leo. 100 Leos. Leo Burnett company

Buzzell, R. and Gale, B. (1987). *The PIMS Principles*, New York: The Free Press

Champy, J. (1995). *Reengineering management*, New York: Harper Business

Clark, K. and Wheelwright, S. (1995). *The product development challenge*, Harvard, MA: Harvard Business Review library

Coca-Cola Retail Research Group Europe (1996). *The future of the food store – challenges and alternatives*

Collins, J. and Porras, J. (1994). *Built to last*, New York: Harper Business

Coopers & Lybrand (1995). *Leadership principles in ECR from the European experience databank of value chain analysis projects* and *The evolution of Joint Category Management*, London and Utrecht

Davidow, W. and Malone, M. (1992). *The virtual corporation*, New York: Harper Business

Dawson, C. (1995) Advertising and the millennium blues. *ADMAP*, October

Deschamps, J-P. and Nayak, P. (1995) *Product juggernauts – how companies mobilize to generate a stream of market winners*, Harvard, MA: Harvard Business School Press

Dougherty, D. and Heller, T. (1994). The illegitimacy of successful product innovation in established firms, *Organization Science*, 5(2)

Drucker, P. All works by

Feather, F. (1994). *The future consumer*, Los Angeles: Warwick Publishing Inc

Fortune Magazine (1993). Brands – it's thrive or die, 23 August

Franzen, G. and Holzhauer, F. (1988) *Brands*, A series of eight books. Amstelveen: BBDO College Edition

Gale, B. (1994). *Managing customer value*, New York: The Free Press

Hankinson, G. and Cowking, P. (1993) *Branding in action*, London: McGraw Hill

Higgins, J. (1995). How effective innovative companies operate – lessons from Japanese strategy. *Creativity & Innovation Management*, 4(2)

Joint industry report on Efficient Consumer Response (1995). *Category management report*, Washington, DC

Kanter, R.M. (1995). *World Class – thriving locally in the global economy*, New York: Simon & Schuster

Kapferer, J-N. All works by

Kapferer, J-N. (1996). Review of *Building strong brands* by Aaker, D. *Journal of Brand Management* 3(4)

Kendall, N. (1995). The brand as entertainment, *Journal of Brand Management* 2(5)

Lannon, J. (1994) Mosaics of meaning : anthropology and marketing, *Journal of Brand Management*, 2(3)

Levitt, T. All works by

Macrae, C. (1993/4). Series on Brand Benchmarking, *brand strategy newsletter*, May 1993 to May 1994, London

Macrae, C. (1994). Rights and wrongs in the name of benchmarking. In Heller, R. *Managing 1994*, Sterling

Macrae, C. (1994). Brand Benchmarking applied to global branding processes, *Journal of Brand Management*, 1(5)

Macrae, C. (1994/5). Series on Brand Chartering, *brand strategy newsletter*, June 1994 to March 1995, London

Macrae, C. (1994/5). Branding – a core business process, *Journal of Brand Management Series*, 2(1–4)

Macrae, C. (1995). Pausing for thought about branding – the Brand Chartering Thoughtpad, *Strategic Direction*, October

Macrae, C. (1995/6). Series on MELNET, *brand strategy newsletter*, August 1995 to Summer 1996, London

Macrae, C. (1996). 3-part series on Brand Chartering and MELNET, *Marketing Business*, February to April, London: The Chartered Institute of Marketing

Macrae, C. (1996). MELNET96 invites you to contribute to the brand learning organisation, *Journal of Brand Management*, 3(4)

Macrae, N. (1984). *The 2024 Report – a concise history of the future*, London: Sidgwick & Jackson

Macrae, C., Devlin, J. and Milton, F. (1993). Brand Reengineering – why and how?, *Journal of Brand Management* 1(2)

Macrae, C., Parkinson, S. and Sheerman, J. (1995). Managing marketing's DNA: the role of branding, *Irish Marketing Review*

Macrae, C. and Cocks, M. (1995). Branding – the Unique Organising Purpose of the World Class company, *Proc. of the 1995 MEG conference*, Bradford Management Centre

Meyer, M. (1961). *Madison Avenue USA*, London: Penguin Books

McDonald, M. and Dunbar, I. (1995). *Market segmentation*, London: Macmillan

McWilliam, G. (1993) A tale of two gurus: Aaker and Kapferer on brands. *International Journal of Research in Marketing*, 10(1)

Mitchell, A. All works by

Mosmans, A. (1995). Brand strategy: creating concepts that drive the business, *Journal of Brand Management*, 3(3)

Murphy, J. (1995). Editorial: changing attitudes to brands, *Journal of Brand Management*, 3(3)

Nicholls, J. (1995). Value to the customer and the strategic leadership star, *Journal of General Management*, 20(3)

Nilson, T. (1995). *Chaos Marketing*, Maidenhead: McGraw-Hill

Nolan, R. and Croson, D. (1995). *Creative destruction*, Harvard, MA: Harvard Business School Press

Normann, R. and Ramirez, R. (1994). Designing interactive strategy – from value chain to value constellation, New York: Wiley

Novaction (1987). *Pocket principles on positioning brands from the Designer/ Catalyst experience databanks*, Paris: Novaction

Parkinson, S. and the Charterered Institute of Marketing (1995) *Manufacturing – the marketing solution. A benchmarking approach to marketing as the core process of business*, London: CIM

Peppers, D. and Rogers, M. (1993) *The one-to-one future*, London: Piatkus

Peppers, D. and Rogers, M. (1995). The end of mass marketing, *Marketing Tools*, March/April

Perks, H. and Carr, C. (1995) An investigation of resource synergy and learning in Anglo/Japanese collaboration, *Proc. of the MEG conference*, Bradford Management Centre

Piercy, N. (1995) Marketing and strategy fit together, *Management Decision*, 33(1)

Rapp, S. and Collins, T. (1994). *Beyond maxi-marketing*, New York: McGraw-Hill

Rubinstein, H. (1995). Brand Chartering – getting to a common understanding of the brand, *Journal of Brand Management*, 3(3)

Ruttenberg, A., Kavizky, A. and Oren, H. (1995). Compositioning – the paradigm shift beyond positioning, *Journal of Brand Management*, 3(3)

Schultz, D., Tannenbaum, S. and Lauterborn, R. (1993). *The new marketing paradigm – integrated marketing communications*, Chicago: NTC

Senge, P. (1990). *The Fifth Discipline – the art and practice of the learning organisation*, New York: Doubleday

Slywotzky, A. (1996). *Value migration*, Harvard, MA: Harvard Business School Press

Stalk, G., Evans, P. and Shulman, L. (1992). Competing on capabilities, *Harvard Business Review*, March/April

Thomas, M., Bureau, J. and Saxena, N. (1995) The relevance of global branding, *Journal of Brand Management*, **2**(5)

Tse, K. (1987). *Marks and Spencer*, Pergamon

Uncles, M. (1995). Branding – the marketing advantage, *Journal of Brand Management*, **3**(1)

Uncles, M., Cocks, M. and Macrae, C. (1995) Brand architecture: reconfiguring organisations for effective brand management, *The Journal of Brand Management*, **3**(2)

Upshaw, L. (1995). *Building brand identity*, New York: J Wiley

Waterman, R. (1987). *The renewal factor*, Bantam

Waterman, R. (1994). *Frontiers of excellence – learning from companies that put people first* (published in the USA as *What America does right*), London: Nicholas Brealey Publishing

Webster, F. (1992). The changing role of marketing in the corporation, *Journal of Marketing*, **56**(October)

Weilbacher, W. (1993). *Brand marketing – building winning brand strategies that deliver*, Chicago: NTC

Wind, J., Green, P., Shifflet, D., *et al.* (1989). Courtyard by Mariott: designing a hotel, *Interfaces* **19**(1)

Indices

Prior to a general index, specific terms relating to fast implementation of Brand Chartering are listed. These detailed references provide Think-Paths for readers who wish to connect up a broader understanding of particular brand organization junctions (see page 21) that have been discussed in depth in *chapters* of this Handbook. By exploring these ThinkPaths it is likely that you will improve Chartering's mastermind quiz for your context-specific organizational learning.

We (co-workers at WCBN) also invite readers to share their own favourite ThinkPaths with our Network of Marketing Expert Learners. To do this:

(1) Interact through MELNET, internet address **http://www.brad.ac.uk/ branding/**
(2) Inform us of your favourite flow of references (pages of this book or other citations) and what learning to expect from taking a mental journey along this ThinkPath.
(3) Remember to tell us whether you wish this contribution to Marketing Expert Learning to be anonymous or signed with your e-mail identity.
(4) We will compile a register of readers' ThinkPaths for 'glocal' access. (This is one of several ways that MELNET will be continuously adding to the ideas in this Handbook as mass marketing precepts of the 20th century pass into history.)

Brand Chartering Implementation Index

General Index